NANCY
Jesus
THE BRIDGE
VOLUME ONE

A Catholic's Journey Toward Truth and Wholeness

JESUS THE BRIDGE: A Catholic's Journey toward Truth and Wholeness

Copyright ©2023 Nancy Salvador

All Rights Reserved. Permission is granted to copy material if you copy it right. For resale purposes, please contact the author.

Most photos, illustrations, and banners used as teaching instruments were made by me. Most proclaim words the Lord spoke to me. Glory be to God, the Author and Finisher of our faith and Publisher of good news.

All Scripture quotations are from the Holy Bible, New King James Version, copyright © 1997 by Thomas Nelson, Inc., unless otherwise noted. Scriptures which contain capitalized words are NKJV from e-Sword.

Scripture quotations marked (KJV) are taken from the King James Version of the Bible, which is in the public domain.

Scripture quotations marked (RSV) are from the Revised Standard Version of the Bible, Copyright © 1946, 1952, and 1971 by the Division of Christian Education of the National Council of the Churches of Christ in the United States of America. Used by permission. All rights reserved.

Scripture quotations marked (NIV) are taken from the *Holy Bible, New International Version*®. NIV®. Copyright © 1973, 1978, 1984 by International Bible Society. Used by permission of Zondervan Publishing House. All rights reserved.

Scripture quotations marked (GNT) are taken from the *Good News Translation in Today's English Version, Second Edition,* Copyright © 1992 by American Bible Society. Used by permission.

Scripture quotations marked (NRSV) are taken from the New Revised Standard Version, copyright © 1989 National Council of the Churches of Christ in the United States of America. Used by permission. All rights reserved.

Scripture quotations marked (NAB) are taken from the Prince of Peace Catholic Edition of The New American Bible by Memorial Bible Publishers, Inc. Copyright © Today, Inc. 1976. All rights reserved.

Published by HigherLife Development Services Inc.
PO Box 623307
Oviedo, Florida 32762
www.higherlifepublishing.com

ISBN 978-1-958211-81-6 (paperback)
ISBN 978-1-958211-89-2 (ebook)
LCCN 2023917645

Contents

Foreword v

Part I—The World's Longest Bridge

Chapter 1: Jesus Is the World's Longest and Shortest Bridge to the Father... 3

Chapter 2: Only He Could Do It...13

Part II—Composition of the Bridge

Chapter 3: The Genuine Bridge 35

Chapter 4: The Choice Was the Father's 51

Chapter 5: Reconcilers Are Components 73

Part III—False Bridges Are Like Mirages

Chapter 6: The Genuine versus the Counterfeit.............................97

Chapter 7: Graven Images Are False Bridges................................121

Chapter 8: What about the Rosary?...141

Chapter 9: Praise God from Whom All Blessings Flow 169

Chapter 10: Divination Is a False Bridge 193

Chapter 11: False Bridges Can Lead to Humiliation 215

Chapter 12: Jesus Claims to Be the Only Bridge 231

Chapter 13: Is Jesus Still a Baby? 263

Part IV—Function of the Bridge

Chapter 14: Jesus Gives Access to God and to Reality 289

Chapter 15: Jesus Reveals the Heart of the Father 311

Chapter 16: Jesus the Priest 339

Chapter 17: Jesus the Prophet and Prophetic Evangelist 409

Chapter 18: Jesus the King 425

Chapter 19: The Ministry of Reconciliation 467

Bibliography 491

Foreword

In the seventies, my Roman Catholic parish had a goal to return to how the church had been around two thousand years before, like it was in the Book of Acts. At that time, I had not even read Acts, but I did have a desire to please God. I had loved Him for as long as I could remember not knowing that anything more than a monologue with Him was possible.

Although I had never read the whole Bible in those days, I had gone to daily Mass for years and loved the little portions of Scripture read there. I had been very religious, praying daily, but little did I know that there was so much more. That is, until the Lord began to break into my life in wonderful ways, speaking to me like Jesus spoke to the woman at the well, and telling me that *"the truth will set you free."*

Like my budgie bird, I did not know that I was not free, so I began a journey to seek truth and wholeness in my life. Surprised to find that Jesus's sheep could hear His voice, I developed a hunger and thirst for His words and righteousness.

This book is dedicated to those who will come out of darkness into His glorious light as the Lord has brought me and countless others. Having met many Catholics and Protestants who also were deceived, I have tried to share what I have learned from Jesus, the Teacher. May you fall more in love with the Beautiful One, Jesus Christ, and come to know more of His truth, the truth that sets His people free when we know it. This story is part of my journey. I hope you will read Book Two afterwards.

The Book of Esther tells of how the king allowed the equipping of her people with weapons to defend themselves against their enemies. The King of kings has allowed the equipping of my people with swords of the Spirit, of the Word of God. This book will help separate what is true from what is counterfeit. Hopefully you will be enriched, equipped to lovingly reach out a hand to others, in His wonderful name.

Happy to have found the true bridge to the Father,

Nancy Salvador

Christian Mission Outreach, www.Jesusthebridge.info

Part I

The World's Longest Bridge

For there is one God and one Mediator between God and men,
the Man Christ Jesus,
who gave Himself a ransom for all, to be testified in due time.
(1 Tim. 2:5–6)

But [Jesus], *because He continues forever, has an unchangeable priesthood.*
Therefore He is also able to save to the uttermost those who come to God
through Him, since He always lives to make intercession for them.
(Heb. 7:24–25)

Chapter 1
Jesus Is the World's Longest and Shortest Bridge to the Father

When I arrived for the first time in Lethbridge, Alberta, an enthusiastic taxi driver proceeded to point out the sights as he drove me to my destination. I had come for the 2002 Dominion Conference at the Miracle Channel, Canada's first 24/7 all-Christian TV station. Among other things, the driver proudly pointed out the railway bridge telling me that it was the world's longest trestle bridge and that it was even in the *Guinness Book of World Records*! He was convinced of it. But then someone else said that it was North America's longest trestle bridge. Was it both or just the longest on this continent? Or neither? If I wanted to know and to quote the truth, I would have to look in the book to find out—otherwise I could be publishing a myth or a fable!

High– Level Bridge

Although the city was on flat land, the terrain was like a slice of bread that had been torn in two and slightly pulled apart. Behind my hotel there was a deep chasm with the Oldman River flowing through the valley at the base of peculiar hills called "coulees" that sprang up in these valleys. The famous CPR High-Level railway trestle bridge spans from the top of the coulees on one side of the city, across the great chasm to the mainland on the other side.

I was told it is the only railway trestle bridge long enough, high enough, and strong enough to span such a long, deep, dividing chasm. In order to carry the trains safely it has intricate, orderly trestlework undergirding it like a series of towers, all joined together by the top piece.

Likewise, because of sin, since Adam and Eve there is a great chasm between mankind and God, and **there is only one bridge in the universe long enough, high enough, and secure enough to bridge that gap so that we may be carried safely to the Father and our eternal homeland, reconciled with God.**

Called to Serve Christ

Peter said, *"Make your call and election sure"* (2 Pet. 1:10). I am a Christian in whose life "Peter" (the Roman Catholic Church) planted and "Paul" (other Christian churches) watered, but God has given the growth. Being from a devout, loving, Roman Catholic (RC) background, I was raised to love God from infancy and often prayed to Him not knowing that a dialogue was possible. I was suddenly surprised around 1979 when I began to experience more than a monologue with Him.

One day while dusting my little daughter's room, as I knelt at the foot of her bed crying to the Lord, thinking my life was useless, the Lord came into my life in a new way with noticeable responses. I was a university graduate who had chosen to be a housewife and stay-at-home mom, but was jaded by the opinions of people around me.

However, the Lord began by revealing to me a threefold calling on my life, not in distinct words but in an understanding. The first was as a housewife and homemaker to feed and care for His sheep, my family and those He sent to us. (Years later, the Lord told me, *"I have called you as a shepherd of sheep."*) Then the other two callings: as my eyes turned to a picture on her wall of the young John the Baptist, I received the understanding that God was calling me as a prophet like John, helping to prepare the way for His next coming, and something to do with Italians.

I found that the Lord was *"my glory and the lifter of my head"* (Ps. 3:3 KJV). I had never thought of my children as being His sheep, so the Lord began to restore dignity to my life. I had not been able to face my childhood teachers because I was not a teacher, a nuclear physicist, or a foreign missionary; but years later I realized that after that day the Lord began to allow me to teach what He was teaching me, sometimes in banner form. Spiritually, I was a nuclear physicist at times, encouraging the nuclear family as the micro version of the body of Christ, which expanded to a church version, national version, and a worldwide macro version of the body of Christ, the family of God—one inside of another. The Lord began to call me as a missionary to home missions and ministry to the nations locally and in a few small places overseas by mail.

We rarely ever mentioned the word "prophet" at church in those days, but since God was calling me to be one, providentially I found a page in my missalette that briefly described the function of this office.

However, I had to rely on the Lord to teach me what He wanted of me. It was not until about fifteen years later that I met others with that calling today and got some teaching at some conferences.

The Lord had shown me that for the Elijah task to which I had been called that I would not be alone. It was like a relay race but with a few of us little ones all holding the rod together as we ran after Him. **I was only *"one of many"* with that calling, He said.** I echo Paul's words: *"But I made known to you, brethren, that the gospel which was preached by me is not according to man. For I neither received it from man, nor was I taught it, but it came through a revelation of Jesus Christ"* (Gal. 1:11–12). What I learned about coming out of spiritual Babylon and its idolatry and immorality, the Lord began to teach me. Thanks and glory be to God, I heard nothing about this in Catholic or Protestant churches in the early days.

Raised as a "Catholic of Catholics," I had always loved God, but we prayed to the saints too in those days. I had been told in RC circles that it was Mary plus the saints in heaven who were chosen to bridge the gap with God, the ones to whom we could and should go to in prayer, and that Mary was the longest bridge (the "Mediatrix of all grace" was what RCs called her), and I was told to pray to Jesus through Mary. We were told we could also pray as the Protestants, directly through Jesus. But then not only did the Protestants not pray to Mary, but they always pictured the cross of Jesus as the bridge. Also, they praised God as the One from whom all blessings flow.

At first, I strongly defended our belief in praying to and through Mary until the Lord Himself began to teach me otherwise in spectacular ways—including by His audible voice in 1981 and by a fresh, strong baptism of fire and the Holy Spirit in 1994, when He "knocked me off my horse" by sticking my feet to the floor for about eleven hours standing and then three and a half more hours stuck down where I fell, lying flat on my back, arms outstretched, as if crucified with Christ. The Lord sent a man to prophesy a word to me that changed my life even more. This was at the Prophetic School at the **Toronto Airport**

Vineyard Fellowship, later called **Catch the Fire,** at the new Attwell Centre.

When I asked the Lord to clarify through the Scriptures the prophetic word brought to me that night: *"They are dead. Do not contact them,"* meaning Mary and the saints, then the Holy Spirit of Jesus began to lead me into truth. As it is written: *"However, when He, the Spirit of truth, has come, He will guide you into all truth"* (John 16:13).

I had already stopped praying directly to Mary and the saints for favors and for healing in 1981 after the Lord gave me *"Isaiah 44"* in an audible voice as an understanding of the second commandment in Exodus 20:4–6. (Normally, though, it was the *"still small voice"* [1 Kgs. 19:12] of the Lord that I heard.) I had been calling our people to come out of the Catholic idolatry of praying to God and the saints through graven images—statues, pictures, and medals. I knew that we were supposed to pray in Jesus's name (see Colossians 3:17; John 16:23), but that was supposed to be to the Father. I mistakenly thought we could ask the heavenly host to pray for us in Jesus's name. So, I had not begun to realize until that night, November 25, 1994, that it was also forbidden to even pray to saints in heaven asking them to pray for us, to intercede in Jesus's name.

Although I asked the Lord for confirmation through His Word, in my heart I knew the answer because **after forty years of daily recitation, I stopped praying the rosary that very night.** The rosary is composed of prayers, some of which are good, but the focal prayer is the "Hail Mary," which asks Mary to pray for us as if she were the eternal High Priest and Mediator, or Mediatrix, the eternal High-Level Bridge.

In effect, I began to ask:

Is it a myth to call Mary the true bridge to the Father and Mediatrix of all grace?

Are the saints and Jesus all stand-alone true "bridges," or is there just one?

And is it Jesus?

To find out, I looked in the **official book** that records such things—**the Bible. There I found that Jesus Christ is the only true bridge, because of what He did on the cross and because His Father firmly set Him in place. There is no other name for us to call upon in prayer. He has no rival or equal.** Since the time of Adam and Eve and their grandson, Enosh, *"Men began to call upon the name of the LORD"* (Gen. 4:26).

> *For there is one God and one Mediator between God and men,*
> *the Man Christ Jesus, who gave Himself a ransom for all,*
> *to be testified in due time, for which I was appointed a preacher...*
> *I am speaking the truth in Christ and not lying—*
> *a teacher of the Gentiles in faith and truth.* (1 Timothy 2:5–7)
>
> *The LORD has sworn and will not relent,*
> *"You are a priest forever according to the order of Melchizedek."*
> (Ps. 110:4)

That is why Protestants usually picture a wooden cross, His altar of sacrifice, as a symbol of Jesus bridging the gap between God and mankind. **Jesus is the one and only way to the Father, the true bridge and Mediator of all grace. He willingly laid down His life for His friends and took it up again.**

Time and again Jesus's name is mentioned in this role in the New Testament, acting as our Mediator and Intercessor, but never is Mary or anyone else mentioned in that role. The Scriptures clearly state that because of His cleansing blood, *"He [Jesus Christ] is the Mediator of the new covenant"* (Heb. 9:15). And John 14:6 is the *rhema* word the Lord gave me for not praying the "Hail Mary." I had asked Him for a *rhema* because the first half of that prayer is scriptural and He had replied, *"I am the way, the truth, and the life. No one comes to the Father except through Me."*

After my Toronto Vineyard fresh baptism of fire experience with the Lord, I began to think of the woman at the well with whom Jesus took the time to converse. I was amazed that He had been talking to me for some time now, and I realized that He is like a jealous husband who does not want His wife to have other lovers. By praying to both God and the saints it was like I had had other lovers. I came to find that I had been trying to take the wrong bridge to the Father all my life, and I was so happy to find that Jesus is the bridge authorized by the Father.

So, I began to tell my people to go to Jesus too. Like that woman, I say, *"Come, see a Man who told me all things that I ever did"* (John 4:29). I know this is the Christ, Yeshua Hamashiach. And He can open in you too a well of living water, with the Holy Spirit bubbling up words to strengthen and lead you.

Believers still on earth, also called *"saints,"* can bridge the gap to the Father only because they are in Christ, parts of His body. As Jesus told His trained disciples, *"Most assuredly I say to you, whatever you ask the Father in My name He will give you"* (John 16:23). But we are forbidden to contact the dead, those who have died on earth, so we are forbidden to pray to saints who have died. **Jesus is all we need. He is more than enough.**

The Holy Spirit Brings Knowledge and Revelation

For years I used to pray to Jesus through Mary, obediently following priests, parents, and schoolteachers who themselves did not know any better—until the Holy Spirit convinced me otherwise. One day at a Ministry of Prayer Counseling class in early 1994 in Belleville, Ontario, a few months before the Vineyard experience, I even had the opportunity to address my classmates—non-Catholics. Not only did I tell these Protestant Christians to honor Mary as our Brother Jesus's mother and as ours, but I tried to tell them how important praying the rosary was. Afterwards, a couple leaders took me aside and tried to tell me what I was doing wrong, and I quietly but determinately defended my Catholic position.

Afterwards, we were supposed to go into small group sessions where I hoped to say more, but the Lord told me to *"sit and wait."* So, I did that, staying there on a chair in the auditorium until we were dismissed to drive home, still wondering why and yet trusting Jesus. It was not until months later, after the fresh baptism of fire November 25, 1994, in Toronto, that Jesus, the Teacher, began to instruct me about this through His Spirit. Although I had received the gift of teaching and had been anointed as a teacher in the midst of my classmates, Jesus has said, *"And do not be called teachers; for One is your teacher, the Christ"* (Matt. 23:10). How can we teach or properly instruct others in righteousness unless it comes from Him?

So now I honor Mary and saints in heaven and look forward to seeing them one day with Jesus. But I pray only to God through Jesus as the Word of God teaches. What Jesus told His disciples is still true today: *"I still have many things to say to you, but you cannot bear them now. However, when He, the Spirit of truth, has come, He will guide you into all truth"* (John 16:12–13).

Although we had tasty bites of Scripture at each Mass, and the Catholic charismatic movement emphasized studying Scripture, most Catholics did not read the whole Bible, including priests and nuns in those days. So, we did not realize some of the truths of Scripture and were in darkness. **I later read that Pope John XXIII had begun to encourage Bible reading after experiencing the moving of the Holy Spirit just prior to Vatican II**, and later Separate schools began to hand out whole Bibles. Priests who received the baptism of the Holy Spirit began to preach wonderful messages when they stuck to the Scriptures. Praise God! However, even in the twenty-first century, many older Catholics still thought reading the whole Bible was only a "Protestant" thing to do. **But reading the Word of God is a Christian thing to do.** *"For the earth shall be full of the knowledge of* [the glory of] *the* LORD *as the waters cover the sea"* (Isa. 11:9; Hab. 2:14).

We are living in exciting times when knowledge is increasing as God said it would, knowledge in so many areas. We know that distance from one part of the world to another is exceedingly long at times, and yet we have jets which will take us there relatively quickly, and cordless phones, mobile phones, and internet which can give us immediate access to nations. Likewise, the distance from earth to heaven, the highest heaven, is even greater. But through the Holy Spirit of Jesus Christ, we can have immediate access—and no long-distance charges.

Chapter 2
Only He Could Do It

Jesus Is the True Bridge

Jesus is the official link between God and mankind designated by God Himself.

God always tells His prophets before He does something.

Years before He sent Jesus to take flesh in the womb of a virgin, God the Father prophesied through David that He was setting His Son in place as His Christ, His anointed King, High Priest, and Mediator between God and mankind. It would be a new order for a new heavenly sanctuary, and Melchizedek was a royal order older than the Levitical priesthood, also established by God. Abraham knew of it.

> *The Lord said to my Lord,*
> *"Sit at My right hand,*
> *Till I make Your enemies Your footstool."*
> *The Lord shall send the rod of Your strength out of Zion.*
> *Rule in the midst of Your enemies!...*
> *The Lord has sworn*
> *And will not relent,*
> *"You are a priest forever according to the order of Melchizedek."*
> (Ps. 110:1–2, 4)

The Book of Hebrews, which refers to this Scripture a few times, I now see is so rich with references to Jesus over and over as being *"the Mediator of the new covenant"* (Heb. 9:15), and the *"High Priest, who is seated at the right hand of the throne of the Majesty in the heavens"* (Heb.

8:1). No wonder one night in the early nineties the Word of the Lord came to me: ***"Study the Book of Hebrews!"*** I did not see this truth at first, but later I did, thank God. Jesus is the Lamb of God sacrificed to atone for the sin of the world and the eternal High Priest, the One who willingly offered the sacrifice. Therefore, being the Chosen One, Jesus is the one Mediator personally designated by God forever, higher than any angel or man. (See Hebrews 1 and 2.)

Jesus the eternal High Priest is the true, permanent, everlasting bridge linking up God and mankind, and the only way to the Father.

In Old Testament times, if anyone wanted to inquire of God, they went to the "go-between"—either the local prophet or the Aaronic high priest. The latter was chosen by God to bring the blood of animals into the Holy of holies in reparation for sin, his own and the people's. Although there were many priests, **no one but he could do it.** Once a year on the Day of Atonement, a high priest in the order of Aaron put his hands on the head of a scapegoat, placing all the sins of the people upon it as he confessed them over it, and then sent it off into the wilderness to die, carrying away their sins. Also, to make atonement for sins, he brought the blood of sacrificed animals into the Holy of holies, the blood of a bull or ram for his own sins and of a second goat for the people's sins *"concerning his ignorance"* (Lev. 5:18). **No one but the high priest was allowed in to meet with God's presence in the Most Holy Place, and not without blood.**

This was a foreshadowing of Jesus. *"Behold! The Lamb of God who takes away the sin of the world!"* (John 1:29). Instead of goats and other sacrifices, at the same time He took our sin upon Himself and became the sacrifice whose blood was shed, sprinkled on the altar of the cross that sins could be forgiven and was also the High Priest who willingly performed the sacrifice and was allowed into the holiest place of heaven. He brought in and sprinkled the blood of the Lamb, His own blood, at the merciful throne of God. **No one but Jesus could do it because He was chosen by God to be the designated High Priest** and His sacrifice only needed to be done once to be effective forever.

It is only because we are *"in Christ,"* members of His body, that we, too, can go boldly into God's presence. **He opened the way to the Father where before we could not go.**

Jesus Is a Long Enough Bridge

Like a train on a railway bridge, **He has gone from one side to the other and back again**—all the way into the real Holy of holies in heaven as the Pioneer of our faith and then back to earth to show Himself to His disciples. This, plus the fact that **Jesus is both God and Man,** shows that He is a long enough bridge. He laid down His life for His people and took it up again. **Jesus has an unending royal priesthood like King Melchizedek,** *"the priest of God Most High"* **(Gen. 14:18), who had no genealogy and existed before Aaron, the first Levitical high priest.** Melchizedek came *"without father, without mother, without genealogy, having neither beginning of days nor end of life, but made like the Son of God, remains a priest continually"* (Heb. 7:3).

Jesus, the actual Son of God who is both God and His Priest forever, is *"the Alpha and the Omega, the Beginning and the End"* (Rev. 1:8). He came in the tribe of Judah, not Levi, Aaron's family tribe, but His birth was miraculous. God was His Father who spoke Him forth as the living *"Word"* of God (John 1:1) and He took flesh in Mary's womb miraculously while she was yet a virgin. She was His mother because she carried Him in her womb, letting Him take flesh and grow as Son of Man inside there. She was His earthly mother, although **He existed before her—and God has no mother**. God testified of Jesus around a thousand years before He came to live on earth, and when He would come.

> *I will declare the decree: the* LORD *has said to Me,*
> *"You are My Son, today I have begotten You."* (Ps. 2:7; John 1:14; 3:16)
>
> *This is My beloved Son, in whom I am well pleased.* (Matt. 3:17)

Jesus called God, *"Abba, Father"* (Mark 14:36), and God called Jesus His only begotten Son and mentored Him as Son of Man, but God Himself has no father or mother. He existed from the beginning and will endure forever.

Jesus will never need to be replaced or repaired as the bridge to the Father because He holds His position forever having a perfect, unending life; so, there is no need to appoint replacement high priests or a mediatrix. God tells the truth.

> *The LORD has sworn and will not relent,*
> *"You are a priest forever according to the order of Melchizedek."*
> (Ps. 110:4)

John saw *"the holy city, New Jerusalem, coming down out of heaven from God, prepared as a bride adorned for her husband. And I heard a loud voice from heaven saying, 'Behold, the tabernacle of God is with men, and He will dwell with them, and they shall be His people. God Himself will be with them and be their God'"* (Rev. 22:2–3). Jesus is coming again.

Aaron's descendants were chosen to replace him because each one would die, but **no saint will replace Jesus because He will never die again.** Saints on earth, holy believers, might accompany Him in fulfilling His duties, or have authority to stand in the gap in His name; but no one will replace Him.

Since I used to pray every day to Jesus through Mary, what a revelation it was for me to realize that not only do we not need to, but we should not go through Mary to get to Jesus! He said, *"I am the way, the truth, and the life. No one comes to the Father except through Me"* (John 14:6). Jesus is the one way to the Father. He will take us there—**to the Father through Jesus.**

Hebrews testifies to Jesus:

> *For He of whom these things are spoken belongs to another tribe, from which no man has officiated at the altar. For it is evident that*

our Lord arose from Judah, of which tribe Moses spoke nothing concerning priesthood. And it is yet far more evident if, in the likeness of Melchizedek, there arises another priest who has come, not according to the law of fleshly commandment [not as a descendant of Aaron], *but according to the power of an endless life. For He testifies: "You are a priest forever according to the order of Melchizedek."* (Heb. 7:13–17)

He, because He continues forever, has an unchangeable priesthood. (Heb. 7:24)

Jesus arose as our permanent bridge, *"according to the power of an endless life."*

He always lives to make intercession for them. (Heb. 7:25)

In Christ, who is true God and true Man, who knew what it was like to face temptation and trials, and yet overcame, the distance has been shortened and restoration has begun. He brought to earth *"the kingdom of God* [which] *does not come with observation; nor will they say, 'See here!' or 'See there!' For indeed, the kingdom of God is within you"* (Luke 17:20–21). When He dwells within us by His Spirit and by His Word dwelling richly, the kingdom can be brought within us. Born again of water and the Spirit, we can enter in and be brought closer to God, in Jesus's name since **being God and Man, Jesus is the longest and the shortest bridge to God.** No wonder both John the Baptist and Jesus began their public ministry by saying, *"Repent, for the kingdom of heaven is at hand"* (Matt. 3:2; 4:17), telling people to believe the good news! The kingdom is that close. Once we receive the forgiveness He purchased by His blood, we can be restored immediately to fellowship with God and man, with fresh resolve to do His will. God Himself, in Christ, will be reconciling us with God, in the Father.

But the righteousness of faith speaks in this way, "Do not say in your heart, 'Who will ascend into heaven?' (that is, to bring Christ down from above) or 'Who will descend into the abyss?' (that is, to bring

> *Christ up from the dead). But what does it say? 'The word is near you, in your mouth and in your heart' (that is, the word of faith which we preach): that if you confess with your mouth the Lord Jesus and believe in your heart that God has raised Him from the dead, you will be saved. For with the heart one believes unto righteousness, and with the mouth confession is made unto salvation. For the Scripture says, 'Whoever believes on Him will not be put to shame.' For there is no distinction between Jew and Greek, for the same Lord over all is rich to all who call upon Him. For 'whoever calls on the name of the LORD shall be saved.'"* (Rom.10:6–13)

Jesus is as close as the mention of His name.

Jesus Is God

Although I did know that Jesus is Son of Man and Son of God, **I used to think that Jesus only began to exist when He was born of a virgin two thousand years ago.** So, I was surprised to find that **He has also been God from the beginning, the living Word spoken forth by God.** It is written:

> *In the beginning was the Word, and the Word was with God, and the Word was God. He was in the beginning with God. All things were made through Him, and without Him nothing was made that was made. In Him was life, and the life was the light of men.... And the Word became flesh and dwelt among us, and we beheld His glory, the glory as of the only begotten of the Father, full of grace and truth.* (John 1:1–4, 14)

Now and forever, He is standing in the gap for us at the true mercy seat, the throne where His Father God sits and allows Him to sit. And yet by His Spirit, He can also be right here with each of us.

Jesus even spoke through His prophets in Old Testament times declaring His triune nature, testifying of Himself with two witnesses.

> *Listen to Me, O Jacob, and Israel, My called:*
> *I am He, I am the First, I am also the Last.*
> *Indeed My hand has laid the foundation of the earth,*
> *And My right hand has stretched out the heavens....*
> *Come near to Me, hear this: I have not spoken in secret from the beginning;*
> *From the time that it was, I was there.*
> *And now the Lord GOD and His Spirit have sent Me.*
> *Thus says the LORD, your Redeemer, the Holy One of Israel:*
> *"I am the LORD your God, who teaches you to profit,*
> *who leads you by the way you should go.*
> *Oh, that you had heeded My commandments!*
> *Then your peace would have been like a river,*
> *and your righteousness like the waves of the sea."*
> (Isa. 48:12–13, 16–18)

God, both the Father and the Son, is called Alpha and Omega, First and Last (Rev. 1:11). God created the heavens and the earth with all three divine Persons involved: Father, Son, and Holy Spirit. His word was spoken, and it was done, while His Spirit brooded or hovered over it until things burst forth. *"All things were made through Him* [Jesus], *and without Him nothing was made that was made"* (John 1:3). Jesus, our Redeemer, is God.

Angels testified of Jesus around His coming into the world, including the one who told His foster father:

> *"Joseph, son of David, do not be afraid to take to you Mary your wife, for that which is conceived in her is of the Holy Spirit. And she will bring forth a Son, and you shall call His name JESUS, for He will save His people from their sins." So all this was done that it might be fulfilled which was spoken by the Lord through the prophet, saying: "Behold, the virgin shall be with child, and bear a Son, and they shall call His name Immanuel," which is translated, "God with us."* (Matt. 1:20–23)

Jesus was, is, and will be with us as God, sometimes through Their Spirit.

Even though the Israelites thought salvation came from doing works of the Law, and obedience to God is important, we see that even from Old Testament times that it was by faith, calling on the name of the Lord, that salvation graciously comes.

> *Our help is in the name of the Lord, who made heaven and earth.* (Ps. 124:8)
>
> *Behold the proud, his soul is not upright in him; but the just shall live by his faith.* (Hab. 2:4) (Faith in whom?)
>
> *And it shall come to pass that whoever calls on the name of the Lord shall be saved.* (Joel 2:32)

Jesus Is High Enough

> *Then Melchizedek ... priest of God Most High ... blessed him and said:*
> *"Blessed be Abram of God Most High, Possessor of heaven and earth; and blessed be God Most High, who has delivered your enemies into your hand."*
> *And he gave him a tithe of all.* (Gen. 14:18–20)

As *"The Son of Man,"* because He is the promised holy Seed of Abraham through His mother, Mary, and foster father, Joseph, like *"Abram of God Most High,"* in Abraham, He is Jesus *"of God Most High."* Like Melchizedek, Jesus is also *"the priest of God Most High."* Yet because He is also *"the Son of God,"* who is God, He is also *"Son of the Highest,"* and **"*God Most High*" Himself**. As Gabriel said to Mary, *"Behold, you will conceive in your womb and bring forth a Son and shall call His name JESUS. He will be great and will be called the Son of the Highest; and the Lord God will give Him the throne of His Father David. And He will reign over the house of Jacob forever, and of His kingdom there will be* *no end"* (Luke 1:31–33). Therefore, Jesus is the highest bridge between God and mankind.

Zacharias's prophecy of his son, John the Baptist, referred to our highest bridge: *"And you, child, will be called the prophet of the Highest* [Most High]; *for you will go before the face of the Lord to prepare His ways"* (Luke 1:76).

Jesus Is Strong Enough

A bridge must be strong. God told His chosen leader Joshua, *"Have I not commanded you? Be strong and of good courage; do not be afraid, nor be dismayed, for the L*ord *your God is with you wherever you go"* (Josh. 1:9). Since an ordinary chosen son of man could become very strong because God was with Him, how much more has the extraordinary Son of Man who is the Son of God become very strong with supernatural strength because as prophesied, the Spirit of *"might"* came upon Him at His baptism to remain there. The seven Spirits of God rest on Jesus. *"The Spirit of the L*ord *shall rest upon Him, the Spirit of wisdom and understanding, the Spirit of counsel and might, the Spirit of knowledge and of the fear of the L*ord*"* (Isa. 11:2).

The Spirit of *might* is holy boldness or fortitude and *might* means "1. Strength; force; power; primarily and chiefly, bodily strength or physical power; as, to work or strive with all one's might. 2. Political power or great achievements."[1]

After rising from the dead, Jesus returned to His position in heaven at the right hand of the Father, forever to be one with Almighty God. He is the Mighty Warrior King and the strongest bridge to the Father.

---

1 Rick Meyers, e-Sword. *Webster's Dictionary of American English* (1828)). https://www.e-sword.net/.

John had a revelation of Jesus. *"I am the Alpha and the Omega, the Beginning and the End ... who is and who was and who is to come, the Almighty"* (Rev. 1:8). **God is Power, and power and might come from Him. Jesus is Almighty God.**

> *God has spoken once,*
> *twice I have heard this:*
> *that power belongs to God.* (Ps. 62:11)

> And the Lord said to me, *"Once, twice, three times I have heard that power belongs to the Lord."*
> *Lift up your heads, O you gates!*
> *And be lifted up, you everlasting doors!*
> *And the King of glory shall come in.*
> *Who is this King of glory?*
> *The* L<small>ORD</small> *strong and mighty, the* L<small>ORD</small> *mighty in battle.*
> (Ps. 24:7–8)

When the high priest asked Jesus if He was *"the Christ, the Son of the Blessed,"* Jesus replied by referring to His Second Coming: *"I am. And you will see the Son of Man sitting at the right hand of the Power, and coming with the clouds of heaven"* (Mark 14:61–62). God the Father is Power, and just as steel reinforcing rods can strengthen a structure, Jesus said, *"Believe Me that I am in the Father and the Father in Me, or else believe Me for the sake of the works themselves"* (John 14:11). Jesus could do great works in His own name because He was God; He was in God, and Almighty God was within Him. We, too, can do great works and *"even greater works,"* if we do them in His name because we are in Christ and God is in us by His Spirit. Unless we are connected to the true bridge, we can do nothing.

Gideon was told by the Angel of the Lord, *"The* L<small>ORD</small> *is with you, you mighty man of valor!"* (Judg. 6:12). Gideon, who felt so weak, became strong because he believed God called him *mighty* and could enable him to be. When God says it, He will do it. As He told Paul, *"My grace is sufficient for you, for My strength is made perfect in weakness"* (2

Cor. 12:9). **Since it is the presence of God with one of His obedient servants that makes him strong, how much more so is Jesus strong!** As Jesus said on earth, *"And He who sent Me is with Me. The Father has not left Me alone, for I always do those things that please Him"* (John 8:29). He continues to be obedient to the Father forever, powerfully doing His will in heaven and on earth and in *"New Jerusalem"* of the new heaven and earth when all things are made new.

> *For their Redeemer is mighty;*
> *He will plead their cause against you.* (Prov. 23:11)

> *You have a mighty arm; strong is Your hand, and high is Your right hand.*
> *Righteousness and justice are the foundation of Your throne;*
> *mercy and truth go before Your face.* (Ps. 89:13–14)

> *Praise the L*ORD*! Blessed is the man who fears the L*ORD*,*
> *Who delights greatly in His commandments.*
> *His descendants will be mighty on earth;*
> *The generation of the upright will be blessed.* (Ps. 112:1–2)

> *The name of the L*ORD *is a strong tower;*
> *the righteous run to it and are safe* [secure, set on high]. (Prov. 18:10)

Multitudes worship God in heaven praising His ongoing strength:

> *…saying with a loud voice:*
> *"Worthy is the Lamb who was slain*
> *to receive power and riches and wisdom,*
> *and strength and honor and glory and blessing!"*
> *And every creature which is in heaven and on the earth and under the earth and such as are in the sea, and all that are in them, I heard saying:*
> *"Blessing and honor and glory and power*
> *Be to Him who sits on the throne,*
> *And to the Lamb, forever and ever!"* (Rev. 5:12–13)

Our Bridge Is a Living Bridge— Seeking and Finding Truth

Pre-Vatican II, we were taught from a catechism and the New Testament, but we were not taught much from the Old Testament. Now some Catholic schools do teach Scriptures from the whole Bible. As a teen I tried once to read the whole Bible starting at Genesis and I am sad to say that I got bored and bogged down in Numbers and shut the Book. But ever since I invited Jesus in to eat the Word with me, I really love to read the entire Bible, even Numbers. He helps me find meaning throughout it, praise God, and He began by magnifying to me certain Scriptures.

Thank God, we did have portions of Scripture in each Mass and I used to love reading them in the missal, often attending daily Mass. Yet chewing on these bits and pieces was like enjoying only a snack pack. However, when my mother, Rose Quattrocchi, became a charismatic Catholic baptized in the Holy Spirit, she gave my husband and me a Bible in 1979, and it sat there for a time until my cousin Sal asked if it was only a decoration to gather dust. Thanks to Mom's encouragement to read the Bible by using *100 Huntley Street's* daily devotional, "New Direction," plus she led me to study it with an ecumenical group of Christian women, I began to get into it and to become very hungry for the Word of God, the living bread of life.

The Protestant ladies asked if I had ever invited Jesus into my heart. I had loved Jesus and prayed to God for as long as I could remember, but since I did not know if I had specifically done it before, I invited Jesus in, remembering a picture I had seen once portraying the words, *"Behold, I stand at the door and knock. If anyone hears My voice and opens the door, I will come in to him and dine with him"* (Rev. 3:20). When I invited Jesus into my heart and home, the most wonderful things began to happen. Jesus began to open the Scriptures to me by His Spirit as we dined on His Word together. Occasionally in those days the Lord even magnified certain words to me as if they were under a magnifying glass with yellow highlighter over them, His *shekinah* glory. **Now I can have the "full meal deal," really enjoying reading the whole Bible.**

Sometimes the Lord will shepherd you to a portion of Scripture, but sometimes He will speak to His sheep directly through the gift of *"prophecy"* (Acts 2:18), where He actually puts His words in their mouths. *"My sheep hear My voice, and I know them, and they follow Me"* (John 10:27). After being baptized in the Holy Spirit, four of the most important words the Lord began to impress upon me in His *"still small voice"* (1 Kgs. 19:12) were,

- *"Our help is in the name of the Lord who made heaven and earth";*
- *"The truth will set you free";*
- *"Prepare ye the way of the Lord";* and,
- *"Fear not for I am with you always."*

And I found they were in the Bible too.

Having assisted a children's choir at Mass when my daughter was in grade two, I had learned a song based on Psalm 23, my mom's favorite psalm, and I would sing it as a prayer-song, beginning,

"Lead me, Shepherd, lead me. I'll follow where You go.
Lead me, Shepherd, lead me. I'm safe with You I know."

("Lead Me, Shepherd, Lead Me" Words and Music by Mary Lu Walker, 1975)

So, I began to seek truth and call upon His name, especially as the Good Shepherd and later by His other names, and I began to see Jesus's shepherding in my life. One of the words the Lord spoke to me was, *"In the last days, I will shepherd My sheep, says the Lord."*

He Himself does shepherd today directly by dreams, visions, and prophetic words, as well as through His under-shepherds. He is a living bridge.

There have been many apparitions or visions of a "Lady" promoting the rosary in different parts of the world and many Catholics and Protestants, including me, assumed that it was Mary. Around 1980, I learned, *"Test all things; hold fast what is good"* (1 Thess. 5:21), so I began to test some of these apparitions. For things to be genuinely of God, they should line up with Scripture and have good fruit. Even with the partial knowledge of the Bible that I had then, I could easily see that some apparitions were not genuine and promoted falsehood, like when the "Lady" said that wearing a rosary around your neck would save you.

Catholics knew that Jesus was the Saviour, but somehow, we did not understand what that name meant. Praise God, I began to get it, to see that this word actually meant that He is the One who saves us. Not only is He the sacrificial Lamb who shed His blood at the cross to purchase our salvation, but He does an ongoing work of salvation in our lives. We just need a childlike faith in His finished work to be saved, not to wear some blessed thing or do some other work. **It is belief in the saving action of Jesus that saves people, not wearing a rosary or a medal.**

After the Word of God came to me one night, *"The truth will set you free,"* and I began to ask Jesus to lead me into more truth, I remembered it is written, *"I still have many things to say to you, but you cannot bear them now. However, when He, the Spirit of truth, has come, He will guide you into all truth"* (John 16:12–13). Later, a woman made this banner for a March for Jesus and left it with me to steward it.

We had a budgie bird at the time, and often we left its cage door open because we knew Buddy would not go far. I later realized that **it had been born in a cage, so it did not know that it was not free**, and I had not known that I was not free either. Sin, even when you are ignorant of doing wrong, can imprison you.

Also, when people do not understand the truth, they sometimes imprison (verbally or physically) those who preach the good news of Jesus Christ.

For a few years, I lived like I was on house arrest, in an open cage like the budgie, allowed out for good behaviour, because my RC husband did not understand the calling on my life. (But thank God, he did before he died.)

Jesus came *"to proclaim liberty to the captives"* (Luke 4:18). When you trust Jesus and receive His saving grace, you shall be free! You do not have to do certain works to get this grace—only believe.

However, to stay free, out of captivity to sin, it is important to both listen to the Word of God and to do what He says to do: *"But be doers of the word, and not hearers only, deceiving yourselves"* (Jas. 1:22); and, *"For God so loved the world that He gave His only begotten Son, that whoever believes in Him should not perish but have everlasting life"* (John 3:16).

We Need This Bridge

John the Baptist warned the people, *"The Father loves the Son, and has given all things into His hand. He who believes in the Son has everlasting* *life; and he who does not believe the Son shall not see life, but the wrath of God abides on him"* (John 3:35–36). That is why the word of the Lord, *"Prepare the way of the Lord,"* came again in our time. As Jesus said, *"For the Son of Man will come in the glory of His Father with His angels, and then He will reward each according to his works"* (Matt. 16:27). *"Taste and see that the Lord is good"* (Ps. 34:8). If we will only believe and follow Him, He can forgive our sins and lead us in His paths of righteousness so we can cross the bridge and have fellowship with the Father and have a righteous judgment. It was done at the cross, but we must appropriate it for ourselves.

It was said to those judging others and yet practicing the same evil, to beware of also receiving God's judgment, just consequences. Even unrepentant Christians can be judged by their words and actions. Thank God grace can teach our hearts to fear the Lord, and grace can relieve our fears. Because of His blood and His intercession, since *"all have sinned and fall short of the glory of God, being* [the repentant can be] *justified freely by His grace through the redemption that is in Christ Jesus"* (Rom. 3:23–24).

The Book of Revelation is full of reminders that His wrath is coming for the wicked, but there are wonderful rewards for the righteous, for those who wash their robes in the blood of the Lamb. The Lord told me that even His vengeance is love.

It is better to have Him deal with someone sooner rather than later, but it is better still when people seek His help to purify their heart and mind. His precious blood can *"cleanse your conscience from dead works to serve the living God"* (Heb. 9:14), washing away the stain of sin. Since people will be judged by what they have done, and nothing is hidden from God, **if we have repented from sins, they will not be held against us in the heavenly books which will be opened. (See Revelation 20:12.) Because of faith in the shed blood of the Lamb,** *"Though your sins are like scarlet, they shall be as white as snow"* (Isa. 1:18).

Jesus is our Saviour and our Mediator, but He expects us to not just listen to Him but to follow Him, to do what is right. He can cleanse and heal us so that we can choose to enjoy fellowship with Him and do His will rather than go back to wallow in the mire. Unbelievers practice evil and risk eternal damnation, but believers should practice righteousness, saved by grace to follow Jesus, and to do the good works God has prepared for them. They can boldly come to the light so they can see to take the right bridge to the Father.

We need Jesus because sin deserves punishment. For believers, Jesus took the heavy part. **I did not realize how much Jesus did on the cross until I read Deuteronomy 28.** There we can see the blessings for obedience to the Word of God and the progressive curses for more and more disobedience under the Law. **Thank God, Jesus gained the victory fulfilling the Law so that believers do not have to get what they deserve. But non-believers ought to beware!** He loves us so much that He desires the gospel to be preached to every nation that more may be saved. Jesus was an overcomer so He can help us be overcomers with His resurrection power and restore our inheritance to us. He left us His Holy Spirit, *"another Helper"* (John 14:16), as the first pledge of our inheritance. His blood which made *"atonement"* *"once for all"* (Rom. 6:10; Heb. 10:10) still speaks mercy over believers.

We need Jesus to prepare us for eternity with Him. His gospel and His Spirit are perfecting us in doing His loving will, but it is a process. O how He loves us!

Our Bridge Is Christ—Our High Priest—God's Chosen Mediator

Who are you going to call? In New Testament times, Jesus is the designated eternal High Priest in the order of Melchizedek, the only name in heaven or on earth or under the earth through whom we are to pray in order to get to God. We can put in our 9-1-1 to Him. As Peter said when others were going elsewhere, *"Lord, to whom shall we go? You have the words of eternal life"* (John 6:68); and Paul declared, *"For there is one God and one Mediator between God and men, the Man Christ Jesus, who gave Himself a ransom for all"* (1 Tim. 2:5–6).

Not only believing the Word of God to be true but having found that other bridges were false and this one was true, even having explored those of eastern religions at one point, **I, too, testify to this truth,** thankful that Jesus set me free!

What about the Prophets?

You might ask, "What about the prophets? Did they not connect with God?"

Yes, they did, and true prophets still do, in Jesus's name. If people wanted to inquire of God, they asked the prophets to do that for them in Old Testament times. But prophets could not save anyone themselves. They could not make atonement for their own or other people's sins so that they could go to the Father in heaven forever. The blood of animal sacrifices prescribed by God as atonement covered their sins but did not remove them, so the high priest had to do it each year, and it was only a foreshadowing of the blood of the Lamb of God who takes away the sin of the world for believers, those before and after His death. Although God raptured up Elijah, even the prophets needed to wait for Jesus, the Great Prophet of whom Moses spoke, to come and lead them to heaven. The prophets were God's chosen messengers who communed with God and pointed towards a coming Messiah, but they were just not long and sturdy enough of a bridge to reconcile God and men by themselves. So, Jesus explained that not only does no one come to the Father except through Him, but, *"It is written in the prophets, 'And they shall all be taught by God.' Everyone who has heard and learned from the Father comes to Me"* (John 6:45). His shed blood was needed for the remission of sins.

All the Old Testament prophets who heard and learned from the Father were also given revelations of the Christ, the Messiah, the

Anointed One appointed by God, who is Jesus. You can see in some of David's songs like Psalm 2 that he prophesied, having heard not only from God as the Father but as the Son. Even when Old Testament prophets died, they could not bridge that final gap to the Father in heaven, but waited for their Messiah Jesus who died and descended to the dead and released them from their captivity there: *"And the graves were opened; and many bodies of the saints who had fallen asleep were raised; and coming out of the graves after His resurrection, they went into the holy city and appeared to many"* (Matt. 27:52–53).

"When He ascended on high, He led captivity captive, and gave gifts to men" (Eph. 4:8). Some had been waiting there hundreds of years before He raised them up on high: *"Nor is there salvation in any other, for there is no other name under heaven given among men by which we must be saved"* (Acts 4:12). **Even for the faithful Jews who lived in Old Testament times, and for all believers today, Jesus was, is, and will be the world's longest bridge between mankind and God.**

Part II

Composition of the Bridge

For there is one God and one Mediator between God and men,
the Man Christ Jesus,
who gave Himself a ransom for all, to be testified in due time.
(1 Tim. 2:5–6)

I am the way, the truth, and the life.
No one comes to the Father except through Me.
(John 14:6)

For as the body is one and has many members,
but all the members of that one body,
being many, are one body, so also is Christ.
(1 Cor. 12:12)

Chapter 3
The Genuine Bridge

If you want to know what a counterfeit twenty-dollar bill looks like, you need to study the genuine one first. Now is the time to study the true bridge so we will not be deceived by the counterfeits.

> *For who in the heavens can be compared to the LORD?*
> *Who among the sons of the mighty can be likened to the LORD?*
> (Ps. 89:6)

Believers are being restored not like God in the sense of equality, but in His image according to His likeness, in the *likeness* of the Father, Son, and Holy Spirit, as He created mankind in the beginning: *"Then God said, 'Let Us make man in Our image, according to Our likeness; let them have dominion over the fish of the sea, over the birds of the air, and over the cattle, over all the earth, and over every creeping thing that creeps on the earth'"* (Gen. 1:26). Jesus is the perfect image and likeness of God, being God and the natural Son of God: *"He is the image of the invisible God, the firstborn over all creation"* (Col. 1:15). Being spiritually born again we have a spiritual family resemblance like adopted children sometimes do. In some ways saints may look like Him, especially their character. But no work of His creation will ever be His equal all the time. Not even the heavenly hosts of angels and saints. Lucifer fell when he thought he was like God. Our only hope to grow to be more like Jesus is to have Him and the Holy Spirit living in us, doing the Father's works through us: *"Christ in you, the hope of glory"* (Col. 1:27).

> *Thus says the LORD, the King of Israel,*
> *And his Redeemer, the LORD of hosts:*

> *"I am the First and I am the Last;
> Besides Me there is no God."* (Isa. 44:6)

No work of God's creation is His equal.

A *mediator*[2] is: "One that interposes between parties at variance for the purpose of reconciling them. 1. By way of eminence, Christ is the mediator, the divine Intercessor through whom sinners may be reconciled to an offended God. 2. Christ is a mediator by nature, as partaking of both natures divine and human; and mediator by office, as transacting matters between God and man."

Shadows and the Real Thing

The Old Testament temple was a *"copy and shadow of the heavenly things"* (Heb. 8:5). God Himself gave Moses instructions like blueprints on how it was to be built and what was to be done there. **Aaron, God's first chosen Levitical high priest mediator** in the wilderness tabernacle, ministered where **the presence of God would meet with him over the mercy seat**. He had priests assist him from his own family, the Aaronic priesthood. This was a shadow of what was coming.

In New Testament times, **Jesus, God's last chosen High Priest**, is seated **at the right hand of the Father Himself at His heavenly throne of mercy and grace**.

The true bridge between God and mankind is the person of Jesus Christ. He Himself is the *"one Mediator between God and men"* who *"always lives to make intercession for them"* at the right hand of the Father. He can be the whole bridge on His own. *"He is also able to save to the uttermost those who come to God through Him, since He always lives to make intercession for them"* (Heb. 7:25). But on earth, He chooses to need Christians like the head needs the rest of the

---

2   Rick Meyers, e-Sword, *Webster's Dictionary of American English* (1828). https://www.e-sword.net/.

body parts. So, the members of His body on earth, like supporting trestlework on the bridge, are called to stand in the gap with Him and in Him in *"supplications, prayers, intercessions, and giving of thanks … for all men, for kings and all who are in authority"* (1 Tim. 2:1–2).

We can ask saintly members of His body who are on earth to pray and mediate for us, to be intercessors, a new royal priesthood of believers with Jesus the High Priest in charge; but they cannot bridge the gap between God and mankind all alone in their own name any more than a piece of trestlework can be the whole bridge. Like trestlework under a bridge, they can only bridge the gap to God for someone if they are in Christ, connected to Him as a functioning part of His body, under His headship, and only in His name. They may pray, and prayers may be answered, but it is all about His name, not their names. Jesus is *"the Mediator,"* and He deserves the glory. As Saint Peter said, *"This is the 'stone which was rejected by you builders, which has become the chief cornerstone.' Nor is there salvation in any other, for there is no other name under heaven given among men by which we must be saved"* (Acts 4:11–12).

Pentecostal churches had a slogan in 2004: **"NO OTHER NAME."** The Bible only records one name *"by which we must be saved"*—Jesus Christ: *"And it shall come to pass that whoever calls on the name of the Lord shall be saved"* (Joel 2:32; Acts 2:21). Jesus told His disciples to abide in Him, loving one another as He had loved them, and to let His words abide in them. Then they would find, *"Most assuredly, I say to you, whatever you ask the Father in My name He will give you"* (John 16:23).

Jesus stands in the gap for us against our enemies too. In Old Testament times, God called Moses and later, Aaron, to stand in the gap for His people. When Joshua led the army to fight with Amalek, Moses stood at the top of the hill, his hands raised, praying with the authority of God. When his hands got heavy, two friends helped him hold them up. Jesus told His apostles after His resurrection, *"All authority has been given to Me in heaven and on earth"* (Matt. 28:18), and

He can give of it to whomever He chooses, that they may uphold Him in His work of reconciling men to the Father and delivering them from evil, and that they may teach what He taught them and release the gifts of the Holy Spirit, part of their inheritance.

Trestlework

Jesus said, *"I am the vine, you are the branches. He who abides in Me, and I in him, bears much fruit; for without Me you can do nothing"* (John 15:5). Can you have a grapevine composed only of branches, with no vine and root system? No. Yet joined together, the unified vine is very productive. Can you have a railway trestle bridge composed only of trestles with no unifying top piece to carry the train? Likewise, no.

Members of the body of Christ alive on earth today who abide in Christ may stand as intercessors before the throne of grace **in His name, like trestlework on the true bridge**. **These parts have been made righteous through faith in Christ.** Their prayer in His name, especially when it is led by His Spirit, connects them, going to the Father through Jesus. They can even ask Him how to pray and for whom to pray.

His one bridge has many functioning parts, just as a body does: *"There is one body and one Spirit, just as you were called in one hope of your calling; one Lord, one faith, one baptism* [into the death and resurrection of Christ]; *one God and Father of all, who is above all, and through all, and in you all. But to each one of us grace was given according to the measure of Christ's gift"* (Eph. 4:4–7). The parts are enabled by what Christ gives them through the will of His Spirit. His grace is truly amazing.

Just as the trestles of a railway bridge are all important, every inch of them including linking pieces, likewise every member and cell in the body of Christ is important. Different parts are made differently because they have different functions. Some are chosen specifically, gifted and prepared with governmental prophetic gifting to stand in the gap with and under Christ, listening to His voice and praying what

He shows them. **The strength of the parts comes from Christ within them, under them, and over them as LORD.** Yet all parts can receive a measure of prophetic gifting as Peter reminded us at Pentecost.

God created us for a purpose and so **Jesus needs the parts of His body, His bride, and bridge, just as we need Him and each other.** Being God and Son of God, Jesus needs nothing, and yet, He chooses to need His human body parts to stand in the gap with Him and to ride behind Him bearing *"the sword of the Spirit, which is the word of God"* (Eph. 6:17).

He created us to each do our own part and yet function together, not completely independently but interdependently; not our way or man's way, but Jesus's way: *"God has set the members, each one of them, in the body just as He pleased"* (1 Cor. 12:18). We are not robots, but children of God to choose lovingly to do His will. We are to connect with one another appropriately. Does not the top of a railway trestle bridge have need of the trestlework supporting pieces attached to it and vice versa? The parts of His body in one church, in one city, in one nation, in all the world, all need one another and most of all, they need the head. And He has humbled Himself to need us even though He could do everything Himself. He has chosen to do it in partnership with us. Wow! What an awesome God we have!

We can go to another geographical location, and immediately find a connection with other members of His body, realizing we are "church family."

> *For as the body is one and has many members, but all the members of that one body, being many, are one body, so also is Christ. For by one Spirit we were all baptized into one body—whether Jews or Greeks, whether slaves or free—and have all been made to drink into one Spirit. For in fact the body is not one member but many. If the foot should say, "Because I am not a hand, I am not of the body," is it therefore not of the body? And if the ear should say, "Because I am not an eye, I am not of the body," is it therefore not of the body?*

If the whole body were an eye, where would be the hearing? If the whole were hearing, where would be the smelling? But now God has set the members, each one of them, in the body just as He pleased. And if they were all one member, where would the body be? [If they were all one trestle, or one railway tie (one church), where would the bridge be?]

But now indeed there are many members, yet one body. And the eye cannot say to the hand, "I have no need of you"; nor again the head to the feet, "I have no need of you." No, much rather, those members of the body which seem to be weaker are necessary. And those members of the body which we think to be less honorable, on these we bestow greater honor; and our unpresentable parts have greater modesty, but our presentable parts have no need. But God composed the body, having given greater honor to the part which lacks it, that there should be no schism in the body, but that the members should have the same care for one another. And if one member suffers, all the members suffer with it; or if one member is honored, all the members rejoice with it. Now you are the body of Christ and members individually. And God has appointed these in the church: first apostles, second prophets, third teachers, after that miracles, then gifts of healings, helps, administrations, varieties of tongues. (1 Cor. 12:12–28)

The "Oldman River" under the trestle bridge in Lethbridge is a reminder of the "old man" that we are to put off when we put on Christ: *"Knowing this, that our old man was crucified with Him, that the body of sin might be done away with, that we should no longer be slaves of sin"* (Rom. 6:6). In Christ, sinful ways can be put under our feet.

Instead of struggling for our lives in the valley, when we humble ourselves before Him, casting all our cares and crowns upon Him (giving Him the glory due His name), because He cares for us and is the One who created and gifted us, He lifts us up into the train on His bridge so we can safely come to the Father through Jesus.

Posture of Prayer

> *At the name of Jesus every knee should bow, of those in heaven, and of those on earth, and of those under the earth.* (Phil. 2:10)

As a child I thought the only posture for prayer was on our knees as Jesus was at Gethsemane, and kneeling is good; but then I saw charismatic people praying standing with hands raised rather than folded and read that Paul told Timothy, a bishop, *"I desire therefore that the men pray everywhere, lifting up holy hands, without wrath and doubting"* (1 Tim. 2:8).

God calls men and women to pray and intercede in faith, and not to be afraid to lift up their hands to Him in doing so. It was an Old Testament way of prayer and praise to God; so I realized that **Jesus, an observant Jew, would have prayed that way at times too.**

I remember when my charismatic Catholic mother began to ask me to try to lift my hands to praise God. She said that people lift up their hands at sports events, so how much more should they be set free to do it unto the Lord since He desires it! I felt self-conscious at first, but now it is natural, supernatural, to do it at times. I find that the physical act of lifting up my hands aids in getting my focus on God rather than my circumstance. It reminds me of the love and trust of a little child in reaching up to her daddy: "

> *Let my prayer be set before you as incense, the lifting up of my hands as the evening sacrifice"* (Ps. 141:2).

> *Behold, bless the* LORD,
> *All you servants of the* LORD,
> *Who by night stand in the house of the* LORD!
> *Lift up your hands in the sanctuary,*
> *And bless the* LORD. (Ps. 134:1–2)

Now today, you can see multitudes lifting up their hands at conferences when worship music is playing. I have noticed a counterfeit though on TV when I have seen portions of rock concerts in the secular world. Multitudes lift up their hands there too now, but in that situation, it has nothing to do with lifting one's hands up to God.

There is a time for people today to *"pray everywhere, lifting up holy hands, without wrath and doubting"* (1 Tim. 2:8). Leaving wrath and vengeance to God and not doubting when you pray is very important.

There was so much emphasis upon lifting up one's hands in prayer a few years ago that I wondered for a time if we were only to worship that way; but I believe the Lord showed me that **we do not have to be legalistic about it**.

Intercession is like the design of a roof truss. A stranger walked into my office when I worked as secretary-bookkeeper of a construction company, and he handed me a couple pages with diagrams of a variety of roof trusses. They were in a variety of configurations to fit the needs, but he said that **each part was very important**. Each truss having an upright king post, top and bottom chords, truss webs (support beams), and bearing points reminded me of Jesus the Intercessor with help from His body.

There can be a variety of postures for prayer, but the upright posture of the heart is important with Jesus as the central component, like the king post. He is *"O Most Upright"* **(Isa. 26:7). Our position is where Jesus places us. Just as every part of a roof truss is important, so is every part of a trestle bridge, and every part of the body of Christ the King. (See Psalm 19.)**

We are admonished by Paul to *"pray without ceasing"* (1 Thess. 5:17), *"praying always with all prayer and supplication in the Spirit, being watchful to this end with all perseverance and supplication for all the saints—and for me, that utterance may be given to me, that I may open my mouth boldly to make known the mystery of the gospel"* (Eph. 6:18–19). We are to keep watchful to follow the Spirit's leading in prayer and to rest on the Rock who is Jesus, supporting one another in prayer agreement. It is the prayer of faith that matters and the follow-through of believing it will come to pass. *"And Ezra blessed the L*ORD*, the great God. Then all the people answered, 'Amen, Amen!' while lifting up their hands. And they bowed their heads and worshiped the L*ORD *with their faces to the ground"* (Neh. 8:6).

Wow! That always reminds me of the angels around the throne of God, and we can begin practicing for heaven by doing it on earth. Our desire should be to worship *"in spirit and truth"* rather than in the flesh, so there are times and places when public expressions are called forth by the leadership for corporate worship and other times when they are better done in private worship. Jesus cautioned, *"And when you pray, you shall not be like the hypocrites. For they love to pray standing in the synagogues and on the corners of the streets, that they may be seen by men. Assuredly, I say to you, they have their reward. But when you pray, go into your room, and when you have shut your door, pray to your Father who is in the secret place; and your Father who sees in secret will reward you openly"* (Matt. 6:5–6).

Although our public worship should not be done to draw attention to ourselves but to pay attention to God, there are some churches where the leadership invites people to be free in their praise and worship and even invites them to go to the front or out in the aisles to dance their praise. Then I have seen the majority enter in with heartfelt expressions as in Ezra's day when they both lifted their hands and bowed their heads.

The first few times I tried putting my whole heart and soul and mind and strength into public worship at church, I was very self-conscious. I was among others who lifted their hands in worship and clapped their hands, and yet sometimes I still needed to ask the Holy Spirit to examine me to be sure it was not to draw attention to myself. Some people are very reserved when they sing praise and worship, but might be engaged nevertheless, so we should not judge by appearance—unless it is blatantly obvious. But especially if the leadership invites people to be free in their worship, then one should worship in the manner that the Holy Spirit is prompting, be it sitting, standing, kneeling, or prostrating oneself in worship, or exuberant dancing and clapping. Yet it should be fitting as worship, in modest dress, as it is in heaven.

We can pray kneeling and David even prayed lying down at times: *"When I remember You on my bed, I meditate on You in the night watches"* (Ps. 63:6). And Jesus prays even sitting down at the right hand of the Father. To those who were formerly lukewarm Jesus sent word, *"To him who overcomes I will grant to sit with Me on My throne, as I also overcame and sat down with My Father on His throne"* (Rev. 3:21).

I have learned that **the most important thing about prayer position is the posture of our heart** with respect for our God to whom we are praying.

Every part of a bridge is important, and every part of the body of Christ is important. When each one is doing his job with Jesus the King over all like the top of the bridge, just as God gave Joshua victory when Moses's hands were held up in prayer assisted by his two friends, so God still wants His people to humble themselves and pray, supporting friends, turning from evil, and seeking His face to give us victory in Jesus. It is like holding up Jesus's hands, although He will never tire out. As members of His body we may be part of His hands.

We do not have to be legalistic about our physical stance though. Sometimes we pray standing with arms physically uplifted; sometimes we are kneeling or sitting, or even lying down. And our arms may be in other positions at times. But there is a place for standing with uplifted arms: *"Therefore strengthen the hands which hang down, and the feeble knees"* [drooping hands and weak knees] (Heb. 12:12).

Saint Paul said, *"I desire that the men pray everywhere, lifting up holy hands, without wrath and doubting"* (1 Tim. 2:8). However, hands and fingers together can help children focus. But keeping one's hands clenched close to one's body a lot can also be a posture of worry. **Freely**

lifting them to the Father can be a childlike posture of faith and expectancy that God is able to answer prayers in line with His will.

In grade two, my daughter learned in catechism class:

Q. How do you bless the Lord?

A. By your prayer of praise and your job well done.

Hebrews 10:5 says, *"But a body You have prepared for Me."* Jesus was begotten of the Father and not created, having existed with Him from the beginning. The Father prepared a physical body for Jesus to grow in after He took flesh and was knit together in Mary's womb. The Father also prepared a spiritual body of believers for the Word of God to dwell in, beginning in the womb of *"Jerusalem above"* (Gal. 4:26). Paul said to those he was training to be Jesus's disciples, *"My little children, for whom I labor in birth again until Christ is formed in you"* (Gal. 4:19). Paul entered into Jesus's intercession that the will and action of Christ might be formed in these new believers.

Jesus can inhabit His spiritual body of believers prepared for Him: *"Moreover whom He predestined, these He also called; whom He called, these He also justified; and whom He justified, these He also glorified"* (Rom. 8:30). Those who answer His call are justified, made right with God, their sins washed away by His blood so that they are cleansed just as if they had never sinned. Because they are united to Jesus with His Spirit dwelling in them, they are also glorified by Him because His glory will shine through them. These believers may form the trestlework bridging the gap in, with and through Him.

The Father had also prepared a glorified body for Jesus to dwell in after His resurrection and He ascended to heaven in it. Thomas saw that His wounds were healed, He could eat food, and go through walls, and slip off the bonds of gravity. Now, at the right hand of the Father, He sits and stands as eternal Mediator where *"He always lives to make intercession for them"* (Heb. 7:25). One day, our bodies will be glorified even more too, and we will form New Jerusalem for Him to inhabit as we join with and worship Him.

Non-Believers Are Not Part of the Bridge, but Could Be

It is Jesus's desire that people believe in Him and abide in Him and He in them so closely that God can do His works in them too, including reconciliation. Jesus has many sheep who can now be intercessors with and in Him, in His name; and there are many others who could be too if they would only come to Him, trust Him, and follow Him. Jesus said, *"And other sheep I have which are not of this fold; them also I must bring, and they will hear My voice; and there will be one flock and one shepherd"* (John 10:16).

Old Testament Bridge Was a Foreshadow—Christ Is the Real Thing

From Moses's time until the death and resurrection of Jesus, **under the Old Covenant, either a recognized prophet like Moses or the high priest in the order of Aaron was the bridge chosen by God to be the mediator between God and man.** The presence of God met with Moses daily and would meet with the high priest once a year between the cherubim on the mercy seat over the ark of the covenant. This was in the Holy of holies of the tent of meeting which was made by Moses according to the pattern given by God, and in the Most Holy Place of the temple Solomon built later in Jerusalem. **But these were only temporary, a foreshadowing of the permanent heavenly tabernacle and of the permanent high priesthood of Jesus Christ, the new bridge, the chosen bridge, anointed and appointed by God.**

> *The priests always went into the first part of the tabernacle, performing the services. But into the second part the high priest went alone, once a year, not without blood, which he offered for himself and for the peoples' sins committed in ignorance....* [In those days,] *both gifts and sacrifices are offered which cannot make him who performed the service perfect in regard to the conscience.... But Christ came as High Priest of the good things to come, with the greater and more perfect tabernacle not made with hands, that is, not of this creation....* [The blood of their sacrifices purified the flesh.] *How much more shall the blood of Christ ... cleanse your conscience from dead works to serve the living God? And for this reason He is the Mediator of the new covenant, by means of death.* (Heb. 9:6–7, 11, 14–15)

Only the high priest could go there beyond the veil where the presence of God would come, and not without the blood of the spotless animal sacrifice, sprinkling it not only on the people but at the mercy seat over the ark of the covenant where the presence of God would meet with him and be enthroned there. **Only he could do it**, and that just once a year on the Day of Atonement. **Likewise, only Jesus could do it** in New Testament times **opening the way to the presence of God for us.** Just as they only went in once a year, not without blood, **He only had to go in once, but once for all time, with His own shed blood, the blood of the Lamb who takes away the sin of the world.** His blood is still sufficient to atone for our sins.

New Testament Bridge Is a Permanent Reality

Jesus is the eternal High Priest, the eternal Intercessor at the heavenly mercy seat, the one Messiah and Mediator chosen, anointed and appointed by God. **Jesus is the bridge built to stand forever.** The order of Melchizedek is an everlasting order, so Jesus is the everlasting High Priest and Intercessor. He has gone into heaven with His atoning blood, the real thing, so believers could wear *"garments of salvation"* by faith. *"With His own blood He entered the Most Holy Place once for all, having obtained eternal redemption"* (Heb. 9:12). No one else needs to do that.

Those who are *"in Christ"* who is *"at the right hand of God"* (Mark 16:19) can prepare their hearts, accept His sacrifice for their cleansing, and join Him in bridging the gap. He is the chosen Intercessor, anointed forever as *"the priest of God Most High"* (Gen. 14:18), and He has given us access to the reality of meeting with God Himself, a privilege we should highly value, purchased by His blood spilled on Calvary's hill. That is why God sent His Son, the Father personified. *"For in Him dwells all the fullness of the Godhead bodily"* (Col. 2:9). His blood shed just once will always keep its effectiveness and He will always be there for us. He loves us so much. Jesus, the bridge, will stand forever. *"He always lives to make intercession for them"* (Heb. 7:25). God is not dead. He is truly alive.

We can have fellowship with Him on an ongoing basis. Jesus shall have His position forever both sitting on the mercy seat at the Father's right hand and standing up for us and for His Father. He is better than an earthly lawyer. He has saved and is saving His people, helping us turn from evil ways and towards His Father.

Hebrews 7:23–24 says, *"Also there were many priests, because they were prevented by death from continuing. But He, because He continues forever, has an unchangeable priesthood."* After His death, His glorified physical body went with Him when He arose and the veil blocking the way into the Holy of holies in the temple *"was torn in two from top to bottom"* (Mark 15:38) at His crucifixion as an indication of this. Since the veil was so high and heavy, and torn from the top, it could not have been torn by mere men. Jesus *"entered for us* [behind the veil]*"* (Heb. 6:20), being and opening the way for members of His spiritual body to enter the presence of God too, not only after death, but in kingdom living now. *"Let us therefore come boldly to the throne of grace, that we may obtain mercy and find grace to help in time of need"* (Heb. 4:16).

But we need to remember what a privilege this is. Old Testament high priests would seek to make their hearts right first before entering the Most Holy Place with animal blood, cleansing their hands and feet first, asking God to be merciful towards their sins and the sins of others. They rejoiced that they were still alive after being in the presence of God. Jesus's own blood cleansed His hands and feet of the sins of mankind which He had carried for us, like when bird dirt is washed off a car.

Today, to be strong trestlework, we, too, should show reverence towards Almighty God knowing that it is from Him that our strength comes. **Although we can call God our heavenly Father by a familiar term, *"Abba,"* and Jesus can even be our best Friend, let us always remember that He is also Almighty God.** Those who have a holy fear of the Lord as well as a great love for Him are blessed. And Jesus, the Word of God, shall live forever.

> *Before the mountains were brought forth,*
> *Or ever You had formed the earth and the world,*
> *Even from everlasting to everlasting, You are God.* (Ps. 90:2)

Chapter 4
The Choice Was the Father's

James and John asked Jesus, *"'Grant us that we may sit, one on Your right hand and the other on Your left, in Your glory.' But Jesus said to them, 'You do not know what you ask. Are you able to drink the cup that I drink, and be baptized with the baptism that I am baptized with?'... Jesus said to them ... 'to sit on My right hand and on My left is not Mine to give, but it is for those for whom it is prepared'"* (Mark 10:37–40). God had already chosen places to prepare for certain people, including His own Son, our Lord Jesus:

> *For David himself said by the Holy Spirit:*
> *"The LORD said to my Lord,*
> *'Sit at My right hand,*
> *Till I make Your enemies Your footstool.'"* (Mark 12:36)

David also prophesied of God Himself choosing and installing His Messiah, God's only begotten Son, who would be King, Judge, High Priest, and Mediator, who would be above all others, with an unending commission ruling, judging, and interceding. Just as a bridge is set in place at the word of the general contractor, the Father set King Jesus in place, in a position to be and do what He was called to be and do, connecting God and man in the priestly order of King Melchizedek. He was set in place even mediating from the cross on the hill of Golgotha where He interceded for the sins of all. *"Father, forgive them, for they do not know what they do"* (Luke 23:34).

Through David, the Father spoke, *"Yet I have set My King on My holy hill of Zion"* (Ps. 2:6). And now Jesus has been set in place first, reigning in ministry over all the power of the devil for three and a half years in Israel, overcoming death by His resurrection, and overcoming gravity by His ascension, and now He has entered into His rest at God's right hand in heaven. He is still trusting the Father for the full completion of His words until the time for Jesus to return in glory as *"KING OF KINGS AND LORD OF LORDS"* (Rev. 19:16).

His enemies are being made to bow before Him. Although the high priest did not recognize Jesus as the Christ yet, interestingly, he knew that the Messiah, the Christ, would have a position in God as His Son. Before His crucifixion, *"the high priest asked Him, saying to Him, 'Are You the Christ, the Son of the Blessed?' Jesus said, 'I am. And you will see the Son of Man sitting at the right hand of the Power, and coming with the clouds of heaven'"* (Mark 14:61–62).

Not only is He reigning now from His position at the Father's right hand, but Jesus is *"the Word, and the Word was with God, and the Word was God. He was in the beginning with God.... No one has seen God at any time. The only begotten Son, who is in the bosom of the Father, He has declared Him"* (John 1:1, 18).

Yet Jesus also takes His place here on earth in the hearts of those who will receive Him and walks amidst His churches: *"And in the midst of the seven lampstands, One like the Son of Man, clothed with a garment down to the feet and girded about the chest with a golden band"* (Rev. 1:13). Our bridge goes from one side to the other with no difficulty because His kingdom can be on earth as it is in heaven.

Jesus's Appointment as Mediator Is Certain because the Father Said So

No man takes the honor of being the mediator, the High Priest, upon himself. He must be *"called by God just as Aaron was. So also*

Christ did not glorify Himself to become High Priest, but it was He who said to Him: 'You are My Son, today I have begotten You'" (Heb. 5:4–5).

Father God permanently appointed His Son, Jesus, as King and High Priest and anointed Him with the oil of gladness at His baptism when the heavens opened. Before coming to earth, Jesus was chosen and *"called by God as High Priest"* (Heb: 5:10). And He is *"a priest forever according to the order of Melchizedek"* (Heb. 5:6).

At His baptism and transfiguration, the audible voice of the Father was heard from heaven testifying to Jesus as being His only begotten Son, above His adopted ones: *"This is My Beloved Son, in whom I am well pleased"* (Matt. 3:17; 17:5). Surely, He was pleased with the way Jesus honored and obeyed His earthly parents and behaved during His first thirty years on earth. The Father also anointed Him with His Holy Spirit and gladness, with joy from above, fulfilling Scripture:

> *Your throne, O God, is forever and ever;*
> *A scepter of righteousness is the scepter of Your kingdom.*
> *You love righteousness and hate wickedness;*
> *Therefore God, Your God, has anointed You*
> *With the oil of gladness more than Your companions.* (Ps. 45:6–7)

John the Baptist also testified of Him saying, *"I saw the Spirit descending from heaven like a dove, and He remained upon Him. I did not know Him, but He who sent me to baptize with water said to me, 'Upon whom you see the Spirit descending and remaining upon Him, this is He who baptizes with the Holy Spirit.' And I have seen and testified that this is the Son of God"* (John 1:32–34).

We know that the Holy Bible is the inspired Word of God who cannot lie; so it is a true book. And the Bible states that *"He* [Jesus] *is the Mediator of the new covenant"* (Heb. 9:15).

God testified to His Son's appointment:

> *...with an oath by Him who said to Him:*
> *"The LORD has sworn*
> *And will not relent,*
> *'You are a priest forever*
> *According to the order of Melchizedek.'.* (Heb. 7:21; Ps. 110:4)

Behold, I Have Prepared a Place for You

Jesus told His disciples they could have a place in Him, in His vine as branches if they did His will, thus remaining attached to Him in love (and so they could be parts of the bridge too): *"If you keep My commandments, you will abide in My love"* (John 15:10). And, *"If you abide in Me, and My words abide in you, you will ask what you desire, and it shall be done for you. By this My Father is glorified, that you bear much fruit; so you will be My disciples"* (John 15:7–8). Thanks be to God, believers are not God, but have been adopted into His family as His children, so they can have a place in Christ, the *"only begotten Son,"* as parts of His body.

Jesus told His eleven chosen ones at the Last Supper, *"Let not your heart be troubled; you believe in God, believe also in Me. In My Father's house are many mansions; if it were not so, I would have told you. I go to prepare a place for you. And if I go and prepare a place for you, I will come again and receive you to Myself; that where I am, there you may be also. And where I go you know, and the way you know"* (John 14:1–4). Functioning members of His body can follow Him there and not only have Jesus be with them where they are, but they can be with Him where He is. Jesus said, *"I am the way, the truth, and the life. No one comes to the Father except through Me"* (John 14:6).

The apostles, being Jews, would understand that these words also referred to how a Jewish bridegroom went away to prepare a place attached to his father's house for his betrothed bride to be with him. And when his father said the house was ready, he would return for her.

Jesus is returning for His bride, the body of Christ, the trestlework on His bridge, ready to lay down her life with Him so that Jesus will reign in her as Lord and Husband of her life. Neither "self" nor *"mammon"* nor any other god or idol will rule over her anymore: *"And those who are Christ's have crucified the flesh with its passions and desires"* (Gal. 5:24). If we want to be with Him, and minister unto God and men at His side, this is important. Like Paul, we can say, *"I have been crucified with Christ; it is no longer I who live, but Christ lives in me; and the life which I now live in the flesh I live by faith in the Son of God, who loved me and gave Himself for me"* (Gal. 2:20).

For those who are *"in Christ,"* because Jesus opened up a way for believers to enter the Father's presence, they too can approach the throne of God as His children, parts of the body of Christ set in place where He desires. Like the prodigal son, those who have gone astray and are repentant can return to the Father just as they are, so that He can restore them to whatever place He chooses. However, it is wonderful if we seek to sanctify ourselves first. Jesus, the Lamb of God, even submitted to baptism with water and the Holy Spirit *"to fulfill all righteousness"* (Matt. 3:15), even though He had committed no sin. How much more should we submit to baptism as an appeal to God for a clear conscience!

Before they put those good clean clothes on the wasteful prodigal son, he probably had to be washed. Hospitality meant that at least hands and feet could be washed. The word and blood of Jesus washes white as snow so that Father God's wayward adopted children who humble themselves can be restored to their rightful place in Him. Praise the Lord!

> *I will arise and go to my father and will say to him, "Father, I have sinned against heaven and before you, and I am no longer worthy to be called your son. Make me like one of your hired servants." And he arose and came to his father. But when he was still a great way off, his father saw him and had compassion, and ran and fell on his neck and kissed him.* [He told his father he had sinned and just

wanted to hear that he was still loved.] *But the father said to his servants, "Bring out the best robe and put it on him, and put a ring on his hand and sandals on his feet."* (Luke 15:18–22)

Knowing people's hearts, Father God knows when people have a desire to return to Him, like the loving father who ran to meet his son even *"when he was still a great way off."* People can come to God just as they are, even while spiritually *"still a great way off."* But He loves them too much to have them stay that way. The father had a feast to celebrate that his lost son was found, having come back from the dead as it were. The humbled son was not looking for his former place as son, but just for a place somewhere nearby as a hired servant. But his father was so merciful and gracious that he even restored him to his former place with authority of sonship signified by the ring. Father God is like that and wants us to serve Him in the place He chooses for us. Sometimes that involves being submissive to human authority, and it always involves a willingness to do His will. The sandals remind us of the equipment of the gospel, and He clothes His children with a robe of His righteousness.

We can serve the Lord and bloom wherever He plants us. I remember around 1986 when my husband decided that I should find a job outside the home. We had both decided when our children were growing that I would be a stay-at-home mother to help raise them, and praise God we managed that way for sixteen years. Besides caring for the family, the Lord had been leading me in prophetic banner making and mission work from my home, so my days were already quite filled. My husband allowed this but did not understand it.

After searching for a job half-heartedly for months, I put it to prayer telling the Lord it would be too much for me; it would kill me to also work outside the home. But the Lord said to me, **"Be obedient even unto death."** However, He also said, **"Behold, I have prepared a place for you,"** so I began to eagerly seek it, desiring to be serving near our Beloved Jesus wherever He would lead me on earth as well as in heaven: *"And if I go and prepare a place for you, I will come again* *and receive you to Myself; that where I am, there you may be also"* (John 14:2–3).

He led me to a humble job, working for a Jewish employer in a drug store. I called on the Lord's name for help, and He blessed me with a wonderful Dutch woman to teach me my job. I had worked in my dad's grocery store years before, but now the cash registers were computerized—a new thing in those days. Then, working alone for a few days, the stress became too great for me at the lead cash register; so they let me work in a quieter area, the cosmetics and perfume section. Since I used to use those things years before, but now no longer wore makeup, I was surprised to be there. But I could help others find what they needed and honestly help the seniors who came there to shop, and it gave me more time to get used to the computerized cash register. Praise God, it was the place God had prepared for me to re-enter the work field.

My own father had taught me about the dignity of each person and of work and that every honest job was important, so I was not ashamed to dust shelves, sweep the floor, or put price tags on a case of eyebrow pencils if it was needed, as well as to help customers. **When work is done as unto the Lord, it is worship:** *"And whatever you do, do it heartily, as to the Lord and not to men, knowing that from the Lord you will receive the reward of the inheritance; for you serve the Lord Christ"* (Col. 3:23–24). Nothing is hidden from His eyes.

And when I told my Jewish employer that I was happy to work there, but not on a Sunday since it was my Sabbath, my Lord's Day to keep holy, he graciously let me have that day off. People could still shop for medicine, but he even decided to close off the cosmetics aisle on Sundays after I told him that people could shop for those things on other days. Praise the Lord!

I worked there for a while and then the Lord led me to two other places of marketplace ministry: a pastry shop run by a wonderful Dutch lady and her son where again I served many seniors as cashier, and had an opportunity to grow the fruit of self-control. I only worked Tuesdays and Fridays, the two days I fasted, and they sold delicious baked breads and sweets. But thank God, the Lord helped me resist temptation. Then occasionally I could buy delicious reduced items to take home for my family.

Then I was asked to be the secretary-bookkeeper of an Italian construction company owned by three brothers. I tried to tell John, who phoned me, that I was not qualified; that I had studied academic, not commercial, at school. However, I had assisted my mother with some office work and she had sent me to take a simple bookkeeping course once. I was surprised when he told me he believed I could do it and the wives of the owners had recommended me. Thank God the office was not computerized yet. When I told him I could not type fast, he told me that honesty and accuracy were more important than speed. And when I asked one of his brothers, Vince, "What if I make a mistake on the books?" he told me, "You will find it."

Like true fathers, they called forth gifting in me. I was amazed at their confidence in me and **I put my confidence in the Lord, calling upon His name** for help each day. If problems arose, the Holy Spirit often reminded me of a song:

> *How great is our God, how great is His name.*
> *How great is our God forever the same.*
> *He rolled back the waters of the mighty Red Sea*
> *and He said, "I'll never leave you. Put your trust in Me."*

I would sing it as prayer reminding God how great He is, and that He had said He would never leave me. Thank God, each time God rescued me from my fears and brought me through. I grew in trust of Him as He rolled back the waters of the sea of circumstances before me, and the problems would get solved.

Again the Lord had prepared a place for me where I could pray and serve Him. And praise God, He gave me many divine appointments there. When I prayerfully asked my employers, they even allowed me to display nativity scenes at Christmas. **Plus, the Lord began to stretch me in following His voice.** This was all preparation.

Jesus said, *"Ask and you shall receive."* When I saw Jesus leading me first to ask for one morning each month to be an hour late for work so I could attend a prayer breakfast for pastors and intercessors, I overcame my fear and asked and was allowed to do so. Glory be to God.

I was often the only one in the office besides one of my employers, Tony, so it meant that he, plus the answering machine, had to cover for me, but he graciously did so. Then the Lord began to call me to attend a few conferences—first for a day and then some for a part-week. Praise God, again I overcame fear and asked and they let me go to be where God wanted me. Since the Lord had called me, I had to trust Him that my work would get done at the construction company and I was always able to catch up when I returned, thank God. **I knew we *"cannot serve two masters"* (Matt. 6:24), and Jesus was to come first as my Lord and Master, who also expected me to be loyal to my employers and to earn my pay**.

Since I was still serving the Lord in banner and mission work as well as raising two children and taking care of household duties, some days I would be so tired when I got home that I would take a twenty-minute power nap/rest. As I would lie there on my bed, I would think of Jesus falling under the weight of His cross and getting up again, and even accepting help to make His burden lighter. So I would get back up, shoulder my cross of responsibilities again and cook dinner, reminding myself, *"The joy of the Lord is my strength."* I would sing praise songs while I worked at home and praise God; family would help me when it was needed. Part of Christian family living is to share in the prayer, work, and play, each doing one's own part, yet helping to bear one another's burden at times.

Employment can be marketplace ministry and a place where prayer is also lifted up at times and the fruit of Jesus can come forth. The construction company, a family business, treated other employees and their clients like family. They had a reputation for integrity, building quality homes. We sowed integrity and mercy and we reaped it, thank God. Especially since I was also the receptionist, many a time people would come to me for encouragement and godly advice, and my employers let me speak to them. Praise the Lord! One couple contemplating divorce even was reconciled, praise God. I worked there for twelve years until after my husband died. Then the Lord told me to leave to follow the Lord in another way.

But each job was the right place at the right time. I was thankful that the Lord had truly provided each place for me in which to love and serve Him. I often thought on how Jesus said, *"In My Father's house are many mansions."* **When you are living in His kingdom here on earth as it is in heaven, there are many mansions where He may place you.** *"And if I go and prepare a place for you, I will come again and receive you to Myself; that where I am, there you may be also"* (John 14:2–3). **He sets us in place for ministry with and through Him.**

We may think we are not qualified for a position, but **Jesus can send someone to graciously train us** as I had in each place when I asked Him for help, and our Father can cause us to do things we never thought were possible. When He told me in 2002, *"Go to Bible School,"* I was fifty-six, but I posted on my bulletin board the encouraging word *Abba* had given me: *"You can do it. Christ is in you."* So, I read the books and did the essays, reminding myself of His Word, and was there for one and a half years. Praise God.

Likewise with intercession. Jesus chooses how His bridge will be constructed and what needs our attention. Just as some trestles are linked together in groups, God can link intercessors together in groups, and change the formation another day if He chooses. Or you could say that He sometimes moves us to another kingdom mansion in His house on earth. But if you know He has set you in place somewhere, I have learned that it is best not to move until or unless He authorizes it. When I was a member of a particular congregation and wanted to leave when I was experiencing their misunderstanding, the

Lord told me, **"DO NOT TAKE OFFENSE."** And, **"You're not going to leave."** So I was given the grace to endure for a time, until they told me to leave. Jesus warned us there would be days like that; so I blessed them, left, and rejoiced in the Lord. I asked Him to show me if there was anything for which I needed to apologize, and asked the Father to forgive them for anything they misunderstood. I also looked for ways to do good unto them. Having trouble finding a peacemaker for years, I asked Jesus to be my Advocate.

Set in Place

It is God who sets His people, the bridgework parts, in place, in His Son. He has been bringing order out of chaos for centuries, interacting with His people: *"I called on the L*ORD* in distress; the L*ORD* answered me and set me in a broad place"* (Ps. 118:5). David spoke of how he could rest assured remembering, *"The L*ORD* is my light and my salvation; Whom shall I fear?"* (Ps. 27:1). Because he sought to stay close to the Lord and to set Him before his face, he knew from experience:

> *"Because He is at my right hand I shall not be moved"* (Ps. 16:8).

> *For in the time of trouble*
> *He shall hide me in His pavilion;*
> *in the secret place of His tabernacle*
> *He shall hide me;*
> *He shall set me high upon a rock.* (Ps. 27:5)

> *I have set watchmen on your walls, O Jerusalem;*
> *They shall never hold their peace day or night.*
> *You who make mention of the L*ORD*, do not keep silent,*
> *And give Him no rest till He establishes*
> *And till He makes Jerusalem a praise in the earth.* (Isa. 62:6–7)

> *For many are called, but few are chosen.* (Matt. 22:14)

Thank God we can have more than the Lord beside us as they had in Old Testament times. We can have Him in us, directing us by

His Holy Spirit. We are all called to pray and worship, but some are chosen for more dedicated times of worship, prayer, and intercession, communing with the King. God can choose whoever He wants to serve day or night watch duty with Him, setting them in place for a season, just as He chose Peter, James, and John to watch and pray going further with Him at Gethsemane. We can volunteer for a position, but it is up to Jesus to choose who and when. Let us be thankful for wherever He sets us. All prayer is important. *"Humble yourselves in the sight of the Lord, and He will lift you up"* (Jas. 4:10).

God can set people in place in His body, in His bridge, with other functions too besides interceding with Him. I know I was so happy after a time of rejection by many loved ones to find that I was *"accepted in the Beloved,"* and set by God in another family of believers. They allowed me to serve in areas I had never served before. God has given me many more **church family members** since then, with God as our Father; He satisfies my thirst, and can do so for you too. We must not despise the day of small beginnings.

> *A father of the fatherless, a defender of widows,*
> *Is God in His holy habitation.*
> *He sets the solitary in families;*
> *He brings out those who are bound into prosperity;*
> *But the rebellious dwell in a dry land.* (Ps. 68:5–6)

Boundaries May Define Your Place

Traveling on His train and standing night watch for His train reminds me of a word the International House of Prayer (IHOP) worship team sang near 5:00 a.m. on June 13, 2012: **"Where I go or don't go, what I do or don't do, there's joy; it's those beautiful boundary lines in pleasant places."** (See Ps. 16:6.)

Sometimes we can hear the Lord tell us to go here but not there, to do this, but not that, and it is wonderful when He leads us with His boundary lines. It is reassuring, like when a surveyor marks out the specific boundaries of a bridge's trestlework.

We can trust Jesus and be joyful, for God is always right. **Hearing His voice can help us choose between good things in order to be in His perfect place for us, in His perfect will and timing,** as well as to choose against what is detrimental, *"that you may prove what is that good and acceptable and perfect will of God"* (Rom. 12:2). Some things are good, but others are better or best for us.

For instance, the night I heard that word watching IHOP, earlier I had fallen asleep at the computer, gone to bed, and then lay awake for a time. So I asked the Lord if He wanted me to get up for night watch. There have been some nights when that has happened and He called me to get up again, refreshing me after only a few moments rest, but this night He told me, *"Don't move,"* so I rested longer. However, just after 3:00 a.m., He allowed me to get up. After making myself a chamomile tea, I asked the Lord if He wanted me to enter into praise and worship with Him. He would not allow me to go into the living room where I could have played the piano or put on a worship CD, but indicated that I was to go into my office where I could participate with live online praise and worship from IHOP, Kansas City. I knew:

> *Unless the LORD builds the house,*
> *They labor in vain who build it;*
> *Unless the LORD guards the city,*
> *The watchman stays awake in vain.*
> *It is vain for you to rise up early,*
> *To sit up late,*
> *To eat the bread of sorrows;*
> *For so He gives His beloved sleep.* (Ps. 127:1–2)

I love it when He tells me where to go and not go, what to do and not do. His boundary lines ARE beautiful. They help us get into the place He wants us to be in for that moment. What we sang, led by His Spirit, including warfare praise, was just right that night. Yet other nights the Lord might have something else in mind, or for me to just sleep. **May the Lord help us to be where He wants us when He wants us there. Then the time will be most fruitful.**

Paul had a time when *"they were forbidden by the Holy Spirit to preach the word in Asia"* (Acts 16:6). But when the time was right, Paul had the vision of a Macedonian man pleading with him to come there and help them. So, the boundary was extended with a door opened into Asia and *"immediately we sought to go to Macedonia, concluding that the Lord had called us to preach the gospel to them"* (Acts 16:10).

Have you ever noticed the symmetry of a tree? It is especially visible when it is resting, in winter. How glorious! Each branch set where the Creator chose.

The grape vine has many branches attached to it, set in place, with a symmetry of three main branches, with others coming from them; and the Father can cut out dead branches, prune others, or even graft in branches where He needs them.

I have seen independent churches wither and close down. But humbly pruned and washed by the blood and Word of God, other churches have been made more fruitful. We are brought into unity by Christ abiding in us and us in Him, by realizing that only He is worthy, and we have been saved by grace, called to be saints on earth and in New Jerusalem. Here we are to seek the Holy Spirit to lead us into all truth with humility and obedience, and churches are to connect and be forged together in unity.

Just as one train may have many different types of cars, so are His churches different. Yet they are each to be an assembly of the called-out ones, *ekklesia*. God has given gifting to us all in various measures, so let us thank Him with no jealousy for what He has given each church and believer; and whether we have much or little of something, use it faithfully for the advancement of His kingdom. We are each accountable for what we have been given for the place He sets us: *"To whom much is given, from him much will be required"* (Luke 12:48).

Parts of the Bridge Are Overcomers

Aaron and his sons had to wash their hands and feet before going into the Holy Place to minister unto the Lord in His inner courts. They were also to have clean hands and a pure heart, and not lift up their souls to an idol. New Testament children of God, reborn from above, who want to join Jesus in His high priestly ministry should also make themselves clean. Once the Holy Spirit descended upon Jesus, He never left Him. Being sinless, the spotless Lamb of God never needed to pray like we do for a clean heart and for help to know what needs changing. He overcame temptation.

Jesus told His disciples, *"Blessed are the pure in heart, for they shall see God"* (Matt. 5:8). When our sins have been forgiven, washed away by the Word and blood of the Lamb, we can overcome the accuser of the brethren, because the righteousness of God will cover us. Our hearts will be pure, and Jesus will help us keep them that way. We will see God working around us, and possibly even in a vision, and one day, face to face.

Jesus promised those eleven chosen ones who had been trained by Him, *"All authority has been given to Me in heaven and on earth. Go therefore and make disciples of all the nations, baptizing them in the name of the Father and of the Son and of the Holy Spirit, teaching them to observe all things that I have commanded you; and lo, I am with you always, even to the end of the age"* (Matt. 28:18–20). Jesus could give them authority over the world, the flesh, and the devil because He had it and He had trained them in the proper way to use it, and they would not operate alone because He would be with them, working through them by His Spirit. Having forgiven them for running away and hiding at His crucifixion, He left them His Holy Spirit as their Helper. He helped them overcome their fears and to do His will. Thank God He is with believers today too and gives believers authority. Jesus also gives ways of escape from temptation. So we, too, can be overcomers.

"Many are called but few are chosen." (Matt. 22:14)

Even today, Jesus can personally call and choose disciples, His trestlework. This especially happens with members of the fivefold ministry. They will need more training, some of which Jesus may personally give, as He did with Paul, and some training they will receive from other chosen ones to whom He leads them. The saints on earth need to be equipped *"for the work of ministry"* by these fivefold gifts from God, who first need to be equipped themselves: *"He Himself gave some to be apostles, some prophets, some evangelists, and some pastors and teachers"* (Eph. 4:11–12). Their part is to follow Jesus and receive His Spirit and scriptural instruction, and thus they will be made more effective parts of His bridge.

> *You are My friends if you do whatever I command you. No longer do I call you servants, for a servant does not know what his master is doing; but I have called you friends, for all things that I heard from My Father I have made known to you. You did not choose Me, but I chose you and appointed you that you should go and bear fruit, and that your fruit should remain, that whatever you ask the Father in My name He may give you. These things I command you, that you love one another.* (John 15:14–17)

Overcomers have a close relationship with Jesus and bear fruit that remains. Even in times of trouble they have *"love, joy, peace, longsuffering, kindness, goodness, faithfulness, gentleness,* [and] *self-control"* (Gal. 5:22–23).

They Should Have the Character of Jesus to Be Good Trestlework on His Bridge

Believers begin as just servants of the living God, rescued from their enemies and slavery to sin. But more than grateful love-slaves to Jesus, they can become His overcoming friends as they do whatever Jesus commands them to do in love. A friend is one you can trust and in whom you can confide, encourage, and be encouraged. Before a person can be a "sent-out one," like the apostles and the seventy-two whom Jesus sent out on mission trips, or the ones the church sent out later, he should first be trained as a disciple by Jesus and His trained leaders. He will receive the power of God to do what he is called to do and to be who he is called to be, and live what he is learning. Thus he can avoid being a hypocrite who tells others what to do but does not do it himself.

John the beloved and Mary of Bethany had that disciple quality of desiring to sit at His feet and be instructed by Jesus first, just as Jesus was instructed by the Father daily.

> *The Lord GOD has given Me*
> *The tongue of the learned,*
> *That I should know how to speak*
> *A word in season to him who is weary.*
> *He awakens Me morning by morning.*
> *He awakens My ear*
> *To hear as the learned.*
> *The Lord GOD has opened My ear;*
> *And I was not rebellious,*
> *Nor did I turn away.* (Isaiah 50:4–5)

It is wisdom to make time daily to spend with the Lord and to journal what He says. He may even wake us Himself. We can ask Him to do so. But we can start small as I did by having a dedicated time one hour per week as well as morning prayer, adding Bible reading. I told my family it was time for my audience with the King.

We become overcomers with His gracious help. As Jesus told Paul, who was acquainted with miracles, but knew God had chosen to leave him with an infirmity to produce the fruit of humility in him, *"My grace is sufficient for you, for My strength is made perfect in weakness"* (2 Cor. 12:9). In order to become *"ambassadors for Christ,"* ministers of reconciliation, we need to crucify our old man with Christ and rise to new life in Him as functioning parts of His body. As John the Baptist said, *"He must increase, but I must decrease"* (John 3:30). As we put Him first, Jesus increases and "self" decreases in disciplined overcomers. An athlete chooses to be disciplined and so should we. Although our old man and his ungodly ways dies with Christ, we are to rise with Him and to love our new man. Otherwise, how can we love our neighbour as ourselves?

> *Finally, there is laid up for me the crown of righteousness, which the Lord, the righteous Judge, will give to me on that Day, and not to me only but also to all who have loved His appearing.* (2 Timo. 4:8)

Bridge Parts Are Worshipers with a Place Close to God

To worship someone is to serve him. Jesus lived a lifestyle of worshiping the Father, spending time with Him in prayer, consulting with Him before He did things, denying Himself by bending His knee to the will of the Father. He lived by the spirit of the Law, not the letter of it. Obeying His Father's commandments, it was *"His custom"* (Luke 4:16) to keep holy the Lord's Day, attending synagogue to worship and read Scripture with the others and to love His neighbour as

Himself. But He taught the commandments in light of the revelation the Father gave Him. Although He rested from labour and would not have worked in the carpenter shop on a Sabbath, He did heal people in need, teaching that we could do good on the Lord's Day. *"And He said to them, 'The Sabbath was made for man, and not man for the Sabbath. Therefore the Son of Man is also Lord of the Sabbath'"* (Mark 2:27–28).

God still wants us to take time to worship Him and rest from our jobs today, doing His will under His direction. Family time is important too, but not at the expense of time with the Lord. I rejoice that so many parents accompany their children to their sports games, but I mourn that they are often at times where Sunday services become neglected. As bridge parts we are to worship Him *"in spirit and in truth"* with our personal spirit lined up with Holy Spirit, keeping Jesus's commandments as He kept the Father's.

I think of Isaiah 58:13–14:

> *If you turn away your foot from the Sabbath,*
> *From doing your pleasure on my holy day,*
> *And call the Sabbath a delight,*
> *The holy day of the* L<small>ORD</small> *honorable,*
> *And shall honor Him,*
> *Not doing your own ways,*
> *Nor finding your own pleasure,*
> *Nor speaking your own words,*
> *Then you shall delight yourself in the Lord;*
> *And I will cause you to ride on the high hills of the earth,*
> *And feed you with the heritage of Jacob your father.*
> *The mouth of the Lord has spoken.*

If we ask the Lord to guide us, we will attend to our duties and responsibilities certain parts of the week but set aside time to worship and learn of Him, and to daily have Jesus lead us in love. He might put on our heart to invite someone to dinner, or to pray for or visit a specific person. He might even put His words into our mouth at times so that we speak His words, not *"your own words. Then you shall delight yourself in the* LORD.*"* With the right attitude, all that we do can become worship.

Jesus loves His Father and often spent time in a quiet place, focused, communing with Him, like a Son, but also like a soldier who gets his orders for the day. He praised Him, saying:

> *"He who sent Me is true; and I speak to the world those things which I heard from Him." They did not understand that He spoke to them of the Father. Then Jesus said to them, "When you lift up the Son of Man, then you will know that I am He, and that I do nothing of Myself; but as My Father taught Me I speak these things. And He who sent Me is with Me. The Father has not left Me alone, for I always do those things that please Him."* (John 8:26–29)

Now, Jesus is seated at the Father's right hand and can stand before Him for us as He did for Stephen. He is still serving Him by reigning, doing the will of the Father from a place of rest and authority and is a model for us. Some will join Him there. *"To him who overcomes I will grant to sit with Me on My throne, as I also overcame and sat down with My Father on His throne"* (Rev. 3:21). Like David we can say: *One thing I have desired of the* LORD,

> *That I will seek:*
> *That I may dwell in the house of the* LORD *All the days of my life,*
> *To behold the beauty of the* LORD *And to inquire in His temple.*
> (Ps. 27:4)

> *Honor and majesty are before Him;*
> *Strength and beauty are in His sanctuary.* (Ps. 96:6)

Just as John the beloved could lean on His bosom as they reclined on couches at a table and ask Jesus questions from a very close place, Jesus can lean on His Father and we can lean on Jesus too, and His *"everlasting arms."* We need His protective input to be an effective bridge. *"No one has seen God at any time. The only begotten Son, who is in the bosom of the Father, He has declared Him"* (John 1:18); and, *"Call to Me, and I will answer you, and show you great and mighty things, which you do not know"* (Jer. 33:3).

As Moses blessed the tribe of Benjamin:

> *The beloved of the LORD shall dwell in safety by Him,*
> *Who shelters him all the day long;*
> *And he shall dwell between His shoulders.* (Deut.33:12)

We *"shall dwell between His shoulders"* if we abide in Christ. We need Him every hour. *"The eternal God is your refuge, and underneath are the everlasting arms; He will thrust out the enemy from before you, and will say, 'Destroy!' Then Israel shall dwell in safety"* (Deut. 33:27–28). I have found His *rhema* word is like arms holding me.

As it was said of Solomon's bride, it is said of the bride of Christ, as she learns to lean: *"Who is this coming up from the wilderness, leaning upon her beloved?"* (Song 8:5).

Chapter 5
Reconcilers Are Components

Therefore, if anyone is in Christ, he is a new creation; old things have passed away; behold, all things have become new. Now all things are of God, who has reconciled us to Himself through Jesus Christ, and has given us the ministry of reconciliation.... Now then, we are ambassadors for Christ, as though God were pleading through us. (2 Cor. 5:17–18, 20)

One day believers will be raptured to heaven or rise from the dead to join Him there. But in the meantime, we can go there in the Spirit. Some are even now being taken up in visions. Psalm 24 says the ones who can ascend His mountain are those who have clean hands, a pure heart, and don't lift their souls to an idol or swear deceitfully. *"Therefore, if anyone is in Christ, he is a new creation; old things have passed away; behold, all things have become new"* (2 Cor. 5:17). Our Redeemer restores us.

By baptism, we appeal to God for a clear conscience. Having turned from evil ways and decided to follow Jesus, we die to sin with Christ (who had no sin of His own), rise to new life in Christ, and in the Spirit we ascend to the Father with Christ. As Forerunner, Jesus opened the way to the Father so that joined to Him we could be here on earth and be there at the throne of mercy not only to receive grace for ourselves, but to become a part of His ministry team. Reconcilers desire that others too will become reconciled. They are facilitators in Christ, *"peacemakers ... sons of God"* (Matt. 5:9).

The Father Is Even Part of the Bridge

"[God] has given us the ministry of reconciliation, that is, that God was in Christ reconciling the world to Himself" (2 Cor. 5:18–19). First God reconciles us to Himself; then He may allow us to work with Christ reconciling others to God and to each other. **God is in Jesus doing His works**, and if we abide in Jesus and He in us, then Christ will do His reconciling works in us too, with the Father. *"If anyone loves Me, he will keep My word; and My Father will love him, and We will come to him and make Our home with him"* (John 14:23).

Having the Father, Christ, and the Holy Spirit in us does not mean that we will never make a mistake again, but if we keep close to the Lord, He will show us the right way. Then it is up to us to follow.

The steps of a good man are ordered by the Lord,
And He delights in his way.
Though he fall, he shall not be utterly cast down;
For the Lord upholds him with His hand. (Ps. 37:23–24)

So, we see that **the Father Himself is part of the bridge and has made reconciled believers parts too with God in them.** Jesus is like the bridge top piece, the cross-piece on which the trains cross over. By His Father and Spirit, Jesus is also like rebar, the strengthening metal within the undergirding trestle pieces and concrete footings. The Almighty Father is in Him with Their Spirit. *"**God was in Christ reconciling the world to Himself.**"* One of the seven Spirits of God is the Spirit of *might*, or *"holy boldness, so that one might do valiantly and not fail or be discouraged."* We can ask *"according to His riches in glory, to be strengthened with might through His Spirit in the inner man"* (Eph. 3:16); and, *"Christ in you, the hope of glory"* (Col. 1:27).

Jesus and His Father have a special relationship and unity, in the power of Their Holy Spirit. Jesus Himself said, *"Do you not believe that*

I am in the Father, and the Father in Me? The words that I speak to you I do not speak on My own authority; but the Father who dwells in Me does the works. Believe Me that I am in the Father and the Father in Me, or else believe Me for the sake of the works themselves" (John 14:10–11). **So when Jesus mediates for us, it is God Himself mediating on our behalf with Himself through Christ**, who also listens to and obeys the words of His Father.

Believers can have Father, Son, and Holy Spirit dwelling within them, interceding. Jesus prayed for those who would believe in Him through the words of His disciples, saying:

> *And the glory which You gave Me I have given them, that they may be one just as we are one: I in them and You in Me, that they may be made perfect in one, and that the world may know that You have sent Me, and have loved them as You have loved Me. Father, I desire that they also whom You gave Me may be with Me where I am, that they may behold My glory which You have given Me.* (John 17:22–24)

With the Father's love upon us and in us, we can be sanctified and transformed to function with Christ, under His leadership.

It Was Necessary for Jesus to Die for Our Sins, to Become the True Bridge

> *But Christ came as High Priest of the good things to come, with the greater and more perfect tabernacle not made with hands, that is, not of this creation. Not with the blood of goats and calves, but with His own blood He entered the Most Holy Place once for all, having obtained eternal redemption.... How much more shall the blood of Christ, who through the eternal Spirit offered Himself without spot to God, cleanse your conscience from dead works to serve the living*

God? And for this reason He is the Mediator of the new covenant, by means of death, for the redemption of the transgressions under the first covenant, that those who are called may receive the promise of the eternal inheritance. (Heb. 9:11–12, 14–15)

There is no forgiveness of sin without the shedding of blood. So the Lamb of God was the perfect sacrifice whose blood atoned for sins before the Father. His blood was so precious that it is effective eternally to purchase our redemption. So Jesus had to die and be resurrected so He would have His blood to bring to the Father on our behalf and then come back to encourage His disciples. *"You have heard Me say to you, 'I am going away and coming back to you.' If you loved Me, you would rejoice because I said, 'I am going to the Father,' for My Father is greater than I"* (John 14:28).

In His holiness, right deeds are rewarded and sin must be punished. Jesus obtained the name, *"Mediator,"* not just because His Father had chosen Him, but because of what He did on the cross in obedience to the Father. For those who will repent, they do not have to get what they deserve. They can say that He has taken the hard part of their punishment, having fulfilled the Law by His death, and pleaded for merciful forgiveness for them: *"So great is His mercy toward those who fear Him"* (Ps. 103:11).

For those who have a holy fear of God, they need not be afraid, because Jesus is Judge, High Priest, and Saviour who saves them by grace because He has done the work of sacrificial offering, fulfilling the Law and paying our expensive ransom with His blood, willingly, according to the Father's gracious love for us. At the same time, with the Father's words in His heart, He made intercession for all who had caused Him to suffer and die by their sin.

Sacrifice and offering You did not desire,
But a body You have prepared for Me.
In burnt offerings and sacrifices for sin
You had no pleasure.

*Then I said, "Behold, I have come—
In the volume of the book it is written of Me—
To do Your will, O God."* (Heb. 10:5–7)

I delight to do Your will, O God. (Ps. 40:8)

Jesus came as a human being to line up His will with that of the Father's, experiencing what man experiences, but without sin, preparing Himself for the role of eternal High Priest and Mediator. In gratitude for all He has done for us, we can seek to do the Father's will too, so full of love for God and one another that we would be willing to lay down our lives if necessary. Jesus did it first—in the Garden of Gethsemane; He even drank the cup of the Father's judgment on mankind's sin, going to the cross the next day. In Old Testament times, sin was forgiven by the shedding of animal blood, but Father God desired the perfect sacrifice, of Jesus, the spotless Lamb and of His will—and ours: *"But a body You have prepared for Me"* (Heb. 10:5).

Jesus replaced the sacrifice of the Old Testament saying, *"Behold, I have come to do Your will, O God.…' By that will we have been sanctified through the offering of the body of Jesus Christ once for all"* (Heb. 10:9–10). Today He is still doing the Father's will and helps believers to do likewise.

"Christ came as High Priest of the good things to come, with the greater and more perfect tabernacle not made with hands, that is, not of this creation" (Heb 9:11). The crucified and resurrected Jesus returned from the Father as the eternal High Priest. The heavenly Holy of holies is more perfect than Solomon's Temple, and so is His body. As Jesus had prophesied, *"Destroy this temple, and in three days I will raise it up"* (John 2:19). **By the power of God Jesus was able to rise from the dead and restore His own body to be a temple of God again; how much more is He able to do that spiritually and physically for the rest of the members of His body!**

His death had to occur for Jesus to become the Mediator because sin deserves the death penalty. He knew how holy God is and how expensive would be the cost to redeem us from captivity to sin. **He had set His will to correspond with the Father's will long before praying in the Garden of Gethsemane** and was able to resist temptation. *"Not My will but Yours, be done"* (Luke 22:42); and, *"Therefore the Father loves Me because I lay down My life that I may take it again. No one takes it from Me, but I lay it down of Myself. I have power to lay it down, and I have power to take it again. This command I have received from My Father"* (John 10:17–18). **So with the joy of expectation that multitudes would be saved, He had the strength to go to the cross and become the bridge.** The *"joy of the Lord"* gave Him strength like that of an expectant mother about to deliver a baby.

We were/are that baby, *"the joy that was set before Him"* (Heb. 12:2), and Jesus is also like the attending Physician, the Deliverer. The pain is forgotten when you see the child, the new life birthed. Likewise, the pain of our sin and its punishment on Him, and also of persecution, is forgotten when He sees us happy to be new creations in Him enjoying kingdom covenant living. Our Mediator cares about us and felt what we deserve. *"By His stripes we are healed"* (Isa. 53:5). **He is very qualified to be our Mediator.**

The Person of Jesus Christ Is the One and Only Eternal Bridge between God and Man

Since God Himself chose Jesus to be High Priest forever, there is no other one necessary; so **no other one is named in the Bible.** Christ alone is the true bridge between God and mankind. But He allows His connected body to unite with Him with Jesus, the head, as the eternal High Priest and Intercessor of the New Covenant: chosen, foretold, anointed, and appointed by God to stand in the gap for us, interceding before the throne of grace and mercy. As Jesus said, *"No one comes to the Father except through Me"* (John 14:6). As the Intercessor, the reconciler, He makes a plea to mankind on behalf of God, and an appeal to God on behalf of man. Jesus is true God and true Man. The parts of His body are not true God, but they are true human beings, reborn as spiritual children of God. When we are born again from above, adopted into His family; we begin to take on the characteristics of our heavenly Father and Brother Jesus. He is already in heaven at the real mercy seat with *Abba*, and those who overcome can become seated with Him.

Even if saintly people are called *"gods, to whom the word of God came"* (John 10:35), we are commanded by God, *"You shall have no other gods before Me"* (Gen. 20:3). What do we have that we did not get from God? Years ago, the Lord told me to **write "body of Christ" with a small "b."** This is a reminder that **even if people are saintly, no one is like God in the sense of equality.** He said through Isaiah,

> *I am the First and the Last;*
> *Besides Me there is no God....*
> *Is there a God besides Me?*
> *Indeed there is no other Rock;*
> *I know not one.* (Isaiah 44: 6, 8)

Even the total sum of all the members of His body is not equal to God, but a *"measure of the stature of the fullness of Christ."* (Eph. 4:13) It reminds me of finding the volume of an irregular shaped object using calculus; it involves calculating **the sum of a series of approximations.**

> *For who in the heavens can be compared to the Lord?*
> *Who among the sons of the mighty can be likened to the Lord?*
> *God is greatly to be feared in the assembly of the saints,*
> *And to be held in reverence by all those around Him.*
> *O Lord God of hosts,*
> *Who is mighty like You, O Lord?*
> *Your faithfulness also surrounds You....*

[And He says of David:] *My arm shall strengthen him.*

The enemy shall not outwit him,

> *Nor the son of wickedness afflict him.*
> *I will beat down his foes before his face,*
> *And plague those who hate him.*
> *But My faithfulness and My mercy shall be with him,*
> *And in My name his horn shall be exalted.* (Ps. 89:6–8, 21–24)

Christ is in us if His Word dwells richly in us and we are in Him keeping His commandments (see John 15). He values us as parts of His body worth dying for, both because He created us to lovingly *"grow up into Him, who is the head—Christ"* and for *"the effective working by which every part does its share"* (Eph. 4:15–16). He fights for us today and equips us to function in Jesus's name. Each part of His body is special, but we are each only a small part of His worldwide body and bridge. **Jesus alone is God, although some people today falsely say that they are Christ or that they become gods equal to Jesus Christ.** This pride of thinking one can be like God in all ways all the time, or that our will overrules the will of God, was Eve's temptation and Lucifer's downfall. Jesus warned, *"Then if someone says to you, 'Look, here is the Christ!' Or 'There!' do not believe it. For false christs and false prophets will rise and show great signs and wonders to deceive, if possible, even the elect"* (Matt. 24:23–24).

No Replacements. Who Is like God?

The Old Testament priests were limited in their mediation because they would die; so God designated the male descendants of Aaron as replacements. They were a foreshadow of who was to come and die, rise again, and never die again. **The Father did not have to designate any replacement for Jesus because He will live forever.** As He told John in a vision, when John was quite old, *"Do not be afraid; I am the First and the Last. I am He who lives, and was dead, and behold, I am alive forevermore. Amen. And I have the keys of Hades and of Death"* (Rev. 1:17–18). He can let people into heaven, or not.

The onetime shedding of Jesus's blood for all, for all time, actually removes the stain of sin forever so believers can start fresh and clean in His service. So **neither the sacrifice of Jesus, the Lamb, nor His death will ever be repeated by Jesus, only remembered. His blood is still effective today and forever.** I praise God for the popes and priests who embraced the coming of the Holy Spirit in the Charismatic Renewal beginning at Vatican II Council, but no one replaces Jesus Christ, not even popes, priests, or evangelists today. So, the myth that arose of the priest being "another Christ" (in Latin: "*alter Christus*") taking Jesus's place in the Mass, confessional, etc., is not correct. Possibly it arose because for some years the baptism of the Holy Spirit and His charismatic gifting were forgotten in the church, and the Bible in its entirety was seldom read. The enemy tries to lead astray God's shepherds as well as the rest of the sheep, **but God likes to restore.**

One moment Jesus could commend Peter for having recognized Him as being the Messiah, saying, *"Blessed are you, Simon Bar-Jonah, for flesh and blood has not revealed this to you, but My Father who is in heaven"* (Matt. 16:17), yet soon afterwards the devil tried to work through Peter. When he rebuked Jesus for saying that He must suffer, be killed, and raised the third day, then Jesus *"turned and said to Peter, 'Get behind me, Satan! You are an offense to Me, for you are not mindful of the things of God, but the things of men'"* (Matt. 16:23). Peter went on to be a great apostle and part of the true bridge because he had the humility to repent quickly when **he realized he had done wrong by acting like he knew more than Jesus. He was not** *"the Christ,"* **nor is anyone greater, or even equal, to Jesus**. Who is like God? He is sinless all the time. An animated image of a flower is not equal to it but is made according to its likeness. We can only hope to be Christlike as we allow Him to mold us and inhabit us, sanctifying and transforming us in the image of the triune God, made according to Him like Adam, *"according to Our likeness"* (Gen. 1:26); and *"You are My witnesses. Is there a God besides Me? Indeed there is no other Rock; I know not one"* (Isa. 44:8).

Although God created Adam *"in Our image, according to Our likeness"* (Gen. 1:26), he was still formed from dust and sinned; but Jesus existed as God before He was born, coming in an earth suit. He always was and always will be sinless. No creature is equal to the Creator, not even Mary. And she did not replace Jesus as High Priest. *"Most assuredly, I say to you, a servant is not greater than his master* [lord]; *nor is he who is sent greater than he who sent him"* (John 13:16). She did not bear mankind's sin and grief on the cross; it was not her blood that was shed so that sin could be forgiven. (That prepared Jesus for His position as Mediator.) Other saints were even crucified, but only Jesus was chosen by the Father to be High Priest forever, the one Mediator between God and men.

In the synagogues, it was read that God had spoken through Isaiah: *"I, even I, am the Lord. And besides Me there is no savior"* (Isa. 43:11). Interestingly, I was asked to read this word in Italian at a Salvador family Mass in Teor, Italy, in 1977: *"Io, Io sono il Signore, e fuor di Me non vi è alcun Salvatore."*

Mary herself acknowledged in her Magnificat that God is greater than her:

> *My soul magnifies the Lord,*
> *And my spirit has rejoiced in God my Savior.*
> *For He has regarded the lowly state of His maidservant;*
> *For behold, henceforth all generations will call me blessed.*
> (Luke 1:46–48)

God wants to restore us to that state where we can be perfect in love. A physical body was prepared for Jesus in the womb of His mother, Mary, while she was still a virgin, *"And the Word became flesh and dwelt among us, and we beheld His glory, the glory as of the only begotten of the Father, full of grace and truth"* (John 1:14), having come to do the will of the Father. And continually, the Father has also been, is being, and will be, preparing a body of believers (of body parts) for Christ to inhabit and display His glory.

Satan, that serpent/dragon, would like to tempt us to be a body for the devil to inhabit instead, or to allow his evil spirits to exist in a stronghold, a house of thoughts within us, but our Father can deliver us from evil if we ask Him. The devil can be resisted and unclean spirits can be cast out in the name of His Son. Let us humble ourselves and *"give to the* LORD *the glory due His name"* (Ps. 96:8).

The Body of Christ Is More than One Denomination

Growing up as a Roman Catholic, we thought we were the complete body of Christ, and some Protestants thought they were, just as early Jewish Christians might have thought they were: *"But now God has set the members, each one of them, in the body just as He pleased"* (1 Cor. 12:18). Like the dry bones Ezekiel prophesied would come together and be revived to form an army of God, we are becoming unified soldiers for Christ, who is the Commander-in-Chief. *"Bone to bone and marrow to marrow,"* the Lord told me in 1994 when I first saw a huge gathering of *"dry bones"* from many spiritual and national backgrounds all drawn to the Toronto Airport Vineyard Fellowship to connect and have the breath of God put into them. And this has happened/is happening in other areas of the world too.

So, **in Christ, in His name**, Christians from any denomination, tribe, or nation can stand before the throne of grace to worship God and intercede for one another *"on earth as it is in heaven"* (Matt. 6:10), and should seek to pray according to the will of the Father, directly to Him through Jesus. He reminds us, *"My House shall be called a house of prayer for all nations"* (Mark 11:17). Believers form that house: *"If anyone loves Me, he will keep My word; and My Father will love him, and We will come to him and make Our home with him"* (John 14:23). What joy it has given me to go to conferences and meet people not only from a multitude of nations, tribes, and tongues but from a multitude of denominations and non-denominations who were *"endeavoring to keep the unity of the Spirit in the bond of peace"* (Eph. 4:3). A touch of heaven!

Revelation Knowledge

I was asked once by a priest to make a banner for a local Roman Catholic Church Diocesan workshop to proclaim, "Without a vision, the people perish." It is a translation of

> *"Where there is no revelation* [prophetic vision], *the people cast off restraint"* (Prov. 29:18).

So, I made it, and the Lord told me to also bring a banner that proclaimed a word He had given me: *"New Jerusalem: Let God mold you into the right shaped stone."* Praise God, the priest allowed me to hang both banners.

God has given us the vision of the holy city through John, revealing that in the *"new heaven and a new earth ... New Jerusalem"* will be seen *"prepared as a bride adorned for her husband"* (Rev. 21:1–2), coming down from God in heaven. In faith, Abraham looked forward to this *"city which has foundations, whose builder and maker is God"* (Heb. 11:10). In it, the body of Christ will be seen in its fullness with Christ as the permanent Mediator, *"the chief cornerstone"* (Eph. 2:20), that joins it all together. By that time He probably will not need to mediate for us anymore.

> *In Him we have redemption through His blood, the forgiveness of sins, according to the riches of His grace ... that in the dispensation of the fullness of the times He might gather together in one all things in Christ, both which are in heaven and which are on earth—in Him. In Him also we have obtained an inheritance, being predestined according to the purpose of Him who works all things according to the counsel of His will, that we who first trusted in Christ should be to the praise of His glory. In Him you also trusted, after you heard the word of truth, the gospel of your salvation; in whom also, having*

believed, you were sealed with the Holy Spirit of promise, who is the guarantee of our inheritance until the redemption of the purchased possession, to the praise of His glory. (Eph. 1:7, 10–14)

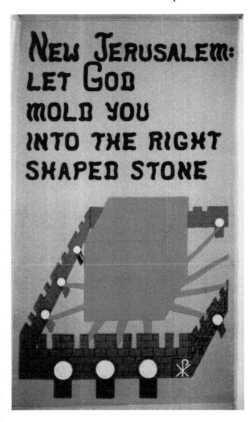

We are God's possession, purchased by the blood of His Son. Our full redemption will be made manifest when Jesus comes again. We will function as parts of His house, His holy city, His bride, and the rehearsal is now. God is fashioning and equipping us to be placed where He chooses, like building blocks, connecting with others. Glory be to God!

A person can be more than one thing at a time. He can be a son, father, friend, husband, and grandchild. That could be compared to being both part of the priestly trestlework of the bridge and passengers carried in the train, parts of the body of Christ and of His bride. Peter referred to God's promise to Moses:

> *You have seen what I did to the Egyptians, and how I bore you on eagles' wings and brought you to Myself. Now therefore, if you will indeed obey My voice and keep My covenant, you shall be a special treasure to Me above all people; for all the earth is Mine. And you shall be to Me a kingdom of priests and a holy nation. These are the words which you shall speak to the children of Israel.* (Ex. 19:4–6; see 1 Pet. 2:9)

But just as building material is to be brought to the bridge builder or the city builder, so we are to come *"to Him, as to a living stone,"* to be in agreement with His blueprint for our life.

> *Coming to Him, as to a living stone, rejected indeed by men, but chosen by God and precious, you also, as living stones, are being built up a spiritual house, a holy priesthood* [bridge], *to offer up spiritual sacrifices acceptable to God through Jesus Christ. Therefore it is also contained in the Scripture,*
> *"Behold, I lay in Zion a chief cornerstone, elect, precious,*
> *And he who believes on Him will by no means be put to shame."*
> *Therefore, to you who believe, He is precious; but to those who are disobedient,*
> *"The stone which the builders rejected*
> *Has become the chief cornerstone* [the head of the corner]," *and*
> *"A stone of stumbling* [that will make men stumble] *and*
> *a rock of offense* [that will make them fall]."
> *They stumble, being disobedient to the word, to which they also were appointed. But you are a chosen generation, a royal priesthood, a holy nation, His own special people, that you may proclaim the praises* [the wonderful deeds] *of Him who called you out of darkness into His marvelous light; who once were not a people but are now the people of God, who had not obtained mercy but now have obtained mercy.* (1 Pet. 2:4–10)

This banner was done as if it was an aerial view of the city, looking down at it from above. The angel told John, *"'Come, I will show you the Bride, the Lamb's wife.' And he carried me away in the Spirit to a great and high mountain, and showed me the great city, the holy Jerusalem, descending out of heaven from God, having the glory of God. Her light* [radiance] *was like a most precious stone* [rare jewel], *like a jasper stone, clear as crystal"* (Rev. 21:9–11).

The wall around it is green reminding of jasper: *"The city is laid out as a square* [lies foursquare]; *its length is as great as its breadth.... The construction of its wall was of jasper; and the city was pure gold, like clear glass"* (Rev. 21:16, 18). The gold cube in the centre with streets of gold leading into it represents the city full of the glory of God. *"But I saw no temple in it, for the Lord God Almighty and the Lamb are its temple. The city has no need of the sun or of the moon to shine in it, for the glory of God illuminated it. The Lamb is its light* [lamp]*"* (Rev. 21:22–23).

And it *"had a great and high wall with twelve gates, and twelve angels at the gates, and names written on them … of the twelve tribes of the children of Israel: three gates on the east, three gates on the north, three gates on the south, and three gates on the west"* (Rev. 21:12–13); and *"the twelve gates were twelve pearls: each individual gate was of one pearl. And the street of the city was pure gold, like transparent glass"* (Rev. 21:21). The white circles represent the gates. I did not include the angels nor the names of the twelve tribes of Israel on the gates nor of the apostles on the foundations because of space limitation.

> *"Now the wall of the city had twelve foundations, and on them were the names of the twelve apostles of the Lamb…. The foundations of the wall of the city were adorned with all kinds of precious stones: the first foundation was jasper, the second sapphire, the third chalcedony, the fourth emerald, the fifth sardonyx, the sixth sardius, the seventh chrysolite, the eighth beryl, the ninth topaz, the tenth chrysoprase, the eleventh jacinth, and the twelfth amethyst"* (Rev. 21:14, 19–20).

I used twelve pillars under the gates to represent the foundations making them of coloured felt to represent the colours of the jewels mentioned.

Although the tribes of Israel camped around the tabernacle starting from the east side in a clockwise rotation in Numbers, I decided to do the twelve jewelled foundations in sequence going counterclockwise beginning on the right side as the east and going north, west, and south because the Revelation Scripture had said, *"…three gates on the east, three gates on the north."* So the first one would be *"jasper"*—green for Peter. Thus, the last foundation for the twelfth apostle was *"amethyst,"* a purplish-rose blend in the south right corner for the one replacing Judas. The Greek symbol for Christ is on the chief cornerstone to the right of it. *"Behold, I am laying in Zion a stone, a cornerstone chosen and precious"* (1 Pet. 2:6).

For a few of my banners, the Lord gave me both the words and a picture in my mind of how to illustrate them. The word on this banner was exactly from the Lord. However, whether the illustration was from me or from the Lord, I do not remember, but it was prayerfully constructed from Revelation 21. I have seen someone picture twelve foundations since then as one wide layer on top of another. But my husband had restored our family cottage keeping it from literally breaking in two by shoring up foundation walls and pillars, so I pictured the foundations as pillars.

The Bride Dwells in Christ and Christ Dwells in His Bride

Apostle Paul said:

> *You are ... fellow citizens with the saints and members of the household of God, having been built on the foundation of the apostles and prophets, Jesus Christ Himself being the chief cornerstone, in whom the whole building, being fitted together, grows into a holy temple in the Lord, in whom you also are being built together for a dwelling place of God in the Spirit.* (Eph. 2:19–22)

The apostles and prophets are also grounded on the Rock who is Jesus Christ. Jesus said, *"A city that is set on a hill cannot be hidden"* (Matt. 5:14). A bridge spanning earth to heaven cannot be hidden either.

The holy city in Revelation is an illustration of the church *"prepared as a bride adorned for her husband"* (Rev. 21:2). It will come down from heaven and have no temple in it because God and Jesus are the temple. The building blocks in Him, the *"living stones"* of the city, form the dwelling place for our King and Beloved. John heard *"a loud voice from heaven saying, 'Behold, the tabernacle of God is with men, and He will dwell with them, and they shall be His people. God Himself will be with them and be their God'"* (Rev. 21:3).

Years after making this banner, I noticed an illustration of foundation pillars which were made up of individual bricks or stones. This made me think of how possibly both the wall and the foundation are made of individual *"living stones"* fitted together since **the holy city is built of people joined together in the unity of the Holy Spirit**. *"Bearing with one another in love, endeavoring to keep the unity of the Spirit in the bond of peace. There is one body and one Spirit"* (Eph. 4:2–4).

True prophecy is the *"testimony of Jesus"* (Rev. 19:10) for the upbuilding of the church. All can receive the gift of prophecy, but only a *"few are chosen"* by Jesus for the office of the prophet or apostle. Jesus had twelve apostles of the Lamb whom He had personally chosen and taught. After the Holy Spirit fell on them, they could also prophesy what they heard from God. God's house is *"built on the foundation of the apostles and prophets"* (Eph. 2:20). Over the centuries, there have been other apostles and prophets, some of whom Jesus personally chose and taught, upon whose teaching some have built. Could it be that some of these are stones in the foundation pillars aligned with the twelve?

For instance, Jesus personally chose Paul to be an apostle. He wanted people to follow him, in as much as he was now following Christ. The early church *"continued steadfastly in the apostles' doctrine [teaching]"* (Acts 2:42). Jesus Himself is the chief *"Apostle and High Priest of our confession"* (Heb. 3:1). Peter urged, *"Coming to Him as to a living stone, rejected indeed by men, but chosen by God and precious, you also, as living stones, are being built up a spiritual house, a holy priesthood, to offer up spiritual sacrifices acceptable to God through Jesus Christ"* (1 Pet. 2:4–5).

The gates are each a single pearl because Jesus is the one way into the presence of God. He is the gate. He said, *"I am the door. If anyone enters by Me, he will be saved, and will go in and out and find pasture"* (John 14:6; 10:9 ESV). He is also the living *"Word"* of God (John 1:1) and *"one pearl of great price."* Jesus is the same at each gate, *"yesterday, today, and forever"* (Heb. 13:8). It could be that people will enter by different ones of His words—which are each pearls of wisdom: *"Again, the kingdom of heaven is like a merchant seeking beautiful pearls, who, when he had found one pearl of great price, went and sold all that he had and bought it"* (Matt. 13:45–46). The names of the twelve tribes are *"written on them,"* on the twelve pearly gates, reminding me that Jesus is concealed in every book of the Old Testament. Shadows and prophecies of Him are throughout those scriptural writings. Also, **New Jerusalem is not complete without His first chosen people who are saved and incorporated into His body. Likewise, His bridge needs them.**

There is a little story about the banner wall's construction. When I made banners, first I waited for the Lord's leading; then I asked the Lord to bless the work of my hands. So, He often brings more out of them than I intended. I made myself thin cardboard stencils for the letters, and paper patterns for the illustrations, cut them out and traced them onto the felt. Then I cut out the felt pieces and glued them onto the background. To line up the letters, I used a huge stainless-steel set-square which my carpenter husband's brother made for him.

Although it is looking down from above, I know that artistically, the perspective is off; but when I drew the walls of the holy city, I had four complete paper walls which all fit onto the banner. However, when I traced and cut out the felt pieces, strangely the wall on the EAST side would not all fit, so I cut part of it away. At first I was upset about it; but then I believed it could be the Lord wanted to show that there is still a breach in the wall of His holy city, the body and bride of Christ. Or **you could say that His bridge has some missing trestlework.** I remembered that if we fast the way the Lord wants us to do it, pouring ourselves out in love for the hungry and afflicted, then a number of blessings will occur in our lives, including the repairing of the breach.

God can have a holy city with repaired walls, His body, His bride, His bridge, with no missing parts, including His people Israel and the Roman Catholic Church. Jesus Himself prayed for unity, showing how it can occur. All Christians today believe in Jesus through the word of the original prophets and apostles, some of whom wrote books of the Bible, and they spread about bringing the gospel to other lands. Just as a branch can be grafted into a fruit tree, missing parts of the wall and bridge can be set in place with Jesus building His structure. Prophecy is for the upbuilding of the church. **If we each get closer to Jesus, our Beloved Kinsman Redeemer who brings restoration of our godly inheritance, and if we live wholeheartedly in His love, seeking His righteousness, we will get closer to one another too.**

> *I do not pray for these alone, but also for those who will believe in Me through their word; that they all may be one, as You, Father, are in Me and I in You; that they also may be one in Us, that the world may believe that You sent Me. And the glory which You gave Me I have given them, that they may be one just as We are one: I in them, and You in Me; that they may be made perfect in one, and that the world may know that You have sent Me, and have loved them as You have loved Me.* (John 17:20–23)

Let us ask Him to *"restore!"* (Isa. 42:22).

The stones for the original temple in Jerusalem were *"prepared at the quarry; so that neither hammer nor axe nor any tool of iron was heard in the temple, while it was being built"* (1 Kgs. 6:7 ESV). So, rather than in heaven, **I believe that God desires to do His work now of molding us into the right shape to fit well with other *"living stones."*** If we choose to cooperate with His refining work, to *"let God mold you into the right shaped stone,* trusting ourselves to a faithful Creator, it will go so much easier. Let us not fight against our Maker nor be rebellious towards Him:

> *For your Maker is your husband,*
> *The LORD of hosts is His name;*
> *And your Redeemer is the Holy One of Israel;*
> *He is called the God of the whole earth.* (Isa. 54:5)

We are to *"let God mold you into the right shaped stone."* Sometimes shaping will occur in interactions with other believers. *"As iron sharpens iron, so a man sharpens the countenance of his friend"* (Prov. 27:17).

Like smooth stones at the water's edge, we will be precious stones, sharp but graciously smooth, if we let the River of God wash over us. Since the stones for God's house are precious jewels, the waves of Holy Spirit will refine and polish us, taking away rough edges so that the glory of God will shine through us.

Revelation 21:3 says, *"Behold, the tabernacle* [dwelling] *of God is with men, and He will dwell with them"*; and Colossians 1:27 says, *"Christ in you, the hope of glory."* The Father will gather His jewels and set them in place preparing a dwelling place. His love will be the mortar and His light will shine through them.

> *So a book of remembrance was written before Him*
> *For those who fear the LORD And meditate on His name.*
> *"They shall be Mine," says the LORD of hosts,*
> *"On the day that I make them My jewels.*
> *And I will spare them*
> *As a man spares his own son who serves him."*
> *Then you shall again discern*
> *Between the righteous and the wicked,*
> *Between one who serves God*
> *And one who does not serve Him.* (Mal. 3:16–18)

The Ongoing True Bridge

So, we see that **the bridge is Christ the eternal High Priest, who allows His bride to be His helpmate, members who have been set in place by Him, spiritually connected with His body and who are under His authority.** Just as the trestlework on the bridge is in sections, prayer towers, which are strengthened by His Spirit and linked together, so saints on earth are to be linked with other Christians, submitted to Christ and His local authority, reaching up to God, and held together by Christ just as the top of the bridge links all the trestle columns. Different parts of the bridge will have different functions.

Jesus alone is the true bridge, the one way to the Father. It is believing in the finished work of Jesus on the cross and responding to His passionate love of ourselves and others that gets us up onto the true bridge, journeying toward the Father on *"the Highway of Holiness"* (Isa. 35:8). Being born again from above, we can both travel on the bridge and become a part of the true bridge's trestlework—part of the living body of Christ, standing in the gap through Christ, with Him, and within Him, holding up other believers in Jesus's name—He in us and we in Him. **But no one is higher than Him.**

> *Lord, You have been our dwelling place* [refuge] *in all generations.*
> *Before the mountains were brought forth,*
> *Or ever You had formed the earth and the world,*
> *Even from everlasting to–everlasting, You are God.* (Ps. 90:1–2)

Part III

False Bridges Are Like Mirages

> "When you cry out,
> Let your collection of idols deliver you.
> But the wind will carry them all away,
> A breath will take them.
> But he who puts his trust in Me shall possess the land,
> And shall inherit My holy mountain."
> And one shall say,
> "Heap it up! Heap it up! Prepare the way,
> Take the stumbling block out of the way of My people."
> (Isa. 57:13–14)

> Give to the LORD the glory due His name....
> Say among the nations, "The LORD reigns." (Ps. 96:8, 10)

> "And what will be the sign of Your coming, and of the end of the age?" And Jesus answered and said to them, "Take heed that no one deceives you.... For false christs and false prophets will rise and show great signs and wonders to deceive, if possible, even the elect."
> (Matt. 24:3–4, 24)

Chapter 6
The Genuine versus the Counterfeit

False Apparitions

People traveling in the desert have sometimes seen mirages. Someone in danger of dying from thirst might see what looks like a lush oasis up ahead and, really believing it is there, walk towards it for miles. However, when he struggles over a hill of dry, sandy ground for a better view of it hoping to see the palm trees and water, he finds that the apparition is only an illusion, a counterfeit of the real thing with a slippery slope down the other side. And like tripping over a stumbling block, down he goes!

The Word of God can be a stepping stone for us if we believe it, or it can also be a stumbling block if we do not. Unbelief and other sin can make us stumble if we give in to the temptation, deceived to think that what is wrong is right or what is right is wrong. But God is so good that He can lift us up again and set us on the right path, in the right train. That is what He did for me.

Do Not Be Deceived

"The disciples came to Him privately saying, 'Tell us, when will these things be? And what will be the sign of Your coming, and of the end of the age?' And Jesus answered and said to them: 'Take heed that no one deceives you. For many will come in My name, saying, "I am the Christ," and will deceive many'" (Matt. 24:3–5).

Deception is on the agenda of our enemy in the end times before Jesus's coming, and we are living in that time now.

Deceive,[3] *planaho,* means "to (properly *cause* to) roam (from safety, truth, or virtue): go astray, deceive, err, seduce, wander, be out of the way."

At a prayer breakfast in November, 1994, the Lord magnified to me the title of a teaching tape I had been given: *"Do not be deceived."* I didn't want to be deceived and did not know I was at the time, so I asked God for help and over time, He began to show me ways in which I had been deceived so I could come out of them. He began when He gave me a fresh baptism of fire at the Toronto Airport Vineyard Prophetic Conference that month. Later I will explain how I came to know that false bridges are an illusion.

There was a time when the Israelites experienced the light of God's truth in a big way. But after Moses and Joshua died, they became deceived and went astray. People had not been paying much attention to the instructions God had already revealed, and many lived contrary to His Word. *"In those days there was no king in Israel: everyone did what was right in his own eyes"* (Judg. 21:25). So they lost their former glory which had come from having God living and reigning among them in Moses and Joshua's time. God's glory, lost through sin, began to return to His people when the word of God suddenly broke into Samuel's life and he listened and obeyed God's voice.

Some people are so convinced that what is wrong is right today that they do not listen to the truth of Scripture. Jesus the King is not in them. But the humble are beginning to listen, praise God, inviting King Jesus to rule in them as He calls to His sheep in various ways. He knows His sheep by name and they can hear His voice. Yet because Jesus warned us that the false prophetic would be around too,

---

3   Rick Meyers, e-Sword. *Strong's Hebrew and Greek Dictionaries* in e-Sword, a downloaded Bible platform from https://www.e-sword.net/.

we must test words against Scripture when people say they hear from God, and examine the fruit. Since Jesus is the true bridge, God's chosen Mediator, and *"the testimony of Jesus is the spirit of prophecy"* (Rev. 19:10). He can speak to us on God's behalf today through true prophetic words.

Separating the True from the False

There can only be a counterfeit if there is already a genuine item; so, they do not make counterfeit fifteen-dollar bills. Jesus warned us, *"Take heed that you not be deceived"* (Luke 21:8). So, **we should pray and study the Bible so we will know what is genuine and be alert. Counterfeit revelation from the wrong source looks good at first glance, but gives a false plan of salvation.** It does not line up well enough with Scripture or twists it; but the true God can give true prophetic revelation and it will be consistent with what He has already revealed as recorded throughout the Bible.

The devil knows Scripture and used God's Word wrongly along with an ungodly shortcut that would have skipped the cross to tempt Jesus. He also tried to rob His identity with doubt, saying, *"If You are the Son of God…"* (Luke 4:3). But Jesus knew that Scripture used properly would refute error and ungodly shortcuts. **Jesus can help us overcome all deception and temptations with the light of His truth if we cry out for truth in our inner being. That is what I did.**

We can be like Solomon who asked God for wisdom and received it. *"Therefore give to Your servant an understanding heart to judge Your people, that I may discern between good and evil"* (1 Kgs. 3:9). Besides natural discernment, God can even give us the Holy Spirit gift of *"discerning of spirits"* (1 Cor. 12:10), so we will know if a spirit comes from God, the devil, or from ourselves. If we ask, we shall receive.

To be able to identify the counterfeit, we should go to the Bible and examine the genuine, as you also saw in the last chapter. Hopefully, this two-book set will help. We no longer need Old Testament

Levitical priests and prophets as mediators, because God has chosen Jesus to be the replacement, as He chose Samuel. But God established a new order of priesthood too. His Son will never die again and will have the position of perpetual High Priest in the order of Melchizedek, sometimes choosing to speak His testimony through His anointed people today. God called Jesus by name at His birth and testified of His Sonship at His baptism, anointing Him with His Holy Spirit. But He foretold His calling years before.

> *And inasmuch as He was not made priest without an oath (for they have become priests without an oath, but He with an oath by Him who said to Him:*
> *"The LORD has sworn*
> *And will not relent,*
> *'You are a priest forever*
> *According to the order of Melchizedek'"),*
> *by so much more Jesus has become a surety of a better covenant. Also there were many priests, because they were prevented by death from continuing. But He, because He continues forever, has an unchangeable priesthood. Therefore He is also able to save to the uttermost those who come to God through Him, since He always lives to make intercession for them.... But now He has obtained a more excellent ministry, inasmuch as He is also Mediator of a better covenant, which was established on better promises.* (Heb. 7:20–25; 8:6)

Jesus replaced the old high priests becoming the eternal bridge. **His is the only name written in Scripture as being chosen by God to be Mediator of the new covenant,** *"Mediator of a better covenant,"* offering His own blood. Nowhere in the Bible is it written that another Mediator or mediatrix was chosen by God or would even be needed. **It is a fable that we need to get to the Father through Jesus's mother, Mary, as if she were closer to Him.** Jesus was an ambassador of reconciliation while on the earth and interceded for us from the cross: *"Father, forgive them for they know not what they do"* (Luke 23:34). **Jesus is one with the Father, being God Himself and is still praying for**

us, mediating at the Father's right hand. He is that close! Mary is blessed but not equal to God and where she sits in heaven is not even named in the Bible. Nor was her blood shed to save us. It is His blood that sanctifies and allows us to be forgiven.

> *But Christ came as High Priest of the good things to come.... Not with the blood of goats and calves, but with His own blood He entered the Most Holy Place once for all, having obtained eternal redemption.... How much more shall the blood of Christ, who through the eternal Spirit offered Himself without spot to God, cleanse your conscience from dead works to serve the living God?* (Heb. 9:11–12, 14)

We have been sanctified through the sacrifice of His will:

> *"Behold, I have come to do Your will, O God...." By that will we have been sanctified through the offering of the body of Jesus Christ, once for all.*

> *And every priest stands ministering daily and offering repeatedly the same sacrifices, which can never take away sins. But this Man, after He had offered one sacrifice for sins forever, sat down at the right hand of God, from that time waiting till His enemies are made His footstool. For by one offering He has perfected forever those who are being sanctified....* [According to His New Covenant,] *says the* LORD: *"I will put My laws into their hearts, and in their minds I will write them," then He adds, "Their sins and their lawless deeds I will remember no more." Now where there is remission of these, there is no longer an offering for sin.* (Heb. 10:9–14, 16–18)

It was done at the cross, so we do not have to repeat the sacrifice, only remember it.

Jesus only died once—yet time for God is different than time for us, so our sins today affected Him two thousand years ago, and what He did then is effective for us today. What good news this is, and what a wonderful Bridge is our eternal Mediator and High Priest!

Yet how sad that our sins crucified Him! I wept when I realized that. **Thank God we do not have to earn our own salvation as I used to think. But neither should we sin purposely:** *"For the wages of sin is death, but the gift of God is eternal life in Christ Jesus our Lord"* (Rom. 6:23).

The Levitical high priest was a prophet too, once a year having the presence of God visit him, enthroned over the mercy seat on the ark of the covenant. Jesus, the eternal High Priest, is also the Great Prophet, the Prophet of prophets, fulfilling God's promise to Moses, *"I will raise up for them a Prophet* [Jesus] *like you* [Moses] *from among their brethren, and will put My words in His mouth, and He shall speak to them all that I command Him. And it shall be that whoever will not hear My words, which He speaks in My name, I will require it of him"* (Deut. 18:18–19). Jesus was and is in contact with His Father every day. He is the *"High Priest, who is seated at the right hand of the throne of the Majesty* [the mercy seat] *in the heavens"* (Heb. 8:1). And since God also promised that many would prophesy in the last days, Jesus can give His words to them: *"And on My menservants and on My maidservants I will pour out My Spirit in those days, and they shall prophesy"* (Acts 2:18); and, *"The testimony of Jesus is the spirit of prophecy"* (Rev. 19:10).

God Can Make Himself Known Today

Psalm 95:7–8 says, *"Today if you will hear His voice: 'Do not harden your hearts as in the rebellion.'"*

God can make Himself known in words, visions, dreams, and baptisms of fire and of Holy Spirit. He can speak to us today in His *"still small voice"* (1 Kgs. 19:12) as He spoke to Elijah at the mouth of the cave, but He can make Himself known in other ways too. One night in the spring of 1981, when the word of the Lord was still *"rare"* (1 Sam. 3:1) in Catholic circles as in little Samuel's time, the Lord began to make me aware of true and false bridges. I was suddenly awakened by a sound and light display by the living God—the audible voice of God telling me understandings of the first three commandments as beams of brilliant yellow light suddenly came into my darkened bedroom. (Later I kept thinking of the lines from the "Battle Hymn of the Republic": *"Mine eyes have seen the glory of the coming of the Lord."*) heard:

1. For what I had learned as, *"I am the L*ORD *thy God. Thou shalt not have strange gods before Me,"* I heard: *"Do not put fear of spending money before Me,"* where money could also mean *"talents."*

2. For Exodus 20:4–6, I heard: *"Isaiah 44: All. (Tell it to a priest.)"*

3. For, *"Do not take the name of the L*ORD *thy God in vain,"* I heard: *"If you call yourself a Christian, act like one."*

With a holy fear of the Lord, knowing it was His voice, I had jumped out of bed as my husband slept on. I also heard the Lord say that night, *"Someone who dips his bread in the same cup with me will betray Me,"* to which I replied, horrified, that surely it could not be me because I had always loved God. I had invited Jesus in to eat the bread of His Word with me. In those days, we were not even taught the true second commandment, but I knew it must be in the Bible somewhere. I read both Isaiah 44 and Exodus 20:4–6, finding them for the first time that night realizing that we had unknowingly practiced many idolatrous things.

Jesus will not lead us astray but some other things can. Love of money, putting before God a fear of spending it, and fear of lack are a type of idolatry. So is praying to saints for favors and through statues.

Near that special night, I went upstairs to receive prayer after my first charismatic meeting on March 25, 1981. (Although my husband had forbade me from attending charismatic meetings for seven years, he allowed me to go to that special one.) I was emptying myself, expecting to hear from God but was completely unprepared for what happened next. When a dear charismatic nun, Sister Grazia, laid hands on my head and anointed it with oil, my head felt very hot and I received a vision of whirling white light that ended in the shape of a dove. I heard the words in my head, *"Fear not for I am with you always."* People prophesied over me too, affirming me and that I would face persecution. (I replied that God had already shown me that I would receive a crown if I endured, and I claimed that I could face persecution from anyone except my husband. Years later a Christian leader told me that I had told the devil where to hit me by saying that, because I experienced a lot of verbal and restricting persecution from him.)

God had made Himself known to me in a baptism of Holy Spirit and prophetic words, but I also felt a strong heat like fire from above that settled in my eyes and right hand. Somehow I knew the vision and words were from God, although in those days I knew no one else who had had that experience. However, a few days later I was deceived to think that the strong, fiery heat which kept coming upon me had come from the devil. So, I turned in the charismatics from that meeting wrongly thinking I was protecting people from evil. (I did not know that there is a fire from God as well as a fire from hell.) It took months before I understood that I had betrayed the Lord in this as He had forewarned me. I was so grateful to receive forgiveness.

There are different types of deception. This was thinking that something right was wrong. However, I kept praying for a healing of the confusion of my mind because I kept vacillating in what I believed like a reed blowing in the wind, and some months later I realized that **when I had asked the Father for bread, He would not have given me a serpent.** The fire I felt along with the baptism of Holy Spirit had actually been a **baptism of fire** of which John the Baptist spoke. It reminds me of how the Holy Spirit drove Jesus into the wilderness to be tempted by the devil after Jesus had been baptized and affirmed by God. Jesus passed all His tests but I failed some of mine.

There are different kinds of stumbling stones. False words can be, but even a true word can be if it is not believed.

> *Therefore, to you who believe, He is precious; but to those who are disobedient,*
> *"The stone which the builders rejected has*
> *Become the chief cornerstone,"*
> *and*
> *"a stone of stumbling*
> *And a rock of offense."*
> *They stumble, being disobedient to the word, to which they also were appointed.* (1 Pe. 2:7–8)

Simeon prophesied to Mary and Joseph, *"Behold, this Child is destined for the fall and rising of many in Israel, and for a sign which will be spoken against"* (Luke 2:34). His people may fall, but Jesus can help them arise again. Years later, Jesus sent word to John the Baptist that he should remember the works Jesus had done, and, *"Blessed is he who is not offended because of Me"* (Matt. 11:6). John too had been tempted—with doubt in prison. If we believe the Word of God and obey it, we will not stumble over it, but rather it will lift us up. We fall when we do not believe His Word, and we rise with the resurrection power of Jesus when we repent, trust Jesus, and obey His Word whether we understand it or not. And then throughout our life we can follow Jesus to the Father.

I had stumbled over the manifestation of God's presence in the refining fire from above—which lasted for days. (Could it be that the 120 felt the heat of the fire on their heads at Pentecost too?) Although confusion lasted a long time, since I had no teaching to help me understand it, one of the words prophesied over me in that upper room had been 1 Peter 2:8–10 and verses 9–10 had given me hope: *"But you are a chosen generation, a royal priesthood, a holy nation, His own special people, that you may proclaim the praises of Him who called you out of darkness into His marvelous light; who once were not a people but are now the people of God, who had not obtained mercy but now have obtained mercy."*

All my life I had tried to obey the commandments, although I would fall short at times with little sins and went to confession to a priest to ask for God's forgiveness. I had no big sins. However, after I betrayed the Lord in my ignorance as He had forewarned, I was shocked to find that the devil did deceive me even more into thinking I had to follow him, and he told me other lies. **My mind got into such confusion, especially after I began to be tempted that I was better off dead than alive.** Since I was afraid the devil would trick me into killing myself, I checked myself into a local hospital psychiatric ward for protection for about a month.

Thank God hospital staff were not allowed to counsel people to have assisted suicide, nor to offer to give me an injection to help me kill myself. **It was a place of safety and protection then.** I did not want to commit suicide and then have to face Father God at the gate of heaven with that grave sin on my record, and I certainly did not want to go to hell! I chose life! That was so many years ago that if Jesus had not come to my rescue, I think of all that I would have missed, including time with my children and grandchildren. And I could not have worked as a secretary-bookkeeper. Plus, I have had so many wonderful experiences as a full-time missionary.

During that time, I began to keep a little journal of my dialogue with the Lord. I wanted to remember what He said to me. Psalm 139 tells us that the love of God can reach us anywhere, so I kept calling on His name as the Good Shepherd and the Great Physician. I felt His love when family visited me. I found that the "medicine" of little *rhema* words which God gave me was much better medicine than the pills the psychologist prescribed—so I "chewed" on the words. I told the psychologist and showed him my little book. Jesus was true to His word, *"Fear not for I am with you always,"* because I had great fear during those days, from which He would deliver me. And when I was healed, some of the words He gave me I proclaimed on banners to help others too, to help make ready a people prepared for the coming of the Lord.

What I really needed was good pastoral care, not psychiatric care. But I knew no one qualified to give it. However, I was grateful for the hospital chapel.

Thank God that Jesus can be our personal Saviour. Although I had loved God all my life, I had not known the plan of salvation, that *"all have sinned and fall short of the glory of God, being justified freely by His grace through the redemption that is in Christ Jesus"* (Rom. 3:23–24). We need forgiveness that can only come because of the shed blood of Jesus.

I had been taught that praying certain prayers to saints a certain number of times would get me saved, but that is not God's plan. Plus, the devil kept lying to me. But thank God I still kept calling on the name of the Lord. I went to a Kingston Charismatic Conference near August 15, 1981. A friend saw me crying during praise and worship in our Memorial Centre and invited me to her place for tea afterwards and asked me what was happening. When I began to tell her some of the lies the devil had been feeding me, that I was lost forever, she told me, "Nancy, did you not know that *Jesus died for us while we were yet sinners*?" Thank God for that word! It pierced my heart. **I knew the Good Shepherd had shepherded me to her house.**

Then the next day the word of the Lord came to me, *"Ask and you shall receive."* So I went to confession at the conference, and when my mother and I asked for prayers for healing of the confusion of my mind, I received that too! God is so good! He truly can pour out of His love into our heart by His Holy Spirit, forgive, save, and heal not only the body but the soul, including mental confusion. God did not disappoint, magnifying to me later that I was His *"child."* For this I am eternally grateful.

Jesus is *"Faithful and True,"* **and** *"the truth."* **But I had not known then that the devil is** *"a liar and the father of it"* (Rev. 19:11; John 14:6; 8:44).

I remember too that the Lord had been magnifying pictures of roosters on a blouse I wore in those days, reminding me of Peter. Thank God I wept like Peter rather than despairing like Judas when I understood that I had betrayed the Lord by turning in the charismatics not recognizing that the strong heat I felt had been a baptism of fire. It was the "sweet anointing from above" Catholics had sung about for years.

I remember the Lord magnifying to me early in the charismatic Renewal,

> *"Trust in the L*ORD *with all your heart, and lean not on your own understanding;*
> *In all your ways acknowledge Him, and He shall direct your paths"*
> (Prov. 3:5–6).

Sometimes there are things about God's Word which we do not even realize we do not understand. But a charismatic priest taught me to pray the two scriptural prayers in Ephesians, in chapters 1:15–23 and 3:14–21, so I began to pray for wisdom and revelation, spiritual strength, and knowledge of His love for myself and others.

During the time of the Judges, God's people had gone astray time and again, trying to serve both Him and false gods, disregarding warnings. God rescued them from captivity and oppression time and again when they humbled themselves to call on His name and repent. In Samuel's time, since priests and people had fallen into great sin again, God was no longer speaking much to His people through prophets, dreams, or visions. When Samuel was a child, true prophetic words from the mouth of God had not been heard much for a long time. *"The word of the LORD was rare in those days; there was no widespread revelation"* (1 Sam. 3:1). So he was surprised when God called him by name with a prophecy for Eli and his house which included, *"For I have told him that I will judge his house forever for the iniquity which he knows, because his sons have made themselves vile, and he did not restrain them. And therefore I have sworn to the house of Eli that the iniquity of Eli's house shall not be atoned for by sacrifice or offering forever"* (1 Sam. 3:13–14).

In Old Testament times, the anointed high priest used to act as a bridge between God and His people, but now Eli was not functioning properly. So God chose Samuel to deliver God's message confirming what He had already told Eli, and Samuel was trained to replace him.

God had provided food for His priests and Levites, but the sons of Eli were stealing from the offerings by taking more and better portions, and they were having sex outside of marriage. Eli spoke to them but did not restrain them, and they did not repent, so God judged them through His chosen prophet and priest, Samuel. Soon Eli and the two sons reaped the wages of sin and were dead.

This gives us food for thought today when well meaning but mistaken people tie up parents, pastors, and teachers by forbidding them to discipline growing and grown children. There are times when God expects us to speak, and He can tell us to speak or not to speak. There is a time to sow and to wait for good seeds to grow or for God to act and a time when further action on our part is required. We see that God judged both the two sons for their unrepented sins and failure to honor and obey their father; and He judged Eli for not using his authority to restrain them. **The world today has tried to strip fathers and mothers and other leaders of their God-given authority. But Jesus** told our charismatic prayer group while we still had teenagers and young adults at home, *"Tell your children often that God loves them and you love them, and bring them up in the discipline of the Lord."*

Jesus warned Thyatira, the corrupt church, **not to tolerate or *"allow"* His servants to be seduced by the false prophetic into serious evil-like sexual immorality and idolatry**, or people could become seriously ill and children could die. **May God help us to fear the Lord rather than fear man.** For if our God is with us, whom then shall we fear?

Are Catholics Automatically Saved?

When I was growing up, especially Pre-Vatican II, we thought that all who were born and baptized as Roman Catholics were automatically saved unless they committed an unconfessed mortal sin. Plus, we thought we could pray certain prayers to the saints a certain number of times and that would take time off our stay in a place between heaven and hell called purgatory. Firstly, I did not know we were supposed to be baptized into Christ and not into a denomination. Then I knew nothing of God's plan of salvation. **But God allowed me to have that experience of getting confused and betraying Him in those who prayed for me when I received the baptism of fire. I had never sinned in a serious way before, and I was able to have *"knowledge of salvation"*** (Luke 1:77). Thank God all who repent can experience the saving grace of the Saviour named Jesus Christ as I did: *"For God has committed them all to disobedience, that He might have mercy on all"* (Rom. 11:32).

Thank God, our God is a forgiving God, if we will only believe and receive the wonderful gift He has ready for us because of what Jesus did at the cross. His precious blood still has power to wash away all our sins if we repent. I am so glad I have *"knowledge of forgiveness."* And since Jesus alone is our Good Shepherd, **He does not give up on His sheep.** *"This is the will of the Father who sent Me, that of all He has given Me I should lose nothing, but should raise it up at the last day. And this is the will of Him who sent Me, that everyone who sees the Son and believes in Him may have everlasting life; and I will raise him up at the last day"* (John 6:39–40).

John the Baptist warned God's first chosen people who came out to be baptized by him, *"Brood of vipers! Who warned you to flee from the wrath to come? Therefore, bear fruits worthy of repentance, and do not begin to say to yourselves, 'We have Abraham as our father.' For I say to you that God is able to raise up children to Abraham from these stones"* (Luke 3:7–8). I found out that we could not just say Peter and the pope were our fathers. **We, too, needed to bear good fruit that continues.** So, I would often ask the Good Shepherd to lead me, and then see it, thank God.

> *He makes me to lie down in green pastures;*
> *He leads me beside the still waters.*
> *He restores my soul;*
> *He leads me in the paths of righteousness*
> *For His name's sake.* (Ps. 23:2–3)

Are We All to Live in Poverty?

I used to think so, although some choose to. Meanwhile, the night I heard God's audible voice, I checked our little daughter's room too, and the Raggedy Ann and Andy pictures on her closet door were suddenly illuminated in that heavenly yellow light bringing them to my attention. Much later I learned in Isaiah 8:19–22 that **praying to the dead can leave families impoverished spiritually and materially. Poverty can be a curse, a punishment for sin** (see Deut. 28:15–19). I knew that greed and avarice were sins, and wealth could be a god for some people if it controlled them: *"For the love of money is a root of all kinds of evil"* (1 Tim. 6:10). We are to beware of *"covetousness, which is* *idolatry"* (Col. 3:5). But I had not realized until then that the flip side of greed, namely the *"fear of spending money,"* could also be a god if it came before the real God.

I was a stay-at-home mom raising two children with the support of my husband, a carpenter. Thanks be to God, trusting in the Word of God changed me from being a worrier to one who seeks to trust our Faithful God and His Son. As I began to seek first His righteousness and His kingdom living here on earth as it is in heaven, obeying His leading, then I found that He truly does provide for our needs so that we are blessed to bless: *"Blessed are the merciful, for they shall obtain mercy"* (Matt. 5:7).

As I began to look for opportunities to share with even *"the least of My brethren"* (Matt. 25:40), freed up to give more to the church and to the needs God magnified, I began to notice the mercy being poured out on us—like a cousin coming to bless our family with big bags full of clothes which his family no longer needed.

I had been deceived for a time to think that God only helped the ones who helped themselves, **but that is what the world says. The Lord magnified to me instead, *"Teach My commandments."*** They are His Father's commandments in the light of the New Testament. **His *agape* love in His commandments is greater than the world's love.** God is so good that He even tells us to *"love your enemies, do good and lend, hoping for nothing in return; and your reward will be great, and you will be sons of the Most High. For He is kind to the unthankful and evil"* (Luke 6:35). Our motivation for giving is important. God will take care of us.

Because Joseph loved God and sought to do His will, the Lord caused all that he did to *"prosper"* (Gen. 39:23; 1 Kgs. 2:3), even when he was unjustly put into prison. **God still wants His obedient people today to prosper in all things, that they may be a blessing.** *"Beloved, I pray that you may prosper in all things and be in health, just as your soul prospers"* (3 John 1:2).

If God is calling us to do something, we can trust Him—even if He tells us to give or sell what we have and give to the poor and follow Him. *"Jesus said to him, 'If you want to be perfect, go, sell what you have and give to the poor, and you will have treasure in heaven; and come, follow Me'"* (Matt. 19:21). He will also give wisdom, timing, and provision for us, so we can give in peace.

That word to the rich young ruler came to me more than once in my life and I began to try to sell some things. However, we did not have much financially, and I began to realize that the Lord wanted me to *"sell"* the riches He had placed inside me. So I began to share more widely when I could and to follow Jesus. And later when that word came again as a widow, I asked the Lord if He wanted me to sell my house. I heard, *"Not at this time."* So, I took it as also to be ready to spend of my monthly allotment to bring in my full tithes and "invest" offerings in His storehouses and do good as the Lord led, trusting His leading. This is what the Acts church did, caring for one another's needs as they were able. Thank God, although in the world's eyes my widowhood income was classified as being below the poverty line at times, living by God's financial plan I always had food, clothes, and a roof over my head, and my provision stretched. I found that I could even *"lend ... [and] not borrow"* (Deut. 28:12; Matt. 6:33). God's ways are perfect.

The true God not only blesses the poor, hearing their cries, but tells us that *"it is more blessed to give than to receive"* (Acts 20:35).

> *No one can serve two masters.... You cannot serve God and mammon. Therefore I say to you, do not worry about your life, what you will eat or what you will drink; nor about your body, what you will put on. Is not life more than food and the body more than clothing?* [God provides for the birds of the air and the lilies of the field.] *...for your heavenly Father knows that you need all these things. But seek first the kingdom of God and His righteousness, and all these things shall be added to you. Therefore do not worry about*

tomorrow, for tomorrow will worry about its own things. Sufficient for the day is its own trouble. (Matt. 6:24–25, 32–34)

I was beginning to learn about Jesus being the Lord who is our Provider and All-Sufficient One, *Jehovah Jireh, El Shaddai*. But that does not mean that we have to live in poverty on earth like beggars in tattered clothing with falling apart houses. The poor who turn to God are *"blessed"* with provision because of the coming of His kingdom. I know He certainly blessed us time and again after I learned to call on His name. Thanks be to God. And **I was reminded of the conditional promise to those who care for the needs of the poor:** *"My God shall supply all your need according to His riches in glory by Christ Jesus"* (Phil. 4:19).

Are We All to Be Rich If We Believe in God?

We do need some people to be rich so they can care for their own needs and their families' needs and run businesses, hopefully in a godly manner, providing work for others. Then those who truly follow Jesus will be happy to help fund the advancement of the kingdom, even being prepared to sell off some assets if He so leads them. This was the spirit of the early church. *"Nor was there anyone among them who lacked; for all who were possessors of lands or houses sold them, and brought the proceeds of the things that were sold, and laid them at the apostles' feet; and they distributed to each as anyone had need"* (Act 4:34–35). **It can be all at once or as needed.**

We can have money, but it should not have us. Plus we need to be willing to receive whatever He wants us to have so we can steward it faithfully. After all, it all belongs to God. We can even ask God how much He would like us to give, and then give it.

All obedient believers are to prosper, but not all are to be rich. God knows who can handle what. It is true that **prosperity was a**

blessing for obedience in the Old Testament (see Deut.28:1–14). But although it is still a blessing in the new, under the law of love even more emphasis is placed on loving our neighbour as ourselves. We need to serve God alone and not let mammon rule over us by being attached to money or possessions. The law of sowing and reaping is true, and we should prosper, body, soul, and spirit if we are serving God. But the prosperity gospel has sometimes gone too far if it has led to:

> *...useless wranglings of men of corrupt minds and destitute of the truth, who suppose that godliness is a means of gain. From such withdraw yourself. Now godliness with contentment is great gain. For we brought nothing into this world, and it is certain we can carry nothing out. And having food and clothing, with these we shall be content. But those who desire to be rich fall into temptation and a snare, and into many foolish and harmful lusts which drown men in destruction and perdition.* (1 Tim. 6:5–9)

It is true that sometimes when we give, God rewards us here on earth. But our giving motivation and how we steward it are important. We should care about the needy and invest into kingdom work not primarily to get money back, but so that souls may be saved and the kingdom of God may advance. *"For we are His workmanship created in Christ Jesus for good works, which God prepared beforehand that we should walk in them"* (Eph. 2:10).

There are extra blessings for those who are obedient to God, and God knows what we need here on earth, but the best place to reap what we have sown is in heaven. *"Do not lay up for yourselves treasures on earth, where moth and rust destroy and where thieves break in and steal; but lay up for yourselves treasures in heaven, where neither moth nor rust destroys and where thieves do not break in and steal. For where your treasure is, there your heart will be also"* (Matt. 6:19–21).

Jesus will not lead us astray, but other spirits trying to guide us with a love of money and a fear of lack are false bridges. They are not of God. *"Command those who are rich in this present age not to be haughty,* *nor to trust in uncertain riches but in the living God, who gives us richly all things to enjoy. Let them do good, that they be rich in good works, ready to give, willing to share, storing up for themselves a good foundation for the time to come, that they may lay hold on eternal life"* (1 Tim. 6:17–19).

Who Is *"the Seed"* of the Woman?

Another Babylonian Catholic fable is that it is the "Lady," the Woman, who will crush Satan's head. There are images of her doing it. But Scripture points to **Jesus, the *"Seed"* of the woman**, as being the One who would bruise his head. It is only *"in Christ"* that we can participate with Him in doing it in our lives. The Lord spoke to the serpent after he deceived Adam and Eve, prophesying of Jesus: *And I will put enmity*

> *Between you and the woman,*
> *And between your seed and her Seed;*
> *He shall bruise your head,*
> *And you shall bruise His heel.* (Gen. 3:15)

Jesus's foster father, Joseph, and Mary, were descended from David and Adam, and so Jesus was the promised *"Seed"* of the woman from this Davidic line. But Jesus was also a supernatural Offspring because Mary supernaturally conceived, Joseph not being involved except as foster father. Mary, a woman who was a virgin until Jesus was born *"was found with child of the Holy Spirit"* (Matt. 1:18). Jesus, *"the Word became flesh"* (John 1:14) in her womb.

Then Satan bruised Jesus's heel at the cross, when he killed Him; but Jesus bruised the serpent's head by triumphing over death and Hades after descending there, not only arising Himself, but leading a host of captives on high who had been awaiting Him and giving gifts to men. That must have given the devil a terrible headache! *"And the dead in Christ will rise first"* (1 Thess. 4:16). *"The graves were opened; and many bodies of the saints which slept arose, and came out of the graves after His resurrection, and went into the holy city, and appeared unto many"* (Matt. 27:52–53 KJV).

Women and men **who are in Christ** can bruise the serpent's head by triumphing over evil and persecution, in Jesus's name, with the resurrection power of Jesus working mightily in them: *"And the God of peace will crush Satan under your feet shortly. The grace of our Lord Jesus Christ be with you. Amen"* (Rom. 16:20). But it is only because we are *"in Christ"* that this becomes reality. He does it. *"To God be the glory."* As David said, *"The battle is* [belongs to] *the* Lord's" (1 Sam. 17:47).

The Righteousness of God Is "Truth and Justice Tempered by Mercy"

When I asked the Lord years ago what His righteousness was, He told me, **"Truth and justice, tempered by mercy."** Jesus can punish unrepentant sin, but even in the midst of judgment He responds with love for His bride, even when she is backslidden like Hosea's adulterous wife, who was a symbol of His people. Once we become part of His family, He never forgets us. God is so good that after He sought truth and justice, with a time-out of withdrawing His mercy and presence from His ungrateful, disobedient people, He mercifully said,

> "Therefore, behold, I will allure her,
> Will bring her into the wilderness,
> And speak comfort to her.
> I will give her her vineyards from there,
> And the Valley of Achor as a door of hope;
> She shall sing there,
> As in the days of her youth,
> As in the days when she came up from the land of Egypt.
> And it shall be, in that day,"
> Says the Lord,
> "That you will call Me 'My Husband,'
> And no longer call Me 'My Master.'
> For I will take from her mouth the names of the Baals,
> And they shall be remembered by their name no more.

> *In that day I will make a covenant for them*
> *With the beasts of the field,*
> *With the birds of the air,*
> *And with the creeping things of the ground.*
> *Bow and sword of battle I will shatter from the earth,*
> *To make them lie down safely.*
> [Our Good Shepherd will take good care of us.]
> *I will betroth you to Me forever;*
> *Yes, I will betroth you to Me*
> *In righteousness and justice,*
> *In lovingkindness and mercy;*
> *I will betroth you to Me in faithfulness,*
> *And you shall know the* LORD.*"* (Hosea 2:14–20)

What a Wonderful God We Have!

HE alone we are to serve. HE alone is worthy of the glory due His name. Although He may allow the unrepentant to experience the just punishment of financial troubles, for those who respond to His love, and who leave behind other "lovers," prosperity can be restored. In heaven, all the angels and saints give Him the glory He deserves. Thanks be to God, we do not have to receive what we truly deserve when we walk in repentance, clothed in His righteousness. Just as He changed the names of two of Hosea's children, so He can change ours when we repent. God is so good! I remember a time when a song about that really ministered to me and gave me hope. **God is so merciful that He changed the name of Hosea's children at one point, giving them mercy and acceptance by Him, and promised me the same in 1981** in a word prophesied to me, including, *"Once you were no people but now you are God's people; once you had not received mercy but now you have received mercy"* (1 Pet. 2:10 ESV).

That Scripture referred to the names of Hosea's second and third children. God commanded the prophet Hosea to marry a prostitute so his family would be a prophetic sign to Israel: *"Go, take yourself a wife of harlotry and children of harlotry, for the land has committed great harlotry by departing from the* LORD" (Hos. 1:2).

Their first child's name, *"Jezreel,"* meant "God sows," and God would avenge his blood. The second child, *"Lo-Ruhamah,"* meant *"No-Mercy,"* for God would no longer have mercy on the house of Israel, but He promised the day would come when He would change her name to *"Mercy-Is-Shown."* The third child was called *"Lo-Ammi,"* which meant *"Not-My-People—"For you are not My people, and I will not be your God"* (Jer. 30:22). (Today, He wants us to remember to act like Christians and not to take His name in vain. *"If you call yourself a Christian, act like one."*) I remember thinking on all this when in the early Catholic charismatic movement God began to speak in prophetic words to Catholics who were seeking Him, calling us *"*[His] *people,"* and to give us *"mercy"* by miracles and healings which were performed in the power and name of Jesus.

God promised the day would come like today when His people would be called *"sons of the living God,"* and His spiritual Fatherhood should be acknowledged and appreciated.

> *I taught Ephraim to walk,*
> *Taking them by their arms;*
> *But they did not know that I healed them.*
> *I drew them with gentle cords,*
> *With bands of love,*
> *And I was to them as those who take the yoke from their neck.*
> *I stooped and fed them.* (Hos. 11:3–4)

Yet there was also a day when the Lord had me bring Hosea 3 to the Catholic church, which tells of Hosea's wife going back to her harlotry and having to be ransomed by him from her slavery. So, we need to learn to be faithful to Jesus who wants to be the Bridegroom of our soul and paid the price for His backslidden bride.

Hebrews 12 reminds us that our Father God raises us with love and discipline. **Father loves His children so much that He may**

chastise us, and **for the obedient, a word of wisdom is sufficient**. But for others, He may have to allow stronger discipline to correct them. He wants us to strive against sin and produce good fruit. You could say that our Father God believes in spanking when necessary, and sometimes He disciplines with a time-out, but that it is not His full righteous wrath. God is not a tyrant or a child abuser. Jesus weeps when His people are abused.

Instead of sin mastering us, holding us in bondage, we can master sin in the freedom and grace of the adopted sons of God.

> *"My son, do not despise the chastening of the Lord,*
> *nor be discouraged when you are rebuked by Him;*
> *for whom the Lord loves He chastens,*
> *and scourges every son whom He receives...."*
> [He allows it] *for our profit, that we may be partakers of His holiness. Now no chastening seems to be joyful for the present, but painful; nevertheless, afterward it yields the peaceable fruit of righteousness to those who have been trained by it.* (Heb. 12:5–6, 10–11)

A grape vine needs to be trained to grow a certain way, fed, sprayed with lime, and pruned to bear good fruit abundantly.

He loves us so much that if we will seek Him, we can receive the benefits of forgiveness which His Son's blood purchased when He bore our chastisement. I have heard from Him, **"His mercy is great on those who fear Him."** The Holy Spirit reminds us not to be afraid because He is with us—and to trust and obey Him: *"Afterward the children of Israel shall return and seek the Lord their God and David their king. They shall fear the Lord and His goodness in the latter days"* (Hos. 3:5).

God is so good!

Chapter 7

Graven Images Are False Bridges

I also went to the living room that night I heard the audible voice of God and for the first time in my life read Isaiah 44. Realizing the Ten Commandments must be in the Bible somewhere, I searched and found them in Exodus 20 and wept realizing that the second commandment is written:

> *You shall not make for yourself a carved image—any likeness of anything that is in heaven above, or that is in the earth beneath, or that is in the water under the earth; you shall not bow down to them nor serve* [worship] *them. For I, the L*ORD *your God, am a jealous God, visiting the iniquity of the fathers upon the children to the third and fourth generation of those who hate Me, but showing mercy to thousands, to those who love Me and keep My commandments.* (Exodus 20:4–6)

I had never heard that before. In those days, not only was I not familiar with Isaiah 44, but we were not even taught the second commandment of Exodus 20:4–6 in Catholic schools or churches my family had attended. Instead, the tenth commandment was split into two separate ones—not coveting a neighbour's wife and not coveting a neighbour's goods.

Thank God, after I shared this with my bishop, Archbishop Francis Spence, the liturgy began to include the biblical commandments of the Exodus 20 passage in some Sunday readings. But sadly, years later, people were still kneeling at statues and shrines, and putting trust in medals, going to the wrong bridge in prayer.

As I read through Isaiah 44, **I found written what I later learned was *"the Promise of the Father"* (Acts 1:4) to send His Holy Spirit *"like water on him who is thirsty"* and how praying to anyone else but God for salvation, favours, or healing was idolatry, as was praying through a graven image.** I was angry at first that our priests, nuns, and relatives had taught us to pray to the saints for everything. But then I realized that they had been ignorant of the Scriptures too in those days. It is written,

> *"I will pour My Spirit on your descendants*
> *And My blessing on your offspring...."*
> *Thus says the* LORD, *the King of Israel,*
> *And his Redeemer, the* LORD *of hosts:*
> *"I am the First and I am the Last;*
> *Besides Me there is no God....*
> *Do not fear, nor be afraid;*
> *Have I not told you from that time, and declared it?*
> *You are My witnesses.*
> *Is there a God besides Me?*
> *Indeed there is no other Rock;*
> *I know not one."* (Isa. 44:3, 6, 8)

Examining Isaiah 44, one can see that idolatry is like a mirage. It is futile, and is not a secure bridge to the Father.

Firstly, no other name is equal to the Lord's: *"Besides Me there is no God."*

Then, the futility of idolatry of graven images is discussed.

[Half a tree is used for firewood]

> *And the rest of it he makes into a god,*
> *His carved image.*

He falls down before it and worships it,
Prays to it and says,
"Deliver me, for you are my god!"
They do not know nor understand;
For He has shut [smeared over] *their eyes, so that they cannot see,*
And their hearts, so that they cannot understand.
And no one considers in his heart,
Nor is there knowledge nor understanding to say,
"I have burned half of it in the fire,
Yes, I have also baked bread on its coals;
I have roasted meat and eaten it;
And shall I make the rest of it an abomination?
Shall I fall down before a block of wood?"
He feeds on ashes;
A deceived heart has turned him aside;
And he cannot deliver his soul,
Nor say, "Is there not a lie in my right hand?" (Isa. 44:17–20)

The Holy Spirit began to open the eyes of my heart as I read those Scriptures. We Catholics had **unknowingly been practicing idolatry by praying to saints and through statues and pictures, using them as false bridges to God**. I could see that trusting in them to save and heal us was very displeasing to God, and that upset me. All sin displeases God. But there is a difference between someone participating unknowingly and knowingly in something which is seriously wrong. So I stopped.

As a child I had been mistakenly taught also to wear every day a medal or crucifix (a cross with an image of Christ on it) if I wanted to be protected. But reading Isaiah 44, I understood that this was trusting in a graven image, acting like the pagans who wear rabbit's feet or amulets thinking they have power to protect. Now I purposely only occasionally wear a cross, **but just as a reminder of what Jesus did on a cross.** My husband and children gave me one with only a tiny diamond on it. That reminded me that the light of the world was crucified and rose again. My salvation does not come from a piece of wood, stone, or metal, but **from what Jesus did** on the cross, atoning for our sins with His blood: *"Shall I fall down before a block of wood?"*

We knew that **Jesus is called the Saviour, but I finally began to understand the obvious,** that this meant that **it is Jesus who saves and protects, not anyone else. A simple, childlike faith in Him is all that is required.** *"For God so loved the world that He gave His only begotten Son, that whoever believes in Him should not perish but have everlasting life"* (John 3:16). As my cousin used to say, "I'm so glad I am a whosoever." **Jesus is the Rescuer.** The Power of God and His Son, Jesus, may reside in His people, and miracles might have been done at their hands, but He is the Source. Perhaps they are hands in the body of Christ. I found that when I call on His name, **He is my defense, thank God.**

I burned, smashed, or discarded all my idolatrous statues and medals, especially if they were **falsely regarded by Catholics as being "miraculous"** like a little statue of the Infant of Prague and the so-called "miraculous medal." **People can no more be protected by wearing a medal, rosary, or cross than by hanging a toothbrush around their neck.**

Instead, I ask Jesus to be my defense and His faithfulness and *"truth shall be* [my] *shield and buckler"* (Ps. 91:4). Now I say as David said,

> *I will love You, O Lord, my strength.*
> *The Lord is my rock and my fortress and my deliverer;*
> *My God, my strength, in whom I will trust;*
> *My shield and the horn of my salvation, my stronghold.*
> *I will call upon the Lord, who is worthy to be praised;*
> *So shall I be saved from my enemies.* (Ps. 18:1–3)

Years ago, especially Pre-Vatican II, I had genuflected and knelt before statues and lit candles before graven images—pictures and statues—trying to pray through them to the persons they represented as

I had been taught, not realizing that God had forbidden this: *"He falls down before it and worships it, prays to it and says, 'Deliver me, for you are my god!'"* (Isa. 44:17).

I had even put a picture of the Sacred Heart of Jesus on my wall and prostrated myself face down on the floor before it in 1981, attempting to worship God through the image because of faulty teaching by the false prophetic. So after I heard the audible voice of God, I asked God for forgiveness for unknowingly making it an idol and tore it off the wall and destroyed it. **No more do I worship Him through a graven image, but I will go down on my face at times to worship the real God** *"in spirit and truth"* (John 4:23). I love the real Jesus and His Father and Holy Spirit. **I no longer need an image as the focal point of my prayers. That is a trap!** I learned, *"Surely He shall deliver you from the snare of the fowler"* (Ps. 91:3).

I honour the Roman Catholic Church for teaching us to have reverence for God. However, in our ignorance of the Scriptures, we talked to the statues and pictures the way a baby talks to her doll or teddy bear. Some people kiss them as if they were real flesh and not hard as stone. Some cover statues in fabric clothing and jewellery or in purple cloth when people are fasting in Lent, and some even turn a statue facing away as if that prevented it from seeing them do something wrong. And in many countries, even into the twenty-first century, some Roman Catholics still carried statues in procession, especially on their feast days, not realizing they were imitating the pagans who carried their idols.

> *Their idols are silver and gold,*
> *The work of men's hands.*
> *They have mouths, but they do not speak;*
> *Eyes they have, but they do not see;*
> *They have ears, but they do not hear;*
> *Noses they have, but they do not smell;*
> *They have hands but they do not handle;*
> *Feet they have, but they do not walk;*

> *Nor do they mutter through their throat.*
> *Those who make them are like them;*
> *So is everyone who trusts in them.*
> *O Israel, trust in the LORD;*
> *He is their help and their shield.* (Ps. 115:4–9)

So my revelation about idolatry and about Jesus being the true bridge did not come initially from Roman Catholics or Protestants, but from the Lord who intervened in my life in spectacular ways that I will never forget. Like Paul, I say, *"To me who am less than the least of all the saints, this grace was given, that I should preach among the Gentiles the unsearchable riches of Christ, and to make all see what is the fellowship of the mystery, which from the beginning of the ages has been hidden in God who created all things through Jesus Christ"* (Eph. 3:8–9). **No one denomination is the whole church any more than one tribe was all of Israel,** and He wants us to let Him mold us according to His plans for our lives. God sees us even when we are in the womb. He alone designed the master plan for our lives with no help from an idol, not even from the woman who bore Him on earth or another saint.

No idol—no person, possession, or position—is above the one true God or equal to Him, not even a Christian who has Christ in him doing God's works in him. He can only hope to be part of the body of Christ, the one true bridge to the Father, by abiding in Crist the Rock.

> *Your eyes saw my substance, being yet unformed.*
> *And in Your book they all were written,*
> *The days fashioned for me,*
> *When as yet there were none of them.* (Ps. 139:16)

> *Thus says the LORD, the King of Israel, and his Redeemer, the LORD of hosts: "I am the First and I am the Last; besides Me there is no God."* (Isa. 44:6)

Now see that I, even I, am He, and there is no God besides Me. (Deut. 32:39)

God is real and human beings are real, while images are only imitations and even counterfeits of the real thing, products of an artist's imagination since we do not know precisely how God looks. Father God even forbade images of Himself.

Flat Nate:

Reality is reality, but a story of make-believe is just that. **Do not be deceived.**

My grandson, Nathaniel, "Nate" for short, did a project in elementary school based on a book about a little boy who became flattened as thin as a piece of paper and was sent by mail to various parts of the world. Each child in Nate's class was to mail a simple picture of himself to someone which showed how he might have looked if he were flattened. In his case, it was called "Flat Nate." Then my daughter who received the picture was to take it to various places in our city and took photos with "Flat Nate" in it, pretending that Nate himself was visiting that city.

Thus, his Aunt Gina took "Flat Nate" to museums and other civic points of interest. For the sake of the school project, it was as if Nate could have been made so flat that he could go through the mail slot and be taken to the various places. Of course, this was all just fantasy, just make-believe. It was not really Nate himself who went; it was only a flat piece of paper with his picture drawn on it. This "Flat Nate" image could not speak or walk or see anything. It was not alive and had to be carried and placed somewhere by somebody's hands, so it was not really him. And even if it had been an animated figure, "3-D Nate," it still would not have been a real boy. My grandson, Nate, is reality, a true boy; but an image, even computerized, is only make-believe.

Likewise, people need to distinguish between reality and fantasy in regard to "Flat Mary" or "Flat Jesus" or "Flat Saint Anthony," etc. Pictures of holy people are only some artist's conception printed onto a piece of paper. Taking that flat image with you somewhere is not really taking Mary or Jesus or Saint Anthony anywhere. **Yet many Catholics in the pro-life movement were deceived into thinking that the image of the "Lady" of Guadalupe, called the Tilma, is miraculous, and that she is the one who can end abortion.** I have seen them lifting high her picture at pro-life rallies.

But let us lift high the name of Jesus! He is the One who can truly end abortion. His name actually has power in it. Yet He wants it used led by His Holy Spirit. As the Lord has told me in regards to seeking justice for the unborn, the battle will be won, *"'Not by power, not by might, but by My Spirit,' says the LORD"* (Zech. 4:6).

I also learned, *"Test all things. Hold fast* [retain] *what is good"* (1 Thess. 5:21), and began to notice years ago that prophetic revelations certain people claimed had come from certain apparitions of a "Lady," who we assumed was Mary, did not line up with Scripture, such as to pray directly to an angel or to wear a rosary around your neck to save you. But it is simple faith in Jesus that saves us and Jesus did warn us that there would be false prophecy coming from the wrong source in the latter days: *"For many will come in My name, saying, 'I am the Christ,' and will deceive many"* (Matt. 24:5). Her false prophets claim that the "Lady" appearing at Fatima said, "Only she can save you." **But that is a lie from the pit of hell. Only Jesus can save you! Basically, the "Lady" is deceptively saying,** *"I am the Christ,"* **and sadly, has deceived many.** In heaven, the redeemed know the truth of Scripture.

John saw in heaven *"a great multitude which no one could number, of all nations, tribes, peoples, and tongues, standing before the throne and before the Lamb, clothed with white robes, with palm branches in their hands and crying out with a loud voice, saying, '****Salvation belongs to our God who sits on the throne, and to the Lamb!****'"* (Rev. 7:9–10).

Flat Lady

Many years ago, I went to see a copy of the Tilma on display at our local cathedral. It was a flat image of the "Lady" of Guadalupe, Mexico. I listened to the speaker and read the material they sent home with us. A false prophet of the "Lady" claimed that by taking the Tilma traveling, that it would be bringing the "Lady" throughout the Americas. But this is false and to believe it would be making the "Flat Lady" into an idol. (See Isaiah 44.) Many pray to her because the image of the "Lady" was supernaturally imprinted upon a Mexican peasant's cloak years ago and I, too, once thought the picture which the man received was a true sign, until the Lord began to teach me more about discerning what is idolatry and that we are not to pray to any saint because only Jesus is the Father's chosen Mediator. As Jesus warned, *"For false christs and false prophets will rise and show great signs and wonders to deceive, if possible, even the elect"* (Matt. 24:24).

There are true signs and wonders and deceptive ones. The evil one can do supernatural signs and wonders too and can come disguised as *"an angel of light"* (2 Cor. 11:14), so do not be deceived into thinking a picture is miraculous, nor talk to it as people also did with the Mother of Perpetual Help image. The "Lady" is not the answer to abortion or anything else. The word of the Lord has come: *"And I heard another voice from heaven saying, 'Come out of her, my people, lest you share in her sins, and lest you receive of her plagues'"* (Rev. 18:4). Glory be to God. He loves us so!

Be aware: *"No temptation has overtaken you except such as is common to man; but God is faithful, who will not allow you to be tempted beyond what you are able, but with the temptation will also make the way of escape, that you may be able to bear it. Therefore, my beloved, flee from idolatry"* (1 Cor. 10:13–14).

The way out of the temptation to pray through a graven image is to stop talking to the picture or statue as if it were truly who it represents. Stop praying through it. Instead of focusing on an image

when you pray, focus directly on God *"in spirit and in truth"* and pray, remembering, *"Our help is in the name of the LORD, who made heaven and earth"* (Ps. 124:8). I made the shift in focus so others can too.

People Carry Idols, but Idols Cannot Carry Them

However, God can carry us. God alone is the real God and Jesus is the way into his presence. Although we can carry Him in our heart, it is really He who carries us. The real God can stand and move around quite well on His own. But a picture or statue of God or of a saint, of Buddha or any other idol, or a crucifix on Good Friday, must be carried as the Baals and Asherim of old were. And **even if it is animated, an image, even a computerized one, only moves or speaks because man has programmed it to do so.** Therefore, it is not really Jesus you are emailing someone (although some say it is) if you pass on a moving picture of Him. So if someone emails me an animated picture of someone, even of Jesus, claiming that the one pictured is visiting my home through the email image, I delete it. And you can break prayer chains because they are only superstition. **Fear not because the Lord is with you. Thank God, the real Jesus, the Good Shepherd, can visit the homes of His people and carry His sheep.** He is always welcome in my home with His Father and Their Holy Spirit.

Deuteronomy 33:27 says, *"The eternal God is your refuge and underneath are the everlasting arms."*

The Lord has held me with a word from Him many a time, especially after my dad, husband, and mom died. The Lord has told me, *"Be not afraid for I am with you always."* I have gray hair and, thank God, **the real Jesus still carries me at times**. But no artist's image can ever completely duplicate Him or be God. God is Spirit and we can carry Him in our heart, although He is really carrying us. **But carrying an image is not carrying God.**

Even to your old age, I am He,
And even to gray hairs I will carry you!
I have made, and I will bear;
Even I will carry, and will deliver you.
To whom will you liken Me, and make Me equal
And compare Me, that we should be alike?
They lavish gold out of the bag,
And weigh silver on the scales;
They hire a goldsmith, and he makes it a god;
They prostrate themselves, yes, they worship.
They bear it on the shoulder, they carry it
And set it in its place, and it stands;
From its place it shall not move.
Though one cries out to it,
Yet it cannot answer
Nor save him out of his trouble. (Isa. 46:4–7)

I remember Jesus ministering to me through words of a song in 1987: *"I have decided to follow Jesus. No turning back, no turning back."* Frank Sinatra used to sing: "I did it my way." But whether others follow or not, God wants us to faithfully follow Jesus, to be His disciples and do things the Lord's way, even if it means overcoming peer pressure or persecution. *"Prepare the way of the Lord."*

Back in 1981, the Lord had been teaching me things for some days, sometimes illuminating words or something with a yellow *shekinah* glory light, like the words, *"Teach My Commandments,"* in my Bible. That night the Lord revealed those understandings of three commandments. I got back into bed shaking with a holy fear of the Lord, realizing I had heard the audible voice of God and seen the glory of His coming. **This was a turning point in my life.** Previously, at another time, I had also made the mistake of trying to pray to Him through a string-art picture on my bedroom wall which had lit up one day to look like an eye and reminded me of God's eye. We need to know that God can see us wherever we are, and He might even draw our attention to something as a teaching instrument by illuminating it with a heavenly light, but the night the Lord gave me *"Isaiah 44"* as an understanding of the second commandment, I realized that talking to Him in prayer through the string-art wall-hanging was treating it like an idol, and shaking as I got back into bed, I repented. It had been a little like a burning bush which I had turned aside to see, but He was not in the art piece.

God got Moses's attention by letting him see a burning bush, and let His voice be heard, but the bush was not God and God was not inside the bush. Likewise God was not in the wall-hanging even though it had been illuminated by a heavenly light. But His voice which seemed to come through the wall behind my bed and His presence in my room was real. Although I did not see Him, I certainly saw the glory of the coming of the Lord in the streams of bright yellow heavenly light.

I had not known that people in some nations worshiped images of God's eye, sometimes putting them on buildings as if they would be protected by God through them, or as if they were portals through which God could see. But our God can see through any wall or ceiling, and even into the depths of our hearts and minds. **He does not need to do it through a graven image or illustration.**

Before I knew this, my daughter innocently made Christmas tree ornaments one year at school in the shape of "God's eye," and I hung some in the window thinking they were pretty decorations. However, after I had had some friends visit from Mexico and learned that in that country people used to hang them in windows thinking that God would see them through the image, I removed them and destroyed them, not wanting to give the appearance of evil. **God does not use man-made or created objects as His eyes or portals. He has plenty of *"eyes"* in heaven including heavenly creatures** *"full of eyes around and within"* (Rev. 4:8), some of which like His Holy Spirit and guardian angels, He sends to earth as *"watchers"* (Dan. 4:17; Ezek. 1:18). The nature of God includes extraordinary, supernatural vision.

Statues and Pictures Can Be Snares

A pastor and his wife gave me a statue of Jesus praying in Gethsemane and I asked the Lord if I could set it up in my living room—not to pray through it, but just as a remembrance, and He said to me, *"Hay and stubble,"* and, *"It would be a snare to them,"* so I smashed it instead.

Perhaps it would have been all right for that pastor to put that statue in their home, but since my family came from a long line of staunch Catholics in Italy who used to pray through statues, some even adorning them with gold jewellery when prayers were answered, the Lord knew it was best not to place it in my living room.

At the word of the Lord, Gideon destroyed his father's idols and worshiped the Lord who led him in battle against their enemies, afterwards giving them peace for forty years. *"Take your father's young bull ... and tear down the altar of Baal that your father has, and cut down the wooden image that is beside it; and build an altar to the LORD your God on top of this rock in the proper arrangement"* (Judg. 6:25–26). However, in his old age, Gideon melted down gold earrings, spoils of battle, making a golden *"ephod and set it up in his city, Ophrah. And all Israel played the harlot with it there. It became a snare to Gideon and his house"* (Judg. 8:27).

I remember right after Vatican II in the late sixties, the Roman Catholic Church removed altars to saints and statues from churches. We were not told why though and unfortunately, statues have become very common again, and have become a snare to some people who kneel and pray before them and even kiss them in their ignorance. **This turns them into idols. That is why they need to know that the second commandment forbids bowing down to or serving graven images.** That means we are not to pray through them or serve the voice of any spirit which might speak through them. *"Now the Spirit expressly says that in latter times some will depart from the faith, giving heed to deceiving spirits and doctrines of demons"* (1 Tim. 4:1).

When false signs and wonders began to happen after people prayed through a "Mother of Perpetual Help" picture, some people ignorantly called it miraculous. But the Lord told me in regard to devotions to her, *"O do not do that abominable thing that I hate!"*

Should All Statues Be Destroyed?

There was a time when I wondered if God wanted people to stop making all statues and images. But **God Himself commissioned images of angels for the top of the ark of the covenant in the Holy of holies** (see Ex. 25:18). **However, they were only to be a remembrance or teaching instrument and not to be prayed through.** Only the high priest entered that part of the tabernacle, and he knew better than to pray to angels, especially through a graven image. Besides that, the real presence of God would meet with him in there, resting between the two angel statues over the mercy seat, as well as in a pillar of cloud or fire at the door of the tent of meeting to talk with Moses. So, God clarified that He was not forbidding the making of all statues and pictures. But right after forbidding them to have other gods before Him, He commanded them not to make carved images to be used as idols: *"You shall not bow down to them nor serve them. For I, the LORD your God, am a jealous God"* (Ex. 20:5–6).

God, through Moses, warned His people to avoid wicked customs of the nations around them. Neither should His people today replace the gods of the nations with Christian "gods." Years ago, instead of setting up statues of false pagan gods, graven images of saints were set up when missionaries went overseas. If they had only been used as teaching instruments or remembrances of what God had done the way that stained glass windows portray Bible stories, it might have been all right. But for people who had just left idolatry, graven images were sometimes a snare trapping them into exchanging one form of idolatry for another. Some burn candles before the images as the pagans burn incense before their idols and treat them as if they are alive. But in one Catholic church, I noticed they removed the picture from behind the candles, so someone could still light one while praying but they did not fall into the snare of praying through an image. And hopefully, they would address their prayers to God in Jesus's name.

> *They served their idols, which became a snare to them.* (Ps. 106:36)

> *Our soul has escaped as a bird from the snare of the fowlers;*
> *The snare is broken, and we have escaped.*
> *Our help is in the name of the L*ORD*, who made heaven and earth.*
> (Ps. 124:7–8)

Interestingly, two of the first words the Lord gave me back in 1981 were, *"The truth will set you free,"* **and,** *"Our help is in the name of the L*ORD*, who made heaven and earth."*

It was not until recently though that I noticed verse 7 and the connection, that idolatry is a snare that causes people to be imprisoned, captive to sin, like a bird in a cage; but by calling on the name of the Lord, one can be set free; and by obeying His Word, we can stay free. No wonder the Lord spoke that to me! God is so good! Before I even understood why, I can remember praying years ago, "Lord, rescue me from the snare of the fowler." And He did, thank God. Jesus is our Rescuer.

After all, although the enemy can do lying signs and wonders, it is God who hears and answers His people's prayers—not idols, neither the images themselves, nor the saints in heaven. God did true signs and wonders delivering His people from Egypt and healing people in the first century, and He still does them today.

Shrines Are False Bridges

> *And the rest of it he makes into a god,*
> *His carved image.*
> *He falls down before it and worships it,*
> *Prays to it and says,*
> *"Deliver me, for you are my god!"* (Isa. 44:17)

Some people carry around statues of Mary from house to house setting up shrines to her. One type they call the Pilgrim Virgin statue, as if it had her life in it. But that reminds me of the Asherah, the Semitic fertility goddess who pagans believed was present in her cult object, often a tree or a pole which would be placed by the altar of Canaanite high places. But rather than a goddess, it really had a demonic spirit that spoke, deceiving the people with false doctrine which her false prophet declared, causing them to worship a goddess through a graven image or her cult object, stealing worship from the one true God.

> *They have no knowledge,*
> *Who carry the wood of their carved image,*
> *And pray to a god who cannot save....*
> *Look to Me and be saved, all you ends of the earth!*
> *For I am God, and there is no other.* (Isa. 45:20, 22)
> *Woe to him who says to wood, "Awake!"*
> *To silent stone, "Arise! It shall teach!"*
> *Behold, it is overlaid with gold and silver,*
> *Yet in it there is no breath at all.*
> *But the* LORD *is in His holy temple.*
> *Let all the earth keep silence before Him.* (Hab. 2:19–20)

Only God is God, and our bodies are meant to be His temple. Instead of visiting shrines to Mary and the saints to pray, we can call on the name of the Lord.

When I read a book about the persecuted Christians in China and it included pictures of pagan practices of **ancestor worship**, I saw the similarity with some Catholic practices. They set up statues of their ancestors, what they called "household gods," and they burned incense before them and bowed to pray to them and put pictures of them on their buildings thinking that then the *"familiar spirits"* of the dead would protect them. To copy these pagan practices, **substituting**

images of dead spiritual ancestors—saints—and praying through them is also idolatry.

The Book of Judges tells of Micah's idolatry. His mother, also an Israelite, paid the silversmith to *"make a carved image and a molded image.... The man Micah had a shrine, and made an ephod and household idols; and he consecrated one of his sons who became his priest. In those days there was no king in Israel; everyone did what was right in his own eyes"* (Judg. 17:3, 5–6). People need King Jesus to rule them. To know whether something truly is right, we need to check to see if it lines up with the Bible, with the Word of God, not with some whim of man. Serving Jesus as King, we should do what is right in God's eyes.

Idolatry Has Been Judged

The Lord awoke me one night in the early 1980s with a vision including tiny rainbow-colored lights and the word of the Lord, *"Love yourself. The truth will set you free,"* and, *"Study the book of Baruch."* It is in the *Apocrypha*, but evidently, Jesus is familiar with it. Baruch was Jeremiah's scribe (see Jer. 36:4). As I studied it, I saw idolatry mentioned as one of the reasons for God's people being prisoners of war in Babylon.

The Jews in captivity in Babylon realized that *"the evils and the curse"* that had come upon them were a consequence of their sinfulness, just punishments foretold in Deuteronomy 28 and in the **song of Moses** in Deuteronomy 32. **Since God is a loving Father who deserves our respectful obedience, this was a chastisement for not listening to His voice or obeying His commandments.** They could see their sins magnified in the lives of the Babylonians; so, **a remnant repented saying that God was right and they had been wrong and waited on the Lord for deliverance.**

> *Integrity belongs to our God and to us the look of shame which we wear today, for we have sinned, we with our kings and rulers, priests and prophets, and with our fathers, from the greatest to the least, have sinned in the Lord's sight, and disobeyed Him. We have*

neither heeded the voice of the Lord, our God, nor followed His commandments. (Bar. 1:15–18, 20 NAB)

Meanwhile, they were to bless the king of Babylon, their enemy and captor.

In Italy, Portugal, the Philippines, and other places, some Catholics have processions carrying idols—statues of the patron saints of their towns. Sometimes they build shrines to them. But in 1984 when I witnessed one such procession in Italy, I remembered what Baruch recorded, and asked family not to idolize the statue, or pray to the Madonna, but to join with me in worshiping God alone: *And now in Babylon you will see borne upon men's shoulders gods of silver and gold and wood, which cast fear on the pagans. Take care that you yourselves do not imitate their alien example and stand in fear of them. When you see the crowd before them and behind worshiping them, rather say in your hearts, "You, O LORD, are to be worshiped!"* (Bar. 6:3–5 NAB)

Because I tried to share these things with his family, my husband would never take me back to Italy with him again. Thank God, he understood and repented before he died.

Chapter 6 goes on to list many reasons why these graven images *"are not gods, do not fear them"* (Bar. 6:28 NAB). People need to follow the real God. It is God who sent forth His Word and the heavens and the earth were created through Him, as Isaiah 42:8 says, *"I am the LORD, that is My name; and My glory I will not give to another, nor My praise to carved images."* It is the pagans who call on the name of patrons, false gods, to protect their areas. But we have the enormous privilege of calling on the name of the One, True God Almighty to *"deliver us from evil."* **He and His hosts of angel armies are on duty** day and night. Instead of calling on the name of angels, or of any saint, we are to call on the name of the Lord who can dispatch one or more angels to our aid. **No one but Jesus Christ the King is the Lord of hosts, the LORD God Sabaoth, the Commander-in-Chief of the hosts of heaven:** *"This is the 'stone which was rejected by you builders,* *which has become the cornerstone.' Nor is there salvation in any other, for there is no other name under heaven given among men by which we must be saved"* (Acts 4:11–12).

In the early twenty-first century, there were still many shrines to saints to which pilgrims flocked, even here in Canada. Plus, many people set up shrines with a statue or picture in their home. But God wants us to stop this pagan practice and worship Him alone.

Chapter 8
What about the Rosary?

Step by step He leads us. Rosaries did not exist two thousand years ago, even though some people hang them on the hands of statues. Years ago, rosary beads with five sets of ten beads called decades, each separated by one bead, were first used by men to pray the 150 psalms. However, for the last couple hundred years or so, the rosary has been a counter for a series of repeated prayers, mainly "Hail Marys" calling on the name of Mary to pray for us as if she were the mediatrix between God and men that they claim she is.

In the early nineties, although I no longer prayed to them for favors or miracles, I still thought it was all right to pray to Mary and the saints if I only asked them to pray for us to God in Jesus's name; so, I still prayed the rosary. I was even in an Italian cenacle praying the rosary in Italian where I often stood in the circle of ladies with my back to the statue of Mary. I did this on purpose to show that idols are nothing: *"We know that an idol is nothing in the world, and that there is no other God but one"* (1 Cor. 8:4). Turning my back to a statue of Mary does not dishonour Mary. **The statue is not alive. But God is truly alive.**

I tried to lead the others out of idolatry as far as I understood it by encouraging them not to pray through graven images. However, I did not get it yet myself that even praying the rosary was treating Mary as an idol! We did not realize that Jesus, not Mary, is the one and only direct *"Mediator of the new covenant"* (Heb. 9:15), and **the rosary is a false bridge**. Nor did many Catholics know that we are forbidden to contact the dead—including dead saints. But the Lord Jesus proceeded to teach me that **He is the one way to the Father.**

I used to pray portions of the rosary many times a day. Even if I awoke in the night or if I had to wait for my children at music lessons or sports, I prayed the rosary. The "Lady" of the apparitions to nations, who we assumed was Mary, told us to do this every day, up to fifteen decades. (That is a counterfeit to 150 psalms, which used to be prayed on the beads). Of course, this cut into my time for talking to God Himself in prayer. **But I stopped once and for all after forty years of daily recitation when I had another very significant encounter with the living God.** As I mentioned in the first chapter, the Lord stuck me to the floor all day and evening and a man brought me a prophetic word that changed my life:

"They are dead. Do not contact them."

This is how it happened: On the last morning of Prophetic School III at the Toronto Airport Vineyard Fellowship on November 25, 1994, they called pastors and missionaries to come down to the front. Although two ladies and I formed a little group called Christian Mission Outreach in 1987, I was not "ordained" by man, so I was not going to go down at first. But then I heard the Lord say to me, *"I have called you as a shepherd of sheep. Go down."* So I did. (Years before, He had said to me, *"Feed My lambs, feed My sheep, even to the bishop,"* so I had been sharing what I was learning from Him.) When the ministry team laid hands on my head, I received another very strong baptism of fire that settled in my lower legs and feet. For about eleven hours, I could feel fire there and I could not move my feet on my own. They felt like someone had glued the soles of my shoes to the floor.

Standing, I felt like a Psalm 1 tree with my roots going deeper, planted by the spiritual River of living water flowing there. I was soaking up love, joy, peace, discipline, and the Lord helped me overcome a fear of crowds that day. After all, when the leaders told the people to go back to their seats, here was I stuck standing right of centre in front of about three thousand people, silently asking the Lord to defend me from what others thought of me. I hoped leaders would not think I was in rebellion when I did not stop standing at the front while everyone else went back to their seats for the rest of the day, because I could not move my feet. Someone offered to put a chair behind me, but I refused it because I heard the Lord say, *"Stand."* The Lord was keeping me standing, immoveable, planted by the River of God, and only a very few people close by me knew the truth of what was happening.

I stood there all day with fire in my feet while speakers taught. I was only hungry for the things of God even when people left for lunch and dinner. But while most people were still gone to supper, a woman came over to me and insisted that I move because she said I was blocking her view. I proceeded to explain to her that I could not, and she threatened to get some men to carry me out. So I silently, desperately, called on the name of the Lord for help, and thanks be to God a leader came over. When I explained to him the situation, he prayed that God would release my feet so that I could move over by a pillar. I agreed to that, and praise God, my feet just barely loosened, feeling very heavy, so that I could manage to shuffle over in front of a pillar where my feet again locked down and would not move.

I began to wonder what people would think when they saw me in a different location and not able to walk away again. Would they think I had been faking it? Surely I could not explain to each one. But again, I called on the Lord in my distress and cast all my cares upon Him. He knew the truth. The Lord told me that this was *"preparation."* Someone said that it could be the Lord was teaching the church how to stand. With Him holding us, we can stand for gospel truth, disregarding what others think, and having the right focus helps. God knows the truth about us, and He is our defense. As He told Abram, *"Do not be afraid, Abram. I am your shield, your exceedingly great reward"* (Gen. 15:1).

I found that **as I purposely focused on the Lord, in love**, desiring that His will be done in my life, that the fear of what man thought left me, thank God. *"Perfect love casts out fear"* (1 John 4:18). **I kept praying, asking the Lord Jesus to be glorified and magnified in my life and in the church. And I asked Jesus, the *"Teacher,"* to purify the teaching of the church.** *"Do not be called Rabbi; for One is your Teacher, the Christ, and you are all brethren"* (Matt. 23:8). **So, He began by purifying mine**, and I felt the fire for days and days. Glory be to God! It was like having the chaff removed from the wheat and burned away, like removing my old shoes and giving me new ones, although I did not realize it at the time. *"Stand therefore, having girded your waist with truth ... and having shod your feet with the preparation of the gospel of peace"* (Eph. 6:14–15).

John Arnott preached that evening, and he began to call for fire on all the "Davids" in the room, right where they were at. As he called for "More, Lord!" over and over, strong waves of fresh fire would come upon me. The feeling in my feet changed. Instead of a pleasant feeling of being planted like a tree with roots drinking from the River, the fire of God now caused my feet to feel like they were being nailed to a cross. As more and more waves of fire came upon me, causing my body to curl down and up like a lily in the waterside grass, it was as if **I was experiencing a taste of the passionate love of Jesus for His sheep.** I had learned at Catch the Fire, October '94, what Song of Solomon bridal "passion for Jesus" was like, and now I was learning what "passion of Jesus" was like, the passion of the Bridegroom for His bride.

His love is so strong and jealous for us that He could endure whatever came His way. He had submitted His will to the Father's in faith and trust and He knew that multitudes would be blessed as a result: *"For the joy that was set before Him He endured the cross, despising the shame, and has sat down at the right hand of the throne of God"* (Heb. 12:2). I remembered how He prayed in Gethsemane, *"Father, if it is Your will, take this cup away from Me; nevertheless not My will, but Yours, be done"* (Luke 22:42).

It was becoming even more important at that point that I focus on Jesus and His Father since the fire was so strong. I had been baptized with strong fire before, but it had never felt like this! Since the pillar behind me reminded me of a rock, I began to lean against it as the fire became more and more painful. Jesus Himself is my true Rock. In the Spirit we must lean on Him. I remembered how David had said,

> *I will love You, O L<small>ORD</small>, my strength.*
> *The L<small>ORD</small> is my rock and my fortress and my deliverer;*
> *My God, my strength, in whom I will trust;*
> *My shield and the horn of my salvation, my stronghold.*
> *I will call upon the L<small>ORD</small>, who is worthy to be praised;*
> *So shall I be saved from my enemies....*
> *The L<small>ORD</small> lives!*
> *Blessed be my Rock!*
> *Let the God of my salvation be exalted.* (Ps. 18:1–3, 46)

Battling what others might be thinking of me again, the Lord held me up by saying to me: *"He will keep him in perfect peace whose mind is stayed on Thee."* (I was used to praying using *Thee* and *Thou* in those days, so sometimes the Lord spoke to me that way.) Years before, Jesus had already taught me to trust Him as the Good Shepherd and as the Great Fisherman. He calmed my anxiety and later I found that word in a Bible: *"You will keep him in perfect peace, whose mind is stayed on You, because he trusts in You"* (Isa. 26:3).

When the fire became even more painful in my feet, and I began to feel faint, I remembered how Jesus also spoke to His Father on the cross, *"Into Your hands I commend my spirit, O Lord."* (See Luke 23:46.) And when I prayed that word, there was a sound like a crack, and for a second, I thought my legs were broken at the knees, but they were not, thank God. I fell over backwards, arms outstretched, feet still stuck, and every part of my body which touched the floor now stuck to it as if glued down, nailed to a cross crucified with Christ. (Except that only He was sinless.)

I thought of the thieves crucified at Calvary who had their legs broken, and in the Spirit, you could say that mine were broken but the Lord would give them new strength. Actually, *"Strengthen weak knees and lift drooping hands,"* was a *"word of knowledge"* they prayed for people's knees that night, and **I knew we were not to bend our knees to anyone but God, and to lift up our hands to Him in worship and prayer.**

Although since 1981, I had been trying to *"give to the Lord the glory due His name"* (Ps. 96:8), later I realized that I, too, had still robbed Him of some glory by asking saints who had died to intercede, because Jesus is the designated eternal *"Mediator of the new covenant"* (Heb. 12:24).

Meanwhile, that night as I lay on the TAVF (later, Catch the Fire Church) carpet, at first my feet were still flat on the floor and only my raised knees and fingertips were still unglued so I asked a girl to check my skirt to be sure I was covered. They asked us to raise our hands if we wanted someone on the ministry team to come to us. Since I could only move my fingertips, I waved them, feeling ridiculous. But knowing that the Lord could see them, I asked Him to send someone over. Praise God, a man on the ministry team came through the crowd. I read his name badge, John Swimner, but had never seen him before or since.

I remembered that Jesus had interceded from the cross: *"Father, forgive them for they know not what they do,"* so I thought I should too, and asked him to pray with me in Jesus's name, forgiving those who had persecuted me in any way for my stand against idolatry in as much as I understood it up to that point, and we interceded on three levels: for my staunch Roman Catholic family, for the RC Church, and for the world, in identificational repentance for our sins, including idolatry.

This man on the ministry team also spoke the prophetic word to me that night that changed my life: *"They are dead. Do not contact* *them,"* and I knew it meant Mary and the saints in heaven. I silently asked the Lord how that could be because the Lord had told me before that they are alive in Christ in heaven, but the Lord told me, ***"Believe, believe, believe."*** They shall live with Christ forever but are dead to us. Interestingly, when the Lord had sent me to Archbishop Francis Spence a few years before to tell him *"Isaiah 44,"* I had told him that I had also learned that the Bible forbids us to contact the dead. I told him I wondered: "Did that mean we were forbidden to contact dead saints too?" The bishop did not answer, but I believe the Lord was answering my question beginning that night.

Therefore, I determined to stop praying the rosary that very night and to never again pray to saints who had died, for anything, even in Jesus's name. And testing the prophecy, I also asked the Lord to confirm from Bible Scriptures that I understood correctly: that the man had brought a true word and exactly what the Lord meant;

1. that not only are we not to pray to those who have died to ask them for favours like salvation and healing,
2. but we are not even to contact them to ask them to pray for us in Jesus's name.

God was patient with me in my ignorance, but **it is really He who hears and answers our prayers, not a saint** in heaven or on earth. **Jesus, His apostles, David, and Moses never prayed to any saints, and neither should we.**

The first Scripture I was led to was Isaiah 8:19 and others are throughout this book: *"And when they say to you, 'Consult the mediums* [psychics, fortune tellers, or those with familiar spirits] *and wizards, who chirp and mutter,' should not a people consult their God? Should they consult* [seek] *the dead on behalf of the living?"* (RSV).

I saw that in Isaiah's time, the Jews had a similar problem. But Isaiah 8:19–22 shows that people who seek the dead, praying to them on behalf of the living, can be thrust into darkness, experiencing oppression and hunger. They will often have a poverty spirit, afraid of lack. I have experienced that, but thank God, He delivered me.

"[Those who lay in darkness and the shadow of death] *have seen a great light*" (Isa. 9:2). I learned that to *"consult the dead on behalf of the living"* was forbidden by God even in Moses's day. It is the one true God alone whom we should seek *"on behalf of the living."* Jeremiah 33:2–3 says, *"Thus says the LORD ... 'Call to Me and I will answer you and show you great and mighty things which you do not know.'"* Moses, Joshua, and David were all great leaders of their people, and they frequently consulted the one true God for advice and good counsel, and they received it. But Israelites were not to pray to them after they died. *"Should not a people seek their God? Should they seek the dead on behalf of the living?"*

We might ask: What about Jesus on the Mount of Transfiguration? But what they saw was an open vision. **In His prayer time, as Son of Man, He always consulted the Father**. It was the Father alone He sought to show Him what to say and do. His three apostles were allowed to see Him transfigured to how He looks as Son of God in heaven, clothed with His heavenly glory, and **taken into a vision** of which Jesus told them afterwards, *"Tell the vision to no one until the Son of Man is risen from the dead"* (Matt. 17:9).

There are other people who have been taken up to heaven in a vision today where people there who had died spoke to them. But those who have died were not to appear or speak to them on earth. Jesus came as Son of Man, but He is also Son of God who could speak to Moses and Elijah as God the Son in a vision.

> *He was transfigured before them. His face shone like the sun, and His clothes became as white as the light. And behold, Moses and Elijah appeared to them, talking with Him. Then Peter answered and said to Jesus, "Lord, it is good for us to be here; if You wish, let us make here three tabernacles: one for You, one for Moses and one for Elijah."*

> *While he was still speaking, behold, a bright cloud overshadowed them; and suddenly a voice came out of the cloud, saying, "This is My beloved Son in whom I am well pleased. Hear Him!" And when the disciples heard it, they fell on their faces and were greatly afraid. But Jesus came and touched them and said, "Arise, and do not be afraid." When they lifted up their eyes, they saw no one but Jesus only.* (Matt. 17:2–8)

The Father had made it very clear to them that **Jesus was the One they needed to hear speak and all they needed**. It is God alone who we are to seek on behalf of the living. We are to hear Jesus and not to be tabernacling with saints of heaven. God said upon Jesus's baptism: *"This is My beloved Son in whom I am well pleased. Hear Him!"*

Saints are not our healers or saviours. It is not saints but God who answers our prayers and takes care of us.

Another of the first Scriptures the Lord led me to was, *"What have I to do with idols? It is I who answer and look after you. I am like an evergreen cypress, from me comes your fruit"* (Hos. 14:8 RSV).

It is God who answers our prayers and from whom gifts and fruit come. We are not even to idolize saints who are still alive on earth. In Acts 3, **Peter would not let people give him the glory which belongs to God when miracles happened at his hand while he was still on earth.** He told the people that it was only by faith in the name of Jesus that the crippled man was healed. Also, Peter prayed that God would *"[stretch] out [His] hand to heal, and that signs and wonders may be done through the name of Your holy Servant Jesus"* (Acts 4:30).

Jesus Himself had said that disciples could go directly to the Father in His name, and God would answer: *"Most assuredly, I say to you, whatever you ask the Father in My name He will give you"* (John 16:23). It is not the saints who heal people, but the power of God through gifts of His Spirit. And it is to the Father that we are to pray through the name of Jesus, not to saints, when we want to intercede for someone.

I had been approximately eleven hours standing and three and a half more hours lying outstretched on the floor, stuck down November 25, 1994. Then feeling a release, I got up and over three and a half years, as I tested the word that had been brought to me—*"They are dead. Do not contact them"*—I experienced extreme warfare especially on the battlefield of the mind. Some call it a dark night of the soul or spirit. My whole belief system was shaken, sifted, so that what was not of the Lord could fall away. But thank God, the Lord graciously proceeded to lead me to Scriptures to solidify in me the truth of His Word. A pastor who did not know me well even prophesied that my belief system would be sifted. This helped me understand what was happening to me.

Sometimes we need to hear a word several times until it is well established in our hearts, especially when we have had years of wrong teaching drummed into us. Our Roman Catholic teachers did not know any better because they did not study the Bible much either, years ago. But the truth that you know makes you free. I found that like the seed planted in rocky soil, I received it with joy, but had trouble standing at first. **I needed to become rooted and well grounded in both the love and Word of God,** so I would not "fall over" when trouble arose on account of the Word. My desire was to become fruitful, but it takes time for a seed to grow deep roots and mature. This illustration[4] could help.

Our God is so good! I still remember the music ministry playing Brian Doerksen *Father's House* music, which ministered to me as I lay there that night in 1994. One song especially was declaring that **I am a child of forgiveness and that my Father God is rich in mercy,** and that children around the world were waiting to hear that song. **I had felt like an "orphan," grateful that my Daddy Warbucks, mighty in battle and rich in mercy, had adopted me and wanted to adopt them too, and to welcome back the prodigals "one by one."**

---

4   Salvador, *The Parable of the Sower* (Belleville, ON: Essence Publishing, 2007) 17.

"Yet he has no root in himself, but endures only for a while. For when tribulation or persecution arises because of the word, immediately he stumbles." (Matt. 13:20-21) He hangs in there for a while but loses heart, like a tackled fooball player who gives up..

Studying the Scriptures could help him and getting to know Jesus who did not take offence and got up again. Jesus' Spirit is both our coach and water boy.

Like Saul of Tarsus who had an encounter with the living God changing him from a zealous Jew, off on a religious tangent, to a fulfilled Jew, a follower of Christ, I became a closer follower of Jesus, a fulfilled Catholic who desired to get back to Acts belief, a Christian who had decided years before to follow Jesus, no turning back. (RCs can trace their history back to Peter.) **No more would I try to get Protestants or Catholics to pray the rosary or to listen to what I later found to be false prophecy coming from Medjugorje.**

I had sent numerous copies of the reports from Medjugorje when I was deceived, so I went about writing those people in other lands telling them what the Lord had shown me, that we had been deceived when we believed the "Lady" of Medjugorje and her false prophets, that it was like going after other lovers when we had prayed to her and the saints. But Jesus is supposed to be our eternal Bridegroom: *"And He came and preached peace to you who were afar off and to those who were near"* (Eph. 2:17).

Thanks be to God. The Lord also had told me earlier, *"I will show you what you must suffer for My name's sake,"* so He had prepared me for persecution I would face when people did not understand. (Up to today, thank God, it has been mainly verbal, and by exclusion, like "house arrest"—what I call "soft" persecution, compared to the "hard" persecution some have faced. I also experienced rejection at one point by all of my family and by some hometown pastors and former close friends.) But through it all I found that Jesus is my Best Friend and my Defense, and He has given me many other church family members and friends. The Holy Spirit reminded me, **"If my God is with me, whom then shall I fear?"**

And He gave me tactics of love and rejoicing always in Him. And, **"Praise is a powerful weapon,"** so I would forgive and put on a mantle of praise singing His praises when a spirit of heaviness began to descend. The heaviness would fall right off, thank God! He's *"my glory and the lifter of my head"* (Ps. 3:3).

Thanks be to God, His loving kindness truly is better than life and *"the joy of the Lord is* [my] *strength"* (Neh. 8:10), and God has even restored some relationships. Disciples are to pick up their crosses and follow Jesus. I could not have made it this far without Him though, and when I have fallen, He has helped me up again. He got up when He fell under the weight of His cross, and we can too, accepting the help the Father sends. Praise the Lord! *"For each one shall bear his own load"* (Gal. 6:5); and, *"Bear one another's burden and so fulfil the law of Christ"* (Gal. 6:2).

Searching the Scriptures for Verification and Going to Jesus, the Word

I remember when my children went to a Catholic school, that at a school play in the eighties I was impressed by the word, *"Those who walked in darkness have seen a great light"* (Isa. 9:2). We did not realize we were spiritually in darkness. The Lord later opened my eyes with the light of His truth and saving grace. He has done it for others too who were willing to have Him lead them in His paths of righteousness: *"Grace and peace be multiplied to you in the knowledge of God, and of Jesus our Lord"* (2 Pet. 1:2).

Although I had stopped going to Catholic masses, I went to Catholic charismatic meetings (and Vineyard-type services) during that three and a half years when I searched the Scriptures. When we sang songs lifting Jesus higher or waited on the Lord for prophetic words, or Scriptures, I took part. Also when we joined hands at the end and prayed the "Our Father," I joined in. But when they began to pray the "Hail Mary," I let go of hands, refusing to do that anymore. However, sometimes it was very difficult to respond when I was bombarded by doubt as to whether I was on the right track—until I was deeper grounded in the Word.

Thanks be to God, besides going to the biblical Word of God for proof, after three years I finally realized that I could go to Jesus Himself (see John 5:39–40). He is the living *"Word of God."* I asked Him for a *rhema* word that showed we should not pray the "Hail Mary," although the first half was scriptural. He gave me John 14:6 and I recorded it in my journal and forgot and asked Him again another day in early 1998. The Lord gave me the same word:

*"I am the way, the truth, and the life.
No one comes to the Father but by Me."*

Thank God, this time I held on to what I had been given. His Word sank into my heart: *"But hold fast what you have till I come"* (Rev. 2:25).

False Bridges Are Illusions

There is no one like Jesus. Earlier, not long after I had ceased praying the rosary, I realized that I had already tested against Scripture many of the words from apparitions of a "Lady" who had appeared in various places. Remembering the Scripture, *"Test all things. Retain what is good"* (1 Thess. 5:21), I had found them to be false. However, a few I had believed, like the apparitions at Fatima, Lourdes, Guadalupe, and Medjugorje. Both Roman Catholics and some Protestants had thought the "Lady" appearing in various nations was Mary, the mother of Jesus.

Each apparition of a "Lady" commanded the praying of the rosary, consisting mainly of repeating a prayer to Mary to ask her to intercede. Yet there had even been some miracles, signs, and wonders in those places. Therefore, recognizing that Jesus said, *"Where two or more are gathered in My name, there am I in the midst"* (Matt. 18:20). I sought the Lord in Jesus's name with a Messianic Jewish pastor. It was **to ask God what He thought about the many apparitions** of a "Lady" whom I had thought was Mary, but who was promoting the rosary as part of a peace plan supposedly from heaven. The reply the Lord gave me about these was,

"Illusion! Illusion! Illusion!"

My Jewish friend then asked me if I knew about Deuteronomy 13, so I looked it up and was amazed to find that **God had been putting us to the test and multitudes who had been deceived by these apparitions, including myself before TACF, had failed the test.** (But God in His mercy will even let people retake tests, and they can be open-Book tests!)

> *If there arises among you a prophet or a dreamer of dreams, and he gives you a sign or a wonder, and the sign or the wonder comes to pass, of which he spoke to you, saying, "Let us go after other gods"—which you have not known—"and let us serve them," you shall not listen to the words of that prophet or that dreamer of dreams, for the LORD your God is testing you to know whether you love the LORD your God with all your heart and with all your soul. You shall walk after the LORD your God and fear Him, and keep His commandments and obey His voice; you shall serve Him and hold fast to Him.* (Deut. 13:1–4)

The devil, Lucifer, has come in the past not only disguised as a serpent to fool Adam and Eve, but also as an *"angel of light"* to fool God's people. So his counterfeit messengers have masqueraded as Mary, as a beautiful lady, with false signs and wonders, deceiving people to worship other gods—the saints, statues, or pictures. Paul warned of *"false apostles, deceitful workers, transforming themselves into apostles of Christ. And no wonder! For Satan himself transforms himself into an angel of light. Therefore it is no great thing if his ministers also transform themselves into ministers of righteousness, whose end will be according to their works"* (2 Cor. 11:13–15). It reminds me of children's Transformer toys. **Remember, when this happens, it is a test from God of our faithfulness.**

Mirror Image versus the Real Thing

If you look at yourself in the mirror, the image looks identical at first glance, but things are not quite right on the sides. Years ago, the Lord helped me understand **the antichrist spirit**. A local shopping centre had a logo that looked **like the capital letter "K" and its mirror image which was back-to-back with it** on the straight line. It was suddenly bathed in a heavenly light and magnified as I drove by once. **The antichrist spirit, like the mirror image backwards "K," looks like the real thing but its members are going in the wrong direction.**

John wrote of its deceiving presence:

> *Little children, it is the last hour; and as you have heard that the Antichrist is coming, even now many antichrists have come, by which we know that it is the last hour. They went out from us, but they were not of us.... But you have an anointing from the Holy One, and you know all things. I have not written to you because you do not know the truth, but because you know it, and that no lie is of the truth. Who is the liar but he who denies that Jesus is the Christ? He is antichrist who denies the Father and the Son. Whoever denies the Son does not have the Father either; he who acknowledges the Son has the Father also.* (1 John 2:18–23)

There were great signs and wonders with some of the apparitions of the "Lady" who looked like Mary, and some twisted truth because the "Lady" wanted the people to pray to her, and go to her as if she were *"the Christ."* And people were to do certain things, *"dead works,"* as if it were these things which would gain them salvation. She told people to be consecrated to her and wear medals or a rosary around their neck or wrapped around their hand to receive favours from her. **But Jesus is our true Saviour. His blood has already made reparation** to God for our sins if we will believe and receive the salvation He offers. **Grace,** *"the gift of God"* **(Eph. 2:8), comes from faith in Him, not the "Lady."** People who have been deceived have only to repent, receive by faith the forgiveness His blood purchased, and start fresh following Him like I did. Not all tests are in school. Now God can speak to people in dreams and make a true prophetic word come to pass, as Peter reminded us at Pentecost, but when signs and wonders are connected with words which lead us to pray to or obey other spirits, to *"go after other gods"* (Deut. 13:2), beware! As the Lord magnified to me earlier that November, ***"Do not be deceived."***

When the Lord gave me the word, *"Illusion! Illusion! Illusion!"* and I also read passages from Revelation, especially chapter 13, I realized there were many signs and wonders at Fatima, Lourdes, Guadalupe, and Medjugorje, **but the fruit was like a ripe pear that looks good on the outside but is rotten at the core.** Since many were making pilgrimages there and repenting of some sin, and there were even some healings (signs and wonders), at first glance things appeared good. However, **idolatry is bad fruit.** Statues of the "Lady" began to be set up there and at people's homes and prayers made to her through them, and shrines and churches were dedicated to her. People carried "Pilgrim Virgin" statues from place to place, worshiping before them. Even high clergy were deceived as I had been, and there were photos of some church leaders kneeling before statues.

The apparition of a spirit disguised as Mary, the "Lady" of this place and that, was telling people about Jesus, but at the same time calling people to pray to her, up to fifteen decades of rosary per day! (Recall, an antichrist spirit looks like the real thing, but its members are going in the wrong direction.) That would take an hour or more daily away from worship meant for God alone, and from Bible study. Besides, God does not want us to have two gods.

I also noticed that the "Lady" of the apparitions in places like Fatima and Medjugorje accepted worship, letting people kneel to her, pray to her, and serve her, **but the real Mary would never accept worship, nor would good angels.**

When Satan (the bad angel Lucifer) tempted Jesus, he wanted worship of himself. He told Jesus, *"Therefore, if You will worship before me, all will be Yours.'* [Jesus replied], *'Get behind Me, Satan!' For it is written, 'You shall worship the LORD your God, and Him only you shall serve'"* (Luke 4:7–8).

When the apostle John fell at a very good angel's feet to worship him, the angel stopped him saying, *"See that you do not do that! I am your fellow servant, and of your brethren who have the testimony of Jesus. Worship God! For the testimony of Jesus is the spirit of prophecy"* (Rev. 19:10; 22:9). **When he forgot, the angel also told John a second time not to kneel before him, but to worship God alone. But many apparitions**

of a "Lady" disguised as Mary accept worship. By even this we know they are false messengers. Jesus also warned, *"For false christs and false prophets will rise and show great signs and wonders to deceive, if possible, even the elect"* (Matt. 24:24).

The Madonna Is a False Bridge

The real Mary humbly acknowledged in the Bible that God is her *"Saviour."* Gabriel had told her that the Son born to her would be named *"Jesus* [Yeshua in Hebrew]," and the angel told Joseph, *"She will bring forth a Son, and you shall call His name Jesus, for He will save His people from their sins"* (Luke 1:31; Matt. 1:21).

There is a falsehood being widely circulated, misusing a capital "S," that "only she can save us," spread by false prophets of the apparition of the "Lady" of Fatima; but even some RC Church leaders have rejected this. **Only Jesus is the spotless Lamb who was slain so sins could be forgiven. Only He can save us.**

The real Mary told Elizabeth that God is her Saviour in her Magnificat:

> *My soul magnifies the Lord*
> *And my spirit rejoices in God my Savior,*
> *For he has looked with favor on the lowly state of His maidservant* [handmaiden];*For behold, henceforth all generations will call me blessed.*
> *For He who is mighty has done great things for me,*
> *And holy is His name.*
> *And His mercy is on those who fear Him*
> *From generation to generation.* (Luke 1:46–50)

She showed by her words that she had an intimate knowledge of God and needed what He supplied to her. **But the real Mary did not claim equality with God or with His Son, her Saviour, the one true bridge. Instead, she offered herself for service unto Him, which is**

true worship. Who is your Lord? *Behold, the maidservant of the Lord! Let it be to me according to Your word"* (Luke 1:38). However, many unscriptural fables have arisen about her.

What about Other Saints in Heaven?

Even though saints who died are still to be parts of *"the holy city, New Jerusalem"* (Rev. 21:2) above, prepared as the body and bride of Christ, and could have been asked to intercede for us **when they were still on earth,** once they have died, we should not be asking them to pray for us anymore. That would make them false bridges, like a mirage in the desert which looks real from a distance but upon closer examination, there is no substance to the report of it. **Let us thank God for the good example they gave though, since they followed the way of the Lord and overcame by faith.** For example, we are to imitate the godly lives of gospel heroes of faith. First Corinthians 11 is full of examples and Paul wrote, *"Imitate me, just as I also imitate Christ"* (1 Cor. 11:1). But since even the lives of saints were sometimes a work in progress, most of all we are to imitate Jesus and do what He would do.

Saints in heaven are alive in Christ and might even be praying for us as well as worshiping God, but they are dead to us so **we should not be trying to talk to them.**

Saints on earth or in heaven are to be honoured, not idolized, and glory is to be given to God. He is the One who answers our prayers. Claiming that saints answered your prayers is robbing God of the glory due His name. As Saint Paul said, *"To God, alone wise, be glory through Jesus Christ forever. Amen"* (Rom. 16:27).

> *Thus says the L*ORD*, the King of Israel, and his Redeemer, the L*ORD *of hosts: "I am the First, and I am the Last; besides Me there is no God."* (Isaiah 44:6)

> *What have I to do with idols?*
> *It is I who answer and look after you.* (Hosea 14:8 RSV)

How surprised I was to see a photo that showed that years ago, my people in Italy, in Termini, Sicily, had mistakenly covered a Madonna statue with gold jewellery, thinking the "Lady" had answered their prayers. The artist had used my great-grandmother's hands as a model making the statue. They had called this grandma a healer because she prayed for people, and they were healed. My own mother served in the healing ministry for a while in the charismatic renewal. But I know now that **Jesus is our true Healer and deserves the glory and honor. People have come to saints on earth who had healing or miracles gifts and were healed, and they have prayed to saints in heaven, and miracles might even have happened, but it is God who answers prayers.** I am so glad that we have the great privilege of approaching Him now with childlike faith, in Jesus's name: *"Little children, keep yourselves from idols. Amen"* (1 John 5:21). The Lord also had magnified Psalm 96 to me November 11, 1981, including:

> *Oh, sing to the LORD a new song!...* (v. 1)
>
> *Proclaim the good news of His salvation from day to day....* (v. 3)
>
> *For all the gods of the peoples are idols, but the LORD made the heavens....* (v. 5)
>
> *Give to the LORD the glory due His name....* (v. 7)
>
> *Say among the nations, "The LORD reigns."* (v. 10)

I noticed in the eighties and nineties at our Catholic charismatic prayer meetings that the Holy Spirit had regularly inspired the music ministry to sing exalting Jesus above others, including, *"For Thou O Lord art high above the earth. Thou art exalted far above all gods."* Praying to saints was treating them like idols or gods. When Israel was deceived, Jeremiah said,

> *But where are your gods that you have made for yourselves?*
> *Let them arise,*
> *If they can save you in the time of your trouble;*

*For according to the number of your cities
Are your gods, O Judah.* (Jer. 2:28)

We can ask the Father ourselves, or we can ask saints who are alive here on earth to pray for us directly, in Jesus's name, as the apostles did. *"Therefore I exhort first of all that supplications, prayers, intercessions, and giving of thanks be made for all men"* (1 Tim. 2:1). *"And whatever you do in word or deed, do all in the name of the Lord Jesus, giving thanks to God the Father through Him"* (Col. 3:17). *"Most assuredly, I say to you, whatever you ask the Father in My name He will give you"* (John 16:23). **We are not to pray or do mighty wonders in our own names or in the name of anyone but Jesus. The apostles knew that.**

"Then Peter, filled with the Holy Spirit," told the religious leaders **the man had been healed not by his own name or power** but *"by the name of Jesus Christ of Nazareth, whom you crucified, whom God raised from the dead, by Him this man stands here before you whole. This is the 'stone which was rejected by you builders, which has become the cornerstone.' Nor is there salvation is any other, for there is no other name under heaven given among men by which we must be saved"* (Acts 4:7–12).

What a privilege we have as adopted children of God! We can approach the throne of grace ourselves because we are in Jesus, His Holy Child. Telling His disciples how to stay in Him, Jesus also told them what the fruit of this closeness would be—by keeping His commandments they would live in His love and joy as He did with His Father and have prayers answered.

> *If you abide in Me, and My words abide in you, you will ask what you desire, and it shall be done for you. By this My Father is glorified, that you bear much fruit.... If you keep My commandments, you will abide in My love, just as I have kept My Father's commandments and abide in His love ... and* [Jesus chose His disciples] *that you should go and bear fruit and that your fruit should remain, that whatever you ask the Father in My name He may give you.* (John 15:7–8, 10, 16)

Patron Saints Are False Bridges

A patron was sometimes a master who had freed his slave, keeping some rights over him after he was set free. A patron could also be a person of distinction under whose protection another placed himself. Therefore, he wassomeone who supports, and protects either a person, a work, or a territory.

Jesus fulfills this definition perfectly. He came that captives, slaves to sin, could be set free. Saints are not meant to be patrons from heaven, nor should we call on their names to intercede for us. **God has appointed the Lord Jesus to do that, and He can send His angels to guard us:** *"Nor is there salvation in any other, for there is no other name under heaven given among men by which we must be saved"* (Acts 4:12).

Centuries ago, regions and nations each had their own gods, and the Promised Land had the one true God. However, although they recognized the God of Israel, Catholics similarly designated saints as patrons not only over villages, cities, and nations, but over solving certain problems—like patrons for finding lost articles or for safety while driving, or for birthing. But now if I am praying about a lost article or for safety traveling, etc., **I ask Jesus or the Father in His name. He can see everything** and Jesus, the Lord of hosts, can dispatch angels to guard the vehicle or the airplane in which a follower travels, or the nation.

I am thankful for many lost articles He has caused to be found or shepherded me to, and for Him finding some lost people too; and for many safe trips in peace, some in which His presence was made manifest. Sometimes when I have had to drive a long distance alone, but asked Jesus to protect me, He would even speak to me on the way so that I would know He was with me without a shadow of a doubt. This was such a comfort to me, especially the first few times I had to drive multiple lane highways after my husband died.

Saints Are False Bridges

Many years ago, relatives took me to Canadian shrines of the saints, and I saw church walls lined with crutches, etc., showing that prayers were answered, we thought by the saints. But it is God who deserves the glory.

A criterion for them being canonized as saints was proof of miracles having been attributed to them. Especially on their feast days, everyone made much of the saints, and sometimes little of God. To some, the feast day was just an excuse for a party, whether they went to church regularly or not—the extreme being like the drunken revellers on Saint Patrick's Day. **But God is the one who hears and answers our prayers.** Plus, alcohol-free partying with the Lord instead, singing praise and worship songs, giving the Lord the glory due His name, is pure fun. He serves the water and wine of His Holy Spirit.

The glory for miracles should not go to Saint Anthony or Mary or to any other saint, alive or dead. When we were babes in the Lord, Father God in His great mercy put up with our ignorant wrong focus, **but now is the time for us to know the truth, that Jesus is our Healer and Saviour, the** *"one Mediator between God and men"* (1 Tim. 2:5), and we do not need patron saints. Nor should we set up shrines to them. We need to *"come out of her,"* out of Babylon, to grow up, and to mature.

> *Ephraim shall say, "What have I to do anymore with idols?"*
> *I have heard and observed him.*
> *I am like a green cypress tree;*
> *Your fruit is found in Me.*
> *Who is wise?*
> *Let him understand these things.*
> *Who is prudent?*
> *Let him know them.*
> *For the ways of the* LORD *are right;*
> *The righteous walk in them,*

> *but transgressors stumble in them.* (Hos. 14:8–9)
>
> *This poor man cried out and the L*ORD *heard him*
> *And saved him out of all his troubles.*
> *The angel of the L*ORD *encamps all around those who fear Him,*
> *And delivers them.*
> *Oh, taste and see that the L*ORD *is good;*
> *Blessed is the man who trusts in Him!*
> *Oh, fear the L*ORD*, you His saints!*
> *There is no want to those who fear Him.* (Ps. 34:6–9)

"There is no want," no fear of lack *"to those who fear Him"* and have come out of idolatry. Paul wrote *"to all the saints in Christ Jesus who are in Philippi, with the bishops and deacons"* (Phil. 1:1). **The saints on earth are believers who fear God and follow Jesus.** They are *"in Christ Jesus,"* parts of His body, and call on His name—not the name of saints in heaven.

Thanks be to God, time after time I have called on the name of the Lord and He has given me good counsel or saved me out of my troubles, even in my widowhood. God truly is good, all the time. I have come to know Him as my Provider, El Shaddai, the All-Sufficient One who is even More Than Enough. He tells us, *"But seek first the kingdom of God and His righteousness, and all these things shall be added to you"* (Matt. 6:33). That is a conditional promise. If we are willing to be and do what we were created for and advance His kingdom in love and right relationship with God, we will prosper and be blessed to bless. Many a time the word of the Lord has come to encourage me, *"Be not afraid."* **Jesus is such an encourager!** As our Husband and Shepherd-King, He takes excellent care of us, and goes after His sheep who go astray. Let us pray, "Lead me, Good Shepherd, in Your paths of righteousness for Your name's sake."

His light comes, not to condemn us but to convict and convince us of sin so we can repent. He can open in us a well of living water that cleanses and refreshes us. His sheep hear His voice, and He is our Kinsman Redeemer. He helped me to see that I had had other "husbands" by praying to saints. **Jesus is supposed to be our eternal Bridegroom, but He is like a jealous husband who wants his wife to be faithful and true to him and to have no other lovers:** *"For you shall worship no other god, for the LORD, whose name is Jealous, is a jealous God"* (Ex. 34:14).

I began to understand spiritual adultery, that going to the saints in prayer was like worship, treating them like other lovers and idols. Jesus, the one Mediator of the New Covenant, set in place by the Father (see Heb. 7–8) has a jealous love for us. He had sent the prophetic word to me, *"They are dead. Do not contact them,"* meaning Mary and the saints, so I had stopped praying to saints, even just to ask those who had died to pray for us, and I now worship the Father *"in spirit and in truth"* (John 4:24). In prayer, I do not focus on a graven image but on God, and I am thankful for the forgiveness He gave me; all my sins washed away because of His blood. I can truly say that I am redeemed because Jesus paid the bride-price at the cross for us, dying *"while we were yet sinners"* (Rom. 5:8). I am thankful for the fellowship I can have with Him now that I am a part of the corporate bride of Christ.

I remember a time when I cried out to the Lord, "I don't want to be a harlot anymore!" knowing that I had treated the saints like other lovers, departing from Him at times in prayer to go to them. Thank God, the day came when I humbled myself before Him at the altar, spiritually washing His feet with my tears, and He changed my name to "Faithful," washed me clean and gave me a fresh start.

I joyfully answered His call to come only to Him in my times of worship, praying to God alone. His Holy Spirit has a job of convincing us of what is sin, righteousness, and judgment so we can repent and be restored. He would not only tell me everything I had ever done, but He has given good guidance, led me, and satisfies my thirst forever. He has given me churches to go to for refreshing *"rivers in the desert"* (Isa. 43:19), and He has shown me how wonderful it is to worship the Father *"in spirit and truth"* (John 4:24), led by His Holy Spirit who gives words, songs, and tongues. And I want that for all His people whom the enemy has tried to lead astray.

Another word He gave me in the late nineties rising up inside of me like the roar of the Lion of Judah at the Celebration City conference was, *"No other love, no other love before Me!"*

We cannot put others before Him, whether they are on earth or in heaven—not even pastors or family.

Jesus is our true God and Husband, our *"First Love,"* and He has been sending word to the church for many years that we are not to go after saints like *"lovers."* Chapter 2 of Hosea is so rich with words from which to learn, including describing idolatry as adultery or prostitution. Plus, the unclean spirit that leads into idolatry also leads into tolerating or taking part in sexual immorality. **We can learn from the past**, seeing that God judged idolatry in His first chosen people time and again. I understood this in a new way. We used to call the Catholic Church our "holy mother, the church." However, *"For the land has committed great harlotry by departing from the L*ORD*"* (Hos. 1:2).

> *Bring charges against your mother, bring charges;*
> *For she is not My wife, nor am I her Husband!*
> *Let her put away her harlotries from her sight,*
> *And her adulteries* [including rosaries and medals] *from between her breasts;*
> *Lest I strip her naked*
> *And expose her, as in the day she was born....*
> (Too many devout Catholics, steeped in idolatry, have already experienced this in hospitals, and in another way in newspapers.)*And make her like a wilderness,*
> *And set her like a dry land,*
> *And slay her with thirst.*
> *I will not have mercy on her children,*
> *For they are children of harlotry.*
> *For their mother has played the harlot;*

> *She who conceived them has behaved shamefully.*
> *For she said, "I will go after my lovers,*
> *Who give me my bread and my water,*
> *My wool and my linen,*
> *My oil and my drink."*
> *Therefore, behold,*
> *I will hedge up your way with thorns,*
> *And wall her in,*
> *So that she cannot find her paths.*
> *She will chase her lovers,*
> *But not overtake them;*
> *Yes, she will seek them, but not find them.*
> *Then she will say, "I will go and return to my first husband,*
> *For then it was better for me than now."*
> *For she did not know*
> *That I gave her grain, new wine, and oil,*
> *and multiplied her silver and gold—*
> *Which they prepared for Baal.* (Hos. 2:2–8)

This prophet's wife was a symbol for God's spiritually adulterous people whom God wanted to be His faithful bride. **She kept thinking that all the abundant provision she received was from her lovers, but God said that it was really from Him. Likewise, our provision does not come from saints, but from our true *"Husband,"* Jesus. Saints are not to be idolized like Baal.**

Hosea's wife used covenant blessings as gifts for her idols. Because she did not repent, God decided to take away all the provision and covering He had provided, exposing her:

> *…lewdness in the sight of her lovers,*
> *And no one shall deliver her from My hand.*
> *I will also cause all her mirth to cease,*
> *Her feast days,*
> *Her New Moons,*

Her Sabbaths—
All her appointed feasts.
And I will destroy her vines and her fig trees,
Of which she has said,
"These are my wages that my lovers have given me...."
I will punish her for the days of the Baals to which she burned incense.
She decked herself with her earrings and her jewelry, and went after her lovers;
But Me she forgot," says the LORD. (Hos. 2:10–13)

"New Moons" reminds me of First Friday and First Saturday devotions, and *"her appointed feasts"* of days devoted to the "Lady" and other saints (*"lovers"*) appointed by the church and not by God. **Remember the devil is a liar and counterfeiter** and can come disguised as Mary or an *"angel of light."* The false prophecy says that by doing the First Saturday devotions to the "Lady" five months in a row that a person will experience salvation at death. But **it is by belief in Jesus that we are saved, because of His shed blood, not because of dead works**.

I used to make the Nine First Fridays and Five First Saturdays, over and over, thinking it was helping people to be saved—**until I learned that Jesus already did the one good work that can bring salvation to all believers. Christ has come! My Redeemer lives!** (We said this but had not realized what it meant.)

Chapter 9
Praise God from Whom All Blessings Flow

"**D**o *not be deceived*" (Gal. 6:1). **Mary is not the Mediatrix of all grace. Jesus, who is true God and Man, is the true Mediator of all grace.**

Grace and blessings do not originate with one of His creatures but with the Creator. **Saint Peter himself wrote**, inspired by Holy Spirit, that we are to submit to God and resist the devil, **calling God the Source,** *"the God of all grace* [who *"gives all grace"* (NCV)]." *"May the God of all grace, who called us to His eternal glory by Christ Jesus, after you have suffered a while, perfect, establish, strengthen and settle you. To Him be the glory and the dominion forever and ever. Amen"* (1 Pet. 5:10–11).

Saint Paul also wrote of where grace comes, of who mediates grace and blessing: *Grace to you and peace from God our Father and the Lord Jesus Christ. Blessed be the God and Father of our Lord Jesus Christ, who has blessed us with every spiritual blessing in the heavenly places in Christ, just as He chose us in Him before the foundation of the world, that we should be holy and without blame before Him in love, having predestined us to adoption as sons by Jesus Christ to Himself, according to the good pleasure of His will, to the praise of the glory of His grace, by which He made us accepted in the Beloved. In Him we have redemption through His blood, the forgiveness of sins, according to the riches of His grace which He made to abound toward us in all wisdom and prudence.* (Eph. 1:2–8)

After I was baptized with the Holy Spirit, God began to teach me like a kindergarten child, one day at a time, as I had asked Him. Some of the names which the "Lady" had us call Mary, like the "Mediatrix of all grace," He began to show to be blasphemous names which elevated her higher than she is. The real Mary was humble. Truly, God is the Source of the River, the One from whom grace, truth, and peace come, and Jesus is the *"one Mediator"* of all grace. **It is written,** *"For the law was given through Moses, but grace and truth came through Jesus Christ"* (John 1:17).

> *One of the seven angels who had the seven bowls filled with the seven last plagues …* [**showed Saint John around the holy city, and the source of grace**]. *And he showed me a pure river of water of life, clear as crystal, proceeding from the throne of God and of the Lamb.* (Rev. 21:9; 22:1)

Jesus said, *"I am the vine, and you are the branches"* (John 15:5), and, *"I am the Root and the Offspring of David, the Bright and Morning Star"* (Rev. 22:16). Grace can flow through parts of His body, in Jesus's name, as sap flows from the root up through the branches of a vine; but just as it does not originate with any of the branches, grace does not originate with a saint. Plus, we are forbidden to contact the dead.

Who Are You Going to Call?

When I was a child, and we did not know any better, I used to pray in the name of Mary as "Our Lady," as if her help were equally valid. We had special prayers to ask her for aid. But it is not written anywhere in the Bible that our help is in the name of the "Lady." No one is a Co-Mediator above or equal to Jesus. We do not have two Gods. It is written that *"our help is in the name of the L*ord*, who made heaven and earth"* (Ps. 124:8).

Actually, after the word of the Lord came to me in 1981, *"The truth will set you free,"* and I began to seek the truth, that is one of the first words of truth that the Holy Spirit often spoke to me, so I began to call upon His name. I discovered from where my help comes. Being one with God, it is Lord Jesus, the living Word of God, *"who made heaven and earth,"* who does help us. *"All things were made through Him, and without Him nothing was made that was made"* (John 1:3). **It is Jesus who is supposed to be the help of Christians, not Mary. He deserves the glory.**

Because of sin, fellowship between Adam, Eve, and God was broken. They no longer spoke together daily in the cool of the evening. But when Adam's grandson, *"Enosh,"* was born, people realized that God was their only hope. So, *"then men began to call on the name of the LORD"* (Gen. 4:26), and now we know His name. It is written: *"What is His name, and what is His Son's name, if you know?"* (Prov. 30:4). The angel Gabriel said the name would be *"JESUS"* and *"Son of God"* for the *"Holy One who is to be* [miraculously] *born"* of the virgin (see Luke 1:31-35).

With Every Temptation, God Offers a Way Out

I grew up believing the fable that we had to go to Mary in order to get to God or to receive blessings and healings, and for years misguidedly prayed the Morning Offering prayer to Jesus through Mary's heart as if she were a bridge. **But one of the deceptive prayers that I discarded was that Morning Offering prayer.** Praise God, the Lord gave me a way out of this giving me a **new focus**—God alone, and purging away another *"dead work."* After I received the Holy Spirit, I began to realize that I needed to address my prayers to God, in Jesus's name. **The Bible says that it is to the Father through Jesus, not to Jesus through Mary, that we are to pray.** He began to prompt me instead, to pray **a prayer of offering to Father God through His Son, Jesus, the great Intercessor, Healer, and Saviour, the true bridge.**

I also began to **ask our true Holy Father, God, what His intentions were** so I could pray for them. The *"interpretation"* of the first expression the Holy Spirit gave me to pray in tongues was, *"Thy kingdom come, Thy will be done."* Then I realized it was the will of the Father, what was on His heart, that we were to seek the coming of His kingdom, of His will to be done *"on earth as it is in heaven"* (Luke 11:2).

A Holy Spirit-filled charismatic priest gave me some Scripture-based prayers and a prayer of trust to the Father, so I began to pray a new prayer in the morning to **daily surrender all to Him in the name of His Son**. In time, I personalized them. I was told also not to leave a vacuum in me which some foreign spirit could fill, which is what some eastern religions do in meditation. **When you empty yourself, you need to fill up with more of God,** so I also ask Him to fill me with gifts and fruit of His Spirit which are appropriate for my life.

I have personalized these two prayers:

Prayer of Trust

God my Father, I praise You for all that You are, and

thank You for all that You do for me through Your Son, Jesus.

In His name, Father, I place myself entirely in Your care—my mind, memory, will, emotions, body, and sexuality.

I place under His Lordship my gifting, talents, and finances.

I hand over to You every person in my life,

every situation, relationship, and concern; and

I trust You to care for me and others in the most loving way.

As I have emptied myself, and handed everything to You,

I ask You, Father, to fill me with Your Holy Spirit and the gifts and fruit of Your Spirit in accordance with Your will for my life.

I desire to receive all that You desire to entrust to me,

that I may be blessed to bless,

not only to care for the needs of my family, but

in loving outreach to others that Your kingdom may advance.

Breathe on Me

Breathe on me, breath of God, fill me with life anew,

That I may love the things You love and do what You would do.

Breathe on me, breath of God, until my heart is pure,

Until with You I have one will, to love and to endure.

Breathe on me, breath of God, my soul with grace refined,

Until this earthly part of me glows with Your fire divine.

Breathe on me, breath of God, so I shall never die,

But live with You the perfect life in Your eternity.

(And I added:)

Breathe on me, breath of God, fill me with Your holy might,

That I may risk my life that lives may be saved, and in Your eyes be a delight.

Revolutionary Thinking

I remember when the Lord ministered to me in song, *"I have decided to follow Jesus. No turning back, no turning back."*

My son, John, learned a song in grade two about great things happening when God mixes with men, and they sure do! In the late eighties, the Lord had told me I needed to be *"more radical,"* so I sought to be more radically rooted in Christ. First, I was led to wear a T-shirt that said, "The cross before me, the world behind me," and to put two pro-life bumper stickers on my car. The Lord had given me the word, *"Focus,"* so I knew some refocusing was needed. My family used to say, "Another day, another dollar," but God gave me a **new focus**: on Him, including living according to His financial system, and being thankful for "another day to love and serve Him." So, I began to declare each morning, gratefully: **"Thank You, Lord, for another day to love and serve You."**

When I became a widow He magnified to me, *"The Lord is my shepherd, I shall not want"* (Ps. 23:1). Instead of thinking that I had to be very poor, or very rich, I could tithe and enjoy some things, but not be attached to them. I found that I could part with them if I believed someone else needed them. **Instead of fearing lack, I began to trust Jesus** to lead me in His paths of righteousness and to prosper me as I *"seek first his kingdom and his righteousness"* (Matt. 6:33 NIV). I learned that the Lord is my Provider, the God who is even More Than Enough, and I am content with that.

To go to the Father through Jesus instead of to Jesus through Mary and the saints was refocusing and revolutionary thinking for someone raised as a Catholic of Catholics! And of course, it is only in Christ that we can bring someone to salvation. We are to be unashamed of the One we love and His gospel message.

We are to be **radically rooted in Christ, in His love, and grounded in the Scriptures, and watered by Holy Spirit,** and **praise God from whom all blessings flow**. Two thousand years ago, Jesus came with revolutionary thinking because His people had gone offtrack and He wanted to get them on course again. It is Jesus who saves, so risking our lives, our jobs, or our positions at His leading that lives may be saved is one way of following Jesus, of laying down our lives for our friends in love. *"For whoever desires to save his life will lose it, but whoever* *loses his life for My sake will find it"* (Matt. 16:24–25); and, *"Restore us, O God; make Your face shine on us, that we may be saved!"* (Ps. 80:3).

Interestingly, *"Restore us"* is sometimes translated, *"Turn us again." "***Turn to Me and be saved, O you people,***"* I heard the Lord sing.

I also began to **pray prayers based upon Scriptures,** including the psalms and noticed God was answering them. God is so gracious, and knows how to lead His children. A prophetic word He gave our charismatic prayer group years ago was, *"For I, the Lord your God, will hold your right hand, saying to you, 'Fear not, I will help you'"* (Isa. 41:13).

I found He truly began to help me as I would put my trust in Him. I began with simple things, like the fear of having company over for dinner. Around 1980, I used to cry for three days after company left, perhaps because dinner was late or I forgot to serve a dish I had prepared. But I began to learn to prepare what I could in advance, to trust that God would provide help or stretch food when I needed it, and not to sweat the small stuff. (If I forgot to serve a dish, there was probably more than enough food anyway.)

Many a time, I heard the Lord say to me, "Fear not," in His *"still small voice"* (1 Kgs. 19:12), and my fear would melt away, thank God, and the good fruit of His love, peace, and joy began to grow in my life.

Jesus also taught His disciples a way of praying according to the *"Our Father"* as in Matthew 6:9–13. I learned that it was not to be just a ritual prayer with every comma in place, but a template, a *"manner"* of praying. *"All your children shall be taught by the Lord, and great shall be the peace* [prosperity] *of your children"* (Isa. 54:13). Jesus said, *"It is written in the prophets, 'And they shall all be taught by God.' Therefore everyone who has heard and learned from the Father comes to Me"* (John 6:44–45).

We see that God is our Teacher and **it is from God that all blessings flow,** either directly through His Son and Holy Spirit or indirectly through parts of His body. We were created to know, love, and serve God who has loved us and given us all that we need. May His glory be praised as it is revealed in us. *"Every good gift and every perfect gift is from above, and comes down from the Father of lights, with whom there is no variation or shadow of turning"* (Jas. 1:17). And 1 Corinthians 12:1–2, 4, and 11 says: *"Now concerning spiritual gifts, brethren, I do not want you to be ignorant: You know that you were Gentiles, carried away to these dumb idols, however you were led.... There are diversities of gifts, but the same Spirit ... distributing to each one individually as He wills."*

Thank God we can come to the Father like a little child. We are to be childlike, but not childish. With His disciples:

> *Jesus called a little child to Him, set him in the midst of them and said, "Assuredly, I say to you, unless you are converted and become as little children, you will by no means enter the kingdom of heaven. Therefore, whoever humbles himself as this little child is the greatest in the kingdom of heaven. Whoever receives one little child like this in My name receives Me. But whoever causes one of these little ones who believe in Me to sin, it would be better for him if a millstone were hung around his neck, and he were drowned in the depth of the sea."* (Matt. 18:2–6)

In Israel, I was surprised to see the excavated outline of an early church with a **millstone flat on the ground at the entrance**. Christians who feared the Lord probably remembered this Scripture as they walked over it.

In the mid- to late nineties, I prayed a song from Dean Baktay's CD, *Exalt Him Together,* which was based on Psalm 51:10–12, which David prayed when he realized his sin and asked for mercy and forgiveness.

> *Create in me a clean heart, O God,*
> *And renew a steadfast spirit within me.*
> *Do not cast me away from Your presence,*
> *And do not take Your Holy Spirit from me.*
> *Restore to me the joy of Your salvation,*
> *And uphold me by Your generous Spirit.*

Our *"Abba, Father"* God loves it when we come running to Him like a child. Many times, tears running down my face He ministered to me through the words of the Father talking to the returned wasteful prodigal in a song, including, *"I forgive you; I love you. You are Mine; go in peace. Sin no more, beloved one."*

I wanted my heart to be clean and God answered my cry by causing some old prayer to surface from time to time, addressed to Mary or another saint. I would then repent of it and not pray it again. I remember there was one I had learned in about grade two and had previously habitually prayed it. But now I have Scriptures and other words to pray to God in Jesus's name.

Jesus is the Saviour of the world. He loves *"pure and undefiled religion"* which is worshiping God alone and reaching out in love *"to visit orphans and widows in their trouble, and to keep oneself unspotted from the world"* (Jas. 1:27). Saints have been treated like idols or gods in the past, and were religiously prayed to, used as false bridges, but **the time has come to renounce that type of defiled religion or ungodly "religious spirit" and worship God alone, praying only to and through Him, and doing the loving works He prepares for us**. And we can ask live saints on earth to pray for us, who are in Christ, but not saints who died, even though they are alive in heaven. Even the highly anointed high priests like Aaron cannot be prayed to. **It was forbidden to contact the dead; otherwise observant Jews would have prayed to Bible heroes to intercede for them. The Book of Acts Christians, Jew and Gentile, prayed only to God, in Jesus's name.**

Years ago, I kept trying to be perfect but would find that I would fall short at times in what I had done and failed to do and would whip myself with words like: "I woulda, shoulda, coulda." But the word of the Lord came to me, **"You're too hard on yourself."** Our God is rich in mercy towards those who fear Him. Just as people could not keep the whole Law without falling short at times, so today we should aim to follow Jesus, but might fail to do some good or may not always do right all the time every day. What good news to find that I only had to believe to receive His forgiveness and a fresh start! **But that does not mean that God does not want us to do right**; yet if we fall short of perfection, what good news it was for me to learn I could still be His loved child and friend! Instead of carrying around the guilt, mentally beating ourselves, **we have the New Covenant promise of forgiveness**. *"For I will be merciful to their unrighteousness, and their sins and their lawless deeds I will remember no more"* (Heb. 8:12). **When God forgives us, we must too.** *"If we confess our sins, He is faithful and just to forgive us our sins and to cleanse us from all unrighteousness"* (1 John 1:9).

We are to *"seek first the kingdom of God and His righteousness"* (Matt. 6:33). He has reminded me, *"I will never leave you nor forsake you"* **(Heb. 13:5),** and of a song about the well of salvation. **Instead of drinking from the well of condemnation, I can now drink from the well of salvation!** *"There is therefore now no condemnation to those who are in Christ Jesus, who do not walk according to the flesh, but according to the Spirit"* (Rom. 8:1). And like the woman He spoke to at the well, I can have a spring of living water welling up in me wherever I go helping me to *"not walk according to the flesh, but according to the Spirit."* That is good news!

> *This hope we have as an anchor of the soul, both sure and steadfast, and which enters the Presence behind the veil, where the forerunner has entered for us, even Jesus, having become High Priest forever according to the order of Melchizedek.* (Hebrews 6:19–20)

Jesus Is to Be the Lover of Our Soul and Spirit—Our Heavenly Bridegroom

Today, we are to recognize that when we live in abundance or when our needs are supplied, the praise belongs to God, not to some patron saint or the "Lady" who could be compared to *"lovers"* or *"Baals."* When I walk into nursing homes and see people trying to uncover themselves, or being put to shame by having to let others bathe them and toilet them, I do not know the reason this is happening in every specific case, but I have wept over some who used to be so delicate. Let us try to cover them and turn them to Jesus, who is rich in mercy. Better yet, let us help prevent this from happening. *"He who believes on [Jesus] will by no means be put to shame"* (1 Pet. 2:6). Let us choose Jesus to save, mediate, and guard us instead of idols or medals.

Some feast day celebrations in bars, like Saint Patrick's Day, remind me somewhat of the revelry around the golden calf that angered God and Moses. Yet **God's jealous love is so awesome that Jesus woos His people today even while they are yet sinners.** He was so gracious to Hosea's wife and **wants to know us and to be known by us intimately, Spirit to spirit.** I remember in the nineties when the Lord used to sing over me the song, especially at a local Diocesan conference: *"**Long have I waited for your coming home to Me and living deeply our new life. The wilderness will lead you there to your heart where I'll speak.**"*

He is so wise, loving and merciful.

> *"Therefore, behold, I will allure her,*
> *Will bring her into the wilderness,*
> *And speak comfort to her.*
> *I will give her her vineyards from there*
> *And the Valley of Achor* [suffering] *as a door of hope;*
> *She shall sing there, as in the days of her youth…*
> *And it shall be in that day,"*
> *Says the* LORD,
> *"That you will call Me 'My Husband,'*
> *And no longer call Me 'My Master,' For I will take from her mouth the names of the Baals,*
> *And they shall be remembered by their name no more."*
> (Hosea 2:14–17)

Let us prepare ourselves to be parts of His corporate bride, His helpmate, and show Him our appreciation. Like Ruth and Naomi, both widows, we have found our *"Kinsman Redeemer"* —Jesus. *Worship* can mean "kissing towards." The Song of Songs (Solomon) is a wonderful allegory of Jesus and His bride, His body, His church.

We are called to be saints while we are still on earth. The epistles addressed believers as *"saints,"* people called out of the world to be God's own people who do not seek to do evil, but to do righteousness. And if they slip, they repent quickly. *"As for the saints who are on the earth, 'They are the excellent ones, in whom is all my delight'"* (Ps. 16:3).

First Corinthians 1:2–3 says, *"To the church of God which is at Corinth, to those who are sanctified* [holy, consecrated, set apart] *in Christ Jesus, called to be saints, with all who in every place call on the name of Jesus Christ our Lord, both theirs and ours: Grace to you and peace from God our Father and the Lord Jesus Christ."* Although God is so good that He even blesses His enemies, there are special blessings like provision, grace, and peace for believers who live saintly lives in a **spirit of excellence.** They *"seek first the kingdom of God and His righteousness"* (Matt. 6:33).

Jesus, the Lord of hosts (of angel armies), is all we need to take care of us, not patron saints. Jesus can do anything someone in heaven can do, and more, and knows who to send to our aid. Plus, He is the One God chose to bridge the gap. *"Oh, fear the* LORD, *you His saints! There is no want to those who fear Him"* (Ps. 34:9).

Jesus moved the apostles from calling Him "Master" to "Friend" after they spent a lot of time with Him and did what He told them to do: *"You are My friends if you do whatever I command you. No longer do I call you servants, for a servant does not know what his master is doing; but I have called you friends, for all things that I heard from My Father I have made known to you"* (John 15:14–15). John the Apostle later wrote, *"We know that the Son of God has come and has given us an understanding, that we may know Him who is true; and we are in Him who is true, in His Son Jesus Christ. This is the true God and eternal life. Little children, keep yourselves from idols. Amen*" (1 John 5:20–21). We can become friends of God too, enjoying His friendship.

Distraction Can Be a Tool of the Enemy

The Holy Spirit was moving so strongly on the Roman Catholic Church through the charismatic movement in the seventies and eighties, but then our attention began to be drawn to Mary and apparitions rather than mainly to Jesus. One day in the early nineties the Lord said to me, *"Focus."* Later I attended a Queen's University reunion and noticed that the artwork done by people of my year all seemed to be out of focus. What should be the focal point of the drawings was off to one side. Later I also realized that the enemy had been trying to take our focus off God alone and put it onto apparitions of a "Lady" of this and that place whom we thought was Mary, giving us a divided heart. **The devil was trying to kill revival, to smother the seed of the Word of God with weeds of idolatry.** So around that time, I made the following illustration for a March for Jesus leaflet:

Birds have to learn to fly. With His grace, we will be stronger than a little bird though. Intercessors will rise up like eagles as they wait upon the Lord and renew their strength, nourished by His Word, and catch the wind of Holy Spirit. *"Do not sorrow, for the joy of the* Lord *is your strength"* (Neh. 8:10). As they go, the Lord will continue to straighten their path just as a GPS will give you course corrections to get you safely to your destination if you accidentally take a wrong turn. That is what He has been doing in my life as I seek an undivided heart and single focus.

> *Trust in the* Lord *with all your heart,*
> *And lean not on your own understanding*
> *In all your ways acknowledge Him,*
> *And He shall direct your paths.*
> *Do not be wise in your own eyes;*

*Fear the L*ORD *and depart from evil.*
It will be health to your flesh,
And strength to your bones. (Prov. 3:5–8)

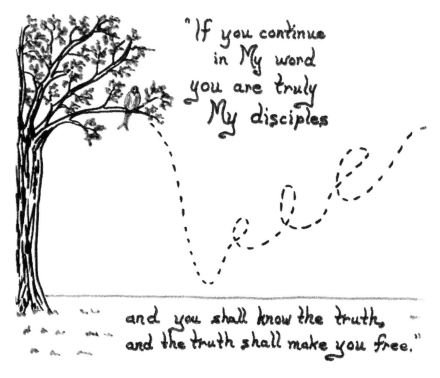

By His cross and resurrection Jesus has set us free if we will believe and receive the everlasting life and the liberty of the adopted children of God which He purchased for us. **Sometimes it takes time to get the truth deeply into one's mind and heart in order to truly know it. It is the truth that you know that makes you free** (see John 8:32). Sometimes we need to read and hear it many times before it sinks in, like when the Lord told me to *"Study the Book of Hebrews."*

*The steps of a good man are ordered by the L*ORD,
and He delights in his way. (Psalm 37:23)

*The steps of a man are from the L*ORD,
and He establishes him in whose way He delights. (Ps. 37:23 RSV)

Jesus is *"the truth,"* who came that captives may be set free since we cannot save ourselves, and idols cannot save us. **Getting to know the Scriptures, the Word of God, and especially to personally know Jesus—the living Word of God—and His Father and Holy Spirit, has made all the difference in my life.** Jesus, *"the life,"* told some Jews, *"Most assuredly, I say to you, he who hears My word and believes in Him who sent Me has everlasting life, and shall not come into judgment, but has passed from death into life.… You search the Scriptures, for in them you think you have eternal life; and these are they which testify of Me. But you are not willing to come to Me that you may have life"* (John 5:24, 39–40). **Scripture alone was not enough for me. I cried out that I wanted to know and love Him more!**

Thanks be to God, Jesus wants to be our personal Saviour. He came to bring release for captives and to lead us. That includes in our prayer life. Once we have been set free from the bondage in which sin holds us, we desire others to know they shall be free too, and to walk in that liberty. Shame disappears; freedom and joy come. His Holy Spirit has been poured out on people, not so that they can return to the distraction of ungodly ways, but so that they can *"be delivered from the bondage of corruption into the glorious liberty of the children of God"* (Rom. 8:21).

Ever since Adam and Eve, the devil has been trying to deceive those whom God has called to be close to Him. But Jesus has been intervening on our behalf, for those who will receive the blessings He desires to give them. Gifts are meant to be unwrapped. If we search **the Scriptures, the writings in the Bible inspired by God Himself**, then we will know the true *"way of the Lord."* We will not fear nor be ignorant of the devil's schemes if we stay close to Jesus. He is our Defense: *"Your word I have hidden in my heart that I might not sin against You"* (Ps. 119:11).

Do Not Give Heed to Fables

Paul urged Timothy not to *"give heed to fables"* (1 Tim. 1:4). Instead he urged him to seek true *"faith"* which produces *"godly edification"* rather than *"disputes"* (1 Tim. 1:4). Sometimes fables can develop even though people start with a truth; but when it is passed on verbally it sometimes gets twisted as they mix in peoples' opinions. Or sometimes people start with a thought which did not originate with God. Years ago, books were rare, so teaching was mostly verbal, but now Bibles are available in so many languages and on listening devices and computers. Many Bible translations are still close to the original Spirit-led Greek and Hebrew, **so we can go back to see what God really said**. *"But reject profane and old wives' fables, and exercise yourself towards godliness"* (1 Tim. 4:7); and, *"Be diligent to present yourself approved to God, a worker who does not need to be ashamed, rightly dividing the word of truth"* (2 Tim. 2:15).

We can be like the Bereans. When Paul and Silas arrived in Berea, *"they went into the synagogue of the Jews. These were more fair-minded* [noble] *than those in Thessalonica, in that they received the word with all readiness, and searched the Scriptures daily to find out whether these things were so. Therefore many of them believed"* (Acts 17:10–12). They did not do what some Thessalonians did when Paul and Silas *"reasoned with them from the Scriptures"*—they did not cause an uproar, or take offense at the Word of God and then assault the household where Paul and Silas had been staying, all because the apostles had presented the good news with which they were not familiar. **Instead of persecuting the messengers or throwing away the Word of God just because it was new to them, the Bereans kept their hearts open to seek truth and searched out the Scriptures to see if God would confirm what Paul had said**. And they found it was true. **Likewise, if someone comes in with some teaching today and it is false, searching the Scriptures should reveal that too.**

We can ask for the gift of *"discerning of spirits"* (1 Cor. 12:10) to see if something comes from God or another source, and examine the fruit. This helps to keep our foot out of the trap of the fowler. Let us stay on the road and out of the ditches, asking Jesus to lead us. Thanks be to God, Jesus will carry us and accompany us as we cross His bridge to the Father, leading us to Him and to one another, that He may be glorified in His body, His temple.

After Francis Frangipane came to speak at Kingston Gospel Temple, in about 1996, I was particularly impressed by his book: *Holiness, Truth, and the Presence of God*. In my quest for these, I asked God to reveal to me any lies which I might have believed and to lead me in His paths of righteousness for His name's sake. While reading it, I began asking Him to **establish truth in my inner being**. I longed for more of this in my life. Jesus did tell us to *"Ask ... seek ... knock"* and we would find results—and He keeps His promises. That is no fable. His light makes things visible, just as both good things and dust are revealed when a shaft of sunlight enters a room.

One night at a Messianic Jewish celebration at the Kingston Gospel Temple, a Jewish believer testified that he used to think that Christ was Jesus's last name, His surname, and that Joseph and Mary were Mr. and Mrs. Christ. I was surprised to hear him say that it was a fable because **I had believed that too!** But I came to learn that *"Christ"* is from the Greek, meaning "Messiah" or *"Mashiach"* in Hebrew.

Matthew began his gospel with a *"genealogy of Jesus Christ, the Son of David, the Son of Abraham"* showing generations from Abraham to His foster father, Joseph, *"until the Christ"* (Matt. 1:1, 17), until the coming of the promised Anointed Son of God, who was also to be the Son of Man, the Seed of Abraham, and David. God has chosen many people to be anointed for special tasks, but showed that Jesus was His specially Anointed Chosen One by anointing Him with the heavenly oil of gladness at His baptism, testifying of Him personally, audibly, *"This is My beloved Son, in whom I am well pleased"* (Matt. 3:17). *"The Christ"* is God's *"only begotten Son"* and no one else is equal to Him. If people say they are another Jesus Christ, do not believe them. But they might be parts of His body being restored according to His likeness.

Who Is Ruler of Heaven and Earth? Whom Do We Worship?

Like other RCs, I used to call Mary the "Mother of God." But the Lord began to impress upon me that **it is also a fable to believe that God has a mother.** Mary was the mother of Jesus who is God, having given birth to Him; but He existed before her. **She is not the mother of God in His entirety.** Some eastern religions try to deify a woman as a goddess that way, making her the mother of other gods and calling her *"queen of heaven"* (Jer. 44:17). Some Catholics in their lack of knowledge have done that with Mary too. But the Creator came before the created ones. The real God in His entirety always was and has no mother, and God chastised the Jews who worshiped this goddess called *"queen of heaven,"* and who offered her food and praises.

Mary truly was the earthly mother who gave birth as a virgin to Jesus when *"the Word"* took flesh as Son of Man. **If she were truly God's mother, then she would be queen of heaven and of saints and angels, as some Catholics mistakenly believed, and** *"Lord of heaven and earth."* **But she is not; the Father is ruler of heaven and earth, and** *"Jesus Christ is Lord"* (Phil. 2:11). When I did not know better, a friend asked me to make a poster proclaiming her as queen of angels and saints. But later, when I knew better, I tore it up and asked God for forgiveness.

Luke 10:21 says, *"Jesus rejoiced in the Spirit and said, 'I thank You, Father, Lord of heaven and earth, that You have hidden these things from the wise and prudent and revealed them to babes. Even so, Father, for so it seemed good in Your sight.'"*

When Joshua was suddenly confronted by a Man standing opposite him with His sword drawn in His hand, *"Joshua went to Him and* said to Him, 'Are You for us or for our adversaries?' So He said, 'No, but as Commander of the army of the LORD I have now come'"* (Josh. 5:13–14). That was a Man, not a woman. He is believed to be the pre-incarnate Jesus, who is One with the Father and is the LORD God Sabaoth, the Lord of hosts, the Lord of angel armies, ready to fight for God's purposes.

Jesus truly is the Son of God who humbled Himself to come like an ordinary human being, and **Jesus is also God and was God from *"the beginning"*** (see John 1:1–2). **But God has no mother.** Saints may reign with Him, but HE is Ruler of rulers. Although I knew He would live forever, I used to think Jesus was only about two thousand years old. **So I was surprised to learn that Jesus began His existence long before His birth** and long before He was conceived of the Holy Spirit, *"for that which is conceived in her is of the Holy Spirit"* (Matt. 1:20).

One night many years ago, a nearby Protestant church invited the RC parish I attended to join with them for an Advent service, and they began by reading Scripture unfamiliar to me from the start of the Gospel of John, including:

> *In the beginning was the Word, and the Word was with God, and the Word was God. He was in the beginning with God. All things were made through Him, and without Him nothing was made that was made. In Him was life, and the life was the light of men. And the light shines in the darkness, and the darkness did not comprehend* [overcome] *it.... [Jesus] was the true Light which gives light to every man coming into the world.... And the Word became flesh and dwelt among us, and we beheld His glory, the glory as of the only begotten of the Father, full of grace and truth.* (John 1:1–4, 9, 14)

I found that my Bible said the same thing!

They had lit one candle in a darkened room, and then all of ours from it. **The light came on for me in more ways than one that night. I began to realize that Jesus,** *"the Word"* **and** *"Light of the world,"* **had

been with the Father before creation, long before His nine months of taking flesh and developing in His earthly mother's womb. True light and revelation come from Him. We might celebrate His earthly birthday at Christmas, His coming to earth as Son of Man, but Jesus, the Word of God, existed and already was God long before Mary was born. *"Do not be deceived"* **(1 Cor. 6:9); God has no mother.** Jesus, who already was God and Son of God, became the Son of Mary, coming to earth as the Son of Man.

Jesus existed long before David too. Wanting people to understand that He was more than the *"Son of David,"* Jesus said, *"If David then calls Him* [the Christ] *'Lord,' how is He his Son?"* (Matt. 22:45; see Ps. 110:1). It was only because He miraculously took flesh in Mary's womb and she and His foster father, Joseph, were of the line of David. **The real Mary calls Jesus *"Lord"* too, but the *"Lady"* of this place and that calls herself by blasphemous names.** Only God is God and only Jesus can save us and give us eternal life.

His coming was revealed to and by the prophets and angels as well as by God Himself audibly at the Jordan and transfiguration. Jesus told some Jews:

> *"If I honor Myself, My honor is nothing. It is My Father who honors Me, of whom you say that He is your God. Yet you have not known Him. And if I say, 'I do not know Him,' I shall be a liar like you; but I know Him and keep His word. Your father Abraham rejoiced to see My day, and he saw it and was glad." Then the Jews said to Him, "You are not yet fifty years old, and have You seen Abraham?" Jesus said to them, "Most assuredly, I say to you, before Abraham was, I AM."* (John 8:54–58)

To Call Mary the "Mother of God" Is Deceptive

Because people on earth sometimes go through an earthly mother to get things from their earthly fathers, and because of the misleading title of "Mother of God" in the "Hail Mary," **A fable also arose that our prayers should go through Mary** because we go through earthly mothers to get things from earthly fathers. That may be logical, but it is not scriptural. "[Jews seek signs and Greeks look for logic] *but we preach Christ crucified, to the Jews a stumbling block and to the Greeks foolishness, but to those who are called, both Jews and Greeks, Christ, the power of God and the wisdom of God"* (1 Cor. 1:22–24).

People thought she was the closest one to God, the one to advocate on our behalf. **But Jesus is the closest and God is one.** *"Hear, O Israel: The L*ORD *our God, the L*ORD *is one"* (Deut. 6:4). **Jesus is God and Lord—He is more than** *"the Son of Man."* **Scripture reveals that it is Jesus whom God set beside Him on His throne where He is to be our Advocate. Mary is not God's mother as if she were the Queen Mother who came before God. Jesus only took flesh in her womb. His Godhood did not come from her.**

David knew the pre-incarnate Jesus, his Good Shepherd: *"The* LORD *said to my Lord, 'Sit at My right hand, till I make Your enemies Your footstool'"* (Ps. 110:1).

Father God is Spirit and has no father or mother. Jesus was God and Son of God from the beginning and lives forever as *"a priest forever according to the order of Melchizedek,"* and Melchizedek was *"without father, without mother, without genealogy, having neither beginning of days nor end of life, but made like the Son of God, remains a priest continually"* (Heb. 7:17, 3). God's wisdom is higher than man's wisdom.

Although Jesus, Son of Man, is also Son of God, He did not inherit His Godhood from Mary's DNA, like "tallness" genes. The blood of a human being comes from the father. Jesus's blood came from Father God and was pure, not tainted by human sin. Mary and His stepfather Joseph raised Jesus as a human being. He may have taken flesh growing in her womb, but Jesus got none of His Godhood from her. Gabriel told her, *"He will be great, and will be called the Son of the Highest.... The Holy Spirit will come upon you, and the power of the Highest will overshadow you; therefore, also, that Holy One who is to be born will be called the Son of God"* (Luke 1:32, 35). His was not an ordinary birth—it was supernatural.

Jesus is closest to God, because He IS God and the Son of God who came as Son of Man too. God the Father even testified of Him at His baptism and on the Mount of transfiguration: *"This is My beloved Son, in whom I am well pleased. Hear Him!"* (Matt. 17:5).He is *"His only begotten Son"* (John 3:16). Besides calling God *"Father"* and allowing God's adopted children to do likewise, Jesus referred to Himself as *"Son of Man"* many times: *"The Son of Man will send out His angels, and they will gather out of His kingdom all things that offend, and those who practice lawlessness"* (Matt. 13:41).

Although she was the mother of Jesus who already was and is God, by calling Mary, the "Mother of God," many have deified her, placing her higher than or equal to God. And we should not be praying to those who died anyway. The living Word of God, *"that Holy One who* [was] *to be born,"* miraculously took on human form in Mary's womb, but **Jesus is no longer a baby and God did not originate in her womb. He existed from the beginning:** *"In the beginning was the Word, and the Word was with God, and the Word was God"* (John 1:1). And the first commandment says, *"I am the* Lord*, your God.... You shall not have other gods before Me"* (Ex. 20:2–3).

God had no mother and He chose His *"only begotten Son"* **Jesus to pray for us, to be our** *"one Mediator,"* **to pray for us now and at the hour of our death. Amen. Stephen saw Jesus doing that for him when he was being stoned to death** (see Acts 7:55–60). **Stephen saw heaven open and only Jesus standing in the gap at the Father's right hand, and Jesus intercedes for all His sheep.** (He sometimes calls intercessors on earth to pray with Him.) When John was an old man many years later, he too saw Jesus at the Father's right hand. Mary could have been dead by then. She was older than John and had lived with him after the crucifixion, but he did not mention seeing her in heaven—although she must have been there somewhere. He did mention the twenty-four elders seated on twenty-four thrones though.

Stephen had told the religious Jews who were judging him that all through history their forefathers had rejected the leaders whom God had raised up for them (like Joseph, Moses, and the prophets). Stephen reminded them that they even rejected God Himself in the wilderness, ungrateful for all that He had done for them. They turned back to worshiping the host of heaven and gods of Egypt, and now they had rejected Jesus, God's Messiah and Son. Stephen told them, *"You stiff-necked and uncircumcised in heart and ears! You always resist the Holy Spirit; as your fathers did, so do you"* (Acts 7:51). Then they stoned him to death *"as he was calling on God and saying, 'Lord Jesus, receive my spirit.... Lord, do not charge them for this sin'"* (Acts 7:59–60).

Jesus alone brought salvation and restoration as the second Adam. *"For as by one man's disobedience many were made sinners, so also by one Man's obedience many will be made righteous"* (Rom. 5:19). It is written: *"At the name of Jesus* **[at whose name?]** *every knee should bow, of those in heaven, and of those on earth, and of those under the earth, and that every tongue should confess that Jesus Christ is Lord"* (Phil. 2:10–11).

Another Fable Is That Mary Is "Ever Virgin"

She will forever be Mary, the one who was a blessed virgin at the time of the miraculous conception of Jesus. However, the Bible speaks of other children that the real Mary had with Joseph after the virgin birth of Jesus, SHOWING THAT SHE IS NOT "EVER VIRGIN." But this does not take away from the fact that she was given the grace to be a "blessed virgin" at the time of the birth of our Saviour.

She had been betrothed to Joseph when Gabriel appeared to her, and betrothal was closer to marriage than an engagement. But after the angel appeared to him and said, *"Joseph, son of David, do not be afraid to take to you Mary your wife, for that which is conceived in her is of the Holy Spirit,"* Joseph *"did as the angel of the Lord commanded him and took to him his wife, and did not know her till she had brought forth her firstborn Son. And he called His name Jesus"* (Matt. 1:20, 24–25). **They lived together as husband and wife then, but he did not "*know her,*" meaning in this context to have sexual relations with her, until after Jesus was born.** *"[Joseph] did not know her till she had brought forth her firstborn Son."*

When Jesus first began to teach in His hometown, people familiar with His family but forgetting that angels announced His birth, not knowing or not believing that Joseph was only His foster father, said, *"Is this not the carpenter's son? Is not His mother called Mary? And His brothers James, Joses, Simon, and Judas? And His sisters, are they not all with us?"* (Matt. 13:55–56). He had brothers and sisters with the same mother but Jesus had a different Father. His half-brother James, birth son of Joseph, is believed to be the writer of the book of James. Jesus was the foster child or adopted child of Joseph the carpenter and only begotten Son of the Father, God. His brothers did not believe in Him at first, but were there in the Upper Room at Pentecost, part of the 120, with Mary.

Chapter 10
Divination Is a False Bridge

*D*ivination[5] is: "1. The act of divining; foretelling future events, or discovering things secret or obscure, by the aid of superior beings, or by other than human means. The ancient heathen philosophers divided divination into two kinds, natural and artificial. Natural divination was supposed to be effected by a kind of inspiration or divine afflatus; artificial divination was effected by certain rites, experiments or observations, as by sacrifices, cakes, flour, wine, observation of entrails, flight of birds, lots, verses, omens, position of the stars, etc."

> *When you come into the land which the* Lord *your God is giving you, you shall not learn to follow the abominations of those nations. There shall not be found among you anyone who makes his son or daughter pass through the fire* [be burned as an offering to an idol], *or one who practices witchcraft, or a soothsayer, or one who interprets omens, or a sorcerer, or one who conjures spells, or a medium, or a spiritist, or one who calls up the dead* ["*or a charmer, or one that consulteth a ghost or a familiar spirit, or a necromancer*" (JPS)] *For all who do these things are an abomination to the* Lord, *and because of these abominations the* Lord *your God drives them out from before you.*

---

5   Rick Meyers, e-Sword, *Webster's Dictionary of American English* (1828). https://www.e-sword.net/.

> *You shall be blameless* [perfect] *before the L*ORD *your God. For these nations which you will dispossess listened to soothsayers [*"who practice sorcery" (WEBA)*] and diviners; but as for you, the L*ORD *your God has not appointed such for you* [not allowed you to do so]. *The L*ORD *your God will raise up for you a Prophet like me from your midst, from your brethren. Him you shall hear....* [God told Moses,] *"I will ... put My words in His mouth, and He shall speak to them all that I command Him."* (Deut. 18:9–15, 18)

This shows the difference between divination and true prophecy and pointed to Jesus, the Great Prophet, who would speak the true prophetic words the Father would put *"in His mouth."* And today, for the true prophetic, God can put His words in a person's mouth, as He did with young Jeremiah. *"For the testimony of Jesus is the spirit of prophecy"* (Rev. 19:10). But we are not to listen to the false prophetic:

> *"An unjust man is an abomination to the righteous, and he who is upright in the way is an abomination to the wicked."* (Prov. 29:27)

Divination, a False Prophetic, Involves Going to the Wrong Source

God forbids it, including divination by contacting the dead. Not only is He exalted above all small "g" gods and idols, but God alone should we contact in prayer, not His creations: *"And take heed, lest you lift your eyes to heaven, and when you see the sun, the moon, and the stars, all the host of heaven, you feel driven to worship them and serve them"* (Deut. 4:19). *"The host of heaven"* is more than the physical stars. We are not to contact Lucifer and his bad angels or serve them. But neither are we to try to contact the heavenly host of good angels and saints to worship them or serve them. We are to go to God through His only begotten Son, Jesus.

Our God alone is called *"the Lord of hosts* [LORD God Sabaoth]*"* (Amos 6:8). Besides being engaged in awesome praise and worship, hosts of saints might be praying for us in heaven, but we are forbidden to contact them, to call them up to speak to them or they to us, or to contact any other ordinary human being who died.

If God wants to call us up to heaven in a vision where we might speak while there in the vision to those who went before us, that is different.

Jesus said it was written, *"He called them gods, to whom the word of God came"* (John 10:35). His Word has come to adopted sons of God as well as to angels, but He does not want us to pray to them, or to stars or to other gods of the nations, and *"feel driven to worship them and serve them."* None of them is *"the Christ,"* the *"only begotten Son"* (John 3:16). **Jesus warned us not to be deceived.** *"Then if anyone says to you, 'Look, here is the Christ!' or 'There!' do not believe it. For false christs and false prophets will rise and show great signs and wonders to deceive, if possible, even the elect"* (Matt. 24:23–24).

A medium uses deception, be it smoke and mirrors, or prophecy by a *"familiar spirit"* who speaks to and through him or her. Rather than be like fortune tellers and psychics who consult the Zodiac or *"familiar spirits,"* or like Masons and New Agers who try to contact Lucifer, or like eastern religions who try to contact other gods and demonic spirits, **we have the great privilege of consulting the one true God— the true Source.** *"Thus says the Lord ... 'Call to Me and I will answer you and show you great and mighty things which you do not know'"* (Jer. 33:2–3). Jesus said, *"Man shall not live by bread alone, but by every word of God"* (Luke 4:4). His Word is truth and life-giving.

First John 1:5 says, *"God is light and in Him is no darkness at all."* Paul prayed for Christians in Ephesus that God would give them revelation, the light of His truth.

The first commandment is: *"I am the L*ORD *your God, who brought you out of the land of Egypt, out of the house of bondage. You shall have no other gods before Me"* (Ex. 20:2–3).

Angels Can Be the Wrong Source Too

Some call themselves Christians and yet they also call on the name of bad angels like Lucifer who fell when he thought he was like God. He did not submit his will to God's will. And he can come disguised as *"an angel of light"* (2 Cor. 11:14).

> *How you are fallen from heaven,*
> *O Lucifer, son of the morning!*
> *How you are cut down to the ground*
> *You who weakened the nations!*
> *For you have said in your heart:*
> *"I will ascend into heaven,*
> *I will exalt my throne above the stars of God;*
> *I will also sit on the mount of the congregation*
> *On the farthest sides of the north;*
> *I will ascend above the heights of the clouds,*
> *I will be like the Most High."*
> *Yet you shall be brought down to Sheol,*
> *To the lowest depths of the Pit.*
> *Those who see you will gaze at you,*
> *And consider you, saying:*
> *"Is this the man who made the earth tremble,*
> *Who shook kingdoms,*
> *Who made the world as a wilderness*
> *And destroyed its cities,*
> *Who did not open the house of his prisoners?"* (Isa. 14:12–17)

But we are not to call on the name of good angels like Michael the archangel either. We can ask God to dispatch angels to our aid though: *"For He shall give His angels charge over you, to keep you in all your ways"* (Ps. 91:11); and, *"In heaven their angels always see the face of My Father who is in heaven"* (Matt. 18:10).

Neither are we to take God's name in vain by inviting any spirit to come inside of us to be our spirit guide—except the Holy Spirit of Jesus Christ: *"If you call yourself a Christian, act like one."* Jesus said, *"My sheep hear My voice, and I know them, and they follow Me"* (John 10:27). What a privilege that is! He is all that we need. And we are forbidden to speak *"in the name of other gods"* (Deut. 18:20). So, to prophesy in other names is false prophecy. **Jesus has taken His place above the angels again and has authority to send** *"stars"* **or** *"angels"* **to His churches** (Rev. 1:20).

For a little while as Son of Man two thousand years ago, He was made *"a little lower than the angels"* (Heb. 2:7). But now He has resumed His place as Son of God at the Father's right hand. God can send angels to minister unto the heirs of salvation as God did to Jesus when He was in the wilderness, but **we are not to worship angels or pray to them:** *"Let no one cheat you of your reward, taking delight in false humility and worship of angels, intruding into those things which he has not seen, vainly puffed up by his fleshly mind"* (Col. 2:18). They are only messengers. God sent angels to announce the birth of His Son and to warn Joseph to flee to Egypt so Jesus would be protected; **but** Mary, Joseph, and the shepherds did not invite the angels into their hearts.

A theology student visited me years ago and she had invited two angels into her heart to guide her. But thank God the Lord led us in a prayer of deliverance for her.

It is the Son of God through His Holy Spirit who is to command us, being our Lord. God can send angels to guard us, and we can ask Him to do so. But we should not be praying to our guardian angels.

> *There are some who trouble you and want to pervert the gospel of Christ. But even if we, or an angel from heaven, preach any other gospel to you than what we have preached to you, let him be accursed.* (Gal. 1:7–8)

> *For to which of the angels did He ever say:*
> *"You are My Son, today I have begotten You"?*
> *And again:*
> *"I will be to Him a Father, and He shall be to Me a Son"?*
> *But when He again brings the firstborn into the world, He says:*
> *"Let all the angels of God worship Him."* (Heb. 1:5–6)

If a good angel prophesies, **God is His source and the angel should not be worshiped.** The apostle John found this out when he tried to worship a very good angel and was stopped. *"See that you do not do that! I am your fellow servant, and of your brethren who have the testimony of Jesus. Worship God! For the testimony of Jesus is the spirit of prophecy"* (Rev. 19:10). God and Jesus were the source.

Ancestor Worship

When I read about Buddhists who sometimes set up pictures or statues of loved ones who died so they could pray to them and asked them to protect them from evil, I realized Catholicism had copied that, burning candles before images. Eastern religions sometimes burn incense before their "gods," including ancestral gods, heaping praise upon them and offering food and drink offerings to them (and sometimes even blood of slain children or animal sacrifices). But we are not supposed to do that. Neither is the killing of children before (abortion) or after their birth permitted by God. **We are to protect all human life from conception to natural death.**

Could it be those early Catholic missionaries, in their ignorance of Scriptures, substituted saints, spiritual ancestors, for the people's household gods?

Ancestor worship, even contacting deceased spiritual ancestors, is forbidden idolatry—spiritual prostitution or harlotry.

Necromancy

Necromancy is consulting with the dead.[6] Divination by means of communication with spirits of the dead is forbidden by God. It is attempting to find out answers **from the wrong source,** and sometimes people have found that it was actually demonic spirits which replied, masquerading as dead loved ones.

Cindy Jacobs, in her book *Possessing the Gates of the Enemy,* related a story about a woman whose fiancé had died and while the woman was worshiping alone, a spirit looking just like him suddenly appeared in her room with her. She thought God had allowed him to visit her in her loneliness. However, her deception deepened and when she told another about it, her friend asked God to show her who the spirit really was so she would be free from its influence. Then the next time it appeared to her, his form looked disgusting and revolting. Only his eyes looked like her fiancé's. The Lord revealed it to be a demonic spirit which had masqueraded as her dead loved one.[7] *"Now the Spirit expressly says that in latter times some will depart from the faith, giving heed to deceiving spirits and doctrines of demons, speaking lies in hypocrisy, having their own conscience seared with a hot iron"* (1 Tim. 4:1–2).

I believe that Catholics have been similarly **deceived by demonic spirits coming to them masquerading** as Mary or other saints in a vision called an "apparition", bringing in *"doctrines of demons."* Demons will disappear if the person calls on the name of Jesus. There is power in His name, Word, and blood: *"For there is no other name under heaven given among men by which we must be saved"* (Acts 4:12). **Now there is such a thing as a true vision from God, but it does not lead to disobeying the Word of God.** James 4:7–8 says, *"Therefore submit to God. Resist the devil and he will flee from you. Draw near to God and He will*

---

6 James Strong, LL.D., S.T.D, "Nave's Topical Bible Reference System" in *The Strongest Strong's Exhaustive Concordance of the Bible,* ed. Kohlenberger and Swanson (Zondervan 2001), 1649

7 6

draw near to you. Cleanse your hands, you sinners; and purify your hearts, you double-minded."

Even when a saintly person dies, we are not to try to contact him or her for counsel or favours. By insisting on trying to talk to these saints who died (ancestor worship), you could be making your church a *"synagogue* [congregation] *of Satan."* There was a place in Ontario where the so-called Christians kept trying to talk to their dead foundress in prayer, although the Lord had sent word that this was sin and to seek the Lord instead. He had told me they were a *"synagogue of Satan,"* as it says in Revelation 2:9: *"I know the blasphemy of those who say they are Jews and are not, but are a synagogue of Satan."*

"If you call yourself a Christian, act like one," is an understanding of the commandment not to take the Lord's name in vain. God said it to me for the church in an audible voice in 1981.

Catholics have good pieces of Scripture at Mass, but many, like me years ago, did not read the whole Bible, so I believe it was in ignorance that they began to use dead saints as bridges to try to connect them with God. But now more need to read the Scriptures in context. **Any other bridge besides Jesus and His body of Christ alive on earth abiding in Him, acting in His name, will crumble or fall short. His Holy Spirit is the only spirit guide we need.**

> *For no other foundation can anyone lay than that which is laid, which is Jesus Christ. Now if anyone builds on this foundation with gold, silver, precious stones, wood, hay, straw, each one's work will become clear; for the Day will declare it, because it will be revealed by fire; and the fire will test each one's work, of what sort it is. If anyone's work which he has built on it endures, he will receive a reward. If anyone's work is burned, he will suffer loss; but he himself will be saved, yet so as through fire. Do you not know that you are the temple of God and that the Spirit of God dwells in you? If anyone defiles the temple of God, God will destroy him. For the temple*

of God is holy, which temple you are. (1 Cor. 3:11–17; see Ezek. 13:9–16)

We should have a holy fear of the Lord and not want to defile the temple of His Holy Spirit by sexual immorality or by inviting in other spirits, false bridges. Not only the churches, but the throne, the mercy seat over our heart and mind upon which the New Testament Law is written, should be reserved for the presence of the one true God alone, Father, Son, and Holy Spirit, with our Lord Jesus as eternal High Priest, Mediator. **No other spirit should be in there.** Otherwise, it reminds me of *"the 'abomination of desolation' spoken of by Daniel the prophet, standing in the holy place"* (Matt. 24:15–16), which could have caused children of Israel to *"flee to the mountains"* when Jerusalem was destroyed in 70 AD, as Jesus warned to do.

Saint Paul delivered a woman from an evil spirit guide that told her some things which were true, but they came from the wrong source and bore the wrong fruit of trying to idolize the men of God.

> *Now it happened, as we went to prayer, that a certain slave girl possessed with a spirit of divination met us, who brought her masters much profit by fortune-telling. This girl followed Paul and us, and cried out, saying, "These men are the servants of the Most High God, who proclaim to us the way of salvation." And this she did for many days. But Paul, greatly annoyed, turned and said to the spirit, "I command you in the name of Jesus Christ to come out of her." And he came out that very hour. But when her masters saw that their hope of profit was gone, they seized Paul and Silas and dragged them into the marketplace to the authorities.* (Acts 16:16–19)

Paul and Silas experienced the demonic backlash of persecution and were imprisoned, but the joy of the Lord was their strength as they sang praises to God at midnight. Praise God, not only were their fellow prisoners touched by their prayers and hymns, but God miraculously caused the cells to all pop open and even the jailer and his family received salvation.

Séances Are Forbidden

In Old Testament times, the High Priest and live prophets of God acted like bridges to Him, but even they were not to pray to the dead. **Sometimes, when people had been greatly displeasing God, He was silent for a time, not answering their prayers, waiting for them to repent.** Sin can cause a breach in our relationship with Him. Sometimes people describe it as their prayers hitting the ceiling. Instead of an open heaven with blessings pouring down, they received the consequences of their actions: *"And your heavens which are over your head shall be bronze, and the earth which is under you shall be iron"* (Deut. 28:23). Inability to contact God—a closed heaven—and unproductiveness were **curses for disobedience to God**.

After November 25, 1994, when I received the word, *"They are dead. Do not contact them,"* I discovered in the Scriptures that **King Saul knew it was forbidden to contact the dead, even dead saints like the prophet Samuel**. In his desperation to know what to do, Saul disguised himself, hoping no one would know it was him. Under cover of night, he visited the medium (or witch) at Endor and asked her to conduct a séance and bring up Samuel. The medium even begged him not to ask her to do that because she knew she could be killed for doing it by order of God and the king (Saul), but he swore to her that she would not be punished.

Fortune tellers and mediums have been known to use illusion and deception in their practice, but sometimes they do bring something up. Some mediums have only pretended to do that by using ventriloquism. For some reason, it looked like Samuel actually appeared and he asked Saul why he had called him up since it was forbidden. Saul told the spirit:

> *"I am in great distress; for the Philistines are warring against me, and God has turned away from me and answers me no more, either by prophets or by dreams; therefore I have summoned you to tell me what to do."*

> Then Samuel said, "Why then do you ask me, since the LORD has turned from you and become your enemy? The LORD has done to you as He spoke by me; for the LORD has torn the kingdom out of your hand, and given it to your neighbor, David. Because you did not obey the voice of the LORD, and did not carry out His fierce wrath against Amalek, therefore the LORD has done this thing to you this day." (1 Sam. 28:3–15)

The penalty for Saul's sin was death, and he soon died and David became king. But Saul was supposed to trust God and not go to the dead for an answer.

Reading this, I could see the similarity with some Catholics. **Sometimes people are tired of waiting for God to answer them and turn to dead saints today to see if they will advocate for them, not realizing that it is forbidden.** So many times in Scripture we are admonished to *"Wait on the LORD"* (Ps. 37:9). We live in a society where so many things are fast, but sometimes when we are waiting on God, He is waiting on us to trust and obey Him in what He has already said. Or it could be that His answer is delayed because there is something He wants to set up for us first or there is a danger He wants us to avoid. Remember, *"The Lord is not slack concerning His promise, as some count slackness, but is longsuffering toward us, not willing that any should perish but that all should come to repentance"* (2 Pet. 3:9).

There Is Deliverance from Darkness and the Land of the Living Dead

Thank God Jesus became a curse on the cross so our curse for disobedience to God could be removed and sin forgiven if we repent. Thanks be to God for the atoning blood of the New Covenant.

Abraham waited twenty-five years until his promised son, Isaac, was born. Perhaps he would have come sooner if Abraham and Sarah had not done things their own way and produced an Ishmael. But

God's promise was fulfilled and Abraham was a hero of our faith for believing God. Psalm 27:14 says, *"Wait on the LORD; be of good courage, and He shall strengthen your heart; wait, I say, on the LORD!"*

As I mentioned, the Lord also helped me to understand:

> *And when they say to you, "Seek those who are mediums and wizards* [who seek familiar spirits], *who whisper and mutter," should not a people consult their God? Should they consult the dead on behalf of the living? To the law and to the testimony! If they do not speak according to this word, it is* because *there is* no light in them. *They will pass through it hard-pressed and hungry; and it shall happen, when they are hungry, that they will be enraged and curse their king and their God, and look upward. Then they will look to the earth, and see trouble and darkness, gloom of anguish; and they will be* driven into darkness.... *Nevertheless, the gloom will not be upon her who is distressed.* (Isa. 8:19–22; 9:1)

NEVERTHELESS, for believers, God will turn their darkness into light. Thank God He did it for me, and for countless others.

> *The people who walked in darkness*
> *Have seen a great light;*
> *Those who dwelt in the land of the shadow of death,*
> *Upon them a light has shined....*
> *For unto us a Child is born,*
> *Unto us a Son is given;*
> *And the government shall be upon His shoulder.*
> *And His name will be called*
> *Wonderful, Counselor, Mighty God,*
> *Everlasting Father, Prince of Peace....*
> *The zeal of the LORD of hosts* [jealous love of the LORD God Sabaoth,
> the God of angel armies] *will perform this.* (Isa. 9:2, 6–7)

People who are deceived into following the devil or *"contact the dead on behalf of the living"* are like those in Isaiah 8 who tried to use a false bridge and as a consequence of their sinfulness, experienced curses like poverty, distress, confusion of mind, and an inability to contact the real God for a time (closed heaven). The glory departed from them and they were in thick darkness spiritually, like in a fog. But God promised that in the latter time, there will be no gloom for her that was in anguish.

Babylon can mean "confusion." The Good Shepherd can even guide someone whose mind has been in a fog if He shines his fog light, His Word, and the person follows Him. **That is what He did for me.** Thanks be to God, even when in deep darkness spiritually and depression many years ago, **feeling like I was in the land of the living dead**, the Lord told me, *"Jesus is the light at the end of the tunnel,"* and I tried to portray that word on this banner. *"I would have lost heart, unless I had believed that I would see the goodness of the* LORD *in the land of the living"* (Ps. 27:13).

Jesus is the Waymaker. I am a witness that the light of Christ can penetrate to your mind, heart, hands, and feet when you feel like you are in a pit, or the womb of the earth, if you humble yourself before Him. His love is so great that it finds His sheep anywhere and **He can birth you into something new**, just as a birth canal suddenly opens at the right time making a way where there is no way.

> *Where can I go from Your Spirit?*
> *Or where can I flee from Your presence?*
> *If I ascend into heaven, You are there;*
> *If I make my bed in hell, behold, You are there.*
> *If I take the wings of the morning,*
> *And dwell in the uttermost parts of the sea,*
> *Even there Your hand shall lead me,*
> *And Your right hand shall hold me.*
> *If I say, "Surely the darkness shall fall on me,"*
> *Even the night shall be light about me;*
> *Indeed, the darkness shall not hide from You,*
> *But the night shines as the day;*
> *The darkness and the light are both alike to You.*
> *For You formed my inward parts;*
> *You covered me in my mother's womb.*
> *I will praise You for I am fearfully and wonderfully made;*
> *Marvelous are Your works,*
> *And that my soul knows very well.* (Ps. 139:7–14)

I traded my sorrow for the joy of the Lord, my fog of confusion for the F.O.G.—the Favour of God. He delivered me from evil. **Jesus is the Deliverer, the chief obstetrician, birthing us into a new thing—the will and action of Christ.**

I had asked the Lord to confirm His word, *"They are dead. Do not contact them,"* with Scriptures and He graciously did. God is so great! I am forever grateful! Although I experienced much warfare on the battlefield of the mind in those three and a half years, probably because RC religious non-scriptural practices had been so entrenched in my life and family history, but the Word of God came to rescue me like a Mighty Warrior. **As I studied His inspired Word, I became more firmly grounded into the truth.**

It cut through dividing biblical truth from generational myth since our ears had been turned *"away from the truth, and be turned aside to fables"* (2 Tim. 4:4).

For the word of God is living and powerful [active], *and sharper than any two-edged sword, piercing even to the division of soul and spirit, and of joints and marrow, and is a discerner of the thoughts and intents of the heart. And there is no creature hidden from His sight, but all things are naked and open to the eyes of Him to whom we must give account. Seeing then that we have a great High Priest who has passed through the heavens, Jesus the Son of God, let us hold fast our confession. For we do not have a High Priest who cannot sympathize with our weaknesses, but was in all points tempted as we are, yet without sin. Let us therefore come boldly to the throne of grace, that we may obtain mercy and find grace to help in time of need.* (Heb. 4:12–16)

Catholic Séance—Contacting Familiar Spirits

I went to an Advent 2010 gathering at a Catholic church and thought we were going to just meditate on and study Scriptures. That would have been great. Therefore, I was surprised when it turned into a "Catholic Séance" calling up dead saints—although the people did not realize that was what was happening.

The leader told us not to use Bibles. (That seemed odd.) He read a portion of Scripture to us and told us to try to contact the biblical people who were involved in that Scripture two thousand years ago to get revelation directly from them on that particular passage. This did not sound right to me because bringing revelation is the job of Jesus, the *"Teacher,"* by the anointing of His Holy Spirit: *"But the anointing which you have received from Him abides in you, and you do not need that anyone teach you; but as the same anointing teaches you concerning all things, and is true, and is not a lie, and just as it has taught you, you will abide in Him"* (1 John 2:27).

Jesus is happy to come in and dine on the Word with us by His Spirit if we invite Him. So, I silently prayed to bind other spirits and asked the Holy Spirit of Jesus Christ to speak to us. When we were asked to share, I shared what I believed He was showing me and was surprised when two people stood up to share what they believed Mary was saying to them.

Saying nothing more, I went right home afterwards to seek the Lord about what had just transpired and Holy Spirit brought to my memory Psalm 2. It is written:

> *Why do the nations rage,*
> *And the people plot a vain thing?*
> *The kings of the earth set themselves,*
> *And the rulers take counsel together,*
> *Against the* Lord *and against His Anointed, saying,*
> *"Let us break Their bonds in pieces*
> *And cast away Their cords from us."*
> *He who sits in the heavens shall laugh;*
> *The* Lord *shall hold them in derision.*
> *Then He shall speak to them in His wrath,*
> *And distress them in His deep displeasure:*
> *"Yet I have set My King on My holy hill of Zion."*
> *I will declare the decree:*
> *The* Lord *has said to Me,*
> *"You are My Son,*
> *Today I have begotten You.*
> *Ask of Me, and I will give You*
> *The nations for Your inheritance,*
> *And the ends of the earth for Your possession.*
> *You shall break them with a rod of iron;*
> *You shall dash them to pieces like a potter's vessel."* (Ps. 2:1–9)

So, I realized that people thought they were contacting Mary, a saint who had died, but they were actually contacting a *"familiar spirit"* **of the dead—which we are forbidden to do.**

I had prayed in Jesus's name binding other spirits, and yet these demonic *"familiar spirits"* had broken *"their bonds,"* the bonds God put on them because what you bind on earth in Jesus's name is bound in heaven. But God just laughs knowing the end from the beginning, and desires that peoples and spirits pay homage to His Son. His Holy Spirit is the only Spirit we are supposed to attempt to contact. God told Moses He would raise up a true prophet to speak the words which God would put in His mouth: *"But the prophet ... who speaks in the name of other gods, that prophet shall die"* (Deut. 18:20). So, people need to realize that it is wrong to contact the dead and repent from this. **It is false prophecy to speak the words *"familiar spirits"* give. Jesus died so the repentant could be forgiven and live.** So I shared in written form what I had found about familiar spirits with the leader and parish priest.

In David's time, God warned the leaders to humble themselves or face the consequences of their actions. *"The Lord reigns"* and *"Jesus is Lord."* We know Him as the gentle Shepherd, but He is also the Judge, and God's chosen Anointed King who comes as Commander of hosts with a two-edged sword and a rod. He has a jealous love for His people. God is the Potter and we are the clay which He can reform into vessels of honour from which living water is served if we are willing and obedient.

> *Now therefore, be wise, O kings;*
> *Be instructed, you judges of the earth.*
> *Serve the L*ORD *with fear,*
> *And rejoice with trembling.*
> *Kiss the Son, lest He be angry,*
> *And you perish in the way,*
> *When His wrath is kindled but a little.*
> *Blessed are all those who put their trust in Him.* (Ps. 2:10–12)

People can humble themselves before Jesus, or risk being humbled by Him. To *"kiss the Son"* is to worship Him with love, and to do His will. It reminds me of how Mary of Bethany kissed His feet, anointing them, wiping them with her hair, and how her life had been transformed by His forgiveness and His teaching as she sat at His feet. Rather than proudly waiting for Him to break her, she humbled herself before Him and broke her vessel of costly ointment instead, pouring it over the head and feet of Jesus. **We have the great privilege of worshiping Jesus in love too, pouring out on Him what is most costly in our lives,** including our humble, heartfelt praise and worship listening to what He has to teach us. His sheep trust and obey Him. I heard a pastor say that **trusting Him also means trusting His timing.**

"Familiar spirits," such as the "Lady" disguised as Mary who appeared in various nations, can go seeking a person to deceive him. Sometimes she just speaks to people in inner locutions. Like the slave girl with *"a spirit of divination"* (see Acts 16:16–19), which gave her things to speak, **the messages might even be true. But they are from the wrong source, and it is really a demonic spirit giving the message** to the person for an evil purpose (which might be hidden).

Many today do not realize our great privilege that if we seek Him, God Himself can speak to us. Jesus said, *"My sheep hear My voice,"* **but we are forbidden to serve** *"familiar spirits,"* **other voices that are not from God.** *"Give no regard to* [do not turn to] *mediums and familiar spirits; do not seek after them to be defiled by them: I am the* LORD *your God"* (Lev. 19:31); and Isaiah 8:19–20 says, *"Should not a people seek their God? Should they seek the dead on behalf of the living?* [People who pray to dead spiritual or natural ancestors do it] *because there is no light in them"* (Isa. 8:19–20).

I have heard the voice of God. But when a spirit with a female voice tried to contact me, calling my name three different nights when I was staying elsewhere, each time I told it to be gone, in Jesus's name, and it left, thank God.

Why go to the wrong source when we have the right Source! John Wesley wrote: "For living men to enquire of the living God, is proper and reasonable; but it is highly absurd for them to forsake him, and to seek dead idols, either to the images, or to the spirits of dead men, which are supposed to speak in them."[8]

Sometimes people who practice consulting the dead end up in great confusion and mental illness. But those who consult the true God and listen for a reply can find He showers them with great blessings for obedience, and confirms His Word to them (see Deuteronomy 28).

> *Thus says the* L*ord* *your Redeemer,*
> *And He who formed you from the womb:*
> *"I am the* L*ord**, who makes all things,*
> *Who stretches out the heavens all alone,*
> *Who spreads abroad the earth by Myself;*
> *Who frustrates the signs of babblers,*
> *And drives diviners mad;*
> *Who turns wise men backward,*
> *And makes their knowledge foolishness;*
> *["I make fools of fortunetellers and frustrate the predictions of astrologers.*
> *The words of the wise I refute and show that their wisdom is foolishness"* (GNT)]
> *Who confirms the word of His servant,*
> *And performs the counsel of His messengers."* (Isa. 44:24–26)

We have the great privilege of praying directly to the Father in Jesus's name and dialoguing with Him. We should desire no other god and put no other god before Him. *"**Familiar spirits**"* are spirits of dead people which mediums, witches, wizards, or psychics are allegedly able to contact. They might claim to have a particular *"familiar spirit"* or

---

8   Rick Myers, e-Sword. *John Wesley's Explanatory Notes* Re: Isa 8:19. https://www.e-sword.net/.

spirit guide who could talk through them either because it was within them or came when they called on it. This is demonic, supernatural prostitution. **Why settle for a counterfeit, displeasing God and risking His wrath, when you can contact the authentic original—the Holy Spirit of Jesus Christ?**

Leviticus 20:6–7 says, *"And the person who turns to mediums and familiar spirits, to prostitute himself with them, I will set My face against that person and cut him off from his people. Consecrate yourselves therefore, and be holy, for I am the* L`ORD` *your God."* Saint Peter even warned Christians that *"as He who called you is holy, you also be holy in all your conduct, because it is written, 'Be holy, for I am holy'"* (1 Pet. 1:15–16). Leviticus 20:26–27 says, *"And you shall be holy to Me, for I the* L`ORD` *am holy, and have separated you from the peoples, that you shall be Mine. A man or a woman who is a medium, or who has familiar spirits, shall surely be put to death; they shall stone them with stones. Their blood shall be upon them."* Today that means that **we are not to ask Mary or any other saint to be a spirit guide for us,** to dwell within us or for us to be in them. **The "Lady" calls people to be part of her body. But rather than be part of her body, we are called to be part of** *"the body of Christ"* (Rom. 7:4).

> *The woman was arrayed in purple and scarlet, and adorned with gold and precious stones and pearls, having in her hand a golden cup full of abominations and the filthiness of her fornication. And on her forehead a name was written:*
>
> MYSTERY, BABYLON THE GREAT, THE MOTHER OF HARLOTS AND OF THE ABOMINATIONS OF THE EARTH.
>
> *I saw the woman, drunk with the blood of the saints and with the blood of the martyrs of Jesus. And when I saw her, I marveled with great amazement.* (Revelation 17:4–6)
>
> *They invited the people to the sacrifices of their gods, and the people ate and bowed down to their gods. So Israel was joined to Baal of*

Peor, and the anger of the Lord *was aroused against Israel. Then the* Lord *said to Moses, "Take all the leaders of the people and hang the offenders before the* Lord*, out in the sun, that the fierce anger of the* Lord *may turn away from Israel." So Moses said to the judges of Israel, "Every one of you kill his men who were joined to Baal of Peor."* (Num. 25:2–5)

We are only to be joined to holy King Jesus. It is His job by His Holy Spirit to guide us. He is *"'Immanuel,' which is translated, 'God with us'"* (Matt. 1:23). **Thank God, He took the death penalty for us so believers could be forgiven and put to death sinful practices in their lives.** After Pentecost His Holy Spirit was not only with His 120 disciples who continued in prayer, but within them. **He was all they needed** then, and *"Jesus Christ is the same yesterday, today and forever"* (Heb. 13:8).

Chapter 11
False Bridges Can Lead to Humiliation

When His people fell into idolatry in Jeremiah's time, praying to the *"queen of heaven,"* many were punished by God by becoming prisoners in Babylon. Later, God brought them out and punished Babylon for her sins too. Isaiah prophesied of **her humiliation** after the Jews had been in captivity there:

> *"Come down and sit in the dust,*
> *O virgin daughter of Babylon ... without a throne....*
> *For you shall no more be called tender and delicate....*
> *Your nakedness shall be uncovered,*
> *Yes, your shame will be seen;*
> *I will take vengeance,*
> *And I will not arbitrate with a man."*
> *As for our Redeemer, the* LORD *of hosts is His name,*
> *The Holy One of Israel.*
> *"Sit in silence and go into darkness,*
> *O daughter of the Chaldeans;*
> *For you shall no longer be called*
> *The Lady of Kingdoms."*

[The Lord tells of how He had been angry with His people so He had given them into her hand; but Babylon treated them cruelly and spoke contrary to God and]

...showed them no mercy;
On the elderly you laid your yoke very heavily....

> [She said in her heart], *"I am, and there is no one else besides me;*
> *I shall not sit as a widow,*
> *Nor shall I know the loss of children";*
> *But these two things shall come to you*
> *In a moment, in one day:*
> *The loss of children, and widowhood....*
> *Because of the multitude of your sorceries,*
> *For the great abundance of your enchantments.* (Isa. 47:1–6, 8–9)

And even spiritual *"Babylon"* will be judged, where many of God's people have been imprisoned even in our time. As I found out, **praying to God through her or** *"the host of heaven"* (2 Kgs. 21:3) **is not pleasing to God, and neither can a graven image protect or save you. It is like sleeping with the enemy.** God gives His people a certain amount of time to exit to avoid being put to shame with her.

> *They shall be turned back,*
> *They shall be greatly ashamed,*
> *Who trust in carved images,*
> *Who say to the molded images,*
> *"You are our gods."* (Isa. 42:17)

Putting your trust in idols and medals can cause people to be put to shame, but if we trust in Jesus, we *"will by no means be put to shame"* (Isa. 44:11; 1 Pet. 2:6). **It is the real Jesus who sets captives free, saves, and protects.**

Ge DeRe asked me to read aloud Isaiah 54 at a charismatic prayer meeting in 1987. There was such a strong anointing on it that I wept as I read it. God is so good!!! It includes:

> *Do not fear, for you will not be ashamed;*
> *Neither be disgraced, for you will not be put to shame;*
> *For you will forget the shame of your youth,*
> *And will not remember the reproach of your widowhood anymore.*
> *For your Maker is your husband.* (Isa. 54:4–5)

I am so grateful that Jesus is alive and I am forgiven, and my people can be too.

I left the Roman Catholic Church on November 25, 1994, the first time (although I went back later hoping to draw out my people from Babylon). Around 1995, during the three and a half years I was seeking confirmation from God, I had asked a prophetess at Kingdom Seed Fellowship, a stranger to me but not to them, to seek God on my behalf. However, I purposely did not tell her what for. She had a vision of me coming out of a house with a glass veranda. When I asked the Lord what it meant, He told me, *"Those who remain in her will be put to shame."* This too was confirmation to me that I was on the right path in those days.

My people had not realized that praying to someone was a form of worship, of idolizing a holy person, and that putting your trust in idols can lead to being put to shame. I came out of the house the "Lady" built to enter the one built by God alone, and shared what I was learning with those whom I could. **The *"one thing"* that I desire, as David did,** is to *"dwell in the house of the LORD all the days of my life, to behold the beauty of the LORD, and to inquire in His temple"* (Ps. 27:4).

Those who bow their knees to gods of silver and gold, etc., praying to what they represent, can become weak in the knees. I had determined not to pray anymore as if I were talking to a statue when the Lord gave *"Isaiah 44"* in 1981. But when I realized that asking Mary to intercede, to pray to God for me even in Jesus's name, was also forbidden and bowing to an idol—**then I knew that I was no better than my ancestors.** So I had to fight discouragement and depression. **But the Lord delivered me from that, strengthening me with His Word** as He led me to confirming Scriptures.

On Mount Carmel, **Elijah asked the priests of Baal who had weak knees from idolatry, how long they would go limping about the altar to their false god**: *"And Elijah came to all the people, and said, 'How long will you falter between two opinions? If the LORD is God, follow*

Him; but if Baal, follow him'" (1 Kgs. 18:21). Today we could say, *"How long will you falter between two opinions? If the* LORD *is God, follow Him; but if Baal ["the Lady of kingdoms"], follow* [her]*."*

God does not want a mixture in our worship.

It is good to seek an undivided heart to pray to and serve (worship) God alone. He enabled me to stop praying the rosary that night in 1994, proved His Word over three and a half years, and He can enable my people to stop and go right to the Source of all Power and Grace in the name of His Son. We have only to trust and obey Jesus.

The "Lady" is full of robbery, lies, and all wickedness: *"BABYLON THE GREAT, THE MOTHER OF HARLOTS AND OF THE ABOMINATIONS OF THE EARTH,"* is pictured as *"a woman sitting on a scarlet beast which is full of names of blasphemy, having seven heads and ten horns.… [*She was wearing] *purple and scarlet, and adorned with gold and precious stones and pearls, having in her hand a golden cup full of abominations and the filthiness of her fornication.…* [She was] *drunk with the blood of the saints and with the martyrs of Jesus"* (Rev. 17:3–5). At first this counterfeit looks good, but she is carried by an antichrist beast, robs God of the glory due His name, and deceives people with her religious *"doctrines of demons"* and kills saints.

People joined to Lady Babylon, joining in on her sins, can take part in her plagues, **so God mercifully has been calling His family out.**

The Babylonian bridge, called the "Lady" of this and of that, *"the Lady of Kingdoms,"* **who we thought was Mary, has been shown to be a mirage, a counterfeit of the real thing. The "Lady" tries to get Roman Catholic priests and people to become parts of her body, her bridge, as her children, not realizing they are becoming parts of the unholy city.**

I, too, was fooled at first by the inner locutions a priest was having who heard a female voice speaking to him who we called, "Our Lady," but who the Lord called, *"Illusion! Illusion! Illusion!"*

Through some of her false prophets, the "Lady" even claimed that she alone can save us—**a lie from the pit of hell.** No wonder the Lord told me to *"repudiate the consecration!"* and to *"come out of her."* **Jesus alone is our Saviour, the spotless Lamb who was slain for the forgiveness of sins.**

Ruth sought to be covered by Boaz as a pledge that he would be her kinsman redeemer. A husband covers his wife if she remains under it. Jesus is also like a very long covered bridge since one of His names is Yahweh Nissi, or Jehovah Nissi, *"The Lord is my banner"* (Ex. 17:15). The Lord is showing us His bridge, the one way to the Father, that His people may be covered as His body parts, that they may repent and not be put to shame any more. Many times in the mid- and late nineties, the Lord sang over me, encouraging me, and I sang it back to Him:

> *"He takes me to His banqueting table. His banner over me is love.*
> *I'm my Beloved's and He is mine. His banner over me is love.*
> *His banner over me, His banner over you,*
> *His banner over us is love, love, love."*

I remember one time especially that He piped that song to me when I attended the outdoor wedding of two friends, Mike and Vicky, who were married under a wedding canopy in a hilltop garden. My husband had gone to visit family in Italy and had refused to take me with him, but our eternal Bridegroom, Jesus, lifted me out of sadness as I rejoiced that I had suffered that type of persecution. His amazing love can cover us like a Jewish wedding canopy or prayer shawl, or like feathers of a great eagle.

> *Behold, I lay in Zion a chief cornerstone, elect, precious,*
> *And he who believes on Him will by no means be put to shame.*
> (1 Peter 2:6)

When John was shown the sixth bowl judgment with demonic spirits coming to kings to perform signs to gather them at Armageddon, Jesus warned that He too was coming suddenly: *"Behold, I am coming as a thief. Blessed is he who watches, and keeps his garments, lest he walk naked and they see his shame"* (Rev. 16:15).

I remember around the year 2000 how moved I was when my cousin parked her car at a restaurant beside a Florida Holocaust museum. In front of her car we saw w a statue of a few naked Holocaust victims huddled in a row, waiting. Mom and I stayed at my cousin's house and I wept softly all night long remembering not only the Jews, His first chosen people, most of whom had not listened to His voice, but also some Catholic chosen people who had rejected the warning, turned from His commandments, and been put to shame recently too. **How I wanted this humiliation to end! When we humble ourselves before Him, it can end.**

God does not want us to be humiliated with *"Babylon."* Those who trust and obey the Lord need not take part in her humiliation. Jesus truly is the world's longest bridge connecting God and mankind, and the only one we need, God's promised Coming One.

Food Offered to Idols

Mary is a model for discipleship in the Bible. She and Jesus's brothers were even present in the upper room at Pentecost (see Acts 1:14), **but she is not the "Mediatrix"** as the Catholic Catechism states saying, "The Blessed virgin is invoked in the Church under the titles of Advocate, Helper, Benefactress, and Mediatrix."[9] God's chosen Mediator is not Mary or the "Lady!" Jesus and the Holy Spirit fulfill those roles of Advocate, Helper, Benefactor, and Mediator. It is written, *"For*

---

9   *Catechism of the Catholic Church* (Ottawa: Publications Service, CCCB, 1994) Article 969, p. 208

there is one God and one Mediator between God and men, the Man Christ Jesus" (1 Tim. 2:5).

It is interesting that the Lord revealed to me that my daughter's little **Marian Prayer Book was *"food offered to idols,"* and told me, *"Destroy it."*** (So, I burned it and bought her another book instead.) It had been full of beautiful sounding prayers, but they were through the intercession of Mary, with a litany to the saints, treating them like idols, praising them and calling on them to pray for us. The Word of God is "bread" and "meat" and **these prayers were food too, but *"food offered to idols,"* with praise offered to saints who had been made into idols instead of praise going directly to God through Jesus with the glory going to Him.**

We are not supposed to be joined to the body of an idol. We are not to be *"unequally yoked.… And what agreement has the temple of God with idols? For you are the temple of the living God"* (2 Cor. 6:14, 16). That is why I discourage Protestants from marrying practicing Catholics until they *"come out of her."* As Jesus warned the church at Pergamos, *"I have a few things against you, because you have those who hold the doctrine of Balaam, who taught Balak to put a stumbling block before the children of Israel, to eat things sacrificed to idols, and to commit sexual immorality"* (Rev. 2:14).

> *They joined themselves also to Baal of Peor,*
> *And ate sacrifices made to the dead.*
> *Thus they provoked Him to anger with their deeds,*
> *And the plague broke out among them.*
> *Then Phinehas stood up and intervened,*
> *And the plague was stopped.*
> *And that was accounted to him for righteousness.* (Ps. 106:28–31)

Jesus sent warning *"to the angel of the church in Thyatira"* (Rev. 2:18) not to tolerate the influence of the Jezebel spirit either. It can result in sickness or death of His servants who are seduced into sexual immorality and eating food offered to idols. God's people are to be led by

His Holy Spirit, not a false spirit of religion. Around 1996, the Lord also gave that word to a local Protestant prayer group of which I was a part; so I asked Him how I was tolerating the Jezebel spirit. Step by step, He helped me see some more Catholic traditions that were not good.

The Jezebel spirit, so prevalent in the world, is a religious spirit and can seduce people into idolatry, putting self or false gods before the one true God, and believing it is alright to commit sexual immorality, including sex outside of marriage with the same or opposite sex, adultery, and rape of little ones. It might start with a thought, a suggestion to the mind which is entertained. So, one may begin by pornography, sexy dressing, or approving of others who commit sexual sin, and then can progress to taking part oneself in spiritual and/or sexual immorality. Jesus taught, *"You have heard that it was said to those of old, 'You shall not commit adultery.' But I say to you that whoever looks at a woman to lust for her has already committed adultery with her in his heart"* (Matt. 5:27–28).

Sadly and tragically, many religious people have been accused even of rape or sodomizing young girls and boys. They have been put to shame worldwide and little ones have suffered or died.

But Jesus can help us to resist temptation and be overcomers if we serve Him alone. He will help people shift their focus. Some Christians are saying like Job, *"I have made a covenant with my eyes; why then should I look* [intently or gaze] *upon a young woman?"* (Job 31:1).

Only Jesus Is Worthy

Over the years, her devotees have made Mary more than she is and I, too, was deceived years ago. A fable arose that Mary never ever committed sin and that she was conceived without even the stain of original sin from Adam and Eve. This misconception came from the false apparition which called herself, "I am the Immaculate Conception." But Jesus, being God, is the only one who stayed immaculate, holy, all His life on earth. He resisted all temptation and had no stain of sin lifelong. "[Jesus] *was in all points tempted as we are, yet without sin*" (Heb. 4:15). For the rest of us human beings:*As it is written:*

> *"There is none righteous, no, not one;*
> *There is none who understands;*
> *There is none who seeks after God.*
> *They have all turned aside;*
> *They have together become unprofitable;*
> *There is none who does good, no, not one."* (Rom. 3:10–12)

Because of man's fallen condition, we needed a model as well as a Saviour. So the Father gave Jesus, not Mary, as the spotless Lamb of God, most pure and perfectly sinless. At a Kingston, Ontario, Aglow meeting around 2000, when the Sniders were singing, the Lord magnified to me:

"Only He Is Worthy!"

We had thought Mary was worthy. But who is worthy to open the scroll and release judgments before the throne of God? Only Jesus. Yet He humbled Himself to be born in a smelly stable, to bear our sin upon Himself on the cross and to plant His Word in our hearts even if areas of it were not clean yet. *"Your word I have hidden in my heart that I might not sin against You"* (Ps. 119:11). Since He was born in a smelly stable, surely He could have been born in a virgin who tried to do right but who fell short of God's glory occasionally!

John saw the vision of the scroll in the hand of the Father and *"saw a strong angel proclaiming with a loud voice, 'Who is worthy to open the scroll and to loose its seals?' And no one in heaven or on earth or under the earth was able to open the scroll or to look at it. So I wept much, because no one was found worthy to open the scroll or to look at it. But one of the elders said to me, 'Do not weep. Behold, the Lion of the tribe of Judah, the Root of David, has prevailed, to open the scroll and to loose its seven seals'"* (Rev. 5:2–5).

Only Jesus was found worthy. But no saint, alive or dead was found worthy, not even Mary, even though they did what they could to obey God and to purify their hearts. She acknowledged her need of a *"Saviour"* in her Magnificat, and if Mary had been without sin all her life, Saint Paul, who lived at the same time as her, would have made an exception when he wrote, *"But now the righteousness of God apart from the law is revealed … through faith in Jesus Christ, to all and on all who believe. For there is no difference; for all have sinned and fall short of the glory of God, being justified freely by His grace through the redemption that is in Christ Jesus"* (Rom. 3:21–24). But he knew that Jesus was the eternal Passover Lamb, the perfect offering who brought redemption. Saint Peter, knowing that Jesus was spotless, wrote, *"Knowing that you were not redeemed with corruptible things, like silver or gold, from your aimless conduct received by tradition from your fathers, but with the precious blood of Christ, as of a lamb without blemish and without spot"* (1 Pet. 1:18–19).

Only Jesus was and is completely righteous all the time. He never fell short of God's glory. He did no dead works, only live ones, only what He saw the Father doing. His experience with sin was when He bore our sin, having none of His own. In John's vision of heaven, he records:

> *Now when* [Jesus] *had taken the scroll, the four living creatures and the twenty-four elders fell down before the Lamb, each having a harp, and golden bowls full of incense, which are the prayers of the saints. And they sang a new song, saying:*
>
> *"You are worthy to take the scroll,*
> *And to open its seals;*
> *For You were slain,*
> *And have redeemed us to God by Your blood."* (Rev. 5:8–10)

He is so holy, He prevailed against evil to the death, was slain, and by His blood ransomed people for God *"out of every tribe and tongue and people and nation, and have made us kings and priests to our God; and we shall reign on earth"* (Rev. 5:9–10).

> *You are My witnesses. Is there a God besides Me?*
> *Indeed, there is no other Rock;*
> *I know not one.* (Isa. 44:8)

From Where Did Devotions to Immaculate Heart of Mary and Sacred Heart of Jesus Come?

In about 1996, when I asked the Lord about the consecrations we had been making to the so-called "Immaculate Heart of Mary," He surprised me by telling me, **"Repudiate the consecration,"** and when I asked Him what that meant, I heard, **"Come out of her."**

I also looked up "repudiate" in the dictionary; it meant, "Dis-vow or divorce," and I said to myself, "These are strong words!"

I was shocked to see that union with her was like joining to a prostitute because we had thought "Our Lady" was Mary. *"Come out of her,"* was also part of the word the Lord had given in regards to the Good Friday veneration of the crucifix, referring to coming out of *"BABYLON THE GREAT, THE MOTHER OF HARLOTS AND OF THE ABOMINATIONS OF THE EARTH"* (Rev. 17:5; 18:4). The "Lady" is not the real Mary but Lady Babylon disguised as Mary—a counterfeit.

I thought I remembered that devotions to the "Sacred Heart of Jesus" and "Immaculate Heart of Mary" were received by a woman who heard a voice reply when she had been praying through a statue of Mary, a graven image. A few days later, the Lord confirmed this when I watched a video of a Mother Angelica program with my mom. So, the instruction the woman heard would have been *"doctrines of demons,"* not from God but from a demonic female-sounding spirit.

> *Now the* [Holy] *Spirit expressly says that in latter times some will depart from the faith, giving heed to deceiving spirits and doctrines of demons, speaking lies in hypocrisy,*
>
> *having their own conscience seared with a hot iron, forbidding to marry, and commanding to abstain from foods which God created to be received with thanksgiving by those who believe and know the truth.* (1 Tim. 4:1–3)

The Roman Catholic Church sometimes commanded us not to eat meat on Fridays and I looked in a booklet I had had from childhood about the story of Fatima and read that the "Lady" who appeared there also promoted these devotions to the "Sacred Hearts." Consecrations to these "Hearts" were also received by the children who knelt and prayed to the "Lady" of Medjugorje, another false apparition of *"the Lady of kingdoms"* (Isa. 47:5). Then I remembered the Lord had said that the apparitions of a "Lady" in these places were *"Illusion! Illusion! Illusion!"* Satan is the father of lies (see John 8:44), and his fallen angels, evil spirits, corrupting demons, can be disguised as something that appears good on the surface.

The Lord had previously taught me in 1981 not to pray through the **images** of those hearts, and that Jesus saves (see Isaiah 44). Now I was beginning to understand that Jesus, not Jesus and Mary, is the only one who was sinless all His life long, the spotless Lamb of God.

The Sacred Heart image had a crown of thorns around the pierced heart, with fire reminding me of His passionate love for us and yellow around it reminding of the glory of God. Since I wondered what His heart was really like, I asked the Lord if we could pray a consecration to the real heart of Jesus. So, He told me to *"remove the thorns."*

Then I remembered I had prayed in the past for people to have a heart like the Sacred Heart image, thinking it was Jesus's true heart today. So I prayed for all those whom I had prayed for in the past, that thorns would be removed from around their hearts. (Words and actions of people are like thorns sometimes.) I also removed crowns of thorns on banners I had made, from around any heart images I had used trying to illustrate the love of Christ.

For some banners, the Lord had given me both the words and a faint picture in my head of how I could illustrate them. For others, I had only heard the words and had used traditional illustrations. **I began to realize how important it is to seek the Lord rather than just use traditional symbols to illustrate banners and in other Christian artwork, unless the Lord approves of them.**

I also remembered that some months earlier, a pastor had had a vision of me as being like a four-year-old clinging to the wrong heart of Jesus, and I began to understand what God meant. I had prayed consecrations to those hearts many times. I felt like the woman at the well who had had five husbands (the saints had been like husbands to me spiritually), to whom Jesus said, *"…and the one you now have is not your husband"* (John 4:18). Thank God for His saving grace.

That very night **I repudiated the consecrations I had made to both "Hearts,"** including consecrations of myself, family, country, and nation(s). When I asked God how to be consecrated properly to Him, the Holy Spirit reminded me of the huge banner I had been asked to make proclaiming the theme of the 1987 Kingston, Ontario, Catholic charismatic conference at the Community Memorial Centre: *"Be consecrated in the truth."*

I think it also had a hand holding a Bible. So, I looked up John 17. The night before He died, Jesus prayed the Father, *"Sanctify* [consecrate, set apart] *them by Your truth. Your word is truth. As You sent Me into the world, I also have sent them into the world. And for their sakes I sanctify Myself, that they also may be sanctified* [consecrated] *by the truth"* (John 17:17–19). So that is what I did. **I consecrated myself in the truth of the Word of God.** We are to sanctify ourselves, letting God wash us with His Word, blood, and Spirit. Jesus, the living *"Word of God,"* is also *"the truth."* Therefore, I prayed that my family, church, and nation(s) may be consecrated in the truth of His Word instead.

May we love Him as His adopted children, saints on earth, and do *"the righteous acts of the saints"* (Rev. 19:8) in Jesus's name.

Then that same night I decided to look more closely at the wording of the consecrations to the two "Hearts" from the "Lady" of Medjugorje that we had been praying at charismatic meetings. In response to His word, **having repudiated the old consecrations, it was like a veil had been lifted off my eyes. I could finally see how deceiving the wording had been.** Now I could see clearly that the Deceiver, the Counterfeiter, the father of lies was behind them. God loves us too much to keep us in darkness if we will come out. In our ignorance at our Catholic charismatic prayer meetings, we had not only been lifting up the name of Jesus, but we had also been praying those two consecrations, so I had these deceptive words on paper. I tore them up and burned them, and told the leadership. But as the Lord had forewarned me, they would not listen at that time, and with the continued split focus, the anointing decreased there, and sadly, most of the leaders have now died.

I have learned that when Jesus gives a word, even if it is not understood fully, that it is trustworthy. Our battle is not *"against flesh and blood, but against principalities, against powers, against the rulers of the darkness of this age, against spiritual hosts of wickedness in the heavenly places. Therefore, take up the whole armor of God, that you may be able to withstand in the evil day, and having done all, to stand"* (Eph. 6:12–13).

We are to worship the Father *"in spirit and truth,"* love and adore the real Jesus, honouring the memory of the real Mary and saints who have died, praising God for what He did through them, believing God's real plan for salvation. **The apparitions of the "Lady" gave a false peace plan which did not take into account what Jesus accomplished at the cross, nor that He always lives to do an ongoing work of saving us at the Father's right hand.**

We had not realized that the counterfeit Mary, **the "Lady" falsely claiming to be the one to save us and mediate for us, was actually the**

harlot bride, *"the Lady of kingdoms"* (Isa. 47:5), Lady Babylon. **Surely we do not want to be part of her, but rather part of the body of Christ, His bride that is consecrated in the truth!**

We can pray:

- **May the Lord give us clean hands and pure hearts.**
- **May we not lift our soul to an idol.**
- **May God help to us be the generation that seeks His face (based on Ps. 24).**
- **Dear Father of the Lord Jesus Christ, forgive us and our ancestors for being part of the body of the** *"Lady of kingdoms,"* **Lady Babylon, the fallen bridge.**
- **We repudiate any consecration to her and cry out to be consecrated in the truth of God's Word instead. Thank You for Your redeeming blood.**
- **May we be part of the one true bridge alone, the body of Christ, forever.**

Jesus the True Bridge Is, and Is Upbuilt on, a Sure Foundation

During those three and a half years I was testing the word, *"They are dead. Do not contact them,"* I attended a 1997 Catholic charismatic conference in Kingston, Ontario, at Regiopolis-Notre Dame High School. My mother and son were there the last night and the Lord gave me a prophetic song to sing out with words similar to "Jesus, Lover of My Soul", an Australian Hillsong Worship song, including:

Jesus, lover of my soul,
Jesus, I will never let You go.
You have taken me from the miry clay.
and set my feet upon the Rock this day.

I love You,
I need You.
Though my world may fall
I'll never let You go.
My Saviour, my closest Friend,
I will worship You until the very end.

I do not seek signs now except the **signs following the preaching of the Word** (see Mark 16:20). There was a sign following this word: As I left the building to get the car so I could drive the others home, it was pouring rain. I had to climb up a slippery, muddy slope which was dimly lit to get to the upper-level parking lot. When I got to the top of the hill, there was solid pavement to walk on and more light, thanks be to God. And in the Spirit, since the Lord had been shaking my whole belief system, the Lord also took me from the miry clay of fused-nugget, sandstone beliefs and set my feet upon the Rock, the solid foundation of Jesus Christ and the scriptural Word of God. I remembered that a minister had prophesied that God was sifting all my belief systems, Catholic and Protestant. What I used to stand on had largely fallen away so I could stand on the truth of Christ alone: *For no other foundation can anyone lay than that which is laid, which is Jesus Christ.* (1 Cor. 3:11)

But let each one take heed how he builds on it. (1 Cor. 3:10)

The foundation of repentance from dead works and of faith toward God, of the doctrine of baptisms, of laying on of hands, of resurrection of the dead, and of eternal judgment. (Heb. 6:1–2)

The apostles' and prophets' teaching is grounded on this: *"Now, therefore, you are no longer strangers and foreigners, but fellow citizens with the saints and members of the household of God, having been built on the foundation of the apostles and prophets, Jesus Christ Himself being the chief cornerstone"* (Eph. 2:19–20).

Chapter 12
Jesus Claims to Be the Only Bridge

January 7, 1998, my confidence was still being shaken a little when I met with Catholics because of war on the battlefield of my mind. Although I had abandoned the rosary and other ungodly traditions of which I was aware, I wanted something concrete to say to them about not praying the "Hail Mary." I journaled that I had asked the Lord for a *rhema* word to confirm to me without a doubt that my understanding was correct—that we are not even to call upon Mary for intercession, as in the "Hail Mary." I forgot and asked the Lord again and God is so gracious that both times He replied,

> *"I am the way, the truth, and the life.*
> *No one goes to the Father but by Me"*

Not only is praying the rosary taking time and glory away from worshiping God, but it is a mixture of prayers, some good and some not. I realized that even though the first half of the "Hail Mary" is based on Scripture, it is used incorrectly, because it is praying Scripture to a saint who has died. (The devil likes to twist Scripture or use it out of context.) Jesus, too, had died, but He was resurrected and ascended into heaven in His glorified body.

I also had journaled another word I had discovered: *"Jesus always lives to make intercession for us"* (Heb. 7:25). Then Protestant ministers asked me to make a banner proclaiming the first half of that John 14:6 Scripture for their ministry to seniors and later gave me stewardship of the banner.

Interestingly, I heard Benny Hinn say in a video that *"the way, the truth, and the life"* are the names the Jews called the three doors into the presence of God in the wilderness tabernacle God instructed Moses to make. *"The way"* was the name for the only door into the outer court. *"The truth"* was the name of the doorway into the Holy Place where only priests could go, and *"the life"* was the name of the way into the Holy of holies where only the High Priest could go. God would meet with him as His presence came over the mercy seat above the ark of the covenant.

These pointed to Jesus as the only way into the Father's presence. He is also the twelve pearly gates into the holy city of God, New Jerusalem, today and tomorrow where *"the tabernacle of God is with men, and He will dwell with them, and they shall be His people. God Himself will be with them and be their God"* (Rev. 22:3). Interestingly, Jesus, our bridge to the Father, said: *"I am the door. If anyone enters by Me, he will be saved, and will go in and out and find pasture"* (John 10:9).

On the banner, I made three panels using the colours of the veil which was the way in to the Holy of holies. *"You shall make a veil woven of blue, purple, and scarlet thread, and fine woven linen.... The veil shall be a divider for you between the Holy Place and the Most Holy"* (Ex. 26:31, 33). Thank God, that is the veil which was torn from above at the crucifixion, signifying for believers that God had opened the way into His presence by the obedience of His Son, Jesus. It was too high and too heavy to have been torn by men. By His death and resurrection, He is alive forevermore, and by faith, we can be too and can enter into His presence.

The Lord pulled me out of the miry clay step by step with every new Scripture to which He led me as He began to solidify the truth in me. They were rocks to climb on and His Spirit was refreshing. Believing in **Jesus,** *"the Way,"* that He is who God says He is, **we enter the first door into the outer court of God's presence, having Jesus with us.** We experience His loving shepherding on our lives as recorded in Psalm 23 and John 10. He even carries us on the way, leading by serving, protecting and providing for us. Purple reminds me of suffering and kingship.

I remember a time when the Lord kept piping to me the song, *"Better is one day in Your courts than thousands elsewhere."* This reminded me of:

> *For a day in Your courts is better than a thousand.*
> *I would rather be a doorkeeper in the house of my God*
> *Than dwell in the tents of wickedness.* (Ps. 84:10)

At that time, Jesus led me from the Catholic church where I had gone back hoping to be a light (which years before had been a strong charismatic church), and going to a second service at a Spirit-filled Protestant church, to full time at the second church. We are to follow the Good Shepherd-King, trusting in Him to lead us to the Father by still waters, restoring our soul and letting us experience His goodness and mercy. He moves His shepherds around, and sometimes He moves His sheep to a different pasture. The best thing is to be where the Owner of the sheep wants you, content to be where He wants you to be fed and to serve. He will discipline and protect you there. This is preparation for the second door.

Jesus is also the second door, *"the Truth,"* the entrance into the first room of the tabernacle sanctuary, the Holy Place, **which only priests could enter.** Those who have received His love and washing from their sins in His own blood will see that He has made them *"a chosen generation, a royal priesthood, a holy nation, His own special people, that you may proclaim the praises of Him who called you out of darkness into His marvelous light"* (1 Pet. 2:9).

Blue is also a royal colour and reminds of revelation. Illustrating *"the Truth,"* I recalled when I was baptized with the Holy Spirit, and I saw a vision of whirling white light that ended in the shape of a dove, and heard the word, *"Fear not, for I am with you always."* Jesus reminded His apostles that the *"Promise of the Father"* (Luke 24:49), **"the Spirit of truth," was coming—God's presence within us.** *"However, when He, the Spirit of truth, has come, He will guide you into all truth: for He will not speak on His own authority, but whatever He hears He will speak; and He will tell you things to come"* (John 16:13). So I pictured a dove and wind-blown white light symbolizing Jesus's *"Spirit of truth"* and seven tongues of fire remembering the seven spirits of God (see Isa. 11:2) enabling us to live life in the Spirit with powerful revelation from the Most High.

The Father has always cared about His people, but now He has more help doing it, *"another Helper"* (John 14:16). At Pentecost, the faithful were **baptized with the Spirit and fire**, visible as *"divided tongues, as of fire"* (Acts 2:3). God's refining love drove fear out of them, enabling them to testify of Jesus and do signs and wonders in His name. His Spirit of *"truth"* comes today baptizing us with fire and the Spirit as He leads us into all truth, empowering us to be and do what God has designed for us.

The Holy Spirit can come upon us with fire and His many gifts, refining and empowering us, and He can guide us into service as members of Jesus's *"royal priesthood"* (1 Pet. 2:9), who know the truth which will set us free. **There is one God with three divine Persons. There is one Holy Spirit with seven Spirits of God. Living within us, He empowers us to follow Jesus for the good of all, and He produces His fruit to feed others.** Revelation speaks of *"seven Spirits of God"* (Rev. 4:5; 5:6), which are like lamps of fire burning before God's throne as well as like horns and eyes of the Lamb.

"Then Jesus said to them again, 'Most assuredly, I say to you, I am the door of the sheep'" (John 10:7). Going through the second door enables us now to go through **the third door,** *"the Life,"* its veil having been opened to us at the crucifixion. Jesus came *"that they may have life and that they may have it more abundantly"* (John 10:10). The Most Holy Place is the inmost room where we encounter the presence of God, corresponding to our heart and the throne room of heaven.

Not only is Jesus within us, but we are within Him, and we can remain so. Otherwise we may be in trouble. Jesus said, *"I am the vine, you are the branches. He who abides in Me, and I in him, bears much fruit; for without Me you can do nothing. If anyone does not abide in Me, he is cast out as a branch and is withered; and they gather them and throw them into the fire, and they are burned. If you abide in Me, and My words abide in you, you will ask what you desire, and it shall be done for you. By this My Father is glorified, that you bear much fruit; so you will be My disciples"* (John 15:5–8).

> *He who dwells in the secret place of the Most High*
> *Shall abide under the shadow of the Almighty.*
> *I will say of the* LORD, *"He is my refuge and my fortress;*
> *My God, in Him will I trust."*
> *Surely He shall deliver you from the snare of the fowler*
> *And from the perilous pestilence.*
> *He shall cover you with His feathers,*
> *and under His wings you shall take refuge;*

> *His truth* [faithfulness] *shall be your shield and buckler....*
> *Because he has set his love upon Me, therefore I will deliver him.*
> (Ps. 91:1–4, 14)

Just as the blood of animals was sacrificed outside the Holy Place in the outer court of the old tabernacle and then brought into the Most Holy Place, so the blood of Jesus was already sacrificed on the altar of the cross and has been brought in to the real heavenly tabernacle in atonement for us so that we can have life: *"For the life of the flesh is in the blood, and I have given it to you upon the altar to make atonement for your souls; for it is the blood that makes atonement for the soul"* (Lev. 17:11).

Believing in Jesus's saving work on the cross, our High Priest bridge, and having been baptized into His death and resurrection, we enter into new life in Christ. If we give Him the reins to our chariot letting Him be Lord, we will both enter into God's rest and do what He inspires us to do. *"For as the body without the spirit is dead, so faith without works is dead also"* (Jas. 2:26). And in John 1:4, we read, *"In Him was life, and the life was the light of men." "If anyone desires to come after Me, let him deny himself, and take up his cross and follow Me. For whoever desires to save his life will lose it, but whoever loses his life for My sake will find it. For what profit is it to a man if he gains the whole world, and loses his own soul? Or what will a man give in exchange for his soul? For the Son of Man will come in the glory of His Father with His angels, and then He will reward each according to his works.* (Matt. 16:24–27)

John 1:3–5 says, *"All things were made through Him, and without Him nothing was made that was made. In Him was life, and the life was the light of men. And the light shines in the darkness, and the darkness did not comprehend it."* Jesus, *"the life,"* lay down His life as the bridge, accepting Simon's help, just as we should accept His in carrying our cross and laying down our life in love for our friends. Yoked to Jesus, we will find rest. Instead of doing just any and all works, we will seek the ones He has prepared for us and leave others for other parts of His body.

Believing in His name, as parts of His body, we have eternal life and can go deeper through Jesus into the presence of God, washed in water and His loving blood. Perhaps going through the gate could be compared to going through a carwash. Instead of sealing it all with wax, we are sealed with the anointing oil of Holy Spirit.

All our sins and accusations against us were washed off Jesus and left behind Him at the cross; so He took up His life again on the third day and His resurrection power can be real in us too. **Even if we encounter persecution and death for His sake, He will give believers everlasting life in Christ.**

In Old Testament times, prophets went right to the Father with belief in the Coming One, the Messiah. Jesus said, *"No one can come to Me unless the Father who sent Me draws him; and I will raise him up at the last day. It is written in the prophets, 'And they shall all be taught by God.' Therefore everyone who has heard and learned from the Father comes to Me"* (John 6:44–45). David even prophesied by the Father and the Son (see Psalm 2). And now, as Jesus said, *"No one comes to the Father except through Me"* (John 14:6). That includes the ones who had died in faith during Old Testament times who were led by Him to the Father and new life after Jesus's resurrection. Jesus is the way in and is interceding for us, forever in the Father's presence. Hallelujah! He wants His people to enter in too.

There Are Not Two Gods

Thank God, the word was made surer by the end of the three and a half years of feeling like I was pinned down on a cross with Jesus, experiencing verbal persecution and exclusion. Having experienced a baptism of fire into His death and resurrection, I also attempted to put to death in myself anything that was not of God, and to warn others.

> *Knowing this, that our old man was crucified with Him, that the body of sin might be done away with, that we should no longer be slaves of sin.... Therefore do not let sin reign in your mortal body,*

> *that you should obey it in its lusts. And do not present your members as instruments of unrighteousness to sin, but present yourselves to God as being alive from the dead, and your members as instruments of righteousness to God. For sin shall not have dominion over you, for you are not under law but under grace.* (Rom. 6:6, 12–14)

Jesus died for our sin so we can walk in newness of life in Him, even if that includes some persecution. With Him we can also be overcomers.

If we disobey traffic laws and plead ignorance, we still might get a fine and even demerit points unless the authorities are merciful. Likewise, we are not to present our body parts to the "Lady," unknowingly making them *"instruments of unrighteousness to sin,"* otherwise we deserve chastisement, unless the Lord is merciful. Instead, I prefer to counsel people to present themselves entirely to God as I was now doing, asking Jesus to have dominion over them, to be their *"Lord,"* and we **His** body parts to do His will. **I came out of her, thanks be to God, and others have and will too.** We are not meant to be both part of the body of *"Christ"* and part of the body of the "Lady." That would be like having two spouses or one spouse and an adulterous affair.

I knew I was finally standing on solid rock and could withstand shaking after a stranger from Toronto prophesied at a citywide intercessory prayer meeting at Kingdom Seed Fellowship. She had a prophecy in tongues with weeping on February 18, 1998. I asked the Father to give us the translation and it came through someone else, again with weeping, confirming all that God was doing in my life. I thank God for His longsuffering with us when we are slow learners. The translation was taped and transcribed:

> *You cannot have a mixed loyalty.*
> *I called out to Ahab and I said,*
> *"You cannot worship Me and you cannot worship Baal."*
> *I called out to Obadiah and I said,*
> *"You cannot worship Me and you cannot worship Baal."*

> *I told you again and again and again that Baal is nothing,*
> *And I have proved My word every single time.*
> *Hear My cry, people! Hear My cry to you!*
> *You cannot serve two Gods. There can be nothing before Me.*

Just as we cannot worship both God and Mammon, God has been teaching His people for centuries that **we cannot serve God plus anyone or anything else**. That is like worshiping Baal too. God chastised His people when they tried to do that.

> *Did you offer Me sacrifices and offerings*
> *In the wilderness forty years, O house of Israel?*
> *You also carried Sikkuth* [tabernacle of Molech] *your king*
> *And Chiun, your idols,*
> *The star of your gods,*
> *Which you made for yourselves.*
> *Therefore I will send you into captivity.* (Amos 5:25–27)

Then I remembered how it is written:

> *Besides Me there is no God....*
> *You are My witnesses.*
> *Is there a God besides Me?*
> *Indeed there is no other Rock;*
> *I know not one.* (Isa. 44:6, 8)

My vision was now clear to see that it was like trying to worship two Gods when I used to ask both Jesus and her to "pray for us sinners," to be our Mediator. **I had been taught that we only have one, not two Gods, but now I realized that praying to her was treating her <u>as if</u> she were another God.** A saint can be a small "g" "god" in the sense that *"He called them gods, to whom the word of God came"* (John 10:35), but gods are not supposed to be worshiped.

For years I had been wrongly taught by misinformed RC teachers that we could have two or more mediators, Protestants using one, and Catholics using many, but now God had reinforced the truth to me that **Jesus alone is the** *"one Mediator between God and men"* (1 Tim. 2:5).

Whose body are we called to be parts of? We should not serve other gods besides the one, true God. That means that we are not to pray to other saints either, asking them for favours, counsel, or to pray for us. That would be treating them as if they were another God, another rock, another mediator, another bridge to the Father. **But God chose only one, His Son and Messiah**. No wonder He had warned me, *"Do not be deceived"!* That had started me on my journey of seeking, "Am I being deceived? And if so, how?" Although I did not think to ask God that question directly, I noticed later that I had recorded in my old Bible that the Lord had actually given me 1 Timothy 2:5–7 back on July 21, 1987! It included, *"For there is one God and one Mediator between God and men, the Man Christ Jesus."*

I was so thankful that the Lord gave me understanding of that verse. Yet I am sad to say that **it took years for me to finally "get it"** and until February 18, 1998 for the truth of that word to solidify in me. So the Lord reminded me years ago to have patience with the RC Church. He opened my eyes to this, and I trust He will remove the veil and open theirs as well. **Sometimes it helps to "chew" or meditate on God's Word, repeating it many times to establish it in our heart.**

In 2007, after having some dreams of turning on a light switch, I asked God to turn on the light for them too, and the Lord reminded me that He had turned on the light switch by sending me to priests and bishops, but it was as if someone kept flicking off the light switch again because they did not believe me. May God forgive them. We have to *"trust Jesus."*

God said in the first commandment, *"I am the Lord your God.... You shall have no other gods before Me"* (Ex. 20:2–3). **No one is His equal. Who have we in heaven that is an awesome God like Him?**

And it was God Himself who chose Jesus to be our one Mediator and Advocate with Him, the eternal High Priest in the order

of Melchizedek: *"The LORD has sworn and will not relent, 'You are a priest forever according to the order of Melchizedek'"* (Ps. 110:4).

Before I received this revelation, I remember in early 1994 being at a Holy Spirit-filled service in Belleville, and my eyes began to well up with tears when we sang, *"As the deer panteth for the water, my soul longs after You. You alone are my heart's desire and I long to worship you."*[10] **Perplexed, I had asked the Lord why I was crying since I thought I worshiped Him every day. However, I was also praying the rosary daily since this was before I realized we should not do that.**  Shortly afterward, months before the November '94 experience, I went to the Toronto Airport church and it was prophesied over me, *"Strengthen weak knees. Lift drooping arms,"* and I experienced a manifestation of that word. My arms shot straight up into the air and were stuck like that for many minutes. I could not bring them down until the Lord released them.

Over time, I realized that praying to saints is like worship and the Lord wanted all my worship. I was to call only on His name, and on no other. Praying the rosary is like calling on Baal; not that Mary is Baal, but if we call on her name, it is putting another god before God. It is like bending our knees to an idol. But *"our help is in the name of the LORD, who made heaven and earth"* (Ps. 124:8), and that is God alone. I

---

10   Martin J. Nystrom, *As the Deer.* Written in 1984.

was to drink only from the pure River of God and not go back to the muddy stream the next day. *"There shall be no foreign god among you; ["There shall no strange god be in thee" (KJV)] nor shall you worship any foreign god"* (Ps. 81:9).

The Jews had a mixed worship of both God and Baal in Elijah's time and, wanting to rid myself of that, I had smashed statues and burned pictures which had been idolatrous. I thought I had removed all idolatry from my life, but now the Lord had begun a deeper work of cleansing in me and burning up some of my old teaching, *"hay and stubble,"* from my life. Since early 1994, **I had been calling out for His refining fire,** and it is like removing the dross from the silver and the chaff from the wheat. He also was answering my prayer to purify my heart so idols would not only be gone from my bedroom wall but from the wall of my heart as well, so my worship would truly involve drinking only from the River of God, the flow which comes from Christ. **This is the pure water I want everyone to enjoy, not the polluted water of false prophecy from broken cisterns.**

In the late nineties, the Lord gave me a Scripture to prophesy aloud at a Catholic charismatic prayer meeting, and it included, *"For My people have committed two evils: they have forsaken Me, the fountain of living waters, and hewn themselves cisterns—broken cisterns that can hold no water"* (Jer. 2:13). That night, two other members who had opposed me were in a car accident going home afterwards. But we prayed for them and thank God they mercifully recovered.

I have wept seeing little children in foreign lands being given muddy, polluted water to drink, and many becoming sick or dying too soon. It always **reminded me of my deceived people who need a "Jesus well"**—to come to Him and drink of the pure water He gives. Thank God, *"There is a river whose streams shall make glad the city of God, the holy place of the tabernacle of the Most High. God is in the midst of her, she shall not be moved; God shall help her, just at the break of dawn"* (Ps. 46:4–5).

And we can worship the Lord alone, in spirit and in truth: *"Like a deer longs for pure running water, my soul longs for the LORD."* People worldwide from every nation, tribe, and tongue thirst for the pure, living water that comes from God and His Christ. Some are just looking for it in the wrong places. **Happy are those who find His River and fountain of living water.** Those who trust in You, O Lord, *"are abundantly satisfied with the fullness of Your house, and You give them drink from the river of Your pleasures. For with You is the fountain of life; in Your light we see light"* (Ps. 36:8–9).

Jesus said, *"If anyone thirsts, let him come to Me and drink. He who believes in Me, as the Scripture has said, out of his heart ["belly" (KJV)] will flow rivers of living water"* (John 7:37–38). I love when a life-giving word bubbles up.

Dead Works Are False Bridges. There Is a Misconception That "Dead Works" Will Save Us

A good, live work is one which the Lord has prepared for us to do: *"For we are His workmanship, created in Christ Jesus for good works, which God prepared beforehand that we should walk in them"* (Eph. 2:10). But *"dead works"* are not authorized by Christ. They come from a different source and lead to death, not life.

Many *"dead works"* have been promoted by well-meaning people who have been deceived, not knowing the Scriptures well. They have tried to bridge the way from man to God, erroneously telling people to follow ungodly traditions causing them to disobey some of His commandments, going offtrack. It is written, *"For false christs and false prophets will rise and show great signs and wonders to deceive, if possible, even the elect. See, I have told you beforehand"* (Matt. 24:24–25). But the Word of God is a beacon of light to get us back on track. *"The elementary principles of Christ … [include] the foundation of repentance from dead works and of faith toward God"* (Heb. 6:1); and Hebrews 9:14 says, *"How much more shall the blood of Christ, who through the eternal Spirit offered Himself without spot to God, cleanse your conscience from dead works to serve the living God?"*

When asked what the signs of the end of the age will be, Jesus said, *"Take heed that no one deceives you. For many will come in My name, saying, 'I am He,' and will deceive many"* (Mark 13:5–6). **I, too, was deceived years ago by devotions** to the so-called Immaculate Heart of Mary and Sacred Heart of Jesus, wrongly thinking they had come from God, **including these dead works:**

- Consecrating Russia, our families, and the entire world to her.
  The false prophets of the "Lady" claim, "Only she can save you," and only she can help us now to peace (as if she were *"He"*). But that is a lie. Jesus brings salvation and peace. True peace is a fruit of His Holy Spirit after seeking His righteousness. Jesus said to His apostles, forgiving them for scattering after His arrest: *"Peace I leave with you. My peace I give to you; not as the world gives do I give to you"* (John 14:27). We are to *"be consecrated in the truth."*

- Making a communion of reparation on the first Saturday of every month, to make up for our own sins and those of others. (But the death of Jesus did that already—Isaiah 53.)

- Making Nine First Fridays and Five First Saturdays in reparation to the two "Hearts," including Mass, confession, and communion, plus the rosary, supposedly as a means of obtaining salvation at the moment of death with graces from Mary. Also, so that nations could be converted to Catholicism (to idolatrous behaviour).
  But grace comes from God through Jesus (see John 3:16), and just believing in His finished work at the cross will

set us on the road to eternal life. *"For by grace you have been saved through faith, and that not of yourselves; it is the gift of God, not of works, lest anyone should boast"* (Eph. 2:8–9).

- Praying the rosary in her honour with an insistence that they must do it.
(People, being bound by this word, feel like they have sinned if they do not.) We are to break unjust bonds, in Jesus's name. Jesus, not Mary, is God's chosen Mediator: *"I am the way, the truth, and the life. No one comes to the Father except through Me"* (John 14:6).

- Setting up their graven images—pictures and statues—to be prayed through.
This too is idolatry, bowing to graven images (see Isa. 44). And the only voice we should seek to speak to us is from God, not from deceiving spirits. For our protection, the second commandment says we are neither to bow to graven images, **nor serve them**, also translated: *"...nor worship them. For I the LORD your God, am a jealous God, visiting the iniquity of the fathers upon the children to the third and fourth generation of those who hate Me but showing mercy to thousands, to those who love Me and keep My commandments"* (Ex. 20:4–6). So, we are forbidden to bow to idols or follow messages from idols or their false prophets.

Reading again the material from Fatima and Medjugorje, I could now see how blatantly demonic some of it was.

Sometimes the RC preaching on Sundays was wonderful, especially if it was done from the Scriptures by a charismatic priest. But if it was mixed, the "Lady" taught a false gospel. The devil wants to get people's focus off Jesus. It is like he plants weed seeds yielding thorns to try to choke out the good seed of the Word of God.

The "Lady" of Fatima had the children constantly making sacrifices *("dead works")* **as if they needed to make reparation for sins, especially sins against her, as if she were the spotless Lamb of God rather than Jesus. But** *"only He is worthy."* **Although fasting as in Isaiah 58 is pleasing to God and training in righteousness, these good works are not to obtain salvation. Mixed with prayer, the fasting God loves involves looking for opportunities to do good** like feeding the hungry, clothing the naked, breaking unjust bonds, and pouring yourself out for the afflicted.

Real atonement for our sins comes simply by faith in the blood Jesus shed at His death. It is already done. Jesus said, *"It is finished!"* (John 19:30); and Saint Paul tells us, *"The just shall live by faith"* (Rom. 1:17). Also, those sacrifices for the "Lady" included **bearing unnecessary pain** like the children whipping their own bare legs with stinging nettles and purposely wearing a knotted rope around their little waists that hurt and cut them, causing bleeding. **Self-mutilation comes from the wrong spirit.** Apparently, the "Lady" approved of this, only telling them not to wear the rope to bed. That reminds me of Satan worshipers who cut their wrists. If a follower of Christ encounters pain as a result of someone persecuting him, that is different, and one is blessed who endures it well. But Christians are not supposed to kill or purposely do harm to the human body, either their own or another's. It is the temple of Holy Spirit: *"Destroy this temple, and in three days I will raise it up"* (John 2:19).

Although Saint Paul encouraged us *"by the mercies of God, that you present your bodies a living sacrifice, holy, acceptable to God, which is your reasonable service"* (Rom. 12:1), we need to also look at the type of sacrifice Jesus called us to make: sacrifices of praise and thanksgiving, the fruit of our lips, and a choice of God's will over our own, denying ourselves and bearing our cross to follow Jesus, being willing to lose our life for His sake. **Resisting sin, if necessary, even to the point of having someone shed your blood rather than choose to sin (see Heb. 12:4), is different than purposely harming yourself.**

I used to believe that carrying your cross was to bear sickness. It could be a part of it at times, but **God has other things for us to bear**, like *"one another's burdens"* (Gal. 6:2) when needed as well as the duties and responsibilities of your state in life. I now know that **instead of having to stay in sickness, I can seek God for healing**, and I have experienced it, thank God. All sickness does not come from sin, but Jesus *"Himself bore our sins in His own body on the tree, that we, having died to sins, might live for righteousness—by whose stripes you were healed. For you were like sheep going astray, but have now returned to the Shepherd and Overseer of your souls"* (1 Pet. 2:24–25). Although even followers of the true Jesus occasionally experience the pain of sickness, as well as persecution and misunderstanding, **our God is a healing God. He is Yahweh Rapha, Jehovah Rapha.** *"For I am the Lord who heals you"* (Ex. 15:26), and Proverbs 4:22 says, *"For they* [the words and instruction of God] *are life to those who find them, and health to all their flesh."*

In Old Testament times they sacrificed animals in reparation for sin, but in New Testament times that is a dead work because the Lamb of God was already sacrificed for sin *"once for all."* His New Testament sacrifice was and ours should be: *"'Behold, I have come to do Your will, O God.' He takes away the first that He may establish the second. By that will we have been sanctified through the offering of the body of Jesus Christ once for all"* (Heb. 10:9–10). As the real Mary said two thousand years ago, *"Let it be to me according to your word"* (Luke 1:38); and at Cana, *"Whatever He says to you, do it"* (John 2:5).

Although we do not need to do every work that we see needs to be done (since we can pray and ask God if it is for us to do, and if not, to provide someone to do it), there are good works He will lead us into. *"Do not grow weary in well-doing"* (2 Thess. 3:13). Jesus said, *"Greater love has no one than this, than to lay down one's life for his friends. You are My friends if you do whatever I command you"* (John 15:13–14). Psalm 37:23 says, *"The steps of a good man are ordered by the* Lord.*"*

Modern Indulgence Peddling Is Promoting the Dead Works Bridge

We are not saved by works but saved by grace so that we can do certain live works, led by God. Martin Luther spoke against dead works like **indulgence peddling** when the church used to sell indulgences. **Now they do it another way, and it is still wrong**—promoting indulgences by telling Catholics to say prayers to a Madonna or saint a certain number of times or to visit Jerusalem, the Vatican, or other shrines as works to obtain "indulgences" of time off their suffering in purgatory after death. **That bridge will save no one.** For instance, I was told even in the nineties to pray certain ejaculations, short prayers to the "Lady" several times, and it would earn me a certain number of years indulgence off time in purgatory, depending on how many times I prayed them. And people flocked to shrines in the new millennium.

Reading about how God hated the *"New Moons"* (Hos. 2:11) of Hosea's adulterous wife reminds me of the Nine First Fridays and Five First Saturdays of the month devotions which people observe **believing they will gain indulgences and get to heaven faster.** Whether or not purgatory exists (Protestants say it does not, and Jesus told the repentant thief on the cross, *"Assuredly, I say to you, today you will be with Me in Paradise"* [Luke 23:43]), rather than doing *"dead works,"* **all we need is a simple faith to be saved by the grace of God, and then to obey Jesus's commandments** walking in the *"good works which God prepared beforehand."*

Ephesians 2:8–10 says, *"For by grace you have been saved through faith* [faith in God, not in the "Lady"], *and that not of ourselves; it is the gift of God, not of works, lest anyone should boast. For we are His workmanship, created in Christ Jesus for good works, which God prepared beforehand that we should walk in them."*

Also, *"if we confess our sins, He is faithful and just to forgive us our sins and to cleanse us from all unrighteousness"* (1 John 1:9).

Jesus Claims to Be the Only Bridge • 249

When asked to make a banner for a church to proclaim a translation of Jesus's words to the woman at the well, *"If you only knew what God gives,"* I asked Jesus, "What do You give?" And He replied, *"Saving grace,"* so I included it on the banner. The atonement has been made *"once for all"* so that we could be reconciled by faith in the finished work of Jesus at the cross. The inside of our vessel washed clean, we can go on to do the good works in love which God has personally designed for us to do. We are saved by grace to love God, ourselves, and our neighbour. It should overflow into how we treat others.

No work of atonement for our sin need be done by us because Jesus's blood was sufficient to reestablish our relationship with the Father. (But if we have stolen from someone, an effort to make amends is good.) Instead of doing works to atone for our sins, we can gratefully receive our forgiveness for debts as we forgive our debtors, by faith, and start afresh to love and serve the Lord with the joy of our salvation restored and overflowing. *"The just shall live by faith"* (Rom. 1:17). That's good news for those who walk in repentance and believe. They can walk according to the Spirit.

Jesus bore our sins and became the perfect sin offering that makes amends. **No one need perform dead works to be saved.** We are told, *"He always lives to make intercession for them"* (Heb. 7:25), *"having obtained eternal redemption"* (Heb. 9:12) in reparation for the sins of people past, present, and future. Jesus is alive forever, a permanent bridge to the Father.

I remember Pre-Vatican II, religiously praying six "Our Fathers," six "Hail Marys," and six "Glory Be to the Father" prayers on All Souls Day because I had been told that each time I said them, these prayers gained enough indulgences to save another soul out of purgatory, atoning for their sins. So I would religiously say these many times thinking I was saving souls. **But now I know Jesus saves.** And many a time I went to confession, Mass, and communion on Nine First Fridays and Five First Saturdays believing what I had been taught, that because of that I would go right to heaven when I died. **I did these works for myself and for others thinking I was saving souls, not realizing that they were what the Scripture calls "*dead works.*"**

Now I know I am redeemed not through merits of my own, but by the blood of the Lamb. All we need is simple faith in Him and to receive His free gift. God takes us from faith in believing about Him, to a faith which is a gift of Holy Spirit which comes from knowing Him personally.

Romans 10:9–10 says, "*If you confess with your mouth the Lord Jesus and believe in your heart that God has raised Him from the dead, you will be saved. For with the heart one believes unto righteousness, and with the mouth confession is made unto salvation.*" Jesus is our Wonderful Saviour, Healer, and Defender, our loving Redeemer who has written His law of love on the hearts and minds of those in covenant relationship with Him: "*For I will be merciful to their unrighteousness, and their sins and their lawless deeds I will remember no more*" (Heb. 8:12). He really loves us!

> *How much more shall the blood of Christ, who through the eternal Spirit offered himself without spot to God, cleanse your conscience from dead works to serve* [worship] *the living God?* (Heb. 9:14)

What about Humanism? Can We Be Good without God?

Humanism is a type of religion where people also do good deeds, but may not believe in God and His Son, Jesus Christ. **All religions are not equal**. People are not saved and connected with the Father just because they are in a service club or some other religion. **They are not saved by works alone, especially dead works, but saved by grace through faith for the specific loving works which God chooses for us to do. But good works plus a fear of the Lord can get God's attention so that He might send someone to the person to present the salvation message as He did with Cornelius.**

In the early nineties, after revealing to me how sinful mankind is, including those who I had thought were *"good,"* the Lord magnified to me Psalm 53, which is also in Psalm 14 and Romans 3:10–18. It includes: *There is none that does good, no, not one.* (RSV)

There is none righteous, no, not one. (NKJV)

As Paul said, *"For all have sinned and fall short of the glory of God"* (Rom. 3:23). All men need the justification that only Jesus can bring to those who believe in Him. He can see the thoughts and motives of one's heart. **Jesus told the rich young ruler,** *"No one is good but One, that is, God"* (Matt. 19:17). Did the man know that **Jesus is both God and good? He was the only perfect person.** *"Only God is good"* all the time. If we abide in His Son, His Spirit living in us can produce in us the good fruit of *"goodness"* (Gal. 5:22).

Even humanists need Jesus, the true Light of the world. Just as dust is not always visible until a shaft of light comes into a room, even though he had tried to live right, Isaiah could not see how he fell short of God's glory until he saw the marvelous glory of God and himself next to it. Then he said, *"Woe is me, for I am undone! Because I am a man of unclean lips, and I dwell in the midst of a people of unclean lips; for my eyes have seen the King, the L*ORD *of hosts"* (Isa. 6:5). The angel purified his lips and purged his sin and then he was prepared to volunteer to answer God's call, *"Whom shall I send, and who will go for Us?"* Isaiah said, *"Hinani"*— in Hebrew, meaning *"Here am I! Send me"* (Isa. 6:8–9).

I found the same in my life. I thought I was so good, raised as a God-fearing Catholic, trained by my parents to do good works (plus *"dead works"*), until God's light examined my heart. My dad, Phil Quattrocchi, had a wall full of awards from every level of government and from service clubs, etc., all proclaiming what a good citizen he was. But it was the blood of Jesus which saved him too. We both needed Jesus.

I remember Ezekiel 36:24–38 had a strong anointing on it for weeks at local Catholic charismatic meetings years ago. **Thank God He promised to give His people a new heart and His Spirit, washing us clean.** I have experienced this.

> *Then I will sprinkle clean water upon you, and you shall be clean; I will cleanse you from all your filthiness and from all your idols. I will give you a new heart and put a new spirit within you; I will take the heart of stone out of your flesh and give you a heart of flesh. I will put My Spirit within you and cause you to walk in My statutes, and you will keep My judgments and do them. Then you shall dwell in the land that I gave to your fathers; you shall be My people and I will be Your God; I will deliver you from all your uncleannesses. I will call for the grain and multiply it, and bring no famine upon you. (Ezek. 36:25–29)*

> *And you He made alive, who were dead in trespasses and sins, in which you once walked according to the course of this world, according to the prince of the power of the air, the spirit who now works in the sons of disobedience, among whom also we all once conducted ourselves in the lusts of our flesh, fulfilling the desires of the flesh and of the mind, and were by nature children of wrath; just as the others. But God, who is rich in mercy, because of His great love with which He loved us, even when we were dead in trespasses, made us alive*

> *together with Christ (by grace you have been saved), and raised us up together, and made us sit together in the heavenly places in Christ Jesus, that in the ages to come He might show the exceeding riches of His grace in His kindness toward us in Christ Jesus. For by grace you have been saved through faith, and that not of yourselves; it is the gift of God, not of works, lest anyone should boast. For we are His workmanship, created in Christ Jesus for good works which God prepared beforehand that we should walk in them.* (Eph. 2:1–10)

His Spirit can perfect us, bringing forth the fruit of *"goodness"* in us. When He comes to separate the sheep from the goats, we will stand with His sheep if we reach out in love to even the least of His brethren. "Live works" like acts of compassion are good and they get God's attention, especially when mixed with reverence for God as Cornelius's were.

He was not a Christian and not a Jew. Did he worship Roman idols too? Probably. We only know he was an Italian centurion, *"a devout man and one who feared God with all his household, who gave alms generously to the people, and prayed to God always"* (Acts 10:2). But humanism and only religious acts are not the bridge to the Father. He still needed Jesus. God can hear the prayers of those who do not know His Christ. He sometimes sends people to bring them the good news. But God even sends Jesus and angels to speak to some in dreams and visions today so they can have an opportunity to be saved. He sent an angel to tell Cornelius to ask Peter to come: *"Your prayers and your alms have come up for a memorial before God. Now send to Joppa, and send for Simon whose surname is Peter.... He will tell you what you must do"* (Acts 10:4–6).

Cornelius and his household heard the good news preached to them by Peter, and God even poured out of His Spirit baptizing them in the Spirit. They believed in His Son, Jesus, were also baptized with water, and were saved.

We Need the Mercy of God, His Unmerited Favour, to Tip the Scales in Our Favour

"All flesh shall see the salvation of God" (Luke 3:6). Some eastern religions think salvation is just through works too, but no one of us is good enough to save himself and to pay God the debt we owe Him, no matter how many good works he does. **We need the blood of Jesus shed in our place and the tender lovingkindness and mercy of God to balance and tip the scales of justice in our favour so that we do not get what we deserve.** *"For all have sinned and fall short of the glory of God"* (Rom. 3:23). No one of us can save ourselves. I know I certainly tried, but there was often some little way by which **I fell short in something I did or failed to do. Thank God, Jesus saves.** He saved us at the cross and continues to do a saving work in our lives. And with His Scriptures to guide us as well as His Spirit within us, the Counselor, *"Emmanuel"* (God with us), points us toward the right choices to make so we can continue to be saved from God's wrath and walk in God's blessings and favour. That is good news!

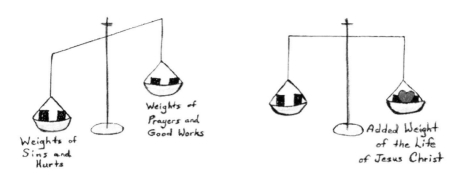

Jesus was the only Son of Man who was perfect all the time. The rest of us cannot balance the scale either by dead works or by our good works alone, but by faith in Him. **His mercy actually tips the scale in our favour.**

When David sinned, he said, *"Against You, You only, have I sinned, and done this evil in Your sight that You may be found just when You speak, and blameless when You judge"* (Ps. 51:4). We can receive God's amazing mercy and grace to walk in repentance and blessing if we choose to follow His Son. Like David, a man after God's own heart who sought to do God's will and sincerely repented when he sinned, we can receive *"the sure mercies of David"* (Acts 13:34).

At the *"great white throne"* judgment, John records: *I saw the dead, small and great, standing before God, and books were opened. And another book was opened, which is the Book of Life. And the dead were judged according to their works, by the things which were written in the books.... Then Death and Hades were cast into the lake of fire. This is the second death. And anyone not found written in the Book of Life was cast into the lake of fire.* (Rev. 20:12, 14–15)

Their good works will not be enough to get them into heaven if their names are not written in the *"Book of Life."* **Although what they have done is important, the mercy and grace which comes through faith in Jesus brings salvation.**

Great People Are Incomplete Bridges

Great people on earth, even saints or great political or military people, may do great exploits, but they alone are not our bridge to heaven. Even if they rescue people, saving them from death or imprisonment, they could do nothing without the power that God gives them. It is good to honour them, but God still deserves the glory due His name. When He raises up a saint on earth to do great things, like Moses, Gideon, Deborah, or David, they are only able by the power and anointing of God working through them. Understanding this as a youth, David told Goliath, *"The battle is the LORD's, and He will give you into our hands"* (1 Sam. 17:47). And the real Mary told the servants to go to Jesus at Cana: *"Whatever He says to you, do it"* (John 2:5). Having a relationship with Jesus, she recognized His wisdom, power, and authority.

Great healing evangelists who do outstanding miracles in our time like Reinhard Bonnke, Daniel Kolenda, and Benny Hinn know they need Jesus and the power of His Spirit. They have given God the glory and others should too. Jesus Himself said, *"Let your light so shine before men, that they may see your good works and glorify your Father in heaven"* (Matt. 5:16). **We are being transformed according to His likeness, but there is no one equal to Him. Saints are to be honoured, not idolized, and glory is to be given to God, who alone is God.** The Book of Revelation shows heaven doing this and we should give Him the glory He deserves *"on earth as it is in heaven."* Peter and Paul did in their epistles.

Sometimes great rulers, like the king of Babylon, were even used by the Lord to carry out the chastisement of His adulterous people. But they were not supposed to take all the credit. God still deserved glory both for judging and redeeming His people.

> *Shall the ax boast itself against him who chops with it?*
> *Or shall the saw exalt itself against him who saws with it?*
> *As if a rod could wield itself against those who lift it up,*
> *Or as if a staff could lift up, as if it were not wood!* (Isa. 10:15)

After God enabled the king of Babylon to take His disobedient people into captivity, the king became very proud. But God humbled him, addressing him by the spirit working through him, *"Lucifer, son of the morning"* (Isa. 14:12). It reminds me of the time that Jesus addressed *"Satan"* in the great apostle Peter because **that was the spirit which was behind his actions at that particular time**. One moment he had been declaring that Jesus was the Christ, something that the Father Himself had revealed to Peter, and then he was acting like the devil. It is a warning to us today to **guard our hearts from deception**. A great person is *"not to think of himself more highly than he ought to think, but to think soberly, as God has dealt to each one a measure of faith"*

(Rom. 12:3). And we should **be thankful for one another's gifts, not jealous, knowing they came from God.** *"God resists the proud, but gives grace to the humble"* (1 Pet. 5:5); and Proverbs 4:23 tells us, *"Keep your heart with all diligence, for out of it spring the issues of life."*

Peter learned his lesson that it was important to trust the Word of God even if he did not understand it. Jesus rose and showed Peter He still cared about him. **He humbled himself and did great things after receiving the Holy Spirit. Peter boldly and humbly made it clear to the people that the apostles were not the ones who healed or saved people,** even on earth, *"as though by our own power or godliness we had made this man walk.... And* [Jesus's] *name, through faith in His name, has made this man strong, whom you see and know. Yes, the faith which comes through Him has given him this perfect soundness in the presence of you all"* (Acts 3:12, 16). **Peter gave the name of Jesus the glory it deserved.**

While living on earth, even Mary, the apostles, and disciples were each only a part of the bridge to God. None of them were the bridge to the Father on their own. As parts of Jesus's body, they were able to be contacted while they were still on earth as intercessors to pray for people and for healing virtue to flow through, in Jesus's name. In His name and love there is strength, power, and hope through His Holy Spirit. Likewise we can ask strong believers alive today, saints on earth, to pray for us in His name, even for healing: *"Therefore I exhort first of all that supplications, prayers, intercessions, and giving of thanks be made for all men"* (1 Tim. 2:1).

In Lystra, when Paul and Barnabas looked so great because they had received His Holy Spirit and God had done great miracles through their hands, the priest of Zeus was going to sacrifice to them, thinking they were the gods Hermes and Zeus in human form. But Barnabas and Paul tore their clothes and gave God His deserved glory, telling the people, *"Men, why are you doing these things? We also are men with the same nature as you, and preach to you that you should turn from these useless things to the living God, who made the heaven, the earth, the sea, and all things that are in them"* (Acts 14:15). Besides miracles, they could stand in the gap for the people, interceding too. But they knew they could only do it in Jesus's name because *"there is one God and one Mediator between God and men, the Man Christ Jesus"* (1 Tim. 2:5), and His Spirit was upon them.

In stark contrast, when King Herod sat in his royal robes and was treated as an idol when he spoke, he did not object. *"And the people kept shouting, 'The voice of a god and not of a man!' Then immediately an angel of the Lord struck him, because he did not give glory to God. And he was eaten by worms and died. But the word of God grew and multiplied"* (Acts 12:22–24).

The Queen of Heaven Is a False Bridge

The Book of Jeremiah speaks of *"the queen of heaven"* (Jer. 7:18; 44:17–19, 25) in reference to a pagan goddess whom the Israelites worshiped. It was a title given to many pagan goddesses in the Mediterranean and Near East, including Isis, Astarte, Aphrodite, Artemis or *"Diana of the Ephesians"* (Acts 19:28), Ishtar, and Asherah.

The Canaanites believed that Asherah ruled the sea, was **the mother of all the gods including Baal**, and sometimes was his deadly enemy. Apparently, the mythology of Canaan maintained that Asherah was the consort of Baal, who had displaced El as their highest god. Thus her sacred objects (poles) were immediately beside altars to Baal, and she was worshiped along with him.

Ishtar was associated with Ashtoreth, or Ashtaroth. The goddess in her various forms was sometimes called the consort or mother of their god and was connected with fertility, sexuality, Venus, and war. **Bible-history.com** states that **the main entrance to Babylon was through the Ishtar Gate** which King Nebuchadnezzar had dedicated to Ishtar. Thus, one could go through the gate of the *"queen of heaven"* coming into Babylon, *"the great city,"* especially for religious processions to the temple of their god, Marduk; and coming out of Babylon you would leave that gate far behind you.

But one must go through the pearly gate of King Jesus, the King of the new heaven and earth, going into or coming out of the greatest city of all, *"the holy city"* **of** *"New Jerusalem."* There you will worship before our God, the Father, and His Son. He is the Most High God and only true God. *"Each individual gate was of one pearl"* (Rev. 21:21).

The so-called queen of heaven, *"the Lady of Kingdoms"* **(Isa. 47:5), is not the bridge to the Father.** The "Lady" of the apparitions, who appears to be Lady Babylon disguised as Mary, falsely claims that you are to go through her to get to God as if she were the Mediatrix of all grace; but Jesus is *"the way, the truth, and the life"* (John 14:6), and said, *"Come out of her"* **(Rev. 18:4), and,** *"No one comes to the Father except through Me"* **(John 14:6).**

When Joshua and the children of Israel, having had the presence of the Lord leading them, entered the Promised Land and later died, a new generation arose who:

> *…did not know the LORD nor the work which He had done for Israel … [and] did evil in the sight of the LORD.… They forsook the LORD and served Baal and the Ashtoreths* [queen of heaven]. *And the anger of the LORD was hot against Israel. So He delivered them into the hand of plunderers who despoiled them; and He sold them into the hands of their enemies all around, so that they could no longer stand before their enemies. Wherever they went out, the hand of the LORD was against them for calamity, as the LORD had said.… Nevertheless,* [in His mercy] *the LORD raised up judges who delivered them out of the hand of those who plundered them. Yet they would not listen to their judges, but they played the harlot with other gods, and bowed down to them.* (Judg. 2:10–11, 13–17)

It was like hockey players being put into the penalty box for longer and longer periods when they kept repeating their actions. God's people could not stand against their enemies anymore because of their sin. They lost the benefit of having Him fight for them. This went on for cycles of idolatry and other sin, oppression by enemies, crying to God for help, God mercifully sending a judge to deliver them, and God would bless them with peace for about forty years. But then the cycle would begin again with another generation and **worse sin growing like weeds, falling away from God, and longer times of punishment cut off from much communication with God before He would have compassion and intervene, until they had seventy years of captivity in Babylon.**

We are supposed to profit by the mistakes of the past and not try to worship gods or goddesses, including the *"queen of heaven."* Let us remember that it is Almighty God who is *"Lord of heaven and earth"* (Matt. 11:25) and *"Lord of hosts"* (Zech. 8:7). Mary is not queen of angels and saints. **It is Jesus, the living Word of God, who is Lord of the heavenly armies of angels and saints.** *"He was clothed with a robe dipped in blood, and His name is called The Word of God. And the armies in heaven, clothed in fine linen, white and clean, followed Him on white horses"* (Rev. 19:13–14).

God hates wickedness and loves righteousness. Because the Israelites kept departing from the way of the Lord to flagrantly go into idolatry and other sin, refusing God's calls to repent, at a certain point He told Jeremiah not even to pray for them, *"nor make intercession to Me; for I will not hear you. Do you not see what they do in the cities of Judah and in the streets of Jerusalem? The children gather wood, the fathers kindle the fire, and the women knead dough, to make cakes for the queen of heaven; and they pour out drink offerings to other gods, that they may provoke Me to anger"* (Jer. 7:17–18). **The wrath of God came down upon them burning hot, especially because they worshiped a pagan goddess called the** *"queen of heaven"* **(Jer. 7:18).**

God appointed four places to go, *"to death ... the sword ... the famine ... the captivity,"* and *"four forms of destruction"* over His disobedient people: *"The sword to slay, the dogs to drag, the birds of the heavens and the beasts of the earth to devour and destroy. I will hand them over to trouble, to all kingdoms of the earth"* (Jer. 15:2–4). **Some died, or experienced pestilence or famine. But in wrath He remembered mercy, so others who would at least obey Him to go into exile, went to Babylon. There, they realized their sins and repented with fasting.**

Baruch recorded for Jeremiah their request to priests in Jerusalem to stand in the gap for them which began: *"Pray for us also to the, Lord, our God; for we have sinned against the Lord, our God, and the wrath and anger of the Lord have not yet been withdrawn from us at the present day"* (Bar. 1:13 NAB). God, the just Judge, imposed a seventy-year sentence of banishment on the Jews, until He redeemed them, setting them free from imprisonment as He had promised. But some years later, sin flourished again. So God stopped sending warnings and after four hundred years of silence, He mercifully sent John the Baptist to announce the coming of Jesus. **Mankind needs Him to be our righteousness.**

The Bible is full of references to Jesus as being the King and Lord and calls Him the *"KING OF KINGS AND LORD OF LORDS"* (Rev. 19:16), but **nowhere does it refer to Mary as being the queen of anything or as the lady in charge** of heaven and earth. **The Word of God does not say she is greater than or equal to Him as many old Catholics believed in their ignorance:** *"Thus says the Lord, the King of Israel, and his Redeemer, the Lord of hosts: 'I am the First and I am the Last; besides Me there is no God'"* (Isa. 44:6).

Jesus is the gate through which we are to pass to go to the temple of the only true God, the gate for fellowship with the Most High God: *"For through Him we both have access by one Spirit to the Father"* (Eph. 2:18).

The "Lady," the *"queen of heaven,"* a counterfeit of Mary, is a gate of *"Babylon,"* the unholy city. God's people are to *"come out of her."* But Jesus is our shepherd and each pearly gate to the holy city, *"New Jerusalem"* (Rev. 21:21–22), the only way in to the presence of the

Father. People are to come out of Babylon and go in to the holy city, His sheepfold, through Jesus. There, our prayers and praises go to God alone.

Jesus said:

> *Most assuredly, I say to you, he who does not enter the sheepfold by the door, but climbs up some other way, the same is a thief and a robber. But he who enters by the door is the shepherd of the sheep. To him the doorkeeper opens and the sheep hear his voice; and he calls his own sheep by name and leads them out. And when he brings out his own sheep, he goes before them; and the sheep follow him, for they know his voice. Yet they will by no means follow a stranger, but will flee from him, for they do not know the voice of strangers.* (John 10:1–6)

When people did not understand, Jesus said:

> *Most assuredly, I say to you, I am the door of the sheep. All who ever came before Me are thieves and robbers, but the sheep did not hear them. I am the door. If anyone enters by Me, he will be saved, and will go in and out and find pasture. The thief does not come except to steal, and to kill and destroy. I have come that they may have life, and that they may have it more abundantly. I am the good shepherd. The good shepherd gives his life for the sheep.... Therefore My Father loves Me, because I lay down My life that I may take it again. No one takes it from Me, but I lay it down of Myself. I have power to lay it down, and I have power to take it again. This command I have received from My Father.* (John 10:7–11, 17–18)

Chapter 13
Is Jesus Still a Baby?

My husband brought back from Italy a beautiful oval picture surrounded by real seashells. It depicted Mary crowned, seated on a raised throne in heaven **with little baby Jesus crowned**, on her arm, and a few saints kneeling before her like to a goddess called *"queen of heaven"* (Jer. 44:17). The Lord caused it to be illuminated with a yellow heavenly light, catching my attention so that I could see that **she was the focal point, the wrong object of worship portrayed**. But King Jesus and His Father alone are worshiped in heaven and should be the One worshiped *"on earth as it is in heaven"* (Matt. 6:10). I hid it for a while, not knowing what to do since it was a present from my husband, Attilio; but with a holy fear of the Lord, I did not hang it. Then much later, overcoming a fear of what Attilio might think, I destroyed it because it was an idolatrous picture.

Through the centuries, artists have depicted their own ideas of what Mary, the saints, and Jesus might look like or be doing. **It is fine to depict Him as one at the nativity, but Jesus is no longer a baby. When John the Apostle was an old man, he was given a revelation of Jesus in heaven.** He saw Him not as a baby, but as a **glorified, radiant Man who had white hair, also seeing Him enthroned at the right hand of God, His Father**, *"the Ancient of days"* (Dan. 7:9). John never mentioned seeing Mary, although she must be there somewhere. But he saw four living creatures and mentioned others he saw: *"Around the throne were twenty-four thrones, and on the thrones I saw twenty-four elders sitting, clothed in white robes; and they had crowns of gold on their heads"* (Rev. 4:4). People all worship Him there including *"a great multitude ... of all nations, tribes, peoples and tongues, standing before the* *throne and before the Lamb, clothed with white robes ...* [praising] *with a loud voice, saying, 'Salvation belongs to our God who sits on the throne, and to the Lamb!'"* (Rev. 7:9–10).

When Jesus no longer would be on earth to fulfill the duties of a son, He gave Mary to John so they would take care of one another. *"He said to His mother, 'Woman, behold your son!' Then He said to the disciple, 'Behold your mother!' And from that hour that disciple took her to his own home"* (John 19:26–27). But that does not mean that we are to pray to her now or to invite her into our home now, as some Catholics, myself included, were deceived to think. **It is the Lord and King, Jesus, whom we should invite in**. He sent word to the Laodicean church, *"Behold, I stand at the door and knock. If anyone hears My voice and opens the door, I will come in to him and dine with him, and he with Me"* (Rev. 3:20). **Jesus spoke of no one else but the Father, Son, and Holy Spirit coming to abide, to dwell in those who keep His commandments and to eat with them**. It is Jesus alone who is the vine in whom we are to abide as fruitful branches.

So John cared for Mary, but at Patmos, an old man now but younger than her, John never wrote of Mary being exalted in heaven with angels and saints bowing before her. **Nowhere in Scripture does it say that saints kneel before Mary, since they only worship God.** In his visions of heaven, **John saw Jesus there as a Heavenly Man—not as a little Child**. He also saw Him as the kingly **Lion of Judah, the Lamb who was slain, and as the Warrior King of kings on the white horse.**

It is a fable to think He is a baby sitting on His mother's lap on her throne in heaven. He is sitting as a mature Man who is God, with His Father, God, *"on His throne"* (Rev. 3:21). Just before Jesus ascended *"into heaven, and sat down at the right hand of God"* (Mark 16:19), *"they* [the apostles] *worshiped Him"* (Luke 24:52). **And in heaven, it was the Father and Jesus, not Mary, whom John saw worshiped by saints and angels, the four living creatures, and all of creation:** *"Every creature which is in heaven and on the earth and under the earth and such as are in the sea, and all that are in them"* (Rev. 5:13).

Madonna icons of the mother holding a little Child should not be prayed through either.

No longer the baby Son of Man who humbled Himself to come lower than the angels for a little while, **Jesus has resumed His status as Son of God who is God, our Lord and King, with the glory He had before mankind was created.**

God has not only Israel but the nations ready to bow before King Jesus. John saw a vision of Him crowned with many crowns as *"KING OF KINGS AND LORD OF LORDS"* (Rev. 19:16), and of the seventh angel sounding the trumpet and *"loud voices in heaven"* declaring, *"The kingdoms of this world have become the kingdoms of our Lord and of His Christ, and He shall reign forever and ever"* (Rev. 11:15). It is the Lord Jesus, not Mary, who reigns as *"Lord of all"* (Acts 10:36). It is written, *"Say among the nations, 'The Lord reigns'"* (Ps. 96:10).

The real Mary is in heaven now, but **nowhere in Scripture is it written that Mary is the queen of heaven who reigns apart from being in Christ, part of the** *"royal priesthood"* **(1 Pet. 2:9).** But the Bible does refer to the queen of Babylon, an adulterous, evil spirit called the *"Lady of kingdoms"* (Isa. 47:5), *"Babylon the Great"* (Rev. 18:17), as being worshiped by misguided religion who joins herself to her, as to a prostitute or to an idol. This *"Lady of kingdoms"* will not be in heaven.

The real Mary was a model of discipleship in the Bible, but not idolized. Jesus obeyed His Father's commandments so He honoured Mary as His earthly mother, was subject as a child to her and His foster father, Joseph, and provided for her after Joseph's death and at His own; but He did not worship or idolize her. He made that clear when she and His unbelieving brothers came, not understanding His dedication and commitment to being about His Father's business. **His Father's will came even before family because He loved God more than these others.**

> *But when His own people heard about this* [that such multitudes came that Jesus did not have time to eat]*, they went out to lay*

hold of Him, for they said, "He is out of His mind" [and the Jews falsely accused Jesus of being possessed by a devil].... *Then His brothers and His mother came, and standing outside they sent to Him, calling Him.* [But Jesus kept on ministering and said,] *"Who is My mother, or My brothers?" And He looked around in a circle at those who sat about Him, and said, "Here are My mother and My brothers! For whoever does the will of God is My brother and My sister and mother."* (Mark 3:21; Mark 3:31, 33–35)

Anyone who births or nurtures the will and action of Christ in themselves or others can be called "the mother of Jesus," as a part of His family, *"the Jerusalem above* [which] *is free, which is the mother of us all"* (Gal. 4:26). **Mary is not worshiped in heaven, and of course we are not to be idolized either.**

Although He normally ate good food to nourish His body, the temple of the Holy Spirit, **feeding His Spirit and doing God's will was even more important to Jesus than food for the body.** He and His disciples could deny themselves when it was appropriate. At the well in Samaria, not only was it evident that He dined on the Word of God, but that Jesus also dined on the action of God. He told them, *"I have food to eat of which you do not know.... My food is to do the will of Him who sent Me, and to finish His work"* (John 4:32–34).

Although as a human Child, Jesus humbled Himself to be subject to Mary, **now she is subject to Jesus.** He is first and foremost God and Son of God, and the eternal High Priest and King of all kings. *"He is Lord of all"* (Acts 10:36). That includes saintly men and women. Nowhere in Scripture is Mary elevated as queen of heaven above Jesus and all else, as some were misled to believe. But to Him belong the kingdom, the power, and the glory.

Who Wears a Crown in Heaven?

John saw King Jesus revealed as *"King of kings and Lord of lords"* suddenly coming on a white horse, *"and on His head were many crowns"*

(Rev. 19:16, 12). But he did not mention Mary specifically. It is up to the Father to choose who sits where in His court and who wears what crown.

Many Catholics had the wrong idea of Mary's position in eternity. **The real Mary surely has a crown in heaven, and will reign with Christ because she is in Him; but so will all believers who persevere. Her Son is the King of all royalty, but His kingship does not come from her—and all humans are less than Him but can also wear a crown if they overcome.**

> *Wisdom is the principal thing; therefore get wisdom.*
> *And in all your getting, get understanding.*
> *Exalt her, and she will promote you;*
> *She will bring you honor, when you embrace her.*
> *She will place on your head an ornament of grace;*
> *A crown of glory she will deliver to you.* (Prov. 4:7–9)

Mary plus all overcomers can reign with Jesus as part of His *"royal priesthood"* (1 Pet. 2:9), and *"the saints of the Most High shall receive the kingdom, and possess the kingdom forever, even forever and ever"* (Dan. 7:18). These saints will only worship God and His only begotten Son, King Jesus. **All overcomers will wear crowns, so Mary surely does, but the real Mary would surely not accept worship as the apparitions do. Nor would other saints in heaven. Although they are crowned, they acknowledge the One who is greatest and deserves the glory.** They lift off their crowns as they worship before Him.

> *The twenty-four elders fall down before Him who sits on the throne and worship Him who lives forever and ever, and cast their* [golden] *crowns before the throne, saying:*
>
> *"You are worthy, O Lord,*
> *To receive glory and honor and power;*
> *For you created all things,*
> *And by Your will they exist and were created."* (Rev. 4:10–11)

Crowns are mentioned in various parts of Scripture:

In that day the LORD of hosts will be for a crown of glory and a diadem of beauty to the remnant of His people." (Isa. 28:5)

Do you not know that those who run in a race all run, but one receives the prize? Run in such a way that you may obtain it. And everyone who competes for the prize is temperate in all things. Now they do it to obtain a perishable crown, but we for an imperishable crown. (1 Cor. 9:24–25)

All believers can get crowns. David listed benefits for believers, blessing the Lord **"who crowns you with lovingkindness and tender mercies"** (Ps. 103:4). Paul said, *"I have fought the good fight, I have finished the race, I have kept the faith. Finally, there is laid up for me the* **crown of righteousness***, which the Lord, the righteous Judge, will give to me on that Day, and not to me only but also to all who have loved His appearing"* (2 Tim. 4:7–8). *"Blessed is the man who endures temptation; for when he has been approved, he will receive the* **crown of life** *which the Lord has promised to those who love Him"* (Jas. 1:12). And Jesus sent word to the faithful church at Philadelphia: *"Behold I am coming quickly! Hold fast what you have, that no one may take your crown"* (Rev. 3:11). Even to Laodicea, the lukewarm church, He said, *"To him who overcomes I will grant to sit with Me on My throne, as I also overcame and sat down with My Father on His throne"* (Rev. 3:21).

Natural and spiritual children can be our *"crown of rejoicing"* (1 Thess. 2:19) too, and there is even a special crown for those who *"shepherd the flock of God which is among you, serving as overseers, not by compulsion but willingly, not for dishonest gain but eagerly; nor as being lords over those entrusted to you, but being examples to the flock; and when the Chief Shepherd appears, you will receive the* **crown of glory** *that does not fade away"* (1 Pet. 5:2–4).

Smashing Idols, Removing Rocks Out of the Way

Stones can be helpful if they are building blocks on a solid foundation. But if stones are blocking our road, they need to be removed. God reprimanded the Jews who prayed to idols, to the host of other gods. God told them that when He brought them in to possess the land to tear down those shrines, the high places where idols were worshiped. **Any person, position, or possession which is treated like an idol, including Self and Mammon, needs to be torn down in our lives and the debris of ungodly practices removed. God should receive the glory due His name.** We are not only to lift the name of Jesus higher, but we are to do what He says to do. We are not to be hypocrites. When we believe in Jesus and His Word, He moves from being a stumbling stone because of *"unbelief"* to a stepping stone or cornerstone in our lives (see 1 Peter 2:4–10). Father, forgive us our trespasses.

For years, in ignorance I used to take part in a Roman Catholic practice called "veneration of the crucifix" on Good Fridays. But the Lord made it clear to me that this is idolatry when every Good Friday for several years after 1981 the word of the Lord would come to me, to bring to the church:

> *"Come out of her, my people,*
> *lest you take part in her sins,*
> *lest you take part in her plagues"*

I had already heard the audible voice of God in 1981 giving me understandings of the first three commandments including, *"Isaiah 44: All. (Tell it to a priest.)"*

> [A man cuts down a tree and says,] *"I have burned half of it in the fire,*
> *Yes, I have also baked bread on its coals;*
> *I have roasted meat and eaten it;*
> *And shall I make the rest of it an abomination?*

> *Shall I fall down before a block of wood?"*
> *He feeds on ashes;*
> *A deceived heart has turned him aside;*
> *And he cannot deliver his soul,*
> *Nor say, "Is there not a lie in my right hand?"*
> *Remember these, O Jacob,*
> *And Israel, for you are My servant;*
> *I have formed you, you are My servant;*
> *O Israel, you will not be forgotten by Me!*
> *I have blotted out, like a thick cloud, your transgressions,*
> *And like a cloud, your sins.*
> *Return to Me, for I have redeemed you.* (Isa. 44:19–22)

It is clear in Isaiah 44 that only God is God and idolatry is foolishness, something of which we should be ashamed. Yet He is so merciful that He is ready to forgive if we return to Him. **Worshiping Him through a crucifix is not worshiping Jesus. Bowing or kneeling to a chunk of wood with or without an image graven on it, or kissing it, is not really adoring Jesus.** It is the pagans who bow before and kiss statues. Nor is kissing a picture kissing a real person. It is kissing a piece of paper. **It is babies who play make-believe with their toys, pretending they are real, until they come out of baby ways.** It is written, *"Shall I fall down before a block of wood?"* (Isa. 44:19).

To pray through a graven image to whomever the craftsman represents is idolatry. A piece of clay, metal, or wood is just that and the spirit of the person is not in it. Therefore, **to call the congregation forward to adore God by kneeling and kissing the feet of a crucifix or bowing to a cross is to make it into an idol, an abomination which God hates.**

Instead, one can adore Him, *"in spirit and truth"* **bowing, kneeling, standing, or prostrating oneself before God, but not worshiping through a graven image.** NOR ARE WE TO HAVE ANY OTHER TYPE OF IDOLATRY. As Jesus told the woman at the well, *"God is Spirit, and those who worship Him must worship in spirit and truth"* (John 4:24).

Today is like the times of Moses and Hezekiah. In Moses's time, the people were sinning greatly, including worshiping both God and *"the host of heaven"*—stars, gods, and goddesses, copying other nations. God took them out of Egypt and worked on taking Egypt out of them in the desert. When He sent fiery serpents among them as a punishment for their ungratefulness and murmuring against Him, He answered their pleas for mercy by having Moses make a bronze serpent and put it on a pole and the Lord said, *"It shall be that everyone who is bitten, when he looks at it, shall live"* (Num. 21:8).

People were healed. However, years later the people made it into an idol. **But it was not the bronze serpent that had healed them, and it is not a crucifix that saves us today**. Neither could even move on its own, let alone bless or curse someone. Just as a crucifix is a reminder looking back to the crucifixion, the bronze serpent was a reminder looking ahead to when Jesus would be lifted up bearing and becoming our sin, and be killed in substitution for us, that we might receive healing and forgiveness. It was when God's first chosen people took a step of obedience by just looking at the brazen serpent on a wooden pole that the power of God for healing was released among them. They were not supposed to pray through it though, or burn incense to it, reverencing it, making it into an idol—they were **just to look at it AND HAVE FAITH IN GOD. Faith in Jesus brings salvation and healing today.** Therefore, because of the idolatry in later times, King Hezekiah *"broke in pieces the bronze serpent that Moses had made; for until those days the children of Israel burned incense to it, and called it Nehushtan"* (2 Kgs. 18:4).

Welcoming an idol was welcoming an abomination and opening the door to the devil. So God had instructed them to burn or smash idols and not to take *"the silver or gold that is on them ... for yourselves, lest you be snared by it.... Nor shall you bring an abomination into your* *house, lest you be doomed to destruction like it. You shall utterly detest it and utterly abhor it, for it is an accursed thing"* (Deut. 7:25–26).

More recently, people have spread myths that some images were miraculous, like a Mother of Perpetual Help icon or Infant of Prague statue. But these are false. **Things in my house which anyone considered to be an idol I have smashed and/or burned,** including idolatrous literature. I do still have a crucifix which we never pray through, but I prefer to hang an empty cross as a remembrance that He died and rose again. Protestant churches do likewise. I have discarded or burned rosaries though because we used to kiss the crucifix on them as if we were pagans; plus the Lord has shown me that we are not to pray to Mary, even for intercession. So praying the rosary is an idolatrous practice.

The Lord has reminded me of His word which came to Elijah when he thought he was the only one left not practicing idolatry, and they wanted to kill him: *"Yet I have reserved seven thousand in Israel, all whose knees have not bowed to Baal, and every mouth that has not kissed him"* (1 Kgs. 19:18).

The Lord encouraged me with this verse. At first I, too, thought I was the only one left and they were seeking *"to take my life,"* but I have found many other Christians who have not bowed, kissed, or served false gods; plus many Christians who used to be Roman Catholics but now worship God alone, praise the Lord! Thank God for His Son, Jesus, whose blood can wash us white as snow again when we repent.

Many people in the world still practice sorcery and witchcraft, but at some Christ for All Nations evangelistic crusades, people have burned their black magic or New Age items. This is like when Paul preached in Ephesus and *"many of those who had practiced magic brought their books together and burned them in the sight of all. And they counted up the value of them, and it totaled fifty thousand pieces of silver"* (Acts 19:19).

Just as God commanded that all His people come out of Egypt and Babylon to worship Him, **it is time not just for Roman Catholics, but for all God's people who have become captives in *"Babylon the Great"* to listen to His call to be set free and go far from her that they may worship God alone. You can begin with a *"baptism of repentance,"* and let Jesus baptize you with Holy Spirit and fire.** Do not commit the sins of Babylon and you will escape her just punishments—the plagues which God has prophesied will come upon her. He has given people a free will and some rebels will end up in *"the everlasting fire prepared for the devil and his angels"* (Matt. 25:41). But **His desire is still *"that all should be saved and none should be lost,"*** as He reminded me October 29, 2005. He commands us, *"Therefore choose life"* (Deut. 30:19), to choose life over death. He writes His law of love on our hearts and minds so that His sheep can follow Him and do loving things to even the least of His brethren as unto the Lord.

Breakthrough in Overcoming Fear—There Is Power in the Name of Jesus

One time when a Catholic woman asked a group of us Christians to "cleanse" and bless her home, I noticed a Madonna picture which was idolatrous on her wall and suggested that she should smash it as I have done. However, she protested that no one would pray through it and that it had a sentimental value. Therefore, I asked her if we could pray about it. As a few of us prayed, the Lord told me, *"Nullify the effect,"* so I prayed nullifying the evil effect of it, in Jesus's name. And I told her that the devil was bound from manifesting through it now. I told her the basics about repenting from idolatry and that Jesus is our nearby defense. There is power in His name. It is written:

> *The nursing child shall play by the cobra's hole,*
> *And the weaned child shall put his hand in the viper's den.*
> *They shall not hurt nor destroy in all My holy mountain,*

> *For the earth shall be full of the knowledge of the* LORD
> *As the waters cover the sea.* (Isa. 11:8–9)

When I destroyed other idolatrous things in my own home, remembering this verse, for a few years I purposely left a couple things through which the enemy had tried to scare me. The Lord had been reminding me, **"Fear not, for I am with you,"** so I had anointed them with oil and prayed for protection, in Jesus's name—and much later I prayed in the name of Jesus to *"nullify the effect."* Even though the enemy had tried to scare me through the designs on them before with a counterfeit yellow light, like snakes from a hole, I now believed that God would protect me and that I had nothing to fear. And thank God I lived as normal around them and slept in peace as I knew His word promised. (Now they are gone.) Hallelujah!!! We are to be strong and listen to His voice. *"Jesus is Lord!"*

Another time, in a faraway place in British Columbia, I stayed overnight at someone's house and noticed many idolatrous things around the rooms. So I prayed in Jesus's name for protection for us all and that He would nullify the effect of them, declared that idols are nothing, and slept in peace and safety. Thank God! *"We know that an idol is nothing in the world, and there is no other God but one"* (1 Cor. 8:4). Later, when the opportunity arose, I prayerfully spoke with my hostess.

Communion of Saints

Somewhere in history, things got offtrack in some circles. Nowhere in the Bible is there reference to the necessity of us to have fellowship or communion with the dead, the old Catholic understanding of "communion of saints." Instead, communication with the dead is forbidden. *"And when they say to you, 'Seek those who are mediums and wizards* [who seek familiar spirits], *who whisper and mutter.' Should not a people consult their God? Should they seek the dead on behalf of the living?"* (Isa. 8:19; see Deut. 18:9–14).

Famous biblical writers like Matthew Henry and John Wesley make mention of a **communion of saints referring to saints on earth having an intimacy with God, a respectful fellowship, and with one another—while still on earth! That is what I now believe too. This is a restoration of what Adam and Eve lost, two-way communication with God, and what Jesus prayed for at the Last Supper.** *"That they all may be one, as You, Father, are in Me, and I in You; that they also may be one in Us, that the world may believe that You sent Me"* (John 17:21). Plus, His death for our sins opened the way to the Father for believers to commune with God.

When we are joined to God, united spirit to Spirit with Jesus and the Father, then we can also have unity with others who have the same unity. **Like the days of Ezekiel, we will be** *"bone to bone"* **in the body of Christ with His Spirit flowing through us.** One day though in New Jerusalem we will have full communion (fellowship) with God and all the saints because there will be a new heaven and new earth, the old ones having passed away.

The apostle John wrote other saintly believers, *"That which we have seen and heard* [concerning the Word of Life] *we declare to you, that you also may have fellowship with us; and truly our fellowship is with the Father and with His Son Jesus Christ.... If we say that we have fellowship with Him, and walk in darkness, we lie and do not practice the truth. But if we walk in the light as He is in the light, we have fellowship with one another, and the blood of Jesus Christ His Son cleanses us from all unrighteousness"* (1 John 1:3, 6–7).

Being led by the light of Christ, by His Spirit and His Word, makes unity with other members of His body who are also living in His love, so much easier. That is what early Christians experienced *"continuing daily with one accord"* (Acts 2:46). *"Now the multitude of those who believed were of one heart and one soul; neither did anyone say that any of the things he possessed was his own, but they had all things in common* [they knew it all belonged to God]*"* (Acts 4:32). They worshiped together and met one another's needs. They knew they were blessed to bless, to steward wisely what God provided for them. They shared the good news. *"And great grace was upon them all"* (Acts 4:33).

Wesley commented on the behaviour of a Christian in the section about *"distributing to the needs of the saints, given to hospitality"* (Rom. 12:13), that **"communion of saints" was among those living on earth**. A believer was to "communicate to the necessities of the saints—Relieve all Christians that are in want. It is remarkable, that the apostle, treating expressly of the duties flowing from the communion of the saints, yet never says one word about the dead." [11]

And in His explanation of many Old Testament Scriptures, like Deut. 30:19, which admonishes us to *"choose life,"* Wesley refers to the desire of God to have communion with His saints on earth, and for them to choose the favour of God and communion with Him, which is to choose life, not death. In the psalms we see that David, as a saint on earth, had communion with God and with Jonathan. We can have communion with God, too, through *"the sure mercies of David"* (Isa. 55:3), which were purchased by the blood of Christ. But we do not talk to Saint David, nor did the apostles.

To Whom Did Jesus and His Disciples Pray? Who Was Their Bridge?

They prayed to the Father who told them to listen to His Son. Jesus would rise early while it was yet dark and pray to His Father, God. Jesus stood night watch with Him, sometimes having apostles join Him. But nowhere is it written that Jesus or the apostles prayed to Saint Moses, Saint Ruth, Saint Isaiah, or any other saint. He taught

---

11 Rick Meyers, e-Sword, *John Wesley's Explanatory Notes*, commenting on Romans 12:13. https://www.e-sword.net/.

the apostles to also pray to God in His name, allowing them to address God as *"our Father"* and believers with Jesus can do that today too.

Jesus had poured out His life as an example to them, and had told them, *"When you lift up the Son of Man, then you will know that I am He, and that I do nothing of Myself; but as My Father taught Me I speak these things. And He who sent Me is with Me. The Father has not left Me alone, for I always do those things that please Him"* (John 8:28–29). He had consulted with His Father in prayer daily when on the earth.

God allowed Jesus on a mountain to be seen by three apostles, Peter, James, and John **transfigured** in a **vision**. They saw Him *"coming in His kingdom"* (Matt. 16:28), *"present with power"* (Mark 9:1), clothed in His resplendent glory which He used to have and would have again in heaven. God knew the enemy was going to fire arrows of doubt and fear at them soon to try to cloud their thinking about who He was; but when the fog lifted, they would remember the vision they had clearly seen.

"He was transfigured before them. His face shone like the sun, and His clothes became as white as the light. And behold, Moses and Elijah appeared to them, talking with Him" (Matt. 17:21). But when Peter, astounded, suggested that they build tabernacles for the three of them, Father God immediately vetoed that. They had no need to consult Moses and Elijah. **Jesus was all they needed. It is to Him, the living Word of God, the very presence of God, that we are to listen! His Father testified of this.** *"While he was still speaking, behold, a bright cloud overshadowed them; and suddenly a voice came out of the cloud, saying, 'This is My Beloved Son, in whom I am well pleased! Hear Him!' And when the disciples heard it, they fell on their faces and were greatly afraid"* (Matt. 17:5–6).

Jesus was only talking to Moses and Elijah **in a vision**. When the vision ended, Jesus told them not to be afraid, and He alone was there looking again as He usually did. He commanded them, *"Tell the vision to no one until the Son of Man is risen from the dead"* (Matt. 17:9).

Hopefully this prophetic vision helped prepare them for His sacrificial death and rising when they would see Him in His glorified body again. As Amos 3:7 says, *"Surely the Lord GOD does nothing, unless He reveals His secret to His servants the prophets"* (Amos 3:7); and, *"Out of Zion, the perfection of beauty, God will shine forth"* (Ps. 50:2).

Moses himself had told the people, in regards to this coming Great Prophet and Messiah, *"Him you shall hear"* (Deut. 18:15).

Even after His ascension they still could listen to the Son, because through His Holy Spirit, they heard Him speak to them prophetically in that *"still small voice"* (1 Kgs. 19:12). Revelation 19:10 says, *"For the testimony of Jesus is the spirit of prophecy."* While Jesus was with His chosen apostles, they could pray the Father or ask Jesus directly for anything since God was dwelling with them in human form. But preparing them for His departure, **He told them to pray to the Father in His name.** *"Most assuredly, I say to you, whatever you ask the Father in My name He will give you. Until now you have asked nothing in My name. Ask, and you will receive, that your joy may be full"* (John 16:23–24). **Nowhere did Jesus tell His disciples to pray to anyone but God, in His name. Of course, the Holy Spirit is part of the Godhead and the Holy Spirit, the Helper, would be given to them to counsel and comfort them, reminding them of what Jesus said.**

A few people today have been taken up to heaven in a vision and spoken to saints living there. But when the vision was over, they were no more to seek to talk or pray to those who died on earth. They have someone far superior—God Himself—to talk to.

The Jews were used to calling on the Aaronic high priests to bridge the gap with the Father. But now the time had come for God to do a new thing, as He had promised. They could pray directly to God themselves. When the apostles were persecuted for using the precious name of Jesus, and told not to speak in His name anymore, **these saints had communion with God and with one another**

because they endeavored *"to keep the unity of the Spirit in the bond of peace"* (Eph. 4:3). They prayed:

> *They raised their voice to God with one accord and said: "Lord, You are God, who made heaven and earth and the sea, and all that is in them.... Now, Lord, look on their threats, and grant to Your servants that with all boldness they may speak Your word, by stretching out Your hand to heal, and that signs and wonders may be done through the name of Your holy Servant Jesus." And when they had prayed, the place where they were assembled together was shaken; and they were all filled with the Holy Spirit, and they spoke the word of God with boldness.* (Acts 4:24, 29–31)

No Collection of Idols Can Be the True Bridge or Bring in True Revival

The leaders of other religions are still dead in their graves; but Jesus rose on the third day, ascended into heaven, and is still alive and active. He is God who sees everything from far off; yet He can be very near, seeing us up close, even abiding within us as He promised and able to bridge the gap. But idols, all false bridges, will not save you, neither Catholic gods nor the gods of the nations. . That includes idols of America.

> *When you cry out, let your collection of idols deliver you!*
> *The wind will carry them off,*
> *a breath will take them away.*
> *But he who takes refuge in Me shall possess the land,*
> *and inherit My holy mountain.*
> *It shall be said,*
> *"Build up, build up, prepare the way;*
> *remove every obstruction from My people's way."*
> *For thus says the high and lofty one*

> *who inhabits eternity, whose name is Holy:*
> *I dwell in the high and lofty place,*
> *and also with those who are contrite and humble in spirit,*
> *to revive the spirit of the humble,*
> *and to revive the heart of the contrite.* (Isa. 57:13–15 NRSV)

God sent word by His prophets to His first chosen people when they became idolatrous time and again. And when He was ignored, a time came when He stopped talking to them for four hundred years, until He sent His Son and Spirit as He promised.

Saint Peter and the other apostles learned to be humble and to exalt God. Although God did great work through them after Pentecost and revived many in Israel because of their willingness to do what He called them to do, **Peter sought God's fame, not His own.** He acknowledged that disciples were not to be idolized; **the credit belonged to God for the mighty outpouring of His Spirit, the many salvations and the power to heal.** The 120 saints who gathered to wait and pray after Jesus's ascension, including *"the women and Mary the mother of Jesus, and with His brothers"* (Acts 1:14), were not a collection of idols, but of broken disciples who knew their weakness and how much they were in need of a personal Saviour. They knew that it was only with divine forgiveness and Christ working through them that they would be strong in the war against sin and fear. As Jesus later told the great apostle Paul, *"My grace is sufficient for you, for My strength is made perfect in weakness"* (2 Cor. 12:9).

> *Proclaim this among the nations:*
> *"Prepare for war!*
> *Wake up the mighty men.*
> *Let all the men of war draw near,*
> *Let them come up.*
> *Beat your plowshares into swords*
> *And your pruning hooks into spears;*
> *Let the weak say, 'I am strong.'"*

Assemble and come, all you nations,
And gather together all around.
Cause Your mighty ones to go down there, O Lord. (Joel 3:9–11)

What Job feared came upon him. But like the believers after Pentecost, what we faith can come upon us. God did even more than they had expected. They humbly obeyed Jesus's word to wait for the Holy Spirit to come with enabling power before going out to all nations with good news and spiritual weapons, and God sent a mighty revival to them at Pentecost. They had prayed in one accord, in great unity. The church grew exponentially, spreading to all nations, and still is. They would never have had the courage to face the other Jews and Romans, etc., if God had not strengthened them, causing them *"to go down there."* Not being idols, they made sure to give Him the glory due His name: *"To Him be the glory both now and forever. Amen"* (2 Pet. 3:18).

This was in contrast to the spirit of Babylon, of self-exaltation and self-righteousreligious pride that gathered together the ones who built the tower of Babel. Those Babylonians thought they could do everything their own way rather than under God's direction. They were unified, but God did not like their pride so He humbled them, confusing their language so they could not understand one another, and He scattered them.

God Gives Us a Choice

Although God gives us a choice, whether to go backward and be a part of an obsolete or false bridge, or to go forward and become a part of the true bridge, He commands us to obey His commands. Let us acknowledge that it is from Him that our blessings actually come. Honour our Father, God, and obey Him in gratitude, and you have a promise *"that you may live, and that it may be well with you"* (Deut. 5:33). When we see backsliders and wasteful ones repent, instead of choosing to blindly stay outside like the prodigal son's elder brother, we can celebrate too, trusting our Father's mercy and entering into His joy. We must not be jealous of the extravagant love He shows some people when the lost return. His abundant love is always there for all His children. God wants His people to acknowledge and receive the truth and to follow Him.

In Old Testament times, people were stoned to death for idolatry. But because of the atoning death of Jesus, we can receive mercy and put to death our sinful actions instead. Our fruit comes from abiding in Christ by obeying His commandments, and then the gap is bridged because the Father, Son, and Holy Spirit will come and live within us. The mercy seat will be that close. Sometimes in the past, when we were in ignorance, when God's people prayed to God through dead saints using them as idols, either God was silent or He mercifully allowed their prayers to be answered, sometimes causing miracles to happen, looking after them like kindergarten children who just did not understand a lot. But it is really God who deserves the glory—not Saint "so and so." It is time to acknowledge Him. We are dust without what God has given us.

> *For the L*ORD *is great and greatly to be praised;*
> *He is to be feared above all gods.*
> *For all the gods of the peoples are idols;*
> *But the L*ORD *made the heavens.*
> *Honor and majesty are before Him;*
> *Strength and beauty are in His sanctuary.*
> *Give to the L*ORD*, O families of the peoples,*
> *Give to the L*ORD *glory and strength!*
> *Give to the L*ORD *the glory due His name;*
> *Bring an offering, and come into His courts!* (Ps. 96:4–8)

For all the gods of the peoples are idols, but the L ORD **made the heavens.**

Let the False Bridges Be Dismantled

The devil is a liar. God is the Father of truth. I encourage people to do what I learned to do—to **cry out to God for truth in your inner being.** Jesus and His Word are truth: *"I am … the truth,"* and He called the Holy Spirit, *"the Spirit of truth"* (John 14:6, 17). It is best to dismantle false bridges ourselves with God's help, rather than waiting for God to order a demolition squad. With a holy fear of the Lord, we dare not bow to idols once we understand, even if we also pray to God. He spoke of the great day of the Lord, and we should want to please Him, not be rebellious.

> *"I will utterly consume everything,*
> *From the face of the land,"*
> *Says the* L*ORD*.…
> *"I will cut off every trace of Baal from this place,*
> *The names of the idolatrous priests with the pagan priests—Those*
> *who worship the host of heaven on the housetops;*
> *Those who worship and swear oaths by the* L*ORD*,
> *But who also swear by Milcom;*
> *Those who have turned back from following the* L*ORD*,
> *And have not sought the* L*ORD*, *nor inquired of Him."* (Zeph. 1:2, 4–6)

Learning from the past, **let the mixture stop** of worshiping and serving the creature plus the Creator.

Jesus honoured Mary and Joseph as parents. He *"was subject to them"* (Luke 2:51), but did not put them on a pedestal and worship them or anyone else. **Mary's blood did not purchase mankind's release.**

> ***Thus says the*** L***ORD***, ***the King of Israel***,
> ***And his Redeemer, the*** L***ORD*** ***of hosts:***
> ***"I am the First and I am the Last;***
> ***Besides Me there is no God***.…
> ***Is there a God besides me?***

Indeed there is no other Rock;
I know not one." (Isa. 44:6, 8)

Who is a God like You,
Pardoning iniquity
And passing over the transgression of the remnant of His heritage?
He does not retain His anger forever,
Because He delights in mercy. (Mi. 7:18)

I used to think that the gods of other religions were the same as our God if people called them "God." However, I came to find that was not true. It reminds me that in the Muslim mosque built on the temple mount, the holy site where Solomon's temple was and where Abraham offered up Isaac, they have inscribed that their god, "Allah has no son." **But their god today is not the same as our God or equal to Him, even when they call him "Lord" or "God Almighty." Their god is certainly not greater than** *"the Most High God,"* **our God, the <u>real</u> God Almighty, El Shaddai, who does have a Son and many adopted children. He has only one** *"begotten Son"* **(John 3:16) though, Jesus, the Christ, the one way to the Father. Jesus died and rose again and is God, and He was God from the beginning.** *"All things were made through Him, and without Him nothing was made that was made"* (John 1:3). There was no god with Him when He did it.

No Man Is the Bridge Alone

"All flesh shall see the salvation of God" (Luke 3:6). **We, by ourselves, are not the true bridge either**, because no man is perfect enough to save himself. Only Jesus is worthy. He laid down His life and rose again so we all might taste salvation. We might think we are living a good life, but we cannot save ourselves apart from Christ, the vine, with His lifeblood flowing through us. *"I am the vine, you are the branches. He who abides in Me, and I in him, bears much fruit; for without Me you can do nothing. If anyone does not abide in Me, he is cast out as a branch and is withered; and they gather them and throw them into the fire, and they are*

burned" (John 15:5–6). Remember, *"All have sinned and fall short of the glory of God"* (Rom. 3:23); and, *"All we like sheep have gone astray; we have turned each one to his own way; and the LORD has laid on Him the iniquity of us all"* (Isa. 53:6). *"For God has committed them all to disobedience, that He might have mercy on all"* (Rom. 11:32).

Jesus willingly laid down His life having had the power both to lay it down and to take it up again, doing it with passionate love for His sheep and for others who could become part of His flock too. None of us can do it without Him. We all need Jesus to bridge the gap as Saviour, Deliverer, Counsellor, and Mediator to restore us to fellowship with the Father and to convey us on our journey to Him.

Over the centuries, people have turned ordinary people into idols, exaggerating their qualities, making them larger than life. The devil loves to steal worship, glory, and praise from God and put it on created beings or things, alive or dead. Beloved, *"We are not ignorant of his devices* [tactics]*"* (2 Cor. 2:11). *"Do not be deceived"* (1 Cor. 6:9). The Most High God is the only bridge high enough. Who could compare? Who would even dare? Saints take off their crowns before His throne acknowledging that all they have comes from Him, and only He is holy all the time. He always is who He is: *"I AM WHO I AM"* (Ex. 3:14).

Let our people realize the truth and repent, and not be left to wander like sheep as Ephraim was for a time and found the heavens closed over him: *"Ephraim is joined to idols, let him alone. Their drink is rebellion, they commit harlotry continually. Her rulers dearly love dishonour"* (Hos. 4:17–18).

Just as centuries ago when His chosen people had gone offtrack, yet God loved them and wooed them unto Himself like Hosea's wife, blessing her children, God is doing the same today.

I remember a time when the Holy Spirit impressed upon me that in seeking the **wholeness of salvation** that I needed the **healing of memories**. I had to go back in my memory and forgive all those who had trespassed against me, and ask forgiveness of those whom I had trespassed against. Of course, that includes asking God for forgiveness. This act of grace and mercy brought reconciliation and the Lord healed my memories too. They no longer control me. Jesus forgave from the cross as our example, leaving sinners to deal with God.

> *Repay no one evil for evil. Have regard for good things in the sight of all men. If it is possible, as much as depends on you, live peaceably with all men. Beloved, do not avenge yourselves, but rather give place to wrath; for it is written, "Vengeance is Mine, I will repay," says the Lord. Therefore*
>
> *"If your enemy is hungry, feed him;*
>
> *If he is thirsty, give him a drink;*
>
> *For in so doing you will heap coals of fire on his head."*
>
> *Do not be overcome by evil, but overcome evil with good.* (Rom. 12:17–21)

Getting to know Jesus as our bridge to the Father has made all the difference in my life. Not that I am perfect yet, but *"forgetting those things which are behind and reaching forward to those things which are ahead, I press toward the goal for the prize of the upward call of God in Christ Jesus"* (Phil. 3:13–14), who even gives a healing of memories when forgiveness is asked for and extended to others.

I used to head towards false bridges in prayer because I did not know any better. I actually thought I was doing the right thing when I asked Mary and the other saints in heaven to pray for us because people I trusted had said to go to Jesus and the Father that way. But once the Lord helped me see how deceived I had been (and many others had been), and we are to have *"no other love before* [Him],*"* **I learned that Jesus Himself is the one way to the Father. I asked Him to forgive and lead me, to wash me clean, and others can too. I thank God for the mercy I received and that we can go to Him directly in Jesus's name.**

Part IV

Function of the Bridge

*Then Melchizedek king of Salem brought out bread and wine;
he was the priest of God Most High. And he blessed him and said:
"Blessed be Abram of God Most High, Possessor of heaven and earth;
And blessed be God Most High,
Who has delivered your enemies into your hand."
And he gave him a tithe of all.*
(Gen. 14:18–20)

*For He [God] testifies: "You are a priest forever
According to the order of Melchizedek."*
(Heb. 7:17; Ps. 110:4)

*Therefore He is also able to save to the uttermost those who come to God
through Him, since He always lives to make intercession for them.*
(Hebrews 7:25)

*Now all things are of God, who has reconciled us to Himself through
Jesus Christ, and has given us the ministry of reconciliation, that is, that
God was in Christ reconciling the world to Himself, not imputing their
trespasses to them, and has committed to us the word of reconciliation.
Now then, we are ambassadors for Christ, as though God were pleading
through us: we implore you on Christ's behalf, be reconciled to God.*
(2 Corinthians 5:18–20)

Chapter 14

Jesus Gives Access to God and to Reality

Around 1990, the word of the Lord came to me one night, *"Study the book of Hebrews,"* so I did, using as a reference a booklet my mother had: *Barclay's Study of Hebrews*. Looking now at my notes on chapter four, inspired by Barclay's, I wrote that the **key thought** of the book of Hebrews is **"Jesus was the one person who gave access to reality and access to God."** Jesus satisfied both Jews and Greeks (non-Jews) in His function as eternal High Priest.

- **To the Jew** – Hebrews says: All your lives you have been looking for the perfect priest who can bring the perfect sacrifice and give you access to God. You have Him in Jesus Christ.

- **To the Greek** – It is said: You are looking for the way from the shadows to reality. You will find it in Jesus Christ.

- **To the Jew** – It is also said: You are looking for that perfect sacrifice which will open the way to God which your sins have closed. You will find it in Jesus Christ.

And I would add: **To the Roman Catholic** – It is said: All your lives you have been looking for the perfect holy person who can speak up for you to the Father; and you have searched for the perfect sacrifice, the perfect sacrificial work that will gain salvation for you. You will find it all in Jesus Christ.

Jesus Functions as THE Mediator of the New Covenant

A mediator between God and men had to have something to offer that included sacrificed shed blood for the forgiveness of sins. So Jesus, the spotless Lamb of God, laid down His life for us. From the cross He offered Himself to God so that the sin of the world may be forgiven.

> *If the blood* [of animals] *sanctifies for the purifying of the flesh, how much more shall the blood of Christ, who through the eternal Spirit offered Himself without spot to God, cleanse your conscience from dead works to serve the living God? And for this reason He* [Jesus] *is the Mediator of the new covenant, by means of death, for the redemption of the transgressions under the first covenant, that those who are called may receive the promise of the eternal inheritance.* (Heb. 9:13–15)

Although I read and studied this passage around 1990, it was not until years later that the significance of it and other Hebrews passages began to dawn on me—I did not have to save myself by doing *"dead works"* **including asking saints to pray for me. Jesus, true God who had come as a real human being, had begun standing in the gap for us from the cross. He offered the perfect sacrifice of shed blood in atonement so that sins could be forgiven for all time if we only believe.**

Hebrews actually says that Jesus functions as God's chosen **holy Mediator forever who does not need to offer up sacrifices daily. His one sacrifice was perfect forever to save us.**

> *He is also able to save to the uttermost those who come to God through Him, since He always lives to make intercession for them. For such a High Priest was fitting for us, who is holy, harmless* [innocent], *undefiled, separate from sinners, and has become higher than the heavens; who does not need daily, as those high priests, to offer up sacrifices, first for His own sins and then for the*

people's, for this He did once for all when He offered up Himself. For the law appoints as high priests men who have weakness, but the word of the oath, which came after the law, appoints the Son who has been perfected forever. (Heb. 7:25–28)

Jesus, who overcame temptations, came as Son of Man to show us that by communing with God, we, too, are able to overcome human weakness. He needed the bread of the Word of His Father in relationship with Him, and so do we. He would go apart to pray, even all night if necessary. By what He suffered, He was made perfectly equipped for the task assigned to Him by the Father, to be the eternal Mediator between God and mankind. Although sinless, He has experienced the punishment that sinners deserve. Having been to Hades and back on our behalf, He desires that captives be set free to have another opportunity to walk in His righteousness and willingly enjoy eternal life with Him. There is no need to choose another high priest because Jesus will never die again. He holds His position permanently. He told John in a vision, *"I am He who lives, and was dead, and behold, I am alive forevermore. Amen. And I have the keys of Hades and Death"* (Rev. 1:18). **He can still set prisoners free.**

Who is He able to save? *"Those who come to God through Him,"* through the power of His name and blood. Jesus, alone, is the everlasting Saviour and Mediator who *"always lives to make intercession for them."* (Heb. 7:25). That is His job *"always."* He can save us spirit, soul, and body. Calling on His name I have experienced protection, provision, healing, and deliverance. Since the soul is composed of our mind, will, and emotions, putting my trust in Him has brought encouragement, counsel, and comfort, saving my soul from being pulled down to despair. God loves us so much that He gave us free will to choose to believe and be saved, or to face the consequences of our behaviour. How much better to believe, to trust, and obey Him!

Jesus was appointed to His mediating ministry by Father God Himself who prophesied it with an oath, and God does not lie. Satan is the father of lies, but God is the Father of truth. *"The Lord has* *sworn and will not relent, 'You are a priest forever according to the order of Melchizedek.'* [In Old Testament times, there were many Aaronic priests who all died.] *But He* [Jesus], *because He continues forever, has an unchangeable priesthood. Therefore He is also able to save to the uttermost those who come to God through Him, since He always lives to make intercession for them"* (Heb. 7:21, 24–25). The early Christians knew this, but some of us got offtrack for a while by turning to saints who have died, not knowing that they were not God's chosen Mediator.

Jesus saves sinners who come to Him. But then as they embark on a life of repentance following Him, if and when they fall short again, Jesus is their salvation doing an ongoing saving work in them. How wonderful that is!

Abraham, Moses, and David, while saints on earth, were chosen mediators of the Old Covenant between God and mankind, as were the Aaronic priests in those days. On Yom Kippur, the Day of Atonement, the holiest day of the year, sins of the people were placed on a scapegoat who was sent into the wilderness; plus the blood of certain animals was shed, including another goat's to atone for their sins and those of the high priest who was the chosen mediator. But the sins were only covered and not washed away until Jesus redeemed by His redemptive death even those who were waiting for Him after death in the holding place of Paradise. *"He has come, not according to the law of a fleshly commandment* [chosen from a particular tribe], *but according to the power of an endless life"* (Heb. 7:16).

Just as Melchizedek *"was the priest of God Most High,"* **the high priestly function of Jesus our bridge is to minister unto God Most High on our behalf and unto men on His behalf, advocating for them, blessing and reconciling many, glorifying God, receiving tithes and offerings into His storehouse and stewarding them, feeding, healing, cleansing, delivering, and blessing people in the name of God, defending them, even raising the dead, and offering sacrifices to God.** Some of these functions Christ performs directly, and some through parts of His body.

Melchizedek blessed both God and Abraham, and Jesus blesses His Father, teaching us to hallow His name, magnifying His name in prophetic words and songs. He also blesses the descendants of Abraham, including spiritual descendants in Christ since He is the promised Seed of Abraham. One way that He blesses God is by leading people in prophetic prayers, songs, dances, or banner ministries which exalt the name of the Lord. And He can bless people with prophetic words, or by answering prayers, or inspiring His people to have compassion on the needy. He blesses the Jews, descendants of Abraham, by bringing many home to Israel and providing for them as He promised, with help from members of His body.

The Bible says it is Jesus alone who is the Father's chosen Mediator for our New Covenant time period, and He will never die again. He is the only one in heaven that we should ask to pray for us. Although some others were martyred, He rose and entered into the heavenly Holy of holies with His own blood, *"once for all"* (Heb. 9:12); and in Hebrews 7:21, *"The Lord has sworn and will not relent, 'You are a priest forever according to the order of Melchizedek.'"*

Why Do We Need Jesus?

I was asked around 2009, "Why do we need Jesus?" I began to give many reasons, including that He will not only be our God and Good Shepherd, but our Best Friend if we love and serve Him. But the reason that the Holy Spirit magnified to me was,

"Because sin deserves punishment."

> *In mercy and truth atonement is provided for iniquity;*
> *And by the fear of the Lord one departs from evil.* (Prov. 16:6)
> *Whoever commits sin also commits lawlessness, and sin is lawlessness.* (1 John 3:4)

> *Whosoever committeth sin transgresseth also the law: for sin is the transgression of the law.* (1 John 3:4 KJV)

> Jesus said: *Do not think that I came to destroy the Law or the Prophets. I did not come to destroy, but to fulfill. For assuredly, I say to you, till heaven and earth pass away, one jot or one tittle will by no means pass from the law till all is fulfilled. Whoever therefore breaks one of the least of these commandments, and teaches men so, shall be called least in the kingdom of heaven; but whoever does and teaches them, he shall be called great in the kingdom of heaven.* (Matt. 5:17–19)

Heaven and earth have not passed away yet, and God does not want us to be lawless, but Jesus fulfills the law. That is good news because believers do not have to die in their sins. **Although Jesus died so those in Christ can be redeemed** from the curse of the law—the just punishment for sin—and receive the free gift of forgiveness and righteousness by faith, **He still expects us to do right**, what is right in God's sight, what God commands us to do. We are still to follow the spirit of the Law and His Law is now written on our hearts and minds. Scripture is true, but some have missed the mark, thinking they are still righteous if they also choose to disobey the essence of the law. They need to plead guilty and repent if they want Jesus to intercede for them so they can wash their clothes. *"For I say to you, that unless your righteousness exceeds the righteousness of the scribes and Pharisees, you will by no means enter the kingdom of heaven"* (Matt. 5:20).

To realize your blessings as a follower of Jesus, and see what curses from which He saved you, read Deuteronomy 28. It was an eye-opener for me. *"The transgressions under the first covenant,"* acts of disobedience, all led to some type of curse as a consequence. However, acts of obedience to God brought blessings. But even when His people did some things right, they, like us, fell short at times. Historically, man could not and cannot keep the whole Law and save himself. Sin deserves punishment and that is why we need Jesus even today. *"Therefore the law was our tutor to bring us to Christ, that we might be justified by faith"* (Gal. 3:24); and, *"The wages of sin is death, but the gift of God is eternal life in Christ Jesus our Lord"* (Rom. 6:23).

The New Testament is a refinement and fulfilling of the Old. We come to Jesus because **He is all we need.** At-one-ment. He is our *"atonement"* so fellowship can be restored with God. Although He had no sin of His own, Jesus was punished in our place. He *"was wounded for our transgressions, He was bruised for our iniquities; the chastisement for our peace was upon Him, and by His stripes we are healed"* (Isa. 53:5).

If we believe and repent, all our sins can be washed away by His Word and His blood. It was done **positionally,** *"once for all,"* at the cross when our High Priest, being the Lamb, shed His own blood for us: *"Christ has redeemed us from the curse of the law, having become a curse for us (for it is written: 'Cursed is everyone who hangs on a tree'), that the blessing of Abraham might come upon the Gentiles in Christ Jesus, that we might receive the promise of the Spirit through faith"* (Gal. 3:13–14). Through Jesus, we are grafted into the Jewish olive tree. Jesus does not have to be sacrificed for us again. His blood is still effective to **experientially** forgive our sins today so we can enjoy the blessings of Abraham. The Lord told him, *"Do not be afraid, Abram. I am your shield, your exceedingly great reward"* (Gen. 15:1).

How wonderful that with our relationship with God restored by Christ, we need not fear, and we have the *"exceedingly great reward"* of having intimacy with Him and God as our protection. **This is because we needed Jesus to not only be our atoning sacrifice, but our Advocate with the Father, the Mediator who stands in the gap pleading for us at His right hand.**

Sin often affects more than the person sinning. For example, adultery or drunkenness in a man affects his whole family. The second commandment states that idolatry can affect our descendants *"to the third and fourth generations of those who hate Me, but showing mercy to thousands, to those who love Me and keep My commandments"* (Ex. 20:4–6). **Fathers need to safeguard their children.**

Jesus became a curse so ours could be taken away, leaving blessings for the family instead. **Experientially,** it is as if we were there at the cross having our sins atoned for now when we need saving grace. Instead of curses coming down on us for bowing to idols and our iniquities affecting our descendants, blessings can come down on us and upon many generations following us. Since He is our Saviour, Jesus will continue to do a saving work in believers, interceding for them and showing the way out of temptation. It is up to us to follow, not just for ourselves but for our children and descendants.

Because Jesus was obedient to the Father, even unto death, offering Himself sacrificially, He was our scapegoat and sacrifice. *"For as by one man's disobedience many were made sinners, so also by one Man's obedience many will be made righteous"* (Rom. 5:19). He modeled obedience and still does, and calls us to follow Him. **Therefore, not only can Jesus intercede for us and administer forgiveness if we are ready to repent, but as our Kinsman Redeemer, He restores the lost inheritance of believers.**

His first chosen people were put out of their inheritance as punishment for sin, being scattered or taken captive among the nations, over and over. But their descendants humbly returning to God meant that He returned them to their inheritance and we can be returned to our spiritual inheritance and the place God has for us. That is what happened to the prodigal who returned to the father in humility—and Jesus, our holy elder Brother, will surely welcome us home.

We also need Jesus because He causes us to *"know"* the Father in an intimate way. *"And this is eternal life, that they may know You, the only true God, and Jesus Christ whom You have sent"* (John 17:3). Believing in Jesus still gives us eternal life, and yet He explains that it means more than living forever and not being destroyed in the lake of fire. It means that we will be married to Jesus, knowing Him and the Father in an intimate way, with the rest of the body of Christ. Our new life begins on earth as it is in heaven.

> *Then I, John, saw the holy city, New Jerusalem, coming down out of heaven from God, prepared as a bride adorned for her husband. And*

I heard a loud voice from heaven saying, "Behold, the tabernacle of God is with men, and He will dwell with them, and they shall be His people. God Himself will be with them and be their God. And God will wipe away every tear from their eyes; there shall be no more death, nor sorrow, nor crying. There shall be no more pain, for the former things have passed away." Then He who sat on the throne said, "Behold, I make all things new." And He said to me, "Write, for these words are true and faithful." (Rev. 21:2–5)

Jesus Christ Is the Eternal Ark of the Testimony

Noah's ark was designed by God and built by Noah and his family **for the saving of a faithful remnant of His people.** Then the ark of the testimony was designed by God and built by Moses and his brethren for the saving of a faithful remnant of God's people in those days. It contained the testimony, the Law of God containing His commandments, His words, written on the two tablets. Since two thousand years ago, God has designed the ark of the testimony of Jesus Christ, the body of Christ, to be prophetically upbuilt by His followers for their salvation. His plans are to be followed. It contains the Law of God written on our hearts and minds, plus prophetic words He has given which line up with sacred Scripture.

The ark of the testimony which Moses built prefigured the current ark of the testimony of Jesus. It was made of acacia wood overlayed *"with pure gold, inside and out you shall overlay it"* (Ex. 25:11). Likewise, the body of Christ is made of flesh which has been glorified by the outpouring of Holy Spirit on it and within it. The Old Testament ark contained the tablets of testimony, and we have the testimony which God has written within us.

Moses's ark had the mercy seat resting on it, made of pure gold and including two golden images of covering angels over it. The presence of God would come down and rest between the angels so that He could communicate with the high priest about impending judgment on His people. The Aaronic priest would intercede for them, offering shed blood so sins of their people could be forgiven, including his own.

Just as the covering angels were a part of the mercy seat, God has angels around His throne in heaven and guardian angels around His people. They are glorious beings. And God reveals impending judgment upon certain "tribes" of His people to Jesus, the New Covenant High Priest and to certain members of His body. Being sinless, His own costly shed blood has been offered once for our sins. He intercedes for His people, sometimes enlisting some of His earthly family to join Him in intercession.

Just as the ark of the testimony was to be carried on the shoulders of Levites, priestly people, the ark of the testimony of Jesus, the body of Christ, is to be carried in prayer by priestly people. The Old Testament mercy seat rested upon the ark. The New Testament mercy seat is the throne of God in heaven above His people, and resting within the body of Christ where His kingdom has come *"on earth as it is in heaven"* (Matt. 6:10). God still wants to meet with His people for their good.

Jesus Is Mediator of the New Covenant because He Offered the Lamb

The goats and the spotless lambs sacrificed at Passover by the high priest, remembering the atoning blood that was put over the doorways of the houses of Jews when God brought His first chosen people out of Egypt, were a foreshadowing of Jesus. He is both the eternal spotless Passover Lamb who was slain in our place to atone for sin so we could receive forgiveness, and the eternal High Priest who selected the Lamb and offered the sacrifice of His own blood in atonement. *"No one takes it from Me, but I lay it down of Myself. I have power to lay it down, and I have power to take it again. This command I have received from My Father"* (John 10:18).

People on earth may bridge the gap between individual persons, or between people and God in Jesus's name, but there was such a long distance to bridge between heaven and earth, between God and mankind because of sin, that **heavenly intervention was required for reconciliation**. The Father had planned it that way from the beginning. **He created Adam in His image, according to His likeness, but God knew that man is not equal to God, and was dust without Him.** Six thousand years later, we need to realize that. **Mankind needs a High Priest Mediator who is also God and Saviour plus the perfect sacrifice, who is no one but Jesus:** *"The Lamb slain from the foundation of the world"* (Rev. 13:8). He was not God's "Plan B."

Long before Jesus took flesh and came to earth two thousand years ago, the Father had a plan. No one could be perfect without Jesus because He gave mankind a free will and since Adam and Eve, sometimes our choices are not good. He gave His people 4,000 years to see that they could not be saved some other way. However, knowing this in the beginning, it was the Father's will that Jesus should die so sin could be atoned for and fellowship with Him could be restored. Then with Christ in us, we can do the Father's will so much easier.

Jesus Opens a Well in Us

Aaronic high priests had various rituals to cleanse the people, including *mikvah*—washing in running water, what they called "living water." Today, Jesus baptizes us, cleansing us with His fire and Spirit, which opens in us a fountain like *"living water,"* and tells us to be baptized with water as well. Like the woman at the well, I gladly received this water which He gives which has become in me *"a fountain of water springing up into everlasting life"* (John 4:14). This satisfies thirst too. Jesus said, *"If anyone thirsts, let him come to Me and drink. He who believes in Me, as the Scripture has said, out of his heart will flow rivers of living water"* (John 7:3–38) for oneself and others. But He also washes us with His living Word and blood. Sometimes a *rhema* word will come bubbling up, prompted by Holy Spirit. This cleanses us spiritually, giving us peace and improving communication with the Almighty.

Jesus, Our Bridge, Truly Can Connect Mankind with God. He Is like a Heavenly Transport System

Jesus told His disciples on the night before He died:

> *Let not your hearts be troubled; you believe in God, believe also in Me. In My Father's house are many mansions; if it were not so, I would have told you. I go to prepare a place for you. And if I go and prepare a place for you, I will come and receive you to Myself; that where I am, there you may be also. And where I go you know, and the way you know.... I am the way, the truth, and the life. No one comes to the Father except through Me.* (John 14:1–6)

Jesus is also like a train engine that goes ahead by itself and then returns to connect to and lead the other train cars with it. To show us the first step in getting onto His train, He preached, *"The time is fulfilled, and the kingdom of God is at hand. Repent, and believe in the gospel"* (Mark 1:15). None of us can do it all on our own. If we walk in repentance and by His Holy Spirit, we can have kingdom living here on earth as it is in heaven. Jesus can shepherd or carry us to a place He has prepared for us here on earth in God's sight, and then one day to one in heaven, that we may be where He is. **He will take us there! Wait eagerly for Him!**

When we are first *"made alive"* by Christ after having been *"dead in trespasses and sins"* (Eph. 2:1), you could say He lifts us up in His salvation train. *"But God, who is rich in mercy, because of His great love with which He loved us, even when we were dead in trespasses, made us alive together with Christ (by grace you have been saved), and raised us up together, and made us sit together in the heavenly places in Christ Jesus"* (Eph. 2:4–6).

Our Bridge is like a heavenly transport system between earth and heaven in more ways than one. We can hop onto the train which is carried by Jesus like my grandson, Nate, carried his. It was prophesied that Jesus Himself would stand in the gap. Just as this little one lifted up his train car, Jesus, the Head, can lift up believers and their prayer requests in intercession, usually with the assistance of parts of His body: *"He saw that there was no man, and wondered that there was no intercessor; therefore His own arm brought salvation for Him; and His own righteousness, it sustained Him"* (Isa. 59:16).

Jesus can take us to the Father, first in the spirit and one day in our glorified bodies. He said the Father chose who to allow onto the bridge though. *"No one can come to Me unless the Father draws him, and I will raise him up at the last day"* (John 6:44).

I remember in 1981 when I went through a time of feeling like I was living in the "land of the living dead" after a preliminary judgment by the Word of God one night. I was encouraged with hope that Jesus, the *"resurrection and the life"* (John 11:25), would raise me up on *"the last day"* into *"the land of the living,"* into kingdom living on earth as it is in heaven. Thank God, when the time came, He did.

> *I would have lost heart, unless I had believed*
> *That I would see the goodness of the L*ORD *In the land of the living.*
> (Ps. 27:13)
>
> *Those who wait upon the L*ORD
> *Shall renew their strength;*
> *They shall mount up with wings like eagles,*
> *They shall run and not be weary,*
> *They shall walk and not faint.* (Isa. 40:31)
>
> *Whoever eats My flesh and drinks My blood has eternal life, and I will raise him up at the last day.* (John 6:54)

To get onto Jesus's salvation train, we have only to believe in Him to receive a free mercy ticket. They are very costly and a privilege to receive, so hold onto yours. **Jesus has already purchased our tickets. He prepaid them with His blood.** And of course He wants us to *"repent, for the kingdom of heaven is at hand"* (Matt. 4:17).

I used to think that all we could confess is our sins, but we can also confess what we believe in regards to faith in God and His only begotten Son, Jesus, our Saviour, and in Their Holy Spirit. Actually, we do that in the Apostles' Creed. Romans 10:9–10 says, *"If you confess with your mouth the Lord Jesus and believe in your heart that God has raised Him from the dead, you will be saved. For with the heart one believes unto righteousness, and with the mouth confession is made unto salvation."*

Since Jesus has opened the way to the Father in the true Most Holy Place, believers who are *"in Christ"* can ascend with Him in the Spirit too. **He will take you there, to a place of which most Old Testament believers only dreamed.** Because of His blood, He can take us all the way into the heavenly Holy of holies, the throne room of God.

Many times in the autumn of 2015, the song of the Lord to me was:

> *Come, now is the time to worship.*

Come, now is the time to give your heart....
One day every tongue will confess You are God, one day every knee will bow.
Still the greatest treasure remains for those who gladly choose you now.[12]

I would remember the night years before when I was at a Prepare the Way Ministries prayer gathering in Memorial Hall, in the Kingston City Hall, when the worship team led us in singing this song. Although there was no formal altar call, I had quickly made my way down to the altar to signify that I had chosen Him before and chose to worship Him now. Thank God, I have found *the greatest treasure* as Abraham did. My *"exceedingly great reward"* (Gen. 15:1) is to experience the presence of Jesus here on earth.

"In Christ," we can worship and dialogue with God Himself, and make return trips. *"Let us therefore come boldly to the throne of grace, that we may obtain mercy and find grace to help in time of need"* (Heb. 4:16). Jesus is our intermediary and gives His disciples the privilege to go, like children, praying directly to Abba Father through His name. *"This is the confidence we have in approaching God: that if we ask anything according to his will, he hears us. And if we know he hears us—whatever we ask—we know that we have what we asked of him"* (1 John 5:14–15 NIV). Jesus gave as a condition for this that we abide in His love. Trust and obey. There is no other way.

Rail System: Churches Joined Together in the Spirit

The churches which are in Christ are like railroad tracks being joined together in the Spirit lining up with His Word and His commandments. After all, whose churches are they and whose churches

---

12   Brian Doerkson, *Come, Now Is the Time to Worship.* (Vineyard Songs, UK/Eire, 1998, Admin. In N. America by Mercy/Vineyard Publishing.)

should they be? They are to welcome Jesus to supervise their installment and maintenance, laying their lives down so believers can get to heaven.

As in the first century AD, there are many churches today worldwide professing belief in Jesus, and He can send them prophetic words of instruction today. Besides the church in Jerusalem, there were seven churches in Asia mentioned in Revelation compared to *"golden lampstands"* (Rev. 1:20), with the presence of Jesus **walking in their midst.** He still does that, overseeing, pointing out things and interceding, speaking through those whom He sends. *"The mystery of the seven stars which you saw in My right hand, and the seven golden lampstands: The seven stars are the angels of the seven churches, and the seven lampstands which you saw are the seven churches"* (Rev. 1:20). So He tells us to listen to what the Spirit says to the churches.

John was amazed as Jesus revealed Himself to him as He is in heaven:

> *…with a loud voice, as of a trumpet, saying, "I am the Alpha and the Omega, the First and the Last," and, "What you see, write in a book and send it to the seven churches which are in Asia…." Then I turned to see the voice that spoke with me. And having turned I saw seven golden lampstands, and in the midst of the seven lampstands One like the Son of Man, clothed with a garment down to the feet and girded about the chest with a golden band. His head and hair were white like wool, as white as snow, and His eyes like a flame of fire; His feet were like fine brass, as if refined in a furnace, and His voice as the sound of many waters; He had in His right hand seven stars, out of His mouth went a sharp two-edged sword, and His countenance was like the sun shining in its strength. And when I saw Him, I fell at His feet as dead. But He laid His right hand on me, saying to me, "Do not be afraid; I am the First and the Last. I am He who lives, and was dead, and behold, I am alive forevermore. Amen. And I hold the keys of Hades and of Death."* (Rev. 1:10–18)

Some churches had more to do than others in order to be functioning properly with Jesus truly as their Lord governing them by His Spirit. **Jesus recognized what they were doing right and also pointed out their shortcomings to their** *"stars,"* **their messengers, so that they could tell the churches,** *"He who has an ear, let him hear what the Spirit says to the churches"* (Rev. 2:7). That takes great humility on the part of His fivefold ministry.

His messengers are in His hand, under His control and protection, and sometimes He has to send them a prophetic word through another messenger, like John, who was an apostle and prophet. Jesus let all the churches hear what He was saying to each one so that they could learn from what He said to others too. **It was not meant to be gossip with other churches pointing their fingers at one another. Rather it was meant to upbuild them all, and they could join Him in interceding.** We are affected by what happens to the rest of the body. After all, there was and is to be one body of Christ, governed under His watchful eyes. Nothing escapes His gaze, even to the depths of our hearts. He sees what needs to be done and tells us how to get there. *"And the government shall be upon His shoulder"* (Isa. 9:6).

Individual churches or ministries are like railroad tracks and ties which are to line up with Jesus. Humbling themselves to seek the unity of the Spirit, they are to be joined with other ministries altogether on top of the railroad bridge—joined together with every railroad track and spike that He supplies. They will carry the train, undergirded by intercessors.

> *But now in Christ Jesus you who were once far off have been brought near by the blood of Christ. For He Himself is our peace ... that He might reconcile them both to God in one body through the cross, thereby putting to death the enmity. And He came and preached peace to you who were afar off and to those who were near. For through Him we both have access by one Spirit to the Father.* (Eph. 2:13–14, 16–18)

If a section of train track or a few railroad ties are off by themselves, unconnected to the rail system and the trestle bridge or bent out of shape, they will not bring the train very far and their service could be shut down. Some churches have already been closed. Indeed, during the COVID-19 pandemic, almost all the churches in many nations were closed down for weeks to *"reset."*

Sadly, in the nineties, I saw a couple vibrant churches in revival close their doors after unrepentant sin was found in the leadership. **We mourned like for a death and it was difficult to worship, until the Lord sent word,** *"Rejoice, the Lord is King!"* Then we offered a sacrifice of praise. Yet a few years later, when a vibrant ministry almost folded because of the same thing, adultery, thank God, following much prayer, the ministry survived. And that humble minister repented and had counseling and a few years later the Lord restored him to ministry elsewhere, praise God.

As Jesus said:

> *I am the vine, you are the branches. He who abides in Me and I in him bears much fruit; for without Me you can do nothing. If anyone does not abide in Me, he is cast out as a branch and is withered; and they gather them and throw them into the fire, and they are burned. If you abide in Me and My words abide in you, you will ask what you desire, and it will be done for you. By this My Father is glorified, that you bear much fruit; so you will be My disciples. As the Father loved Me, I also have loved you; abide in My love. If you keep My commandments, you will abide in My love, just as I have kept My Father's commandments and abide in His love. These things I have spoken to you, that My joy may remain in you, and that your joy may be full. This is My commandment, that you love one another as I have loved you. Greater love has no one than this, than to lay down one's life for his friends.* (John 15:5–13)

This is like train tracks laid down under the loving command of the master builder. If individual churches and members abide in

Christ, getting their red and green signals from His Word, the train of souls will be routed to salvation and brought to the Father, and He will be glorified in His church.

Jesus expects us to pray desiring the Father's will to be done on earth as it is in heaven, and **there is power in agreement**: *"Again I say to you, if two of you agree on earth about anything they ask, it will be done for them by My Father in heaven. For where two or three are gathered in My name, there am I in the midst of them"* (Matt. 18:19–20). **The tracks will be orderly with none missing when multitudes of churches throughout the world agree with Jesus and with one another.** But Jesus begins by getting two or three sections of His "rail system" to line up with one another, adding on. **His Word is the plumb line. We must not despise the day of small beginnings** which He has initiated. How wonderful it has been at conferences with ministers from many denominations and nations, gathering together in one accord to pray and serve in Jesus's name!

Jesus Receives New Believers and Transports Them to the Father

He will transport His sheep, His passengers, into His kingdom and carry His kingdom into us even while we live here on earth. *"He has delivered us from the power of darkness and conveyed* [transferred] *us into the kingdom of the Son of His love, in whom we have redemption through His blood, the forgiveness of sins"* (Col. 1:13–14).

Since we have been saved *"by grace ... through faith, and that not of yourselves; it is the gift of God, not of works, lest anyone should boast"* (Eph. 2:8–9), we can return as His little ones to the throne room of God in the Spirit. What a great privilege that is, to take Jesus's glory train. **Jesus will take us there.**

Humility is so important. James 4:10 says, *"Humble yourselves in the sight of the Lord, and He will lift you up."* Jesus yearns jealously for

His bride, so He continues to give us grace so we can resist the devil and submit to God: *"God resists the proud, but gives grace to the humble"* (Jas. 4:6).

When I have humbled myself, bowing before Him on my face or knees in repentance, in worship or in seeking His aid because a task seemed too big, there have been times when after a few moments I have heard the Lord graciously tell me to *"stand up."* He lifted my spirit too with His permission, presence and grace, sometimes reminding me, *"Fear not,"* because He was with me, or that, *"You can do it. Christ is in you."* His joy truly is our strength. *"[He's] my glory, and the lifter of my head"* (Ps. 3:3 KJV).

Another way for believers to humble themselves before Him is to do whatever He tells them to do, whether anyone understands or not. Jesus always obeyed His Father's instruction, including at Gethsemane even when His trained disciples did not understand at first. So God gave Him strength to stand.

The servants at the wedding at Cana trusted and obeyed Jesus, filling water jugs at His word, and their obedience was rewarded. **God lifted their spirits** when they saw the result—water turned into excellent wine for the days of celebration. **By faith, Jesus saw the result even before it came to pass,** so He was encouraged, trusting and obeying His Father at all times. *"For the joy that was set before Him* [He] *endured the cross, despising the shame, and has sat down at the right hand of the throne of God"* (Heb. 12:2). **When we trust Jesus and the Father, trusting in His grace and that His Word will work mightily in us, we can do more than we could otherwise.** The joy He gives us is our supporting strength, like strong hands under us, and He is our defense.

When Jesus began His ministry, **He announced and described in parables the coming of the kingdom.** We can pray to the Father today for His kingdom to come and His will to be done *"on earth as it is in heaven"* (Matt. 6:10). Then when He sent His apostles out on a mission trip, He told them, *"And as you go, preach, saying, 'The kingdom* *of God is at hand.' Heal the sick, cleanse the lepers, raise the dead, cast out demons. Freely you have received, freely give"* (Matt. 10:7–8). People are not sick, lepers, dead, or demon-controlled in heaven, so believers can experience this freedom on earth too because the power of God comes through Jesus and in His name. He still calls His disciples to repent today, recognizing that the kingdom of God is near and to ask the Father for its manifestation in our midst. **Jesus still lifts us with God's kingdom living today.**

Chapter 15

Jesus Reveals the Heart of the Father

Jesus told Philip, *"He who has seen Me has seen the Father; so how can you say, 'Show us the Father'? Do you not believe that I am in the Father and the Father in Me? The words that I speak to you I do not speak on My own authority; but the Father who dwells in Me does the works. Believe Me that I am in the Father and the Father in Me, or else believe Me for the sake of the works themselves"* (John 14:9–11). Jesus revealed the heart of the Father before, and **He still does**. *"Worthy is the Lamb who was slain to receive power and riches and wisdom, and strength and honor and glory and blessing!"* (Rev. 5:12).

Jesus is *"the Prince of Peace"* **(Isa. 9:6), so His Father is the King of Peace.** When we are reconciled and living in right relationship with Him, and even when we are ready to do it again but are confused, we can experience His peace as the apostles did when they were reconciled with Jesus again. They had run off when Jesus was arrested, afraid of being captured too. They received His peace by faith after He rose from the dead, proved to them He was really resurrected, and forgave their sins.

He manifested the Father's mercy. Supernaturally, He entered:

> *…when the doors were shut where the disciples were assembled, for fear of the Jews. Jesus came and stood in the midst, and said to them, "Peace be with you." When He had said this, He showed them His hands and His side. Then the disciples were glad when they saw the Lord. So Jesus said to them again, "Peace to you! As the Father has*

sent Me, I also send you." And when He had said this, He breathed on them, and said to them, "Receive the Holy Spirit. If you forgive the sins of any, they are forgiven them; if you retain the sins of any, they are retained." (John 20:19–23)

A benefit for believers is that through His Son, our Father *"forgives all your iniquities.... As a father pities his children, so the LORD pities those who fear Him. For He knows our frame; He remembers that we are dust"* (Ps. 103:3, 13–14).

Years ago, the Lord magnified to me this word, *"Glory to God in the highest, and on earth peace among men with whom He is pleased"* (Luke 2:14 RSV), as the understanding of the angel's message to the shepherds at His birth. Jesus acted and still acts according to what He saw and heard from His Father. He saw how the sin of mankind grieved

His Father, and deserved punishment. Yet God's love for the world was so great that He gave His only begotten Son so that believers could obtain forgiveness and eternal life. The Father loves His Son and He loves the works of His creation too. But those who have faith and obey His will, including walking in repentance, please Him the most. **When we seek His righteousness, we receive His peace.**

> *So then, those who are in the flesh cannot please God. But you are not in the flesh but in the Spirit, if indeed the Spirit of God dwells in you.* (Rom. 8:8–9)

> *But without faith it is impossible to please Him, for he who comes to God must believe that He is, and that He is a rewarder of those who diligently seek Him.* (Heb. 11:6)

The Father **desires that all should be saved** and none should be lost, and yet **He gave us free will to choose** to become His children. Jesus did and does everything He can to seek and save the lost and lead His people to the Father for all eternity. He does it all for love of God and mankind. He even warned people in parables that those who refuse to obey God or have Him reign over them, would be punished. *"The LORD is righteous in all His ways, gracious in all His works"* (Ps. 145:17).

"Blessed are the peacemakers, for they shall be called sons of God" (Matt. 5:9). **Jesus is the best peacemaker.** He is one with His Father and pleads with Him on our behalf and with us on His behalf. God is one. **He knows God's heart because no one is closer to God than Jesus.** *"Hear, O Israel: The Lord our God* [Elohim], *the Lord is one!"* (Deut. 6:4) And Hebrews 1:1–3 tells us that *"God ... has in these last days spoken to us by His Son, whom He has appointed heir of all things, through whom also He made the worlds; who being the brightness of His glory and the express image of His person, and upholding all things by the word of His power, when He had by Himself purged our sins, sat down at the right hand of the Majesty on high."* As a matter of fact, the Hebrew word *Elohim* is

used for God here. This is a plural word referring to Father, Son and Holy Spirit, our God, being one.

God wants us to pray for more than ourselves or our family, but for all men, including the leadership, good or bad, political and spiritual. So Jesus can remind us to pray to *"our Father."* The fruit of our labour in the name of Jesus can be *"that we may lead a quiet and peaceable life in all godliness and reverence"* (1 Tim. 2:2). **People can humble themselves or be humbled, coming down like a melting mountain.** When the Jews were exiled by God to Babylon, **God even commanded them to pray for their captor, the king of Babylon.** And evil leaders may even come to realize that their authority comes from God, not themselves, as King Nebuchadnezzar admitted after God humbled him: *"The Most High rules in the kingdom of men,* [and] *gives it to whomever He will, and sets over it the lowest of men"* (Dan. 4:17).

The king was restored to sanity after being judged by God for seven years as God had foretold him in a dream Daniel had interpreted. When restored, the king humbly testified, *"My understanding returned to me; and I blessed the Most High and praised and honored Him who lives forever: For His dominion is an everlasting dominion, and His kingdom is from generation to generation"* (Dan. 4:34).

Jesus reveals the loving heart of the Father, telling His disciples to *"love one another as I have loved you"* **(John 15:12), and even to** *"love your enemies, do good to those who hate you, bless those who curse you, and pray for those who spitefully use you"* (Luke 6:27–28). Some of His parables show that we are to humble ourselves before God rather than have Him humble us. **The heart of the Father is for us to react well to others according to the Golden Rule, and leave the person in God's hands**. If we do unto others as we would have them do unto us, rather than what they did unto us, it just could be a seed of a turning point in their lives. After all, Jesus loved us when we did not deserve it. Each of the names of Jesus reveals more of who the Father is.

Jesus reveals the mercy of God in so many ways, yet acknowledging that He *"by no means clearing the guilty"* (Ex. 34:7) when they do not repent. When Moses wanted to see God's glory, He let His goodness and mercy pass by him. The Father proclaimed His name to Moses having said, *"I will be gracious to whom I will be gracious, and I will have compassion on whom I will have compassion."* (Ex. 33:19) Jesus was and is full of compassion and tender mercies. Healings and miracles still happen today, in Jesus's name, according to the Father's will.

Zacharias, father of John the Baptist, prophesied of Jesus coming:

> *That we should be saved from our enemies*
> *And from the hand of all who hate us,*
> *To perform the mercy promised to our fathers*
> *And to remember His holy covenant....*
> *To grant us that we,*
> *Being delivered from the hand of our enemies*
> *Might serve Him without fear,*
> *In holiness and righteousness before Him all the days of our life.*
> [And John would] *prepare His ways,*
> *To give knowledge of salvation to His people*
> *By the remission of their sins,*
> *Through the tender mercy of our God,*
> *With which the Dayspring from on high has visited us;*
> *To give light to those who sit in darkness and the shadow of death,*
> *To guide our feet into the way of peace.* (Luke 1:71–72, 74–79)

The Son Still Follows the Father's Leading and So Should We

Jesus said, *"I can of Myself do nothing. As I hear, I judge; and My judgment is righteous, because I do not seek My own will but the will of the Father who sent Me"* (John 5:30). **That is humility!** He compared doing the Father's will to eating: *"My food is to do the will of Him who sent Me and to finish His work"* (John 4:34). And we know that, *"Jesus Christ is* *the same yesterday, today, and forever"* (Heb. 13:8). We, His trestlework, His *"royal priesthood"* (1 Pet. 2:9), can know His will from the Bible and from listening to the *rhema* words which He gives us, instruction specific for our situations. His sheep can hear His voice even today, thanks be to God.

If a cell phone is turned off, you cannot receive calls. But if it is on stand-by, there might be a ring or a vibration to alert you to an incoming call, even if it comes from overseas. It is not too difficult for God to communicate with us either. God can call us. Keep the connection available and recharge your receiver with worship.

If I awake in the night, since I asked the Lord to make it clear to me whether it was because He wanted me to rise and pray, at times I have heard a *"song in the night"* (Ps. 77:6), or a knocking sound or a ring in the spirit awakening me, sounding like a phone; but it was not, because no incoming call was recorded on my phone. We have just to answer His call and invite Him in.

I have heard the Lord say, *"Jesus is coming soon."* He is coming in His glorified body to receive the raptured church, but He is also making visitations and habitations by His Spirit. Let us also be ready to meet with Him Spirit to spirit, no matter what hour He comes. The bride of Christ should be willing to follow the Bridegroom's leading, able to say, *"I sleep, but my heart is awake; it is the voice of my beloved! He knocks, saying, 'Open for me, my sister, my love, my dove, my perfect one'"* (Song 5:2).

We need to keep our hearts open for Jesus, ready and willing to rise and meet with Him in love. He might want us to worship the Father with Him, or to intercede with Him according to what is on the Father's heart, or to give us revelation and eat it with us, or to prepare to go somewhere with Him. He might want us to go deeper into intercession with Him, like Peter, James, and John at Gethsemane. **The Father's heart is to have fellowship—communion with His children.**

May God forgive us for times when we have not responded well to His calls. Let us be like little Samuel who was taught to say, when he heard God calling his name (like dialing his number), *"Speak, LORD, for Your servant is listening"* (1 Sam. 3:9). Sometimes Christ has a "text message" for us too, leading us to a Scripture. **Part of His function today is to connect with His people so that they may join with Him in praise and worship and intercession, or for revelation.** *"True worshipers will worship the Father in spirit and truth"* (John 4:23), loving Him with their whole heart, soul, mind, and strength, and waiting on the Lord to lead them. Let His Word enter our hearts and minds like seed; trust and obey it with a deep trust, and enter into His rest. As it is written, *"Today, if you hear His voice, do not harden your hearts"* (Heb. 4:7).

Jesus is still sowing His Word which He gets from the Father, into the hearts of men. [13] If our hearts are not hard, we can receive the precious seed and go on to bear fruit in repentance and love.

Not only is He the Teacher, the Sower, and the Author and Finisher of our faith, but Jesus said, *"No one comes to the Father except through Me"* (John 14:6). The Father draws men to Jesus and then Jesus leads them to the Father, manifesting His will. What a great privilege it is to assist Jesus in lifting up people to God with words of encouragement and prayer through His name! He said, *"This is the will of the Father who sent Me, that of all He has given Me I should lose nothing, but should raise it up at the last day"* (John 6:39). **Jesus brings forth a mighty harvest of souls.** Mankind has only to repent and believe in the gospel to enjoy kingdom living beginning here on earth. It is done and it is being done *"on earth as it is in heaven"* (Matt. 6:10).

Jesus Tells His Disciples to Pray Down the Father's Kingdom and His Will

We are to ask the Father, *"Your kingdom come, Your will be done, on earth as it is in heaven"* (Matt. 6:10). Having His kingdom with its King within us, our joy increases. If we ask Him to lead us in intercession, He will. It's His train, His people, and His bridge. Our prayers in His name rise like incense before His throne. We can have the presence of God among us, leading and guiding us, healing and delivering us from evil. It is an atmosphere with foundations of love and honor for God, and for our neighbours as ourselves.

King Jesus, like His Father, is rich in mercy, but also just. *"So great is His mercy toward those who fear Him"* (Ps. 103:11). He wants *"to settle accounts with his servants"* (Matt. 18:23) while they are still on

---

13   Salvador, Cover page

earth, forgiving and healing; but He wants them to *"go and sin no more"* (John 8:11). **This is being set free for kingdom living now, before we face Him when He comes again to judge the living and the dead.** He is like the king who was so merciful to the servant who owed him a huge debt and forgave it all because the man begged him. But let us not be like that man who turned around and refused to forgive another servant a relatively small debt when he asked for mercy. Therefore, his master *"threw him in prison till he should pay the debt...*. [Then the king became angry with his wicked servant] *and delivered him to the torturers until he should pay all that was due to him.* [And Jesus continued,] *So My heavenly Father also will do to you if each of you, from his heart, does not forgive his brother his trespasses"* (Matt. 18:30, 34–35). Jesus shows us the right way to live, as He has mercifully treated us, warning us that otherwise we could face the consequences of our actions.

God Is the One to Choose Where and How His People Will Serve

Jesus foreknew His apostles and personally called and trained them and sent them out to specific places. Yet sometimes they were slow in grasping things: *"Thomas said to Him, 'Lord, we do not know where You are going, and how can we know the way?' Jesus said to him, 'I am the way, the truth, and the life. No one comes to the Father except through Me'"* (John 14:5–6).

Jesus was proclaiming that He is the one Mediator, reconciling man to God and the way to get there. He gives direction as the King, Lord, and Head, giving authority to believers to use His name to go to the Father and in prayer.

God chose where His Son would serve, both two thousand years ago and in the time following that. Speaking through David in Psalm 2, the Father revealed beforehand His plan to set in place His Chosen One, His only begotten Son, Jesus, as the reigning King of Israel and of the nations. He calls the Son, *"His Anointed,"* which means He is God's *"Christ,"* or Messiah, *Hamashiach*, His Commissioned One.

> *He who sits in the heavens shall laugh* [at] ...
> *the rulers* [who] *take counsel together,*
> *Against the* LORD *and His anointed....*
> *"Yet I have set My King*
> *On My holy hill of Zion."*
> [Then He spoke through the Son,]
> *"I will declare the decree:*
> *The* LORD *has said to Me,*
> *'You are My Son,*
> *Today I have begotten You.*
> *Ask of Me and I will give You*
> *The nations for Your inheritance,*
> *And the ends of the earth for Your possession.'"* (Psalm 2:4, 2, 6–8)

God is supposed to be the one who chooses and sets in place the king and high priest who will minister unto Him and His people, and so He personally chose Saul and David to be Old Testament kings and promised a chosen Seed of David to reign forever, who is actually Jesus. God also chose Aaron and his sons to be high priests in the Old Testament tabernacles. But they were but a foreshadowing of Jesus.

God's real desire was to have Jesus, Son of Man and Son of God, as His chosen, everlasting, King and High Priest, serving now at His right hand. The other Old Testament judges, kings, and priests, only sons of men, all had sin in their lives to a greater or lesser degree and were temporary; but Jesus is eternally the spotless Lamb of God and High Priest. Years after the shepherd-king David died, Ezekiel prophesied of his Seed, the Good Shepherd-King, and of the reuniting of God's divided people: *"David My servant shall be king over them, and they shall all have one shepherd ... and I will set My sanctuary in their midst forevermore"* (Ezek. 37:24, 26). His sanctuary is now within His people who acknowledge Him as Saviour and Messiah (Christ) and will be within more Jewish people as they come to really know the truth.

We are to wait on the Lord, the *"possessor of heaven and earth"* (Gen. 14:19), to let Him possess us by His Holy Spirit and to position us as sons and daughters, trained by the Father, Son, and Spirit. He gifts and trains His disciples, calling them forth by speaking words like, *"Fear not, for I am with you"* (Gen. 23:24); and, *"All your children shall be taught by the Lord, and great shall be the peace of your children"* (Isa. 54:13).

I used to really worry about how and where I could serve the Lord, until I learned to trust Jesus and let Him lead. He had ministered to me through a song which proclaimed that the love He had for me and the faith He had in me was greater than what I had for Him, and that His love and light in me would grow. So my part was to exercise that love and faith. As my mom used to tell me, "Bloom where you are planted." And body parts need to be connected to the body of Christ where God wants them, like trestles in a bridge.

God's Word is true and says:

> *From the rising of the sun to its going down*
> *The Lord's name is to be praised.*
> *The Lord is high above all nations,*
> *His glory above the heavens.*
> *Who is like the Lord our God,*
> *Who dwells on high?* (Psalm 113:3–5)
> *Wait on the Lord,*
> *And keep His way,*
> *And He shall exalt you to inherit the land.* (Psalm 37:34)
> *A man's gift makes room for him,*
> *And brings him before great men.* (Proverbs 18:16)

God can send His people to where they can receive training. Afterwards, I have been amazed at where He has sent some of His people to serve and even some divine appointments I have had. To God be the glory!

The Lord can lead us to the church where He wants us to be a part and worship, and even to where He wants us to work. I have experienced those things. Our job is to seek the place He has for us and to stay there until He releases us. That is the place where we can be and receive the greatest blessing as a member of the body of Christ.

There is a micro and macro view of where God is placing people. We can be part of the body of Christ in our home church, a functioning member. And we can be part of the citywide body, which is in the provincewide and nationwide body; and at the same time be a part of the global body of Christ. Sometimes the connection is only by mail or internet. But there is one God orchestrating it all. *"There is one body and one Spirit, just as you were called in one hope of your calling; one Lord, one faith, one baptism; one God and Father of all, who is above all, and through all, and in you all"* (Eph. 4:4–6).

Already, *"bone to bone and marrow to marrow,"* the Lord is bringing together people with similar callings to connect at conferences where the singing of praise and worship is often awesome—because it is anointed and heartfelt. In these days of Ezekiel, He has begun to set the dry bones in place, fill them with His Spirit and to release the captives bringing restoration. His watchmen *"see eye to eye"* at prayer and fasting gatherings like The CALL and The CRY. We are to be Christlike, but no one is His equal. With Jesus leading His watchmen, seeing with the vision of Holy Spirit and washed in the blood of the Lamb, they will be clean when they worship and lift up the people in prayer as part of His holy arm.

> *Your watchmen shall lift up their voices,*
> *With their voices they shall sing together;*
> *For they shall see eye to eye*
> *When the LORD brings back Zion.*
> *Break forth into joy, sing together,*

> *You waste places of Jerusalem!*
> *For the LORD has comforted His people,*
> *He has redeemed Jerusalem.*
> *The LORD has made bare His holy arm*
> *In the eyes of all the nations;*
> *And all the ends of the earth shall see*
> *The salvation of our God.*
> *Depart! Depart! Go out from there,*
> *Touch no unclean thing;*
> *Go out from the midst of her,*
> *Be clean,*
> *You who bear the vessels of the LORD.*
> *For you shall not go out with haste,*
> *Nor go by flight;*
> *For the LORD will go before you,*
> *And the God of Israel will be your rear guard.* (Isaiah 52:8–12)

He has been bringing His Jewish people back to their homeland in the natural and some in the spiritual, causing us to rejoice and break forth in singing. How we did that in gatherings in Jerusalem, and how His people have been comforted by Christians! Glory be to God! He leads them out of *"Babylon"* and tells them to wash themselves. (He did that for me too.) Jesus leads and defends.

His people are finding that Jesus, the Good Shepherd-King, overrules all. He can also set certain people in place as leaders or shepherds under Him. They are not to act like hirelings, though, because He can help them.

> *I am the good shepherd. The good shepherd gives His life for the sheep. But a hireling, he who is not the shepherd, one who does not own the sheep, sees the wolf coming and leaves the sheep and flees; and the wolf catches the sheep and scatters them. The hireling flees because he is a hireling and does not care about the sheep. I am the*

> *good shepherd; and I know My sheep, and am known by My own.* (John 10:11–14)
>
> *I will gather the remnant of My flock out of all countries where I have driven them, and bring them back to their folds; and they shall be fruitful and increase. I will set up shepherds over them who will feed them; and they shall fear no more, nor be dismayed, nor shall they be lacking, says the L*ORD*.* (Jeremiah 23:3–4)

"Jesus called a little child to Him, set him in the midst of them" (Matt. 18:2), and used him as an example for His Jewish disciples to follow that they might humble themselves in order to enter the kingdom of heaven. This childlike trust of and obedience to the Father means He can set Jewish and Gentile believers as an example, as a light, to others, in Jesus's name, *"for salvation." "The* LORD *has commanded us: 'I have set you as a light to the Gentiles, that you should be for salvation to the ends of the earth'"* (Acts 13:47).

In Christ the Mediator, in His body, as parts of the trestlework of His bridge, set in place by Him, we are all important: Jews and Gentiles, Roman Catholics and Protestants, non-denominational and mainline church members, Evangelicals and Pentecostals, male and female, all races and colours. May He bring the hearts of believers together in His praise and in common sorrow for their sins. People should repent of any serious sin which causes division in the church so that breaches can be repaired, and we will be a fuller, more complete bridge with trestles intact and in place. His righteousness leads to peace. May the Father make us one so the world will know that He sent His Son.

Function of Watchmen

Watchmen are trestlework. They are called and set in place by Jesus. He took all eleven apostles with Him to the Garden of Gethsemane to pray with Him. But He chose three to come closer to Him, *"a stone's throw away,"* to watch and pray there—like the top of a tower of trestlework. They could have helped Him hold His hands up by agreeing with His prayers. Sadly though, they kept falling asleep after hearing a little. *"Then He came to the disciples and found them sleeping, and said to Peter, 'What? Could you not watch with Me one hour? Watch and pray, lest you enter into temptation. The spirit indeed is willing, but the flesh is weak'"* (Matt. 26:40–41).

Jesus can call people even today to **watch with Him, and to pray into what they are seeing.** It could be in the day or in the night, sometimes for a one-, three-, or six-hour watch with Him. Occasionally it could be all night as He sometimes prayed with His Father. He can even call them up to heaven in the Spirit as He did John, to see things more clearly from a higher perspective.

If a watchman sees that a wall is broken down or in need of repair as protection against the enemy, he might be led to pray that God would rebuild it with better material or that the wall be called "Salvation." **But they should do it according to the Lord's blueprint and not speaking things into existence just out of their own heart. They need to see and hear from Him**—even in a vision.

> *"Son of man, prophesy against the prophets of Israel who prophesy and say to those who prophesy out of their own heart, 'Hear the word of the LORD!'"*
>
> *Thus says the Lord GOD:* "*Woe to the foolish prophets, who follow their own spirit and have seen nothing!... You have not gone up into the gaps to build a wall for the house of Israel to stand in battle on the day of the LORD."* (Ezekiel 13:2–3, 5)

We can pray:

Cleanse me from secret faults.
Keep back Your servant from presumptuous sins;
Let them not have dominion over me,
Then I shall be blameless,
And I shall be innocent of great transgression. (Psalm 19:12–13)

Instead of bronze I will bring gold,
Instead of iron I will bring silver,
Instead of wood, bronze,
And instead of stones, iron.
I will also make your officers peace,
And your magistrates righteousness.
Violence shall no longer be heard in your land,
Neither wasting nor destruction within your borders;
But you shall call your walls Salvation,
And your gates Praise. (Isaiah 60:17–18)

Watchmen are supposed to be responsible, seeing what God shows them and praying for themselves and others: *"Watch therefore, and pray always that you may be counted worthy to escape all these things that will come to pass, and to stand before the Son of Man"* (Luke 21:36).

There was a time in Isaiah's day when they did not behave responsibly, and it is a warning for us today. *"Thus says the LORD: 'Keep justice, and do righteousness, for My salvation is about to come, and My righteousness to be revealed'"* (Isa. 56:1). The Lord had reminded them that His salvation and righteousness were coming. They were supposed to give the people warning of things, but were missing opportunities.

His watchmen are blind,
They are all ignorant;
They are all dumb dogs,
They cannot bark;
Sleeping, lying down, loving to slumber.
Yes, they are greedy dogs
Which never have enough.
And they are shepherds
Who cannot understand;
They all look to their own way,
Every one for his own gain, from his own territory.
"Come," one says, "I will bring wine,

> *And we will fill ourselves with intoxicating drink;*
> *Tomorrow will be as today,*
> *And much more abundant."* (Isaiah 56:10–12)

There are times when God gives them rest and times when He wants them to be on the job, alert, doing their duty. God blesses His watchmen, but they need to remember that **they are blessed to be a blessing and not to be greedy.** They need to be satisfied with what God provides for them, for He will supply their needs abundantly so that they can share with others. **He knows what they need, so the advancement of the kingdom of God and His righteousness should be their priority.** They should care about the sheep that Jesus entrusts into their care and understand their needs, following the Good Shepherd themselves. They need the Holy Spirit and to have others receive Him too, and there are times, especially initially, when the Holy Spirit might fill them so full with His new wine, His intoxicating presence, that people think they are drunk as they thought the 120 disciples were at Pentecost. **But the purpose of being filled is not to keep being drunk, but to refresh, invigorate, and enable you to serve. We are to *"be fruitful, not fruity,"* the Lord said once at a conference.**

> *Therefore He says:*
> *"Awake, you who sleep,*
> *Arise from the dead,*
> *And Christ will give you light."*
>
> *See then that you walk circumspectly, not as fools but as wise, redeeming the time, because the days are evil. Therefore do not be unwise, but understand what the will of the Lord is. And do not be drunk with wine, in which is dissipation; but be filled with the Spirit, speaking to one another in psalms and hymns and spiritual songs, singing and making melody in your heart to the Lord, giving thanks always for all things to God the Father in the name of our Lord Jesus Christ, submitting to one another in the fear of God.* (Eph. 5:14–21)

There are times when watchmen need to be persistent in prayer, in faith believing until what is already done in heaven is manifested on earth.

> *For Zion's sake I will not hold My peace,*
> *And for Jerusalem's sake I will not rest,*
> *Until her righteousness goes forth as brightness,*
> *And her salvation as a lamp that burns....*
> *I have set watchmen on your walls, O Jerusalem;*
> *They shall never hold their peace day or night.*
> *You who make mention of the* L{\scriptsize ORD}*, do not keep silent,*
> *And give Him no rest till He establishes*
> *And till He makes Jerusalem a praise in the earth.*
> (Isaiah 62:1, 6–7)

There are times when the Lord shows watchmen that it is time for something to happen, like when He was bringing His scattered remnant home. They need to let the people know, declare God's Word and intercede, praying for His saving grace.

> *For there shall be a day*
> *When the watchmen will cry on Mount Ephraim,*
> *"Arise, and let us go up to Zion,*
> *To the* L{\scriptsize ORD} *our God."*
> *For thus says the* L{\scriptsize ORD} *:*
> *"Sing with gladness for Jacob,*
> *And shout among the chief of the nations;*
> *Proclaim, give praise, and say,*
> *'O* L{\scriptsize ORD}*, save Your people,*
> *The remnant of Israel!'"* (Jeremiah 31:6–7)

Sometimes watchmen give warning even today. Hopefully people will take notice and be saved from trouble. But if God has them sound a warning and people do not listen, then the watchmen know they have been faithful, but that is something about which others will have to answer to God: *"Also, I set watchmen over you, saying, 'Listen to the sound of the trumpet!' But they said, 'We will not listen'"* (Jer. 6:17).

Jeremiah warned that Babylon would drink the cup of the Lord's wrath (as she will today) but it was time for His people to *"come out of her"* and any who stayed prostituting themselves with her could also experience her plagues. This is so we can learn from the past.

> *Flee from the midst of Babylon,*
> *And every one save his life!*
> *Do not be cut off in her iniquity,*
> *For this is the time of the L*ORD*'s vengeance;*
> *He shall recompense her.*
> *Babylon was a golden cup in the L*ORD*'s hand,*
> *That made all the earth drunk.*
> *The nations drank her wine;*
> *Therefore the nations are deranged.*
> *Babylon has suddenly fallen and been destroyed.*
> *Wail for her!*
> *Take balm for her pain;*
> *Perhaps she may be healed.*
> *We would have healed Babylon,*
> *But she is not healed.*
> *Forsake her, and let us go everyone to his own country;*
> *For her judgment reaches to heaven and is lifted up to the skies.*
> *The L*ORD *has revealed our righteousness.*
> *Come and let us declare in Zion the work of the L*ORD *our God.*
> *Make the arrows bright!*
> *Gather the shields!*
> *The L*ORD *has raised up the spirit of the kings of the Medes.*
> *For His plan is against Babylon to destroy it,*
> *Because it is the vengeance of the L*ORD*,*
> *The vengeance for His temple.*
> *Set up the standard on the walls of Babylon;*

Make the guard strong,
Set up the watchmen,
Prepare the ambushes.
*For the L*ORD *has both devised and done*
What He spoke against the inhabitants of Babylon.
O you who dwell by many waters,
Abundant in treasures,
Your end has come,
The measure of your covetousness. (Jer. 51:6–13)

God sent word by His watchmen then and He does the same now.

Jesus Also Chooses People and Sends Them Out

When Jesus sent out the seventy, He told them to ask for reinforcements: *"The harvest truly is great, but the laborers are few; therefore pray the Lord of the harvest to send out* [thrust] *laborers into His harvest. Go your way; behold I send you out as lambs among wolves"* (Luke 10:2–3). When they asked the Lord of the harvest to send out workers, He would inspire worthy people, compelling them to help. When He calls someone to go somewhere, He equips them and provides for them.

When I worked at a Christian-run thrift store, sometimes we were short-staffed. So a couple times I led the others in morning prayer that the Lord of the harvest would send out helpers, and praise God, other workers would soon show up.

One of the functions of our High Priest and King, Jesus, even today is to send His chosen servants where He wants them to go and to provide for them. There is a general call in the Great Commission, but there are also times when He will call people individually, especially when they are already willing to volunteer. That is what happened with me. I remember a song about being chosen and set apart by God ministering to me in those early days. *"You did not choose Me, but I chose you and appointed you that you should go and bear fruit, and that your fruit should remain, that whatever you ask the Father in My name He may give you"* (John 15:16).

Those He has chosen He will be sure to lead and direct and command. *"This is My commandment, that you love one another as I have loved you. Greater love has no one than this, than to lay down one's life for his friends. You are My friends if you do whatever I command you"* (John 15:12–14). He will not ask people to do anything He would not have done Himself.

When Jesus sent out His apostles and seventy disciples on mission trips, they were **not to charge** for their services. However, He made it clear to them that **since they were obediently working the works God was calling them to do, seeking first the advancement of His kingdom and His righteousness, God would see that their needs were met.** *"As you go, preach.... Heal the sick, cleanse the lepers, raise the dead, cast out demons. Freely you have received, freely give"* (Matt. 10:7–8; see Luke 9:3–4). They were to have faith that He would provide for them, including food, clothes, shelter, and transportation, rather than haggling over a wage. God knows that *"the laborer is worthy of his wages"* (1 Tim. 5:18). Since God had called ("hired") and sent them out to work in His harvest, He would see that their needs were met. *"Whatever city you enter, and they receive you, eat such things as are set before you. And heal the sick there, and say to them, 'The kingdom of God has come near to you.' But whatever city you enter, and they do not receive you, go out into its streets and say, 'The very dust of your city which clings to us we wipe off against you. [That city is liable for judgment]'"* (Luke 10:8–12). The Lord provides materially and spiritually for His obedient children. Jesus gives them faith and peace through His Spirit, not anxiety.

Some disciples may have functioned only as hired help, as hirelings; but others functioned as sons, as shepherds of His sheep—with more authority, responsibility, and hopefully, loving concern for them. It is God who gives His workers their wages, sometimes even extravagantly as the landowner did with the workers who were hired on at the *"eleventh hour"* (Matt. 20:6, 9), who helped the other workers complete the job. But that is His kingly prerogative since every worker is important to Him. **We are blessed to bless, and blessed when we bless, and are not to have any jealousy over how God provides for our brethren.** *"For everyone to whom much is given, from him much will be required; and to whom much has been committed, of him they will ask the more."* (Luke 12:48)

By Baptism, We Participate in His Death, Resurrection, and Intercession

In order to be trestles in His bridge, we need to die to sin and rise to righteous living with Jesus, our Saviour and Mediator.

> *Or do you not know that as many of us as were baptized into Christ Jesus were baptized into His death? Therefore we were buried with Him through baptism into death, that just as Christ was raised from the dead by the glory of the Father, even so we also should walk in newness of life. For if we have been united together in the likeness of His death, certainly we also shall be in the likeness of His resurrection, knowing this, that our old man was crucified with Him, that the body of sin might be done away with, that we should no longer be slaves of sin.* (Rom. 6:3–6)

Jesus calls us to be baptized with water and His Holy Spirit, not into a denomination, but into Christ so He can do His life-giving, saving work in us and we can become ministers of reconciliation with Him.

Since His job now as the resurrected Christ is to be the eternal High Priest, we participate in that as part of His *"royal priesthood"* (1 Pet. 2:9). Jesus *"loved us and washed us from our sins in His own blood, and has made us kings and priests to His God and Father, to Him be glory and dominion forever and ever. Amen"* (Rev. 1:5–6). We can minister unto God and man now if we are *"in Christ,"* calling upon the name of the Lord and letting His Word and Spirit flow through us.

The devil is *"the accuser of our brethren,"* (Rev. 12:10) but Jesus is the *"Advocate"* of the brethren (1 John 2:1), advocating for our defense. So just as He prayed from the cross, *"Father, forgive them for they do not know what they do"* (Luke 23:34), we need to follow His lead and intercede for others, forgiving as we would have God forgive us. *"Blessed are the pure in heart, for they shall see God"* (Matt. 5:8).

Jesus Is Perfecting His Followers. This Makes for a Stronger Bridge It takes time for fruit to mature, so God calls it forth how He sees it in heaven as if it were already here, and intercessors in tune with Him do likewise. As Solomon said to his bride, *"You are all fair, my love, and there is no spot in you. Come with me from Lebanon, my spouse"* (Song 4:7–8).

Jesus sees His bride as the finished product of His workmanship in her. He sees her as beautiful even though He knows there is more to be dealt with. This fact helped me to keep serving Him, seeking maturity, and to stop being so hard on myself. Even though He knew how we would disappoint Him at times, Jesus prayed for trained believers to have a true unity with Him, a communion, clothed in His righteousness and glory, *"that they all may be one, as You, Father, are in Me, and I in You; that they also may be one in Us, that the world may believe that You sent Me. And the glory which You gave Me I have given them, that they may be one just as We are one: I in them, and You in Me; that they may be made perfect in one, and that the world may know that You have sent Me, and have loved them as You have loved Me"* (John 17:21–23).

Therefore, **the true bridge, the bride of Christ united to the Bridegroom, shall bear the name of her Beloved from whom she obtains her righteousness, and she shall do righteous deeds:** *"And this is the name by which she will be called:*

'THE LORD OUR RIGHTEOUSNESS'" (Jer. 33:16; 23:6).

The righteousness we receive at salvation is a free gift, but we are expected then to choose righteous living. Thus, the bride's clothing is *"fine linen, clean and bright, for the fine linen is the righteous acts of the saints"* (Rev. 19:8).

In expressing appreciation for the saints living on earth in his days, David, who was also a saint, a man after God's own heart who repented from sin, humbly noted his own need for God. All saints have needed the Lord. **The fruit of goodness comes from Him. Only God is good all the time.**

> *O my soul, you have said to the* L<small>ORD</small>*,*
> *"You are the* L<small>ORD</small>*,*
> *My goodness is nothing apart from You."*
> *As for the saints who are on the earth,*
> *"They are the excellent ones, in whom is all my delight."*
> (Psalm 16:2–3)

People who chose to turn away from evil and follow the way of the Lord were called "saints" by their contemporaries in both the Old and New Testaments. They were very holy, morally blameless people. The Philippians were told to greet other saintly, faithful believers: *"Greet every saint in Christ Jesus. The brethren who are with me greet you. All the saints greet you, but especially those who are of Caesar's household"* (Phil. 4:21–22). Yet Paul also reminded living saints to be humble and not puffed up: *"…not to think of himself more highly than he ought to think, but to think soberly, as God has dealt to each one a measure of faith"* (Rom. 12:3). Like Paul, we can acknowledge that what we have comes from God, not from ourselves, and that His power is made perfect in our weakness. **Bridge trestlework is humble and sincere, yet full of inner strength, dependent on the top to keep them standing upright together.** Jesus said, *"Blessed are the meek, for they shall inherit the earth"* (Matt. 5:5).

Jesus is both Lion of Judah with holy boldness, and *"gentle* [meek] *and lowly in heart"* (Matt. 11:29). **Meekness is strength under control.**

I awoke from a dream February 5, 2014, hearing, *"And there shall arise a meek people."*

The *"poor in spirit"* are often meek and Jesus said they are *"blessed"* too—*"for theirs is the kingdom of heaven"* (Matt. 5:3). They *"wait on the Lord"* as Jesus does and experience kingdom living here on earth. They are well trained, but not robots. They use the authority of the believer as God's children should. Although one with the Father, Jesus holds His Father in high honour, submitting His will to the Father's, and the Godhead allows believers to approach the throne of grace with holy boldness in Jesus's name because they are in Christ, born again from above. *"As many as received Him, to them He gave the right to become children of God, to those who believe in His name: who were born, not of blood, nor of the will of the flesh, nor of the will of man, but of God"* (John 1:12–13). We adopted children of God are chosen children.

God's Word perfects us. Jesus helps us line up our life with His Word as a plumb line—such as the Beatitudes and the teaching of His apostles. John distinguishes between those who choose to be saints, set apart unto God following Jesus, and those who choose to remain sinners, captives of Satan. With Jesus, many can be kept back from hell though. John notes that even saints sometimes fall short, but *"ought . . . to walk just as He walked"* (1 John 2:6), and keep His commandments and His Word if they say they abide in Him; and to purify themselves *"just as He is pure"* (1 John 3:3). *"Now by this we know that we know Him, if we keep His commandments."* (1 John 2:3)

> *God is light and in Him is no darkness at all. If we say that we have fellowship with Him, and walk in darkness, we lie and do not practice the truth. But if we walk in the light as He is in the light, we have fellowship with one another, and the blood of Jesus Christ His Son cleanses us from all sin.... If we confess our sins, He is faithful and just to forgive us our sins and to cleanse us from all unrighteousness. If we say that we have not sinned, we make Him a liar, and His word is not in us. My little children, these things I write to you, so that you may not sin. And if anyone sins, we have*

> *an Advocate with the Father, Jesus Christ the righteous. And He Himself is the propitiation for our sins, and not for ours only but also for the whole world.* (1 John 1:5–7; 1:9–2:2)

Our Advocate is the Lion of Judah, the Lamb who was slain. **Those who are truly crucified with Christ do not have a lifestyle of sin, but of righteousness.** That pleases the Father.

Jesus As Bridge Functions as Priest, Prophet, and King

In His office as eternal High Priest and Mediator of the New Covenant in the order of Melchizedek, Jesus functions as Priest, Prophet, and King, and sometimes those roles overlap. Those who receive baptism with water and the Spirit into His death and resurrection, can join Jesus as the faithful saints on earth, helpmates in His prophetic *"royal priesthood"* (1 Pet. 2:9). But Jesus will never die again—therefore, saints will not replace Him as the sons of Aaron replaced Aaron.

Each called to be *"an apostle of Jesus Christ, by the will of God"* (2 Tim. 1:1), Peter and Paul wrote to believers on earth calling them *"saints."* Paul wrote to *"the saints who are in Ephesus, and faithful in Christ Jesus: Grace to you and peace from God our Father and the Lord Jesus Christ"* (Eph. 1:1–2). Even though there was idolatry in places like Rome and Ephesus, there were also true believers who sought to do the will of God and to pray for one another in His name only. These saints were communing with God and one another, praying for one another in Jesus's name while living on earth, and we can too. **By baptism, we share in Christ's ministry as priest, prophet, and king.** *"You are a chosen generation, a royal priesthood, a holy nation, His own special people, that you may proclaim the praises of Him who called you out of darkness into His marvelous light"* (1 Pet. 2:9). **But no saint will replace Jesus as High Priest/Mediator of the New Covenant.**

Hebrews 7:23–25 tells us, *"Also there were many priests, because they were prevented by death from continuing. But He because He continues forever, has an unchangeable priesthood. Therefore He is also able to save to the uttermost those who come to God through Him, since He always lives to make intercession for them."*

Chapter 16
Jesus the Priest

Jesus Is the Perfect High Priest Knowing What It Is Like to Be Both God and Man

[Gabriel said to Mary]: *"And behold, you will conceive in your womb and bring forth a Son, and shall call His name JESUS. He will be great, and will be called the Son of the Highest; and the Lord God will give Him the throne of His father David. And He will reign over the house of Jacob forever, and of His kingdom there will be no end."* (Luke 1:31-33)

Inasmuch then as the children have partaken of flesh and blood, He Himself likewise shared in the same, that through death He might destroy him who had the power of death, that is, the devil, and release those who through fear of death were all their lifetime subject to bondage. For indeed He does not give aid to angels, but He does give aid to the seed of Abraham. Therefore, in all things He had to be made like His brethren, that He might be a merciful and faithful High Priest in things pertaining to God, to make propitiation for the sins of the people. For in that He Himself has suffered, being tempted, He is able to aid those who are tempted. (Hebrews 2:14–18)

Through the life and death of Jesus, sacrificed so sins could be forgiven, and through His resurrection, Jesus could and can set people free from their bondage to sin and fear of death. In order to give this help to His brethren, **it was necessary for Jesus to be made like them *"in all things"* when He took on flesh in His mother's womb.** She was a virgin at that time, but He grew within her womb until it was time to be birthed. All His life on earth was preparation for His calling to be the Saviour and the chosen *"merciful and faithful High Priest in things pertaining to God."* **He had to experience what man does, including the draw toward a temptation, the pressure of iniquity—except that He resisted the temptation to sin**; however He felt the sting of the sin of others when He was on the cross.

When I was studying *Restoring the Foundations* by Chester and Betsy Kylstra, **the Lord told me,** *"Put a star beside that,"* when I got to a certain part. They had written that not only the fathers, but the mothers can contribute to the iniquity, which is passed on to their children, as happened in the case of Ahaziah, son of Ahab and Jezebel (see 1 Kings 22:51–53).

They said that one theory states that when Jesus was born of a human mother and *"yet was without sin,"* that no iniquity or sin was passed on to Him from the mother and all that He inherited was from His Father, God, who was without sin. (I had believed this.) They said, "Yet, if this were the case, then Jesus would not have experienced any temptation. Remember, **iniquity is the tendency and the pressure to rebel and enter into sin.** This doesn't automatically mean that we **have to** sin, but that we are likely to"[14] They also made it clear that the iniquity that comes down to the third and fourth generation "does cause a 'pressure' to be applied to us [and our descendants], but it does not **force** us to sin. It does not mean automatic condemnation or death"[15]

---

[14] Chester and Betsy Kylstra, *Restoring the Foundations: An Integrated Approach to Healing Ministry* 2nd *Edition* (Hendersonville, NC: Restoring the Foundations Publications. 2,000), 116. Copying material allowed for limited use within a teaching.

[15] Kylstra, *Restoring the Foundations,* 108.

We know that Jesus did experience temptation—the pressure to rebel against His Father's will. The pressure was so great at Gethsemane that He sweat great drops of blood, but had the strength from God to submit His will to the Father's. *"God cannot be tempted by evil"* (Jas. 1:13), but in His earth suit as Son of Man, Jesus was **"tempted in every way ... yet hedid not sin."** *"For we do not have a high priest who is unable to sympathize with our weaknesses, but we have one who has been tempted in every way, just as we are—yet he did not sin"* (Heb. 4:15 NIV).

Having God as His Father did not make it easier for Jesus, except that He knew who to call for help: *"Since the children have flesh and blood, He too shared in their humanity.... He had to be made like His brothers ... in every way.... Because He Himself suffered when he was tempted, He is able to help those who are being tempted"* (Heb. 2:14, 17–18 NIV). The Kylstras (and now I, too) believe these passages, plus those describing His temptations by the devil:

> ...actually support the opposite theory: that Jesus **was able** to be tempted precisely because He did have a human mother and did receive the iniquity of the Israelite family line through Mary. It was because He "entered the sheep pen by the gate," i.e., by being born through the womb of a woman, that He "legally" entered the domain of Adam and so could be the second Adam. This made it possible for Him to be *"made like His brothers in every way,"* including having the ability to be tempted, to suffer in temptation, to be pressured by the iniquity of His mother. Yet He did not sin. He chose not to sin, in spite of the iniquity inherited from Mary.[16] ***(This is where I heard the word of the Lord:** "Put a star beside that."*)

Mary was a holy woman, but *"all have sinned and fall short of the glory of God"* (Rom. 3:23). Only Jesus was the spotless Lamb of God. The devil had no "cookies" of *"evil desires"* or past sins in Him. *"I will no*

---

16   Kylstra, *Restoring the Foundations*, 117.

longer talk much with you, for the ruler of this world is coming, and he has nothing in Me" (John 14:30). Yet Jesus felt the pressure of temptation, especially the night before His death. *"He began to be troubled and deeply distressed"* (Mark 14:33). *"Father, if it is Your will, take this cup away from Me; nevertheless, not My will, but Yours be done"* (Luke 22:42).

Three apostles were supposed to be supporting Him in prayer, but kept falling asleep three times. He told them, *"Watch and pray lest you enter into temptation. The spirit indeed is willing, but the flesh is weak"* (Mark 14:38). He was in agony and sweat blood. **So He prayed to His Father and chose to submit His will to the Father's rather than give in to the temptation. So the devil fled instead of Him.** An angel was sent to strengthen Him so His flesh would be willing and able to endure what was coming.

High Priesthood: His Time Here on Earth, Including His Suffering and Triumphs, Was All Preparation

Jesus *"has been perfected forever"* (Heb. 7:28), made perfectly equipped for His role as bridge to the Father, to bear His name in truth while saving His own to the uttermost:

> *Who in the days of His flesh, when He had offered up prayers and supplications, with vehement cries and tears to Him who was able to save Him from death, and was heard because of His godly fear, though He was a Son, yet He learned obedience by the things which He suffered. And having been perfected, He became the author of eternal salvation to all who obey Him, called by God as High Priest "according to the order of Melchizedek."* (Hebrews 5:7–10)

Jesus was perfect and always did what His Father wanted. But having overcome twice the temptation, the pressure, to not go to the cross (firstly in the second temptation in the wilderness and secondly at Gethsemane), *"He learned obedience by the things which He suffered."*

This helped to perfect Him, to make Him perfectly prepared for His work as High Priest and New Covenant Mediator.

He understands mankind having encountered all types of situations on earth: joys and sorrows, and grief at the death of His foster father, Joseph, and of Lazarus, protection from wild beasts around him during forty days in the wilderness, and He was tempted by the devil at opportune times. But He kept close communion with His heavenly Father throughout and passed all tests with flying colours. Having faith in God, the authority of the believer and perfect love instead of fear, He resisted temptation, was protected from harm and was ministered to by angels. Jesus was nourished by the heavenly, life-giving *"daily bread"* of *rhema* words from His Father. He experienced the blessings of Abraham of having His Father as a *"shield"* and as His *"exceedingly great reward"* (Gen. 15:1). God increased His followers, blessed Him, made His name great, and made Him a blessing (see Genesis 12:2).

His Father gave Jesus wisdom and words to say when lawyers and Pharisees tried to trap Him. He still knows what to say and it can come in a prophetic word. Also, He can give His followers the right words to say today in situations.

We know He tasted the rewards for obedience under the Law because He always did what His Father told Him to do. He received blessings of favour, prosperity, health, and lovingkindness so that He could continue to be a blessing, and He still is blessing many. Jesus said He is returning as *"the Son of Man"* (Matt. 24:37). The Lord hears the cry of the poor, so He responds with compassion, and gives teachings so the people can be shepherded on the right path. He encountered persecution and was protected from being thrown off a cliff and stoned to death. The enemy was not allowed to kill Him until the appointed time, and then He even tasted death for all mankind, before and after His time on earth,. tThe curses for our disobedience were the penalty for sin—for our sin since He had none of His own. He was our substitute, for those who believe in Him. Then He was resurrected victoriously on the third day. He can keep His people alive today until they have completed the work the Father has for them to do.

Living life perfectly as Son of Man with God's Spirit resting on Him and tasting firsthand the rewards for obedience and for our disobedience (on the cross) enabled Jesus to become perfectly prepared for His eternal calling at the Father's right hand. At my nephew Michael's funeral, I realised that He not only bore all our sin and sicknesses, but He can empathize with us further: *"Surely He has borne our griefs and carried our sorrows"* (Isa. 53:4) too. No wonder He is the *"God of all comfort"*!

> *Blessed be the God and Father of our Lord Jesus Christ, the Father of mercies and God of all comfort, who comforts us in all our tribulation, that we may be able to comfort those who are in any trouble, with the comfort with which we ourselves are comforted by God. For as the sufferings of Christ abound in us, so our consolation also abounds through Christ* (2 Cor. 1:3-5).

Jesus knew His Father would provide for Him and His disciples when they were doing His will and experienced many blessings, including the multiplication of food when people were hungry. Grateful healed and delivered women traveled with them and *"provided for Him from their substance"* (Luke 8:3). Jesus still reassures His disciples that when He sends them out on mission trips today that God will provide for them too, through the generosity of worthy people. What God authorizes, He provides for.

Just prior to His crucifixion, Jesus told the Pharisees to tell Herod, *"Behold I cast out demons and perform cures today and tomorrow, and the third day I shall be perfected"* (Luke 13:32). God allowed Jesus to *"taste death for everyone ... in bringing many sons to glory, to make the captain of their salvation perfect through sufferings"* (Heb. 2:9–10). Having come as Son of Man, experiencing what we experience and made perfect through what He suffered, He was made perfect in love for God and for others, even blessing His enemies, a perfect example for us. He calls us *"brethren"* and can see things from our perspective. Thus He can better speak up for us to God, empathizing with us, and encouraging us to be made perfect too. He never tells us to do anything He was not willing to do.

Perfecting His Bride, His Glorious Ministry

Taking up His glory again as the only begotten Son of God, Jesus sees things from God's perspective and can speak to us for Him, mediating disagreements and bringing good counsel, bridging the gap as the Father's *"righteous right hand."* And some can be parts of Jesus's *"righteous right hand,"* clothed in His righteousness. He can lift us up to see things from His perspective. His Word is entirely trustworthy: *"Fear not, for I am with you; be not dismayed for I am your God. I will strengthen you, yes, I will help you, I will uphold you with My righteous right hand"* (Isa. 41:10).

When I hear a *rhema* word for me, that word of God is like a hand holding me and strengthening me. Thanks be to God.

"For by one offering He has perfected forever those who are being sanctified [set apart]*"* (Heb. 10:14). He put on our sin so we could put on His righteousness. Then it is up to us to keep under His covering, to keep ourselves sanctified or consecrated in the truth of His Word.

First John 2:4–6 says, *"He who says, 'I know Him,' and does not keep His commandments, is a liar, and the truth is not in him. But whoever keeps His word, truly the love of God is perfected in him. By this we know that we are in Him. He who abides in Him ought himself also to walk just as He walked."* He has perfected us and is perfecting us.

Jesus was perfected so that He could be the way of perfection for us. *"Let us go on to perfection* [maturity]*"* (Heb. 6:1). His blood washes us clean so that by faith, not works, we are perfected, clothed in His righteousness. But to maintain that perfection to which Jesus calls us, living faith needs to be mixed with works. *"Faith without works is dead"* (Jas. 2:26). We need to be rooted and grounded in His love, with His Word and Spirit dwelling within us, and Jesus, our chief Pastor, will shepherd us into the good works He has prepared for us. *"If we love one another, God abides in us, and His love has been perfected in us"* (1 John 4:12). By encouraging this love, He still works to perfect that love in us. We cannot give the excuse that it is too hard, because the Lamb has overcome and will help us to as well. As Jesus told Paul, *"My grace is sufficient for you, for My strength* [power] *is made perfect in weakness"* (2 Cor. 12:9).

Jesus taught His Father's commandments in the light of the New Testament, clarifying them but not eliminating them.

Then He said:

> *You have heard it was said, "You shall love your neighbor and hate your enemy." But I say to you, love your enemies, bless those who curse you, do good to those who hate you, and pray for those who spitefully use you and persecute you, that you may be sons of your Father in heaven; for He makes His sun rise on the evil and on the good, and sends rain on the just and on the unjust.... Therefore you shall be perfect, just as your Father in heaven is perfect.* (Matt. 5:43–45, 48)

Now He writes His laws on our hearts, minds, and in His Word, **perfecting us**, because He is coming for a pure and spotless bride, **perfect in love for God, self, and others and keeping His Word**: *"But whoever keeps His word, truly the love of God is perfected in him"* (1 John 2:5).

If we do not love God, He calls us to it, reminding us of His great love for all the world that He even gave His only begotten Son that we should taste salvation. He pours out His love on us while we are yet sinners. If we love ourselves too much and become selfish, He calls us to repentance. But we also have to beware of the other extreme. **When I was trying to die to self too much, going too deep, influenced by eastern programs on TV, the Lord sent His word to me:** *"Love yourself."* We cannot love neighbours properly if we do not have a healthy love for ourselves. He teaches us leading in ways in which we can *"love one another as* [Jesus has] *loved you"* (John 15:12), ready to *"deny"* (Matt. 16:24) ourselves when it is appropriate.

Ephesians 5:26–27 says, *"Christ also loved the church and gave Himself for her, that He might sanctify and cleanse her with the washing of water by the word, that He might present her to Himself a glorious church, not having spot or wrinkle or any such thing, but that she should be holy and without blemish."* He only died once, but now He washes us by the *logos* word of Scripture which we hear or read, and by the *rhema* word which comes prophetically either directly to us or through another. He is perfecting all of His church, His corporate bride, saints on earth in various locations, *"that they may be one just as We are one: I in them, and You in Me; that they may be made perfect in one, and that the world may know that You have sent Me, and have loved them as You have loved Me"* (John 17:22–23). May we have a teachable spirit.

This is part of the glorious ministry of our eternal High Priest: *"Herein is our love made perfect* [love has been perfected among us], *that we may have boldness on the day of judgment: because as He is, so are we in this world"* (1 John 4:17 KJV).

Perfect[17] in the Greek is *"teleioo,"* meaning "to perfect, complete, finish(ed); (pass) to reach a goal, be fulfilled, completed, make/made perfect; consecrated." *"Perfect,"* as in, *"You shall be perfect, just as your*

---

17   James Strong, LL.D., S.T.D., *The Strongest Strong's Exhaustive Concordance of the Bible*, ed. Kohlenberger and Swanson, (Zondervan, 2001)

Father in heaven is perfect," is *"teleios,"* meaning "perfect, mature, finished, full age."[18]

Biblical perfection has the major idea of being complete or whole, having come to maturity rather than without fault or shortcoming since all have fallen short of the glory of God and can be forgiven to start afresh. This can only happen when we are united with Christ, a body part doing His will, a fruit bearing branch in the vine. Unity with the members of the body of Christ on earth is so important. There is a commanded blessing when brothers dwell in unity—*"Life forevermore"* (Ps. 133:3). One day we will be united with the saints in heaven too as His full body: *"New Jerusalem, coming down out of heaven from God, prepared as a bride adorned for her husband"* (Rev. 21:2). **The finished work at the cross perfected His bride positionally, so Christ calls into being what He expects in her, and experientially, she is being perfected.** In heaven it is done, and it is being done. Part of our job is to desire this and pray that it will be done here on earth as it is in heaven. May our will be aligned with the Father's as Jesus's was.

Jesus calls forth our love for our neighbour to be of a higher quality than that of sinners. They sow to reap on earth. We can do that too, but our motive should be higher, and we should be prepared to wait until heaven to reap some blessings. Since He is still perfecting us in love, calling into being what He knows He can accomplish in us as He meets with us like fire to a candle wick, Holy Spirit to our personal spirit, therefore with passionate love Jesus says to the bride, as Solomon does to the Shulamite, *"Open for me, my sister, my love, my dove, my perfect one"* (Song 5:2). Our hearts need to be open so Jesus can come in by His Spirit and do His works in us. *"Let us go on to perfection* [maturity]*"* (Heb. 6:1). **Calling her *"perfect"* reminds me of when the angel called Gideon a *"mighty man of valor"* while he was still hiding from his enemies. God sees the finished product from heaven and will be faithful to complete the work in His corporate bride.** This

---

18   Strong, James, *The Strongest Strong's*

helped me immensely because I often seemed to fall short of the glory of God, even though I tried to be perfect in love.

> *Lift up your heads, O you gates! ... and the King of Glory shall come in.* (P. 24:9)

> *To them God willed to make known what are the riches of the glory of this mystery among the Gentiles: which is Christ in you, the hope of glory.* (Col. 1:27)

> *Let us be glad and rejoice and give Him glory, for the marriage of the Lamb has come, and His wife has made herself ready. And to her it was granted to be arrayed in fine linen, clean and bright, for the fine linen is the righteous acts of the saints.* (Rev. 19:7–8)

Her wedding gown is being made up of perfect pieces sewn together, of *"righteous acts,"* of *"good works which God prepared beforehand that we should walk in them"* (Eph. 2:10).

Jesus's Helpmate

The body of Christ is to become His bride, His helpmate, as Eve was to be for Adam. Yet **Jesus leads by example, by humbly being a helper for us, and sending His Spirit who can be** *"another helper"* (see John 14:15–16) **to people all over the world at the same time. A loving bride and groom serve one another willingly without even being asked.**

Jesus said, *"The Father who dwells in Me does the works. Believe Me that I am in the Father and the Father in Me.... And whatever you ask in My name, that I will do, that the Father may be glorified in the Son. If you ask anything in My name, I will do it"* (John 14:10–11, 13–14).

Like Solomon's bride we learn that **Jesus loves us even when we are immature and He calls us to confidence even in a time of weakness.** From time to time He has told me, *"You can do it. Christ is in you"*, and *"You're going to make it"*. When the bride keeps seeking the One she loves, she finds that **no flood can quench this love**, and a time comes when she can enter mature partnership with our Beloved ready to go where He wants her to go and do what He wants her to do, trusting Him. She/we will also love one another willingly as He has loved us: *"Who is this coming up from the wilderness leaning upon her Beloved?"* (Song 8:5).

It is only because we are *"in Christ"* that saints on earth dare to *"come boldly to the throne of grace, that we may obtain mercy and find grace to help in time of need"* (Heb. 4:16). The Israelites knew that if God had set up a boundary to His presence, they were not to break through it or they could die. Only priests could even go into the first chamber of the tabernacle. That is why having the veil into the second chamber, the Holy of holies, torn in two from the top, from heaven, was such a blessing for us, signifying opening the way to the Father once we have obtained entry to the heavenly tabernacle by baptism. Believers here on earth can intercede for one another in Jesus's name. We can be individual pieces of trestlework, or like individual living stones taught about intercession by Jesus, our Rock, and led by Him.

David called on the name of the Lord to help him in battles and the bride needs His help too for spiritual battles. *"We do not wrestle against flesh and blood, but against principalities, against powers, against the rulers of the darkness of this age, against spiritual hosts of wickedness in the heavenly places"* (Eph. 6:12).

Psalm 18:32–33 says, *"It is God who arms me with strength, and makes my way perfect. He makes my feet like the feet of deer, and sets me on my high places."* Just as the Lord taught David how to fight against his enemies, Jesus leads and helps us and His people help Him, even in the job of intercession.

The Chosen Mediator/High Priest Commands His Army of Intercessors

A childlike example of faith is that of the Roman centurion whose faith was commended by Jesus when he said, *"Lord, I am not worthy that You should come under my roof. But only speak a word, and my servant will be healed. For I also am a man under authority, having soldiers under me. And I say to this one, 'Go,' and he goes; and to another, 'Come,' and he comes; and to my servant, 'Do this,' and he does it"* (Matt. 8:8–10). It reminds me of the *"throne set in heaven, and One sat on the throne. And He who sat there was like a jasper and a sardius stone* [green and red] *in appearance; and there was a rainbow around the throne, in appearance like an emerald"* (Rev. 4:2–3). The green and red remind me that God can tell us, *"Go,"* and yet sometimes He says, *"Stop,"* or *"Wait,"* like to wait for the promised Holy Spirit and power to come before obeying the Great Commission. Since we call Him Lord and should desire the Father's will to be *"done on earth as it is in heaven"* (Matt. 6:10), we should listen for His commands, ready to obey them.

When God gives a *rhema* word, a current word prophetically spoken forth by Him, **it will come to pass when the time comes**. (Unless it is a word promising just and true judgment and He decides to be merciful because the people repent like Nineveh.) God is trustworthy so we should believe Him and wait for it expectantly. *"So then faith comes by hearing, and hearing by the word of God"* (Rom. 10:17).

> *Now faith is the substance of things hoped for, the evidence of things not seen. For by it the elders obtained a good testimony. By faith we understand that the worlds were framed by the word of God, so that the things which are seen were not made of things which are visible.... But without faith it is impossible to please Him, for he who comes to God must believe that He is, and that He is a rewarder of those who diligently seek Him.* (Hebrews 11:1–3, 6)

Jesus can lead as we pray the Scriptures, and we can war in prayer with the prophetic word God gives, sometimes in song: *"He teaches my hands to make war, so that my arms can bend a bow of bronze"* (Ps. 18:34).

Jesus teaches us how to battle in intercession, how to assist Him under His leadership and fire arrows of deliverance and of double fruitfulness. He also teaches how to wield the *"sword of the Spirit"* (Eph. 6:17), declaring as truth what God has spoken, giving praise and thanks to God that it is done and being done. Positionally it is done. Experientially it is being done.

The Lord told us around 2005 at a prayer meeting at Kingston Gospel Temple, *"Praise is a powerful weapon,"* so **we asked Him to lead us in songs of praise, and He did, week after week.** Sometimes I would shout out, "You lead, Lord!" When one or another of us would hear Him within and sing out the song, we would all join in singing it to God prayerfully. Glory be to God! I love when the Lord leads like that! He is the Commander of the hosts.

Mark 11:22–24 says, *"Have faith in God. For assuredly, I say to you, whoever says to this mountain, 'Be removed and be cast into the sea,' and does not doubt in his heart, but believes that those things he says will be done, he will have whatever he says. Therefore I say to you, whatever things you ask when you pray, believe that you receive them, and you will have them."* Our battles are ultimately spiritual. As David said, God is the One who teaches us what we need to know and equips us, and fights on our behalf.

> *I will call upon the L*ORD*, who is worthy to be praised;*
> *So shall I be saved from my enemies....*
> *For by You I can run against a troop,*
> *By my God I can leap over a wall.*
> *As for God, His way is perfect;*
> *The word of the L*ORD *is proven;*
> *He is a shield to all who trust in Him.*
> *For who is God except the L*ORD*?*

> *And who is a rock, except our God?*
> *It is God who arms me with strength,*
> *And makes my way perfect.* (Psalm 18:3, 29–32)

Just as God fought for David, He will for us. His meekness makes us great.

> *Seek the LORD, all you meek of the earth,*
> *Who have upheld His justice.*
> *Seek righteousness, seek humility.*
> *It may be that you will be hidden in the day of the LORD's anger.*
> (Zephaniah 2:3)

> *You have also given me the shield of Your salvation;*
> *Your right hand has held me up.*
> *Your gentleness has made me great.*
> *You enlarged the path under me,*
> *So my feet did not slip.*
> *I have pursued my enemies and overtaken them;*
> *Neither did I turn back again until they were destroyed.*
> (Psalm 18:35–37)

Sometimes our enemies are sickness or deadly sins like pride, anger, etc.

> *The LORD lives!*
> *Blessed be my Rock!*
> *Let the God of my salvation be exalted.*
> *It is God who avenges me*
> *And subdues the peoples under me.* (Psalm 18:46–47)

In the old days, a king riding on a white horse would lead his troops into battle. Jesus is pictured in Revelation 19 as the King of kings and LORD of lords riding a white horse leading the hosts of heaven.

Jesus wants His people to follow Him in battle-prayer today. The church is also compared to His war horse, but the victory belongs to the Lord who can surround us and our enemies with His host of angel armies: *"For the L*ORD *of hosts will visit His flock, the house of Judah, and will make them as His royal horse in the battle"* (Zech. 10:3). "Judah" means "praise". *"The horse is prepared for the day of battle, but deliverance is of the L*ORD*"* (Prov. 21:31).

We are admonished in Ephesians 6:10 and 2 Corinthians 10:3–6:

Finally, my brethren, be strong in the Lord and in the power of His might. (Eph. 6:10)

For though we walk in the flesh, we do not war according to the flesh. For the weapons of our warfare are not carnal but mighty in God for pulling down strongholds [houses of thoughts], *casting down arguments and every high thing that exalts itself against the knowledge of God, bringing every thought into captivity to the obedience of Christ, and being ready to punish all disobedience when your obedience is fulfilled.* (2 Cor. 10:3–6)

An **evil stronghold** is like a house made of bundles of *"hay and stubble,"* composed of various thoughts or words which someone harbours. It might appear to be strong, but God can burn it up with His refining fire or blow it down like a house of cards with the wind of His Holy Spirit.

Sometimes our enemy likes to try to attack us on the battlefield of the mind. That is why we need to **seek the mind of Christ to rule us, to have our mind filled with the thoughts of the Lord**. A Christian can have a good stronghold within him and an evil one as well walled off in an area of his mind or heart. But he should want to be rid of it. A good stronghold is made of thoughts and words of God used appropriately. Both **the Lord, who is** *"Faithful and True,"* **and His name are compared by David in Scripture to a godly stronghold, one that is rock-solid:**

> *I will love You, O Lord, my strength.*
> *The Lord is my rock and my fortress and my deliverer;*
> *My God, my strength, in whom I will trust;*
> *My shield and the horn of my salvation, my stronghold.* (Ps. 18:1–2)

> *The name of the Lord is a strong tower; the righteous run to it and are safe.* (Proverbs 18:10)

But an evil stronghold should be surrendered to Jesus. It is composed of actions, words, or thoughts from our enemy, the father of lies, the deceiver, which may be twisted Scriptures—God's Word used inappropriately—or wrong ideas, and even *"doctrines of demons"* (1 Tim. 4:1). Like David, we can ask God to search our heart to see if there is any wicked way in us of which we were unaware.

Or an evil stronghold may be something that you know is the will of God but you feel is impossible because doubt has crept into your mind. That is why we are not to be led by feelings; rather they should follow appropriately after the Word of God, in line with it, not in opposition to it. So when a storm rose up when Jesus had said they were going to the other side and He had slept in their boat, Jesus rebuked His disciples for their lack of faith. Jesus wants a disciple to trust Him, not circumstances, willing to do whatever He tells him to do, even if it is to walk on water. (Notice: **Peter did not get out of the boat until he was sure it was Jesus talking.** He did not put God to the test, but he did test the spirit to be sure it was Jesus before taking a leap of faith.)

Jesus can give us victory demolishing strongholds, leading us to repent and resist temptation, to cast *"down arguments and every high thing that exalts itself against the knowledge of God, bringing every thought into captivity to the obedience of Christ"* (2 Cor. 10:5), as we replace the lie or misconception, the deception of the enemy, with the truth—and continue to believe the truth.

Jesus has armour for us today:

> *Therefore take up the whole armor of God, that you may be able to withstand* [against the wiles of the devil] *in the evil day, and having done all, to stand. Stand therefore, having girded your waist with truth, having put on the breastplate of righteousness, and having shod your feet with the preparation of the gospel of peace; above all, taking the shield of faith with which you will be able to quench all the fiery darts of the wicked one. And take the helmet of salvation, and the sword of the Spirit, which is the word of God; praying always with all prayer and supplication in the Spirit, being watchful to this end with all perseverance and supplication for all the saints—and for me, that utterance may be given to me, that I may open my mouth boldly to make known the mystery of the gospel.* (Eph. 6:13–19)

Our High Priest Maintains and Reestablishes Godly Connections

Psalm 121 speaks of how God "*keeps*" us like a shepherd, that *"the Lord is your keeper"* (Ps. 121:5), that He helps, defends, preserves, shields His people who seek Him. That is part of His function. *"The Lord shall preserve you from all evil; He shall preserve your soul* [mind, will, and emotions]" (Ps. 121:7). Jesus prayed for His disciples who followed Him, interceding for them, pleading on their behalf that they may remain connected with God and one another since He was about to leave the world, and the Holy Spirit had not yet been abundantly poured out.

> *Holy Father, keep through Your name those whom You have given Me, that they may be one as We are. While I was with them in the world, I kept them in Your name. Those whom You have given Me I have kept; and none of them is lost except the son of perdition, that the Scripture might be fulfilled. I have given them Your word; and the world has hated them because they are not of the world, just as I am not of the world. I do not pray that You should take them out of*

the world, but that You should keep them from the evil one. (John 17:11–15)

Unrepented sin can break the connection with God. Jesus came that sin may be forgiven and that we may welcome Him in and be kept by Him. He goes after the ones who lose the way: *"But if we walk in the light as He is in the light, we have fellowship with one another, and the blood of Jesus Christ His Son cleanses us from all sin"* (1 John 1:7).

> *I will not forget you.*
> *See, I have inscribed you on the palm of My hands;*
> *Your walls are continually before Me....*
> *Even the captives of the mighty shall be taken away,*
> *And the prey of the terrible be delivered;*
> *For I will contend with him who contends with you,*
> *And I will save your children....*
> *All flesh shall know*
> *That I, the* L<small>ORD</small>, *am your Saviour,*
> *And your Redeemer, the Mighty One of Jacob.* (Isa. 49:15–16, 25–26)

God is still fighting on our behalf.

One way the connection with God can be broken is by robbing God, by holding back what is rightfully His. He owns everything, so we should be happy to return to God a tithe and offerings so it can be stewarded wisely by His servants to meet needs. I know the Lord stretched me into doing that and I was blessed for doing so. I remember an autumn night when He gave me a portion of Malachi 3 to prophesy at a prayer gathering It began with: *Yet from the days of your fathers you have gone away from My ordinances*

> *And have not kept them.*
> *Return to Me and I will return to you," says the* L<small>ORD</small> *of hosts.*
> *But you said, "In what way shall we return?"*
> *Will a man rob God? Yet you have robbed Me!*

> *But you say, "In what way have we robbed You?"*
> *In tithes and offerings.*
> *You are cursed with a curse.*
> *For you have robbed Me,*
> *Even this whole nation.*
> *Bring all the tithes into the storehouse,*
> *That there may be food in My house,*
> *And try Me now in this.* (Mal. 3:7–10)

(This is one time when we can test God.)

It continues with abundant blessings for tithers, including rebuking the devourer. But those who do not bring in tithes and offerings when they are able are robbing God, and just punishments could come down as a result on individuals, families, or even nations. They could reap what they sowed by their fear of lack, or their selfish, withholding spirit, and it could affect their families. Thank God, repentance and the blood of Christ can remove the curse today so blessings can flow instead. **Rather than it being a matter of compulsion, it should be a matter of love for God and our neighbour as for ourselves. Thus we see that giving is evidence of love.**

There was a "sign" following that word too, because my garden had become so fruitful with me giving my "first fruits," plus tithes and offerings to the Lord, that I had brought about three tall pails full of produce to the church to give to the pastor and others that night from the back of the church. Then, shortly afterward, although it was the end of the tomato season and the plants had begun to wither, God rebuked the devourer and they suddenly came back to life bearing more large abundant tomatoes to share again!

Our High Priest Receives Tithes and Offerings

Some people wonder if we need to tithe now, since we are not under the letter of the Law but the spirit of the Law. **But we do need to obey the Law that God has written on our heart and mind as Abraham did many years before Moses received the Law.** It often reminds me of when Jesus was asked:

> *"Tell us, therefore, what do You think? Is it lawful to pay taxes to Caesar, or not?" But Jesus perceived their wickedness, and said, "Why do you test Me, you hypocrites? Show Me the tax money." So they brought Him a denarius. And He said to them, "Whose image and inscription is this?" They said to Him, "Caesar's." And He said to them, "Render therefore to Caesar the things that are Caesar's, and to God the things that are God's."* (Matt. 22:17–21)

We pay taxes to earthly government so they can care for the nation; how much more does our heavenly government help us! How wonderful that we were created in the image and according to the likeness of God! When we are polished up so it can be seen that His image is on us, then we should be happy to return to Him not only 10 percent of our increase whenever possible, but even ourselves! Some wealthy people return close to ninety percent and live on the remainder.

Jesus, being our High Priest *"according to the order of Melchizedek"* **(Heb. 7:17), can receive tithes after the Law since Melchizedek did before the Law.** Thus, I like to think that **my tithes and offerings go to King Jesus**.

When Gentiles began to become Christians, the church at Jerusalem met and decided that they did not have to keep the whole Law: *"For it seemed good to the Holy Spirit and to us, to lay upon you no greater burden than these necessary things: that you abstain from things offered to idols, from blood, from things strangled, and from sexual immorality"* (Acts 15:28–29). But since the Lord gave me that word from Malachi

3 to proclaim at that gathering, I believe it is close to His heart for us to *"return"* to Him by observing at least the spirit of tithing.

Abraham's tithing is only mentioned once so we do not know how often he did it, but many Christians are happy to do it weekly and to even give more. If we seek first the advancement of the kingdom of God and His righteousness in love, we will be happy to bring in tithes to King Jesus that there may be food in His house and church and ministry expenses may be paid. That is something that flows from a right relationship with Him. And He will take care of our needs, not greeds. Beware of judging others, because some needs are not greeds, even if they look that way, like a plane for an evangelist who travels frequently with his team, And our God is an extravagant, loving giver.

> *Guve and it will be given to you: good measure, pressed down, shaken together, and running over will be put into your bosom. For with the same measure that you use, it will be measured back to you.* (Luke 6:38)

When I knew nothing about tithing, the word of the Lord came to me, *"Do not put fear of spending money before Me,"* as an understanding of the first commandment, **gently** setting me on the road towards full tithing and offerings. My husband was a hardworking carpenter and I was a housewife, concerned that our family would have enough. The Lord began by stretching me so that I could give more in love, according to His provision, to my home church and to those whose needs He placed upon my heart. I learned that for all I have, even my health, and especially my salvation, I owe gratitude to God. A few years later, He magnified to me a song about how the Lord hears the cries of the poor and so should we. As I began sharing more with others, I could see that God was blessing us. *"Blessed are you poor, for yours is the kingdom of God"* (Luke 6:20). Then when I became a widow, He stretched me into full tithing and giving offerings, and has blessed me time and again, thank God. He is my Provider.

Adam and Eve could eat of any permitted tree in Paradise. Thank God, Jesus restores many blessings to us. The Lord provided used materials my husband recycled into furnishings like desks and beds for our children. Some other blessings were sufficient work, food, and shelter, plus bags of used clothing for us, fulfilling His conditional promise: *"Seek first the kingdom of God and His righteousness, and all these things shall be added to you"* (Matt. 6:33). He also taught me that **grace can be undeserved and God even helps those who cannot help themselves.** Not only does He bless those who deserve it, but there are times when **He is even kind to the selfish and ungrateful**, so we should be too, whether they return the favor or not. God will take care of His children. *"But love your enemies, do good, and lend, hoping for nothing in return; and your reward will be great, and you will be sons of the Most High. For He is kind to the unthankful and evil"* (Luke 6:35).

Those who rob God are like His people to whom God sent Haggai. **They looked after building their own houses but neglected His.** By trying to live on 100 percent, withholding God's 10 percent, they found that they fell into economic ruin.

> *"Is it time for you yourselves to dwell in your paneled houses, and this temple to lie in ruins?"*
> *"Consider your ways!*
> *You have sown much and bring in little;*
> *You eat, but do not have enough;*
> *You drink, but you are not filled with drink;*
> *You clothe yourselves, but no one is warm;*
> *And he who earns wages,*
> *Earns wages to put into a bag with holes."*
> *Thus says the LORD of hosts: "Consider your ways! Go up to the mountains and bring wood and build the temple, that I may take pleasure in it and be glorified," says the LORD.* (Haggai 1:4–8)

Churches as well as Christians themselves are *"the temple of the Holy Spirit"* (1 Cor. 6:19) in which God should be glorified. We can go up the mountain in prayer in Jesus's name to ask God to *"restore!"* His house is in ruins and we can send money so missionaries can go do His will. **Jesus is the contractor** who has paid the price to purchase the building material for the temple, and the one who chooses which boards will fit where, which living stones will fit where, and cuts them to size. It is in cooperation with Him that they are set in place to rebuild the broken walls of the house of God. When we invest tithes and offerings into kingdom purposes, it is like going there ourselves, and we store up treasure where no moth or rust will corrupt. The Lord is our Provider, blessing us to be a blessing. Like those who gathered manna from heaven and the Acts church, He will ensure we receive our daily bread: *"He who gathered much had nothing left over, and he who gathered little had no lack"* (2 Cor. 8:15).

As Eternal Mediator, He Leads Us to Value God above Mammon

Jesus is the eternal *"Mediator of the new covenant"* (Heb. 12:24). **He is more precious than gold, silver, or precious jewels** because being the perfect Son of God and Son of Man, wisdom personified, **He faithfully passes to us what He receives from His Father, enabling kingdom living on earth as it is in heaven**. *"Again, the kingdom of heaven is like treasure hidden in a field, which a man found and hid; and for joy over it he goes and sells all that he has and buys that field. Again, the kingdom of heaven is like a merchant seeking beautiful pearls, who, when he had found one pearl of great price, went and sold all that he had and bought it"* (Matt. 13:44–46). We need to put first things first, seeking divine *"treasure"* or the *"pearl of great price,"* guarding it when we find it. We need to listen to His voice with all that God has given us or placed inside of us at the Lord's service.

Solomon sought wisdom when he became a leader. Because he did not ask for riches, but how to be a good leader, God gave him these too. Although he became the richest man worldwide, God had not wanted him to just accumulate wealth. He later learned that some things were more valuable than others, like wisdom and understanding (see Proverbs 16:16).

> *Receive my instruction, and not silver,*
> *And knowledge rather than choice gold;*
> *For wisdom is better than rubies,*
> *And all the things one may desire cannot be compared with her....*
> *Riches and honor are with me* [wisdom],
> *Enduring riches and righteousness.*
> *My fruit is better than gold, yes, than fine gold,*
> *And my revenue than choice silver.*
> *I traverse the way of righteousness,*
> *In the midst of the paths of justice,*
> *That I may cause those who love me to inherit wealth,*
> *That I may fill their treasuries.* (Prov. 8:10–11, 18–21)

I loved when we sang about how Jesus was more precious than silver, gold, or diamonds and *"nothing I desire compares with You."* Many times the Lord has piped it to me. **The most important wealth is spiritual—having His presence. Jesus is wisdom personified** and releases to us installments of our heavenly inheritance through His Spirit. This should cause us to live with His character, His fruit, evident in our lives.

God is our source for both spiritual and material wealth. He told His people to *"remember the Lord your God, for it is He who gives you power to get wealth, that He may establish His covenant"* (Deut. 8:18). Although those who obey God will prosper and be blessed, it is to be a blessing even under the New Covenant—they will have sufficient for their own needs and to advance the kingdom. God knows we need money but we are not to be selfish hoarders. **Money is useful, but it should serve us, not we it:** *"The love of money is a root of all kinds of evil"* (1 Tim. 6:10).

No one can serve two masters; for either he will hate the one and love the other, or else he will be loyal to the one and despise the other. You cannot serve God and mammon. (Matt. 6:24)

Now godliness with contentment is great gain. For we brought nothing into this world, and it is certain we can carry nothing out. And having food and clothing, with these we shall be content. But those who desire to be rich fall into temptation and a snare, and into many foolish and harmful lusts which drown men in destruction and perdition. For the love of money is a root of all kinds of evil, for which some have strayed from the faith in their greediness, and pierced themselves through with many sorrows. (1 Tim. 6:6–10)

God will prosper the obedient, but we should not set our heart on riches. Check your motivation.

Jesus knew He could have had anything He desired while on earth. Yet He humbled Himself to work as a carpenter before His public ministry and to rely on His Father providing for His needs when He sent Him out afterwards. Jesus did not sit at home doing nothing, expecting provision. He worked, fulfilling His ministry.

During His first thirty years as an obedient Jew and a carpenter, Jesus prospered but did not just accumulate material wealth. Instead, He used it to return tithes to the Lord's storehouse, to honour His widowed mother by supporting her and the family, to give to the poor, and later to finance kingdom work. In His public ministry, He also gave abundantly, spiritually enriching us tremendously. As God, He was rich, but became poor for our sake, humbling Himself in love and compassion. Therefore God blessed Jesus by publicly acknowledging Him, giving the Holy Spirit as His constant companion, having others willingly contribute to His ministry and open their hearts and homes to give food and lodging to Him and His disciples on their mission trips, and He exalted Him after His resurrection. *"For you know the grace of our Lord Jesus Christ, that though He was rich, yet for your sakes*

He became poor, that you through His poverty might become rich" (2 Cor. 8:9).

God could get it to Him because He could get it through Him. This is different than a poverty spirit, a curse which I used to live under. **God does not intend that His children go about in rags and broken-down houses.** Doing things God's way is great gain. **He prospers them, body, soul, and spirit, as well as materially so they can be blessed and be a blessing.**

God dispenses grace and mercy even to the undeserving, He is so good. But He also has special blessings for those who act like His children should. He rewards them at the right time. He sits enthroned in heaven and should be on the throne of our hearts as well, from which He can guide us.

Jesus reprimanded the scribes and Pharisees, those who put their tradition ahead of God's commandment. *"For God commanded, saying, 'Honor your father and your mother'; and, 'He who curses father or mother, let him be put to death.' But you say, 'Whoever says to his father or mother, "Whatever profit you might have received from me is a gift to God"—then he need not honor his father or mother.' Thus you have made the commandment of God of no effect by your tradition. Hypocrites!"* (Matt. 15:4–8). **Yes, we should be willing to *"gift,"* to surrender all of our resources to God, in accordance with His will. But studying His Word helped me see that part of His will is that we care for the needs of our own parents and of our family—to love God and our neighbour as our own self.** The poor widow commanded by God to feed Elijah was also to feed her son and herself. The Lord rewarded her obedience with lasting provision. *"A good man leaves an inheritance to his children's children, but the wealth of the sinner is stored up for the righteous"* (Prov. 13:22).

When I was in Jerusalem a year after my husband died, a woman from South Africa had a prophetic word for me that confirmed that God would take care of me. It was, *"'The silver is Mine and the gold is*

Mine,' says the Lord *of hosts"* (Hag. 2:8). That year, the Lord had led me to leave my job to be freer to follow Him, and I knew He had His hand under me with the adequate survivor's pensions I received each month. (Thank God my husband had paid into them.) He had also stretched me into cheerfully returning my full tithe and offerings to His storehouses, delivering me from a fear of lack, and blessed me for it.

But Jesus warned His servants not to take advantage of widows presumptuously, devouring their houses. They do not know how many others have already asked each widow for her two cents. I know I had some months when it was very difficult with so many requests, including telemarketers and strange charities coming like Philistines who tried to rob the children of Israel. In a service one day, when the pastor spoke of David's mighty man, Shammah, the Lord told me to *"stand up."* I prayed that I would be like Shammah who defended his crop which was for blessing God, His people, and his family. He *"stationed himself in the middle of the field, defended it, and killed the Philistines. So the* Lord *brought about a great victory"* (2 Sam. 23:12).

Jesus can be our financial adviser. I had asked Him to be mine and my children bought me a phone that could screen calls. I would prayerfully go through the "mountain" of monthly requests to give where I could, and if the Lord gave me an amount, I would give it—trying not to have a motive of getting something in return, but to advance His kingdom. Thankfully, He always blessed me, stretching finances. He had given me a word, including, *"Love your enemies, do good, and lend, hoping for nothing in return, and your reward will be great, and you will be sons of the Most High. For He is kind to the unthankful and evil. Therefore be merciful, just as your Father also is merciful"* (Luke 6:35–36).

Even sinners know the law of sowing and reaping, that they can expect a return on their investments, but God expects more from His children. **Our motive is important. He is to be our God, not mammon.** He desires to bless His people, making them a blessing as they remember Him and steward it well. **One day we will give an accounting of our stewardship.**

Tithes and Offerings Replenish His Storehouse and Maintain His Bridge

"Blessed are the merciful for they shall obtain mercy" (Matt. 5:7). Those who consider the poor and walk in the good deeds God has for them are like ones who lend to God. Although He repays abundantly when the time is right, let us do it out of love. *"And let us not grow weary while doing good, for in due season we shall reap if we do not lose heart. Therefore as we have opportunity, let us do good to all, especially to those who are of the household of faith"* (Gal. 6:9–10). **The Lord can receive graciously what we return and offer to Him and teach us to do it with right motives, taking good care of us.** *"Do not lay up for yourselves treasures on earth, where moth and rust destroy and where thieves break in and steal; but lay up for yourselves treasures in heaven, where neither moth nor rust destroys and where thieves do not break in and steal. For where your treasure is, there your heart will be too"* (Matt. 6:19–21).

Tithes are not strictly a gift, because they belong to God, so we are to *"return"* them to Him. He has abundantly invested in us, even giving us His Son. Everything belongs to Him so His people were to return a tithe of their increase and steward the rest. In the New Testament, Jesus obeyed His Father so He would have willingly brought in tithes so that there would be provision in His Father's house for those who ministered there and for those in need. In Deuteronomy 14:22–29 and 26:12–13, we see that tithes were brought in of their increase of grain, animals, oil, and produce, some being returned year by year, and some every three years. They would travel to the temple with their tithes at the time of the Lord's three great feasts, and if it was too far they could bring money and buy whatever they wanted for the feast at the place the Lord indicated. Some of the tithes would be stored up until needed.

The levites, a great number, including the Aaronic priesthood, singers, musicians, and doorkeepers, each had specific duties in the tabernacle of meeting. All these **priestly workers in God's house were provided for** when the Levites received tithes and offerings from the people **and they were commanded to return tithes themselves.** Thus food and lodging was provided for them and their families, since they were to have no other job but their duties in the temple. **Tithes were also to be used for assisting people in their need**, especially *"the Levite, the stranger, the fatherless, and the widow"* (Deut. 26:12–13).

"Speak to the children of Israel, that they bring Me an offering. From everyone who gives it willingly with his heart you shall take My offering" (Ex. 25:2). **Besides tithes, the Jews in David's time willingly gave offerings for building, maintaining, and furnishing the Lord's house, just as things are needed today for that purpose. They knew that everything belonged to God,** *"both riches and honor come from You"*, **and gratefully blessed His house with what was needful.**

> *Then the people rejoiced, for they had offered willingly, because with a loyal heart they had offered willingly to the* Lord; *and King David also rejoiced greatly.*
> *Therefore David blessed the* Lord *before all the assembly; and David said:*
> *"Blessed are You,* Lord *God of Israel, our Father, forever and ever.*
> *Yours, O* Lord, *is the greatness,*
> *The power and the glory,*
> *The victory and the majesty;*
> *For all that is in heaven and in earth is Yours;*
> *Yours is the kingdom, O* Lord,
> *And You are exalted as head over all.*
> *Both riches and honor come from You,*
> *And You reign over all.*
> *In Your hand is power and might;*

In Your hand it is to make great
And to give strength to all.
Now therefore, our God,
We thank You
And praise Your glorious name.
But who am I, and who are my people,
That we should be able to offer so willingly as this?
For all things come from You,
*L*ORD *of Your own we have given You.*
For we are aliens and pilgrims before You,
As were all our fathers;
Our days on earth are as a shadow,
And without hope.
*"O L*ORD *our God, all this abundance that we have prepared to build You a house for Your holy name is from Your hand, and is all Your own. I know also, my God, that You test the heart and have pleasure in uprightness. As for me, in the uprightness of my heart I have willingly offered all these things; and now with joy I have seen Your people, who are present here to offer willingly to You."* (1 Chron. 29:9–17)

They did not have to turn the temple into a marketplace or house of thieves by selling things or having lotteries and bingos to collect money equal to tithes and offerings, nor did the temple need a myriad of other money-making "marketplace" projects. God simply told the people they were going to take up an offering and **many willingly gave according to their means out of a heart of love for Him and His house**. There were even times when they gave so much that they were told to stop! **No wonder Jesus had a righteous anger** when His Father's house was turned into *"a den of thieves"!* (Matt. 21:13; Jer. 7:11).

Paul commended Gentiles who willingly gave, although he did not ask them at first: *"For it pleased those from Macedonia and Achaia to make a certain contribution for the poor among the saints who are in Jerusalem. It pleased them indeed, and they are their debtors. For if the Gentiles* have been partakers of their spiritual things, their duty is also to minister to them in material things" (Rom. 15:26–27). He had told the Corinthians to regularly lay up something for this collection on Sundays, according to how God prospered them (see 1 Cor. 16:1–3).

Jesus's Refining Fire Produces a Heart to Give Right Offerings

John the Baptist told the people Jesus would baptize them with His fire and Holy Spirit. Jesus will suddenly come to us who are His temple of the Holy Spirit where He has placed His name and refine us like gold and silver. I have experienced this. **He is restoring His people today with His cleansing fire so we will give right offerings unto the Lord** and offerings in a state of *"righteousness"* (Mal. 3:3). It is much easier on us when we submit to it, surrendering to Him in love.

When Melchizedek blessed Abram, bringing out bread and wine, Abram gratefully responded by giving him a tithe, one-tenth of all. **This was long before tithing was revealed to Moses as a law of God.** Abraham lived before the Law was written and delivered to the people by Moses. By giving a tithe to God's priest, Melchizedek—before it became a Jewish law to do so, Abraham was returning it to God.

As a Catholic, I never heard any teaching on tithes as I was growing up. I do not think our priests knew about them then, but now some do. Melchizedek *"whose genealogy is not derived from [Levi] received tithes from Abraham and blessed him who had the promises. Now beyond all contradiction the lesser is blessed by the better. Here mortal men receive tithes, but there he receives them, of whom it is witnessed that he lives"* (Heb. 7:6–8).

Immortal King Jesus is undoubtedly the greatest One, *"He who lives"* (Rev. 1:18), and a priest *"in the order of Melchizedek"* (Ps. 110:4).

Neither Jesus's nor Melchizedek's genealogy is derived from the Levites, but **King Jesus** today, and God through Him, **receives tithes and offerings, being the New Covenant High Priest** serving in His Father's house. Jesus received the little boy's five loaves and two fishes offering, and the other person's *"seven loaves and a few little fish"* (Matt. 15:34), blessed them and fed thousands of men, including Himself and His disciples who were helping Him, plus women and children (see Matthew 14:13–21; 15:32–38). **He made a withdrawal from the storehouse of heaven** that there might be food in His Father's house, which we are. He is an example of receiving not to be rich but to steward wisely.

God does love when we give cheerfully and not under compulsion. *"And though I bestow all my goods to feed the poor, and though I give my body to be burned, but have not love, it profits me nothing"* (1 Cor. 13:3). It should not be a legalistic thing either. *"But without your consent I wanted to do nothing, that your good deed might not be by compulsion, as it were, but voluntary"* (Phm. 1:14).

Just as Abraham willingly gave his tithes to King Melchizedek, so today, we should willingly give to King Jesus in thanksgiving for all that God is and all that He does. Usually this is done by bringing tithes and offerings and the "first fruits" of our increase into our home church or to other ministry leaders to be received in His name and stewarded wisely. Jesus has a number of "storehouses." Like the Jews, we should give where He indicates—**not so any one preacher can become rich, but so that ministries will be provided for and be rich in mercy.** They can then distribute from the storehouse to fulfill needs as the apostles did. When we ask God to provide our *"daily bread,"* He knows what we need, and sometimes His love is extravagant, so we can pass it on. *"Worthy is the Lamb who was slain to receive power and riches and wisdom, and strength and honor and glory and blessing!"* (Rev. 5:12).

"It is more blessed to give than to receive" (Acts 20:35). **People will know we are Christians by our love.** But those who selfishly horde their wealth will be judged. God sees everything. Jesus told the story of the rich man and the starving beggar Lazarus to warn some *"Pharisees, who were lovers of money"* (Luke 16:14). God wants us to know the truth sooner rather than later.

> *Come now, you rich, weep and howl for your miseries that are coming upon you! Your riches are corrupted, and your garments are moth-eaten. Your gold and silver are corroded, and their corrosion will be a witness against you and will eat your flesh like fire. You have heaped up treasure in the last days. Indeed the wages of the laborers who mowed your fields, which you kept back by fraud, cry out; and the cries of the reapers have reached the ears of the Lord of Sabaoth.* (Jas. 5:1–4)

Jesus baptizes us with His refining and empowering fire and teaches us.

> *But this I say: He who sows sparingly will also reap sparingly, and he who sows bountifully will also reap bountifully. So let each one give as he purposes in his heart, not grudgingly or of necessity; for God loves a cheerful giver. And God is able to make all grace abound toward you, that you, always having all sufficiency in all things, may have an abundance for every good work. As it is written: "He has dispersed abroad, he has given to the poor; his righteousness endures forever." Now may He who supplies seed to the sower, and bread for food, supply and multiply the seed you have sown and increase the fruits of your righteousness, while you are enriched in everything for all liberality, which causes thanksgiving through us to God.* (2 Cor. 9:6–11)

Paul showed we need not be afraid of giving, and that includes more than money.

In Old Testament times, God took care of His priests and Levites, providing for their needs as they did what He called them to do. Today, **God takes care of His ministers working in His house and field who do what He has called them to do.** Sometimes this depends upon the generosity of His people. God has a generous spirit. Jesus demonstrated that with the parable of the workers in His vineyard and when He sent out the twelve and the seventy. These missionaries were to stay in the homes of those who were worthy, and their meals were provided for them there, and if they needed clothing or finances, someone moved by their ministry would offer these to them. They could receive an offering, as Jesus received the loaves and fishes and as Jesus received offerings from disciples like the holy women who followed Him. This was so that people could be fed: body, soul, and spirit. *"Freely you have received, freely give"* (Matt. 10:8).

Today, missionaries who are sent out can pray beforehand **asking God to supply all that is needful for them,** and praise God, many testify that He does. Like Paul (who sometimes did not use his right to receive offerings, especially among new converts), others have a "tent-maker ministry" to help support them—a job on the side that they can work at when they are able. Much of the time, Paul ministered like that. He wrote:

> *If we have sown spiritual things for you, is it a great thing if we reap your material things? If others are partakers of this right over you, are we not even more? Nevertheless, we have not used this right, but endure all things lest we hinder the gospel of Christ. Do you not know that those who minister the holy things eat of the things of the temple, and those who serve at the altar partake of the offerings of the altar? Even so the Lord has commanded that those who preach the gospel should live from the gospel.* (1 Cor. 9:11–18)

People pay for their dinner in a restaurant, so **they should not think pastors are doing something wrong when they receive an** offering. **Of course the pastor is accountable to God for how he collects it and how he stewards it.**

Later, having learned to be content whether he had plenty or little, praising God who strengthened him so that he could *"do all things through Christ"* (Phil. 4:13), Paul commended the new church at Philippi for **their generosity which helped him to plant new churches:** *"No church shared with me concerning giving and receiving but you only. For even in Thessalonica you sent aid once and again for my necessities. Not that I seek the gift, but I seek the fruit that abounds to your account"* (Phil. 4:14–17). He called the things they willingly sent *"an acceptable sacrifice, well pleasing to God"* with *"a sweet-smelling aroma"* (Phil. 4:18). **Because of their compassionate giving, God rewarded them:** *"And my God shall supply all your need according to His riches in glory by Christ Jesus. Now to our God and Father be glory forever and ever. Amen"* (Phil. 4:19–20). Since Paul was one of Jesus's little brothers, supporting his ministry, they were doing it as unto the Lord Jesus and would be rewarded. God deserves glory for this.

Especially when bringing the good news to a new area, it is good to have people and established churches fund the missionary effort so good news and miracles can be offered without charge. **God takes care of His workers.** Free will offerings are sometimes collected. Then, as new believers grow in the Lord, they will willingly desire to bring in their tithes and give offerings so the work of ministry can continue.

> *Ho! Everyone who thirsts,*
> *Come to the waters;*
> *And you who have no money,*
> *Come, buy and eat.*
> *Yes, come, buy wine and milk*
> *Without money and without price.* (Isa. 55:1)

In the early church, from time to time, believers would sell a field or possession, and they laid the proceeds at the feet of the apostles who distributed to any who had need, especially caring for the needs of the saints and missionaries, but loving their neighbours as themselves. Believers invested into the work of the gospel and it paid dividends in their heavenly bank account, and they were blessed on earth when they needed it too.

My husband, a carpenter, answered numerous calls for help after he came home from his regular job. He did not ask for pay for these although a few gave us something, like some fresh-caught fish. But when the time came that we needed help, numerous people volunteered to help us—even a river of mercy flowed, praise God. *"Blessed are the merciful for they shall obtain mercy"* (Matt. 5:7).

> *Let him who is taught the word share in all good things with him who teaches. Do not be deceived, God is not mocked; for whatever a man sows, that he will also reap. For he who sows to his flesh will of the flesh reap corruption, but he who sows to the Spirit will of the Spirit reap everlasting life. And let us not grow weary while doing good, for in due season we shall reap if we do not lose heart. Therefore as we have opportunity, let us do good to all, especially to those who are of the household of faith.* (Gal. 6:6–10)

God is our Provider. The purpose of our giving should not be to get, but to do good; yet knowing that God faithfully rewards givers.

When the rich young ruler wanted to be perfect but walked away not realizing that **the heart of the gospel is love,** and our supply depends upon obedient service to Jesus, not on our own personal accumulation of wealth, Jesus reassured His disciples who had learned to trust in Him and had overcome a fear of lack: *"Assuredly, I say to you, there is no one who has left house or brothers or sisters or father or mother or wife or children or lands, for My sake and the gospel's, who shall not receive a hundredfold now in this time—houses and brothers and sisters and mothers and children and lands, with persecutions—and in the age to come, eternal life"* (Mark 10:29–30).

Jesus, still alive today, receives tithes and offerings now when they are given to storehouse-keeper members of His body. This builds and maintains the railway trestle bridge and provides for those traveling on the train to visit the Father. Gifts given cheerfully, in love, are good fruit borne on the branches. *"But you, O mountains of Israel, you shall shoot forth your branches and yield your fruit to My people Israel, for they are about to come"* (Ezek. 36:8).

"And the King will answer and say to them, 'Assuredly I say to you, inasmuch as you did it to one of the least of these My brethren, you did it to Me'" (Matt. 25:40). If you do something for His little toe, you do it to Jesus.

Blessings Promised to the Believing Giver

Jesus dispenses blessings too: *"Beloved, I pray that you may prosper in all things and be in health, just as your soul prospers"* (3 John 1:2). He prospers those who love Him and seek to do His will *"in all things,"* not just blessing finances.

I got to know Him as El Shaddai, the Almighty, All-Sufficient One, our God who is even More Than Enough, who has taught me that we should not grumble and complain if things are tough as when the Israelites did in the wilderness, displeasing Him. Rather, with an attitude of gratitude, do as Jesus taught and pray to the Father, hallowing His name, seeking His kingdom and will among us, asking for our daily bread, for needs not "greeds," and we shall receive. Even in my widowhood, praise God, I found that *"I shall not want"* **with the LORD as my Good Shepherd** (Ps. 23:1). He delivered me from the evil of a fear of lack.

We show the good fruit of longsuffering when we can be content in all circumstances: *"Let your conduct be without covetousness; be content with such things as you have. For He Himself has said, 'I WILL NEVER LEAVE YOU NOR FORSAKE YOU'"* (Heb. 13:5).

But if we are greedy and covet things that belong to our neighbour, we might even get them, but that is following mammon, not God. Beware of all *"covetousness, for that is idolatry. Because of these things the wrath of God is coming upon the sons of disobedience"* (Col. 3:5–6).

However, there are many blessings promised for the believing tither and giver. Jesus still gives them today.

> *"Bring all the tithes into the storehouse,*
> *That there may be food in My house,*
> *And try Me now in this,"* [It is one of the few times we are allowed to put God to the test.]
> *Says the* Lᴵᴼᴿᴰ *of hosts,*
> *"If I will not open for you the windows of heaven*
> *And pour out for you such blessing* [spiritual and material blessings]
> *That there will not be room enough to receive it.*
> *And I will rebuke the devourer for your sakes,*
> *So that he will not destroy the fruit of your ground,*
> *Nor shall the vine fail to bear fruit for you in the field,"*
> *Says the* Lᴵᴼᴿᴰ *of hosts;*
> *"And all nations will call you blessed,*
> *For you will be a delightful land,"*
> *Says the* Lᴵᴼᴿᴰ *of hosts.* (Malachi 3:10–12)

After all, *"'The silver is Mine, and the gold is Mine,' says the* Lᴵᴼᴿᴰ *of hosts. The glory of this latter temple* [the body of Christ] *shall be greater than the former,' says the* Lᴵᴼᴿᴰ *of hosts. 'And in this place I will give peace,' says the* Lᴵᴼᴿᴰ *of hosts"* (Hag. 2:8–9). Since the silver and gold belong to God who created them and so much more, He has a right over His creation and He asks for at least 10 percent to be returned to Him. **Today, the glory will be greater** with *"Christ in you, the hope of glory"* (Col. 1:27), and *"the peace of God which surpasses understanding"* (Phil. 4:7).

Stewarding

Genesis 26:12–13 says, *"Isaac sowed in that land* [in the time of famine] *and reaped in the same year a hundredfold; and the L*ORD *blessed him … until he became very prosperous."* We can steward well the overflowing blessing that God gives tithers, **sure of God's provision, even while others are worried about economic insecurity.** I remember being in that situation during the Great Ice Storm that hit Kingston in 1998 and the COVID-19 global pandemic during 2020-2022. While others were starving, scrambling to get government aid, I was lending and giving to others. I was not rich but had overflowing blessings, more than enough. Glory be to God! And when I developed a problem with my leg, restricting mobility during COVID-19, I was blessed abundantly with food and supplies from my daughter and others. Praise God! And the Lord healed my ailments.

Jesus receives and stewards the tithe today through members of His body. When he saw that the multitude was hungry, **He blessed and broke the offering** of loaves and fishes and **handed them to His disciples to distribute, to steward in His name, to miraculously continue to break off pieces.** We can give as unto the Lord, ask God to bless it, and distribute what He provides with wisdom and compassion.

In Old Testament times, tithes were for the Levites, including the priestly descendants of Aaron to steward *"as an inheritance in return for the work which they perform, the work of the tabernacle of meeting"* (Num. 18:21).

They were not to have an inheritance of land among the children of Israel, but the congregation provided accommodation for them. (This reminds me of a church manse today.) The Lord said, *"I am your portion and inheritance"* (Num. 18:20). In stewarding the tithes and offerings, they began by tithing on it. The best part was to be given to the Lord and then the Levites and their household could eat of it *"for it is your reward for your work in the tabernacle of meeting"* (Num. 18:31). **But the entire tithe was not for themselves.** A portion of the tithe was to be stewarded so that strangers, the fatherless, and widows could also eat (see Deut. 14:29). Our God cares.

God also provided for needy people by allowing them to glean after the harvesters like Ruth did. Parts of the field edges were set aside for them too, and they could pick up the leftovers. **Today, obeying the spirit of the Law rather than the letter, soup kitchens and food banks steward fresh food and leftovers which homes and businesses contribute. But even in New Testament times, the recipients were not to be lazy. If they were able, they were to do work.**

Jesus reminded people not only to tithe from their animals and garden, but also to stay alert to what was going on around and tithe more important things which God has deposited within like **justice, mercy, and faith**. This is another aspect of giving lovingly.

> *Woe to you, scribes and Pharisees, hypocrites! For you pay tithe of mint and anise and cumin, and have neglected the weightier matters of the law: justice and mercy and faith. These you ought to have done, without leaving the others undone. Blind guides who strain out a gnat and swallow a camel! Woe to you, scribes and Pharisees, hypocrites! For you cleanse the outside of the cup and dish, but inside they are full of extortion and self-indulgence. Blind Pharisee, first cleanse the inside of the cup and dish, that the outside of them may be clean also.* (Matt. 23:23–26)

We can also steward our gifts and talents in Jesus's name, looking for other opportunities to love our neighbour as ourselves and seeing that justice is done, helping others in need while caring for our own household. **Hospitality, including to strangers, is still important, but extortion and self-indulgence are evil.**

> *Above all things have fervent love for one another, for "love will cover a multitude of sins." Be hospitable to one another, without grumbling. As each one has received a gift, minister it to one another, as good stewards of the manifold grace of God. If anyone speaks,*

> let him speak as the oracles of God. If anyone ministers, let him do it with the ability which God supplies, that in all things God may be glorified through Jesus Christ, to whom belong the glory and the dominion forever and ever. Amen. (1 Peter 4:8–11)

Members of the body of Christ are to steward well what is entrusted to them, for one day we will have to give an accounting of what we have done with them.

> Who then is that faithful and wise steward, whom his master will make ruler over his household, to give them their portion of food in due season? Blessed is that servant whom his master will find so doing when he comes. Truly I say to you that he will make him ruler over all that he has. But if that servant says in his heart, "My master is delaying his coming," and begins to beat the male and female servants, and to eat and drink and be drunk, the master of that servant will come on a day when he is not looking for him, and at an hour when he is not aware, and will cut him in two and appoint him his portion with the unbelievers. And that servant who knew his master's will, and did not prepare himself or do according to his will, shall be beaten with many stripes. But he who did not know, yet committed things deserving of stripes, shall be beaten with few. For everyone to whom much is given, from him much will be required; and to whom much has been committed, of him they will ask the more. (Luke 12:42–48)

Our Bridge Defends the Poor and Widows in Their Affliction

Psalm 82:3–4 says, "Defend the poor and fatherless; do justice to the afflicted and needy. Deliver the poor and needy; free them from the hand of the wicked."

In the early church, **Jesus's training was followed and no believer lacked provision.**

> *The multitude of those who believed were of one heart and one soul; neither did anyone say that any of the things he possessed was his own, but they had all things in common. And with great power the apostles gave witness to the resurrection of the Lord Jesus. And great grace was upon them all. Nor was there anyone among them who lacked; for all who were possessors of lands or houses sold them, and brought the proceeds of the things that were sold, and laid them at the apostles' feet; and they distributed to each as anyone had need.* (Acts 4:32–35)

They could have brought in everything at once, or some at a time, as needed.

People speak today about the importance of relationship with God above ritualistic religion. **True love of God flows out into love of others, especially believers, as Jesus loved us**. *"Pure and undefiled religion before God and the Father is this: to visit orphans and widows in their trouble, and to keep oneself unspotted from the world"* (Jas. 1:27).

Paul admonished families to lovingly take care of their relations who were widows as part of their responsibility, their cross to carry as Jesus's disciples with *"the joy of the Lord"* **as their strength.** *"Honor your father and mother, that your days may be long upon the land which the* LORD *your God is giving you"* (Ex. 20:12). *"But if anyone does not provide for his own, and especially for those of his household, he has denied the faith and is worse than an unbeliever"* (1 Tim. 5:8). They made sure that widows who were *"worthy,"* who had insufficient support, were taken care of. It was the church, not the government, that did this. The Acts church acted in that spirit, feeding widows who did not have family to perform that duty. There was a *"daily distribution"* (Acts 6:1), and deacons, *"seven men of good reputation, full of the Holy Spirit and wisdom* [were appointed] *over this business"* (Act 6:3), waiting on tables so the apostles could attend to their other duties.

Jesus even warned religious leaders to beware of devouring the houses of widows. He protected them acting as an advocate for

their defense. *"For your Maker is your husband"* (Isa. 54:5). *"Beware of the scribes ... who devour widows' houses, and for a pretense make long prayers. These will receive greater condemnation.... For they all put in out of their abundance, but she out of her poverty put in all that she had, her whole livelihood"* (Mark 12:38, 40, 44).

Jesus made the point that her couple coins were a high percentage, all that she had to live on, but some do not see that **He was also warning them so that they would not** *"devour widows' houses,"* **like wolves in sheep's clothing.** As a widow myself, I know how many appeals for funds I receive, and how I desire to do what I can. And God has blessed me for what I have done and wants my family to have food too. But it reminds me of how I loved to give blood so that lives might be saved, and I thank God I was able to donate over fifty times when I was younger. But some years ago they changed the regulations to protect the donors. Sometimes I wept because they refused to receive an offering from me, saying that my iron level was high enough for my health, but not high enough to give blood to others. But I understand now, and another day, I could give again, thank God.

Although seniors may be willing to lay down their lives for their friends, and sometimes they do, sometimes leadership might need to watch that seniors are not overworked and oppressed.

Jesus knew as well as they did that there were times in history when **God specifically commanded a widow to care for a prophet** whom He had sent to her house, so it had not been robbery for Elijah to accept the shelter and hospitality of the widow of Zarephath and her son, **sharing** the last of their food: *"He who receives a prophet in the name of the prophet shall receive a prophet's reward"* (Matt. 10:41). He knew she would be blessed because God had told him:*Arise, go to Zarephath, which belongs to Sidon, and dwell there. See, I have commanded a widow there to provide for you....* [First he asked for water from the starving widow.] *And Elijah said to her, "Do not fear; go and do as you have said, but make me a small cake from it first, and bring it to me; and afterward make some for yourself and your son. For thus says the* L<small>ORD</small> *God* of Israel: 'The bin of flour shall not be used up, nor shall the jar of oil run dry, until the day the LORD sends rain on the earth.'" (1 Kings 17:9, 13–14)

So God allowed all three to eat and abundantly blessed the stranger, fatherless, and widow for their obedience, hers to give and his to receive.

We can remember Jesus in the breaking of the bread. The Lord has reminded me, *"Little becomes much when God is in control."*

Jesus Is an Obedient High Priest

He was obedient to the Father in the past so He is now and always will be. *"Jesus Christ is the same, yesterday, today, and forever"* (Heb. 13:8). *"Then Jesus said to them, 'When you lift up the Son of Man, then you will know that I am He, and that I do nothing of Myself; but as the Father taught Me, I speak these things. And He who sent Me is with Me. The Father has not left Me alone, for I always do those things that please Him'"* (John 8:28–29). **He is forever faithful to the will of His Father, full of compassion and righteousness.**

He both showed compassion to the woman caught in adultery and stood up for what is right. He protected her, yet said, *"Go and sin no more"* (John 8:11). Jesus demonstrated His righteousness—*truth and justice tempered by mercy*. They knew she had done wrong, as had the missing man, a sin that deserved death for both (see Lev. 20:10). Knowing that at the cross He was going to fulfill the death penalty she deserved, **Jesus acknowledged that she had sinned and offered her mercy, but commanded her to repent. He can do that today too.**

As parts of the body of Christ, we can approach the mercy seat of God in His name and ask for what is needful. His Spirit produces good fruit in our lives. Like a tree, we can go through dormant seasons. But if we are like a Psalm 1 tree planted near His River, His lifeblood runs through us like sap again. New life will spring forth like putting forth leaves for healing and fruitfulness. **God is faithful with**

the natural trees bringing forth new life every spring, so how much more faithful is He with us if we do not lose heart? He gives strength to endure in a dry season. I remember a time when the word of the Lord came to me: *"You have need of endurance."* That strengthened me.

> *Blessed be the name of God forever and ever,*
> *For wisdom and might are His.*
> *And He changes the times and the seasons;*
> *He removes kings and raises up kings;*
> *He gives wisdom to the wise*
> *And knowledge to the understanding.* (Daniel 2:20–21)

Our High Priest can lead us in praise of the Father in the dry, dormant seasons and in the times of flourishing, so we can provide fruit for Him and parts of His body, even to the least of His brethren. *"Let my beloved come to his garden and eat its pleasant fruits"* (Song 4:16).

> *Blessed is the man who trusts in the L*ORD*,*
> *And whose hope is the L*ORD*.*
> *For he shall be like a tree planted by the waters,*
> *Which spreads out its roots by the river,*
> *And will not fear when heat comes;*
> *But its leaf will be green,*
> *And will not be anxious in the year of drought,*
> *Nor will cease from yielding fruit.* (Jer. 17:7–8)

Jesus gives hope that one day in New Jerusalem there will be no more dormant seasons: *"In the middle of the street, and on either side of the river, was the tree of life, which bore twelve fruits, each tree yielding its fruit every month. The leaves of the tree were for the healing of the nations"* (Rev. 22:2). Meanwhile, let us stay by the River of God, yield much fruit and partake of the fruit borne by others.

Jesus was so one with the Father that He only did what the Father showed Him. Yet at Gethsemane, for our sake, He showed more humility by asking the Father to help Him line up His will to the

Father's. He drank deeply from His living water which proceeded from the true temple, *"from the throne of God and of the Lamb"* (Rev. 22:1). Thus He was ready and willing for Messianic prophecy to be fulfilled as in Isaiah 53 about Him being lifted up as the suffering Servant of Yahweh who interceded for men who were yet sinners.

> *For He was cut off from the land of the living;*
> *For the transgressions of My people He was stricken....*
> *When you make His soul an offering for sin,*
> *He shall see His seed....*
> *By His knowledge My righteous Servant shall justify many....*
> *And He bore the sin of many, and made intercession for the transgressors.* (Isa. 53:8, 10–12)

"Jesus Christ is the same ... forever" (Heb. 13:8), but He never has to die again. When He was on earth He answered many pleas for mercy, like that of the man who was blind yet could tell who He was and cried out, *"Jesus, Son of David, have mercy on me!"* (Luke 18:38). Even in his blindness, the man had better spiritual eyesight than some.

With this same compassion, humility, and faithfulness coming to do the will of the Father with the power of God, Jesus continues to do His job very well. He often works through members of His body but can deal directly with us. His sheep hear His voice. He is not a statue, but Jesus is the living Word of God, who said, *"I always do those things that please Him"* (John 8:29). **His blood has already satisfied the requirement of the Law—the death penalty for sin—so Jesus, the eternal High Priest, can enter a plea of mercy for us and remind the Father** at His right hand that believers can receive justification. They can be made right with God just as if nothing had happened. We can join with Him in this plea for mercy and the people can choose to receive the saving grace God gives. He bids us to keep asking, seeking and knocking, and we may see the fruit of our labour.

He has a concern for God and men but puts God first. For those who are willing, He will give priestly instruction through His *rhema* and *logos* word, in His timing. He still extends compassion today and multitudes have been healed in His name, inside and outside.

Jesus Heals

Jesus, the great priestly physician, Jehovah Rapha, is alive and active! When people wondered why Jesus ate with sinners and was healing and cleansing any who came to Him, He told them, *"Those who are well have no need of a physician, but those who are sick. But go and learn what this means: 'I desire mercy and not sacrifice.' For I did not come to call the righteous, but sinners, to repentance"* (Matt. 9:12–13). He still eats with sinners today because they need His saving grace and to chew on the prescriptions He gives and then to go on to repentance. Levitical priests were given instruction by God regarding the healing and cleansing of certain people, so how much more our High Priest, Jesus, heard and hears from God! **Jesus still comes to heal and to call people to repentance. In the power of His name, working with and within His disciples, He even does many miracles and healings today, cleansing some who are treated like lepers.**

Although God has inspired the written *logos* word in biblical Scripture, and it is helpful, it's not just a matter of "take two psalms and call me in the morning" (unless His Spirit actually gives you two psalms). Rather, people need to listen to the verbal *rhema* word prescription God gives from Jesus especially for them and meditate on it. Not all sicknesses are the result of someone's sin, but some are. As Jesus told the man healed at Bethesda, *"See, you have been made well. Sin no more lest a worse thing come upon you"* (John 5:14). Instead of reaping just punishments for their sins, people can receive a gift they do not deserve—forgiveness, debt cancelation, healing, and amazing grace. Afterwards they can walk in repentance and follow Him down the road like blind Bart did. Experiencing His goodness leads to experiencing repentance and more of His goodness and saving grace.

Jesus came to save men's lives, and *save*[19] in the New Testament is *"sozo."* It means "to save, that is, deliver or protect; heal, preserve, do well, be (make) whole." So, part of the way Jesus saves us body, soul, and spirit, is by healing us and making us whole.

Sometimes the healing comes first and sometimes the repentance. The Mighty Healer helps people keep their healing by calling them to repentance. He did that with me in 1981. He called me to repentance with 2 Chronicles 7:14 so I knew there must be sin in my life. Then when I acted upon it, He healed me from the inside out. Glory be to God, my health was generally good for years after. Not every sickness is the result of one's sins, but a benefit for believers is that He:

> *...forgives all your iniquities,*
> *Who heals all your diseases,*
> *Who redeems your life from destruction,*
> *Who crowns you with lovingkindness and tender mercies,*
> *Who satisfies your mouth with good things,*
> *So that your youth is renewed like the eagle's.* (Ps. 103:3–5)

But Jesus can also sovereignly heal people. Don't put Him in a box.

Normally a person's own *"faith"* in Jesus saves them. *"Your faith has saved you. Go in peace"* (Luke 7:50). Yet we do not know the faith condition of the man lowered through the roof by his four friends so Jesus could heal him. But Jesus had compassion on him, so he experienced both forgiveness and healing. The four men were so determined not to leave until he got his blessing that it was like they were standing in the gap for him, and, *"When Jesus saw their faith, He said to the paralytic, 'Son, your sins are forgiven you'"* (Mark 2:5). The people knew that only God can forgive sin, so being the Healer too, He healed him as well, removing the consequence of sin. Because He bore our chastisement,

---

19   James Strong, *Strong's Hebrew and Greek Dictionaries*, in Rick Meyer's *e-Sword*. https://www.e-sword.net/.

Jesus still heals today. We *"were healed"* by His stripes—and *"we are healed"* (Isa. 53:5; 1 Pet. 2:24), immediately or progressively. Only believe!

However, once we have tasted His goodness, let us not fall away; for those who do choose to go back to a life of sin *"crucify again for themselves the Son of God, and put Him to an open shame"* (Heb. 6:6). Their ungodly lives give Christ and Christians a bad name. It is as if they were there two thousand years ago, piercing Him again with their sins.

> *Or do you despise the riches of His goodness, forbearance, and longsuffering, not knowing that the goodness of God leads you to repentance? But in accordance with your hardness and your impenitent heart you are treasuring up for yourself wrath in the day of wrath and revelation of the righteous judgment of God, who "will render to each one according to his deeds": eternal life to those who by patient continuance in doing good seek for glory, honor and immortality; but to those who are self-seeking and do not obey the truth, but obey unrighteousness—indignation and wrath, tribulation and anguish, on every soul of man who does evil, to the Jew first and also to the Greek; but glory, honor and peace to everyone who works what is good, to the Jew first and also to the Greek. For there is no partiality with God.... For not the hearers of the law are just in the sight of God, but the doers of the law will be justified* [even if the law is only written on their hearts] ... *in the day when God will judge the secrets of men by Jesus Christ.* (Rom. 2:4–11, 13, 16)

We are saved by grace through faith but saved to have a fresh start in loving and obeying God, walking in the good works He has planned, loving others as He loves us. **As the Lord has said to me, *"If you call yourself a Christian, act like one"* And *"His mercy is great on those who fear Him"*. Thank God! Let us trust and obey God as Jesus does.**

Jesus Actually Made the Greatest Plea from the Altar of Sacrifice, the Cross

Jesus sympathizes with His people, pleading today for their forgiveness rather than condemning them, but some people choose to be condemned. The wise will choose to follow Jesus, who said:

> *As Moses lifted up the serpent in the wilderness, even so must the Son of Man be lifted up, that whoever believes in Him should not perish but have eternal life. For God so loved the world that He gave His only begotten Son, that whoever believes in Him should not perish but have everlasting life. For God did not send His Son into the world to condemn the world, but that the world through Him might be saved. He who believes in Him is not condemned; but he who does not believe is condemned already, because he has not believed in the name of the only begotten Son of God. And this is the condemnation, that the light has come into the world, and men loved darkness rather than light, because their deeds were evil. For everyone practicing evil hates the light and does not come to the light, lest his deeds should be exposed. But he who does the truth comes to the light, that his deeds may be clearly seen, that they have been done in God.* (John 3:14–21)

Jesus knew He would come again to judge the living and the dead, so on the cross by appealing, *"Father, forgive them, for they do not know what they do"* (Luke 23:34), **He opened the way for reconciliation with the Father for any who would repent**. That was for all even today because our sins helped crucify Him. In the midst of His agony, His love for mankind was so great. His plea then was for us now.

In God's presence, one can be so in awe of Him that other matters fade away. Aaron as high priest needed to wear precious stones engraved with names of the twelve tribes on his shoulders and over his heart each time He entered the Holy of holies to encounter God's presence. I believe it was partly so he would not forget to pray for the people. He would remember them before God, foreshadowing Jesus.

Since God would reveal to Aaron when judgment was coming to each tribe, he would bear their judgment on his heart and shoulders, and having come with shed blood, he pleaded for them before the mercy seat. Like the Aaronic high priest, Jesus offered the chosen sacrificial Passover Lamb—Himself—for the forgiveness of sins. **Jesus prayed on the cross from the order of Melchizedek fulfilling the Aaronic priesthood.** He said He will not forget His own: *"See, I have inscribed you on the palms of My hands"* (Isa. 49:16).

God revealed to Jesus the judgment that was coming so He agreed not only to stand in the gap, but to drink the cup of judgment in our place and bore the judgment upon His heart and shoulders going to and on the altar of the cross and the sword in His heart once for all. There, He cried out to God. **Before He died He remembered to pray for all, making the greatest plea from the cross for Jews and Gentiles that whosoever will believe should be saved**—*"Father forgive them, for they do not know what they do"* (Luke 23:34). It is up to us how we respond.

The Father suffered too. As the Father asked me once, *"Don't you care about My sacrifice? Don't you care about the sacrifice of My Son?"*

It is written, *"And I will pour on the house of David and on the inhabitants of Jerusalem the Spirit of grace and supplication; then they will look on Me whom they pierced. Yes, they will mourn for Him as one mourns for his only son, and grieve for Him as one grieves for a firstborn"* (Zech. 12:10).

This refers to the Jews, but **how I wept when I suddenly realized that it was not the sins of the Romans and Jews alone that crucified Jesus! It was the sins of all mankind before and since, including my own which drove the nails into Him.** I grieved that my sins had pierced Him. But how happy I was to receive the great pardon the Father offers!

He *"humbled Himself and became obedient to the point of death.... Therefore God also has highly exalted Him and given Him the name which is above every name"* (Phil. 2:8–9). **He is still standing in the gap.** So, all should kneel and bow to Him alone, not to a picture or carving. Let us confess that *"Jesus Christ is Lord,"* obeying His Word. Paul wrote, *"Work out your own salvation with fear and trembling; for it is God who works in you to will and to do for His good pleasure"* (Phil. 2:12–13); and, *"For we must all appear before the judgment seat of Christ, that each one may receive the things done in the body, according to what he has done, whether good or bad"* (2 Cor. 5:10).

Jesus even resisted the temptation to die with unforgiveness and bitterness in His own heart, dying instead for love of us with a broken heart emptied of blood and water. He did everything He could for us so He understands the broken-hearted. Because He believed the Father heard His prayer, Jesus could later sit on His throne with Him in His healed and glorified body, reigning as King and trusting God to make His enemies a footstool for Him. He would forgive those who sought it. He could not have done that if He harboured unforgiveness and bitterness. He was sinless.

God Gave Us a Free Will, but Commands Us to Choose Rightly, Even Today .

God's willingness to forgive now leaves mankind the choice as to whether to accept His atonement and follow Jesus, walking covered by His righteousness or to continue walking in sin, heading in the wrong direction. But Jesus began His public ministry commanding people to repent and believe the gospel, and that is still His desire and will. God still commands us, as He told me years ago, *"I have set before you life and death Therefore choose life. Every tree that does not bear good fruit is cut down and thrown into the fire. Bear fruit that lasts"* .

Praise God, some of the Jews who had shouted, *"Crucify Him,"* could very well have been among those who repented at Pentecost. Three thousand repented that day, fruit of the labour in prayer and deed of Jesus, the 120, and Peter. **Jesus offers a partnership with Him in this work. Evangelists today call people to repentance and multitudes have been saved in Jesus's name.**

Similar to an expectant mother's labour, **intercession is a labouring that the new life of Christ, the will and action of Jesus, may be birthed in someone** for the first time or in a fresh way. In His name, we can enter into Jesus's intercession and see the good fruit come forth in people's lives and give the Father, our heavenly Father, praise. *"He shall see the labor of His soul, and be satisfied. By His knowledge My righteous Servant shall justify many, for He shall bear their iniquities"* (Isa. 53:11).

Jesus remembers our prayer needs. His wounds are healed now, but the holes remain as a continual reminder. The Father can communicate face to face with Him, the everlasting High Priest. Jesus remembers the names and judgments of His people before the Father *continually*, and may let some intercessors know so they can join Him in interceding, asking that the atonement and mercy obtained for us *"once for all"* (Heb. 10:10) by the blood of the Lamb, may be applied to us now, *"on earth as it is in heaven"* (Matt. 6:10).

Melchizedek and Jesus Served Bread and Wine

Melchizedek did not sacrifice an animal to God when he met Abram. He *"brought out bread and wine"* (Gen. 14:18) instead. But it looked forward to a future event, the sacrifice of the Lamb of God. Likewise, Jesus brought out bread and wine when He met with His disciples at the Last Supper. **It too was a remembrance of a future event, the sacrifice of the Lamb of God, slain so that sins could be forgiven. Jesus wants us to share an offering of bread and wine today as a remembrance of a past event—the same one-time sacrifice of the Lamb of God.

Melchizedek served it to Abram to celebrate with thanksgiving the victory won by *"God Most High, Possessor of heaven and earth"* **(Gen. 14:22), in setting Lot and the other captives free. Symbolically, this looked ahead to the atoning death of Jesus whereby we could gain victory over sin and death by the grace of God, and captives could be set free to walk in newness of life.** At the Last Supper, Jesus began to serve as a humble *"priest forever according to the order of Melchizedek"* (Ps. 110:4), leading the Passover meal in which He shared bread and wine bringing in the New Covenant, praying His priestly prayer in John 17, and serving His disciples, washing their feet. *"Whoever desires to become great among you, let him be your servant. And whoever desires to be first among you, let him be your slave—just as the Son of Man did not come to be served, but to serve, and to give His life a ransom for many"* (Matt. 20:26–28).

Jesus, the living Word of God, claimed, *"I am the bread of life"* (John 6:48), and the cup is a reminder that He poured out His life as blood. *"For the bread of God is He who comes down from heaven and gives life to the world"* (John 6:33). As He had at the Last Supper, on the road to Emmaus, Jesus served spiritual and material bread. After chastising them for being *"slow of heart to believe in all that the prophets have spoken"* (Luke 24:25), He broke open the Word of God, which is the bread of life, and had a meal with them. **After He taught them, they recognized Him in the breaking of the bread at table.** The persons were nourished, body, soul, and spirit, as Abraham was at his encounter with Melchizedek.

Jesus still brings out bread and wine today through His priestly people. Let us remember Him in the breaking of the bread.

394 • Jesus the Bridge

The Good Shepherd Is Active Today

Isaiah 53:6 tells us that *"all we like sheep have gone astray; we have turned, every one, to his own way; and the LORD has laid on Him the iniquity of us all."* Just as Abraham risked his life going after Lot to rescue him, Jesus laid down His life so lost sheep could be rescued. **He is the Good Shepherd who goes after His lost sheep today and wants us to follow His leading.**

"Between a rock and a hard place? Put your trust in the Good Shepherd," the Lord said to me years ago, so I proclaimed it on a banner.

Sometimes well-meaning sheep can be looking for God in the wrong places, going up the wrong mountain, but put your trust in the Good Shepherd. Jesus is alive and working today. He will come down from His holy mountain and rescue them, even carrying them, shining the light of His face on them and tending to their needs.

How many times have I called on His name for Him to shepherd me and He has been so faithful! He rescued me when I was stuck going up the wrong mountain like worshiping God and "Baal" by praying the rosary, and He led me through the darkest valleys of my life, providing for me, refreshing me, and giving me rest. Plus, He calmed my anxieties about my husband as I trusted in Jesus, and He brought him down from the wrong mountain too. Jesus is so faithful and true!

We need not fear even death traveling with Him. Now that is cause to celebrate the goodness of God Most High!

> *He restores my soul.*
> *He leads me in*
> *The paths of righteousness*
> *For His name's sake....*
> *You prepare a table before me in the presence of my enemies;*
> *You anoint my head with oil;*
> *My cup runs over.*
> *Surely goodness and mercy shall follow me*
> *All the days of my life;*
> *And I will dwell in the house of the* L<small>ORD</small> *forever.* (Ps. 23:3, 5–6)

The Lord said to me years ago, **"In the last days, I, I will shepherd My sheep."** We can see Him doing that if we look, leading them in His paths of righteousness for His name's sake.

When some Jews asked if He was the Christ, Jesus replied:

> *The works that I do in My Father's name, they bear witness of Me. But you do not believe, because you are not of My sheep, as I said to you. My sheep hear My voice, and I know them, and they follow Me. And I give them eternal life, and they shall never perish; neither shall anyone snatch them out of My hand. My Father, who has given them to Me, is greater than all and no one is able to snatch them out of My Father's hand. I and My Father are one.* (John 10:25–30)

Jesus still cares for His sheep today. His love for us is so great, He keeps looking out for us, saving us, continuing His work from heaven and from within those who dwell in (are attached to) Him. **And He will care for us eternally.** The victory is the Lord's and God is One: Father, Son, and Holy Spirit. John saw the Lamb in heaven shepherding:

> ...*the ones who come out of the great tribulation and washed their robes* [and serve God] *day and night in His temple. And He who sits on the throne will dwell among them. They shall neither hunger anymore nor thirst anymore; the sun shall not strike them, nor any heat; for the Lamb who is in the midst of the throne will shepherd them and lead them to living fountains of waters. And God will wipe away every tear from their eyes.* (Revelation 7:14–17)

As Priest, Jesus Glorifies God

Jesus Leads Worship Lifting Up the Name of His Father

Melchizedek, God's prophet, priest, and king, declared the name of God to Abram (Abraham) as *"God Most High, Possessor of heaven and earth"* (Gen. 14:19). He gave God glory for being who He is and who He was called to be. This encouraged Abram to worship God too. He responded by serving God, giving a tithe, praising Him, declaring God's name to *"the king of Sodom ...* [as] *'the LORD, God Most High, the Possessor of heaven and earth'"* (Gen. 14:19, 21–22).

Jesus also declared the name of God as *"Father, Lord of heaven and earth,"* revealing Him to chosen descendants of Abraham.

> *At that time Jesus answered and said, "I thank You, Father, Lord of heaven and earth, that You have hidden these things from the wise and prudent and have revealed them to babes. Even so, Father, for so it seemed good in Your sight. All things have been delivered to Me by My Father, and no one knows the Son except the Father. Nor does anyone know the Father except the Son, and the one to whom the Son wills to reveal Him."* (Matt. 11:25–27)

Jesus does not reveal the Father to all. Only those to whom He wills. But He sent His apostles to preach the gospel and teach all nations, that all could choose to believe, be baptized, and be saved. *"But he who does not believe will be condemned"* (Mark 16:16).

Years before, when Moses was a go-between, in the second **song of Moses**, Deuteronomy 32, he too published the name of God. It was to remind them of who God is and to warn them what would happen when they would forsake Him. He wanted them to know both how great God is and that He was acting as a Father to them, not only having made them from the dust of the earth, but spiritually making them and raising them. Yet Moses went on to proclaim that God is also the Avenger and the Redeemer in His holy righteousness.

The **Song of the Lamb** also reveals the Father. In John's revelation of Jesus, he was shown:

> *…those who have the victory over the beast, over his image and over his mark and over the number of his name, standing on the sea of glass, having harps of God. They sing the song of Moses, the servant of God, and the song of the Lamb, saying:*
> *"Great and marvelous are Your works,*
> *Lord God Almighty!*
> *Just and true are Your ways,*
> *O King of the saints!*
> *Who shall not fear You, O Lord, and glorify Your name?*
> *For You alone are holy,*
> *For all nations shall come and worship before You,*
> *For Your judgments have been manifested."* (Rev. 15:2–4)

Jesus's name proclaims who He is as God. The angel told Joseph, *"You shall call His name JESUS, for He will save His people from their sins"* (Matt. 1:21), and He still does. By living with us and in us, He continues to glorify the Father. *"They shall call his name 'Immanuel,' which is translated, 'God with us'"* (Matt. 1:23).

Jesus is a confident Advocate, not an anxious one, because **He knows the heart of the Father**. He said from the altar of the cross, *"It is finished!"* (John 19:30). He knows it is done and it is done. So in faith, hope, and love, He can sing songs of deliverance over us and of praise to His Father *"in the midst of the seven golden lampstands* [churches]*"* (Rev. 1:13), ministering unto God and men. Prophetic songs and music come forth from Jesus, glorifying God.

> *I will declare Your name to My brethren;*
> *In the midst of the assembly I will praise* [sing to] *You....*
> *My praise shall be of You in the great assembly;*
> *I will pay My vows before those who fear Him.* (Ps. 22:22, 25)

I have experienced the Lord declaring the name of God to me, names like Good Shepherd, Alpha and Omega, Rescuer, Love, Redeemer, Just Judge, Faithful and True, Name above All Names, Desire of Nations. Sometimes it is just so I will get to know Him more, but sometimes it has been so I will proclaim His name to others. This was especially as I served in banner and dance ministry glorifying God, led by His Word. And **He declares the name of God to others today too, through His *logos* and *rhema* words.**

When John was taken up to heaven in a vision, Jesus proclaimed who He is, having obtained His Father's name, being one God with Him. Jesus said, *"'I am the Alpha and the Omega, the Beginning and the End,' says the Lord, 'who is and who was and who is to come, the Almighty.... Do not be afraid; I am the First and the Last. I am He who lives'"* (Rev. 1:8, 17–18). Jesus declared it to John and His churches several times in the book of Revelation.

Even while He was physically on earth, Jesus took an active part in regular services of worship and openly taught, so He was called Teacher or Rabbi. *"He taught in their synagogues, being glorified by all. So He came to Nazareth where He had been brought up. And as His custom was, He went into the synagogue on the Sabbath day, and stood up to read. And He was handed the book of the prophet Isaiah"* (Luke 4:15–17). He would have sung the psalms of praise to the Father too on the Sabbath and at feasts of the Lord. He was an observant Jew who loved God, His Father.

Part of His priestly function now is to be a **worship leader**, glorifying God, proclaiming His Word, and giving God's name the credit and honour it deserves with **sacrifices of praise and thanksgiving**, the fruit of His lips, and blessing the people. Those in Christ, can participate in this type of sacrifice, and especially worship leaders, by keeping a grateful heart and keeping their ears open to what He magnifies—His words, music, songs, and instruction through His Spirit. *"But thanks be to God, who gives us the victory through our Lord Jesus Christ"* (1 Cor. 15:57).

Jesus is now on the throne with the Father again, in constant communication with Him, glorifying Him and giving us the Father's love, leading us sovereignly from there and through those He has anointed and appointed. **John also saw Jesus walking among His churches** from where He can observe, lead, and give prophetic messages.

While He was on earth two thousand years ago, Jesus glorified the Father, and the Father glorified the Son and the Holy Spirit did too. **He manifested the name of the Father and gave to His disciples the Father's words and eternal life, and He still does.** Jesus prayed:

> *Father, the hour has come. Glorify Your Son, that Your Son may glorify You, as You have given Him authority over all flesh, that He should give eternal life to as many as You have given Him. And this is eternal life, that they may know You, the only true God, and Jesus Christ whom You have sent. I have glorified You on the earth. I have finished the work which You have given Me to do.* (John 17:1–4)

He blessed the Lord by His prayer of praise and His job well done, and so can we.

Like a restaurant owner who moved from chef to overseer, Jesus is resting at the Father's side, yet doing His heavenly work as eternal High Priest, still being about His Father's business, judging and having compassion on many but *"by no means clearing the guilty"* (Ex. 34:7), again glorifying the Father. Jesus still gives us the Father's words through the Bible and when He puts a prophetic word in someone's mouth to be spoken forth. *"For the testimony of Jesus is the spirit of prophecy"* (Rev. 19:10). He also wants us to listen like Mary of Bethany to His teaching and instruction that we may know and love God and one another as He loved us.

The Aaronic high priest **burned incense in worship** on the golden altar *"before the veil that is before the ark of the Testimony, before the mercy seat that is over the Testimony, where I* [God] *will meet with you"* (Ex. 30:6–8). It's sweet fragrant smoke rose as a symbol for prayer and worship. Aaron did it each day at twilight when he lit the lamps, and in the morning when he tended the lamps. Jesus is now the eternal High Priest who Himself is like burning incense and sets His priestly people on fire, lighting our lamps as we worship. *"And walk in love, as Christ also has loved us and given Himself for us, an offering and a sacrifice to God for a sweet-smelling aroma"* (Eph. 5:2). *"Now thanks be to God who always leads us in triumph in Christ, and through us diffuses the fragrance of His knowledge in every place. For we are to God the fragrance of Christ"* (2 Cor. 2:14–15).

Since He is also the Lord of hosts, Jesus is Commander-in-Chief to the hosts of angels. One night in Kingston, Ontario, at a particularly intense time of citywide worship in the nineties, a worshiper saw a vision of a whirlwind funnel of angels at the altar area of St. Paul's Anglican Church. They were ascending to heaven with a bowl full of our prayers.

The prayers of Jesus and of His saints seeking His kingdom and righteousness are effective and bring results from heaven. Jesus said, *"I came to send* [cast] *fire on the earth, and how I wish it were already kindled!"* (Luke 12:49). **He can send a baptism of fire on believers, cleansing and empowering them.**

As a Priest, Jesus Offers Gifts and Sacrifices

Hebrews 8:3 says, *"For every high priest is appointed to offer both gifts and sacrifices. Therefore it is necessary that this One also have something to offer."* As eternal High Priest, He already offered the sacrifice of the Lamb, Himself, on the cross. *"They shall look on Him whom they pierced"* (John 19:37). His blood is effective forever as a sin offering. We just reap the benefits of His action if we believe, and in gratitude we can love as He loved us. **Jesus only needed to bring His atoning blood in to the presence of God once. But He still offers gifts and sacrifices of praise and thanksgiving** to the Father in prophetic *rhema* words and as our Worship Leader with, through, and in those attuned to His Spirit. It is for us to respond.

God was not surprised when Adam and Eve were found to be unequal to Jesus in obedience. They were created according to the image and likeness of God, but of dust and were not equal to Him. *"For He knows our frame; He remembers that we are dust"* (Ps. 103:14).

His living Word is daily bread and meat and vegetables which He serves us. He gives us the gifts and fruit of His Holy Spirit, including love, so that God can be glorified in us as we offer them back to Him in Jesus's name.

When the parts of His body do things at His command, Jesus is doing it through them. His holy priesthood is chosen to offer acceptable gifts and sacrifices joined to Him. *"But you are a chosen generation, a royal priesthood, a holy nation, His own special people, that you may proclaim the praises* [the wonderful deeds] *of Him who called you out of darkness into His marvelous light"* (1 Pet. 2:4–9). We do this in gratitude, acknowledging who God is and what He does. *"Let them do good, that they may be rich in good works, ready to give, willing to share"* (1 Tim. 6:18). Sometimes God says, *"No,"* or *"Wait."* Yet doing just what the Father chooses for us to do is best, because to obey like Jesus is the *"living sacrifice"* of the New Testament.

When it is appropriate, these are some sacrifices bridge pieces can offer with Jesus:

- **Sacrifice of Will** – Instead of animal sacrifices, Jesus said:

  "Behold, I have come to do Your will, O God…." By that will we have been sanctified through the offering of the body of Jesus Christ once for all. (Heb. 10:9–10)

  Father, if it is Your will, take this cup away from Me; nevertheless not My will, but Yours, be done. (Luke 22:42)

  Obey those who rule over you, and be submissive, for they watch out for your souls, as those who must give account. (Heb. 13:17)

  Yet, obey God above men whose will conflicts with His: *"We ought to obey God rather than men"* (Acts 5:29). For, *"Jesus Christ is Lord"* (Phil. 2:11).

- **Sacrifice of Righteousness** – Psalm 4 speaks of seeking the *"God of my righteousness"* who knows the truth about each situation and can vindicate one who is falsely accused. He is Yahweh Tsidkenu, *"THE LORD OUR RIGHTEOUSNESS"* (Jer. 23:6). Our righteousness comes from Him.

  Hear me when I call, God of my righteousness….
  Be angry and do not sin.
  Meditate within your heart on your bed and be still.
  Offer the sacrifices of righteousness [truth and justice tempered by mercy]
  And put your trust in the Lord….
  [Then you will] *both lie down in peace and sleep;*

For You alone, O Lord, make me dwell in safety. (Ps. 4:1, 4–5, 8)

But do not forget to do good and to share, for with such sacrifices God is well pleased. (Heb. 13:16)

Defend the poor and fatherless; do justice to the afflicted and needy. (Ps. 82:3)

To do righteousness and justice is more acceptable to the Lord than sacrifice. (Prov. 21:3)

Behold, to obey is better than sacrifice, and to heed than the fat of rams. (1 Sam. 15:22)

- **Sacrifice of Joy** – When we see how real the Lord is in our lives, it gives us great joy! We need not fear when He is our light and salvation, giving us victory.

  When we seek to dwell in His house like David: *"All the days of my life, to behold the beauty of the Lord, and to inquire in His temple"* (Ps. 27:4), we find that *"in the time of trouble He shall hide me in His pavilion; in the secret place of His tabernacle He shall hide me; He shall set me high upon a rock. And now my head shall be lifted up above my enemies all around me; therefore I will offer sacrifices of joy in His tabernacle; I will sing, yes, I will sing praises to the Lord"* (Ps. 27:5–6).

  Who are kept by the power of God through faith for salvation ready to be revealed in the last time. In this you greatly rejoice, though now for a little while, if need be, you have been grieved by various trials, that the genuineness of your faith, being much more precious than gold that perishes, though it is tested by fire, may be found to praise, honor and glory at the revelation of Jesus Christ, whom having not seen you love. Though now you do not see Him, yet believing, you rejoice with joy inexpressible and full of glory, receiving the end of your faith—the salvation of your souls. (1 Pet. 1:5–9)

*Blessed are you when men hate you,
And when they exclude you, and revile you,
And cast out your name as evil,
For the Son of Man's sake.
Rejoice in that day and leap for joy!
For indeed your reward is great in heaven,
For in like manner their fathers did to the prophets.* (Luke 6:22–23)

Rejoice in the Lord always. Again I will say, rejoice! (Phil. 4:4)

- **Sacrifices of God** – *"The sacrifices of God are a broken spirit, a broken and contrite heart—these, O God, You will not despise"* (Ps. 51:17).

  Humble yourselves in the sight of the Lord, and He will lift you up. (Jas. 4:10)

- **Sacrifice of Praise** – Giving Him the glory He deserves (see Ps. 96).

  Therefore by Him let us continually offer the sacrifice of praise to God, that is, the fruit of our lips, giving thanks to His name. (Heb. 13:15)

  [There shall be heard again in the desolate streets of Judah and Jerusalem] *the voice of joy and the voice of gladness, the voice of the bridegroom and the voice of the bride, the voice of those who will say:*

  "Praise the L{\scriptsize ORD} *of hosts,
  For the* L{\scriptsize ORD} *is good,
  For His mercy endures forever"—*

And of those who will bring the sacrifice of praise into the house of the LORD. *For I will cause the captives of the land to return.* (Jer. 33:11)

To Him be glory in the church by Christ Jesus to all generations, forever and ever. Amen. (Eph. 3:21)

I will praise the name of God with a song,
And will magnify Him with thanksgiving. (Ps. 69:30)

Praise Him [everywhere with all kinds of instruments] *for His mighty acts;*
Praise Him According to His excellent greatness!...
Praise Him with the timbrel and dance;
Praise Him with stringed instruments and flutes!...With clashing cymbals!
Let everything that has breath praise the LORD. *Praise the* LORD*!* [Hallelujah!] (Ps. 150:2, 4–6)

- **Sacrifice of Thanksgiving** – *"Be anxious for nothing, but in everything by prayer and supplication, with thanksgiving, let your requests be made known to God; and the peace of God ... will guard your hearts and minds through Christ Jesus.* [Meditate on the things for which we can be thankful: things true, noble, just, pure, lovely, of good report, praiseworthy]*"* (Phil. 4:6–8). In Christ, in His name, these sacrifices will sometimes just flow forth from our hearts. Other times, we may be so attuned to Christ that we will hear His prompts to do so. *"O that men would give thanks to the* LORD *for His goodness.... Let them sacrifice the sacrifices of thanksgiving, and declare His* [wonderful] *works with rejoicing"* (Ps. 107:21–22).

- **Living Sacrifice** – *"I beseech you therefore, brethren, by the mercies of God, that you present your bodies a living sacrifice, holy, acceptable to God, which is your reasonable service. And ... be transformed by the renewing of your mind"* (Rom.

12:1–2). "Worship" is also "service" which God expects and deserves. In thanksgiving for God's indescribable gift, we can offer our lives to God as living sacrifices, as a form of worship, denying ourselves and bowing our will to His in love like Jesus in Gethsemane. When we choose to bow low before Him, humbling ourselves because we love Him and honour Him with a holy fear and reverence, He lifts us up and sets us higher with Him: *"For the love of Christ compels us, because we judge thus: that if One died for all, then all died; and He died for all, that those who live should live no longer for themselves, but for Him who died for them and rose again"* (2 Cor. 5:14–15). All that we have and all that we are can be offered to Him to be at His service, under His Lordship, taking care of our own families as well, loving our neighbour as ourselves: *"And do not present your members as instruments of unrighteousness to sin, but present* [yield] *yourselves to God as being alive from the dead, and your members as instruments of righteousness to God"* (Rom. 6:13).

Jesus gave praise offerings to Father God on earth saying that the works He did were in the name of the Father and lifting up His name: *"I have come in My Father's name"* (John 5:43). Jesus continues to offer sacrifices like praise and thanksgiving to God and can prompt us to do likewise through His Spirit. Members of His body can participate in this royal priesthood of believers, learning from the Scriptures and sometimes hearing directly from God too, being helped to minister unto God and men and to intercede as parts of the bridge, and to finish the work they are called to do. *"Now thanks be to God who always leads us in triumph in Christ, and through us, diffuses the fragrance of His knowledge in every place"* (2 Cor. 2:14).

Melchizedek prayed for Abram and blessed him, recognizing that Abram was God's chosen man. **Jesus, the seed of Abraham and David (yet He was before them), prays for those who come to Him,**

blessing them with covenant blessings too: *"In you all the families of the earth shall be blessed"* (Gen. 12:3). **Thank God, we can be blessed and become a blessing to others because we are in Christ and Abraham.**

Chapter 17
Jesus the Prophet and Prophetic Evangelist

Jesus is the Great Prophet of whom Moses prophesied:

> *The LORD your God will raise up for you a Prophet like me from your midst, from your brethren. Him you shall hear....* [The Lord said,] *"I will raise up for them a Prophet like you from among their brethren, and will put My words in His mouth, and He shall speak to them all that I command Him. And it shall be that whoever will not hear My words, which He speaks in My name, I will require it of him."* (Deut. 18:15, 18–19)

Peter referred to this prophecy of Jesus when preaching in Solomon's Portico, as did Stephen when he was on trial.

The Father speaks to Jesus and He speaks to His prophets, who in turn can tell us. The prophetic angel told John not to kneel before him because he was not God. He only carried His *rhema* word. *"I am your fellow servant, and of your brethren who have the testimony of Jesus. Worship God!* [Not angels or the prophets.] *For the testimony of Jesus is the spirit of prophecy"* (Rev. 19:10).

Jesus is the Great Prophet through whom God would speak two thousand years ago, the Prophet of prophets, and **the One who speaks to true prophets now.** He is the only prophet who deserves worship because He is also God. The Father speaks to Jesus, *"the Word"* (John 1:1), and He bears witness of this by speaking to His prophets through His Holy Spirit. They in turn can tell us, proclaiming the *rhema* word of the Lord. And He can speak directly to any of His servants once the Holy Spirit is poured out. *"I will pour out of My Spirit on all flesh; your sons and your daughters shall prophesy"* (Acts 2:17).

A true prophet hears from God, and sometimes is a seer as well like Jeremiah, Ezekiel, and Daniel, seeing what God reveals to him or her in dreams and/or visions, and seeing with supernatural insight. Melchizedek spoke to Abraham a revelation from God that it was *"God Most High, who has delivered your enemies into your hand"* (Gen. 14:20). Elisha had God open the eyes of his servant so that he too could see the cohort of angels fighting on their behalf. *"Do not fear, for those who are with us are more than those who are with them....' The mountains were full of horses and chariots of fire all around Elisha"* (2 Kgs. 6:16–17).

The apostle Nathanael recognized Jesus to be the Great Prophet and the woman at the well did too when He told them what He had seen in the Spirit the first time He met them. But as usually happens with prophets, most of His own townsfolk did not honor Jesus when He first came among them, but people in other places did. Thus Elijah and Elisha were sent by God to heal and cleanse specific people in other regions. Likewise, others to whom God sent Jesus then and now, did and still do recognize Him, glory be to God! Praise God, just as His own brothers recognized Him after Pentecost, more and more of His first chosen people are also recognizing Him today.

Jesus's teaching and preaching modeled prophetic evangelism. It was led by God with signs and miracles following since as He said:

> *Most assuredly, I say to you, the Son can do nothing of Himself, but what He sees the Father do; for whatever He does, the Son also does in like manner. For the Father loves the Son, and shows Him all things that He Himself does; and He will show Him greater works than these, that you may marvel. For as the Father raises the dead and gives life to them, even so the Son gives life to whom He will.* (John 5:19–21)

The Father gave Him *"words of knowledge"* (1 Cor. 12:8) of healings or things He would do. *"I do nothing of Myself; but as My Father taught Me, I speak these things. And He who sent Me is with Me. The Father has not left Me alone, for I always do those things that please Him"* (John 8:28–29). The Father showed Him even greater things to do and will show things to those to whom Jesus reveals Him. *"Nor does anyone know the Father except the Son, and the one to whom the Son wills to reveal Him"* (Matt. 11:27). After Pentecost, the disciples, with the aid of the Spirit, performed great miracles in His name. And **Jesus is still working through prophetic evangelists today**.

Jesus the Prophet Is a Builder

Prophecy is for the edifying or **upbuilding of the church**. God promised to pour out the Spirit and is doing so again in our time as He did at Pentecost. So, people who have the gift of *"prophecy"* (1 Cor. 12:10) from the Holy Spirit are supposed to prophesy by the word or vision which God gives to them, **prophesying what Jesus Christ in them today testifies about the situation**. The words which God puts into their mouths are *"the testimony of Jesus,"* so **Jesus is still prophesying today**. If it is true prophecy, it will line up with Scripture and have good fruit. Whether it is in tongues or in one's native language, prophecy upbuilds God's people: *"But he who prophesies speaks edification and exhortation and comfort to men. He who speaks in a tongue edifies himself, but he who prophesies edifies the church"* (1 Cor. 14:3–4). *"For the LORD shall build up Zion; He shall appear in His glory* [He will reveal His greatness]*"* (Ps. 102:16).

I had a dream once about a huge wrecking ball about to hit a skyscraper. It bothered me until I realized that sometimes an old stronghold must be torn down first like a condemned house on prime land, so a solid structure can be built and planted on it.

Some people just have an Acts 2 occasional gift of prophecy, but others have been given the **office of prophet**. When God told Jeremiah He had chosen him to be a prophet in that office, he replied:

> *"Ah, Lord G*ᴏᴅ*!*
> *Behold, I cannot speak, for I am a youth."*
> *But the* Lᴏʀᴅ *said to me:*
> *"Do not say, 'I am a youth,'*
> *For you shall go to all to whom I send you,*
> *And whatever I command you, you shall speak.*
> *Do not be afraid of their faces,*
> *For I am with you to deliver you," says the* Lᴏʀᴅ*.*
> *Then the* Lᴏʀᴅ *put forth His hand and touched my mouth, and the* Lᴏʀᴅ *said to me:*
> *"Behold I have put My words in your mouth.*
> *See, I have this day set you over the nations and over the kingdoms,*
> *To root out and to pull down,*
> *To destroy and to throw down,*
> *To build and to plant."* (Jer. 1:6–10)

Jeremiah was shown visions too. He had a seer anointing. But there were ungodly practices that he needed to *"root out and to pull down, to destroy and to throw down"* before he could *"build"* and *"plant."* When God destroys something, it is for a good purpose. He also restores and makes things new.

If we call Jesus, *"Lord,"* there are times to seek the Lord and wait on Him to speak about situations rather than running in with our own opinions. How great that we can ask Him how to pray for a situation! We need His counsel! **A true prophet prophesies the words Jesus puts into his mouth. Jesus does not want His disciples to be false prophets** who *"prophesy lies … of the deceit of their own heart"* (Jer. 23:26).

> *I have not sent these prophets, yet they ran.*
> *I have not spoken to them, yet they prophesied.*

> *But if they had stood in My counsel,*
> *And had caused My people to hear My words,*
> *Then they would have turned them from their evil way,*
> *And from the evil of their doings.* (Jer. 23:21–22)

In the office of the Prophet, Jesus was in communion with His Father daily, rising early to stand in His counsel, to listen to what He had to say and to see what He had to show Him. Even Jesus needed His private devotions as Son of Man, meditating, chewing on His *"daily bread"* —the words His Father spoke to Him, so He could preach and teach, heal, and do miracles according to the Father's blueprint. **He was a pattern for us,** *"the way."* Knowing the Father so well, **Jesus as** *"Son of Man"* **and** *"His only begotten Son"* (John 3:16), **revealed the Father to men by what He said and what He did, and He still does.** *"He is the image of the invisible God, the firstborn over all creation"* (Col. 1:15).

He prayed to the Father for His apostles, referring to His prophetic activity:

> *I have manifested Your name to the men whom You have given Me out of the world. They were Yours, You gave them to Me, and they have kept Your word. Now they have known that all things which You have given Me are from You. For I have given to them the words which You have given Me; and they have received them, and have known surely that I came forth from You; and they have believed that You sent Me.* (John 17:6–8)

Jesus was physically with them then, putting His words into their mouth, and He can do that now for us by His Spirit. We are not to add to them or take away from them. Jesus is still in communion with the Father. But we are warned, *"Do not add to His words, lest He rebuke you, and you be found a liar"* (Prov. 30:6).

We are not to just prophesy what we want, but what the Lord is saying: *"Unless the* LORD *builds the house, they labor in vain who build it;*

unless the LORD *guards the city, the watchman stays awake in vain"* (Ps. 127:1).

Jesus Leads in Healing, Prophecy, and Deliverance, Etc.

They all should be done in communication with the Lord. Jesus gives power and authority and teaching in using God's gifts, and He **wants us to check with Him today so we will not be using His name in vain.**

> *Not everyone who says to Me, "Lord, Lord," shall enter the kingdom of heaven, but he who does the will of My Father in heaven. Many will say to Me in that day, "Lord, Lord, have we not prophesied in Your name, cast out demons in Your name, and done many wonders in Your name?" And then I will declare to them, "I never knew you; depart from Me, you who practice lawlessness!"* (Matt. 7:21–23)

Paul reminded us: *"*[Lay hands suddenly on no man.] *Do not lay hands on anyone hastily, nor share in other people's sins; keep yourself pure"* (1 Tim. 5:22).

Sometimes a person is not ready to receive a miracle so we may have to wait before laying hands on him. **But all those who came to Jesus believing, seeking mercy, received mercy:** *"Then He touched their eyes, saying, 'According to your faith let it be to you'"* (Matt. 9:29). The purpose was so that they could have a fresh start to follow Jesus, healed and delivered. Sometimes it was so that God could be glorified in the healing, like with the man who was born blind, his infirmity not the result of sin. And if their affliction was the result of sin, they could go in repentance and new life like the man healed at Bethesda: *"See, you have been made well* [whole]. *Sin no more, lest a worse thing come upon you"* (John 5:14).

Jesus can call us to build or use gifting or to stand on night watch with Him, but we are not to be just doing our own thing if we want even more than the *"acceptable"* but the *"perfect will of God"* (Rom.

12:2). Rather than be like the ones who call Him, *"Lord, Lord,"* yet do things their own way, we are to be like those who come to Him and follow His instructions. If we claim Jesus as Lord, we are to listen to what He says, study His Word, and do it. He prophesied that John was sent to *"prepare the way of the Lord"* (Isa. 40:30). We are not to follow false revelators. We are to even seek more than His *logos* written Word. His *rhema* personal word is also important. **We need both Scripture and His Spirit, and to both trust and obey. Then we will be an effective part of His bridge.**

> *Whoever comes to Me, and hears My sayings and does them, I will show you whom he is like: He is like a man building a house, who dug deep and laid the foundation on the rock. And when the flood arose, the stream beat vehemently against that house, and could not shake it, for it was founded on the rock. But he who heard and did nothing is like a man who built a house on the earth without a foundation, against which the stream beat vehemently; and immediately it fell. And the ruin of that house was great.* (Luke 6:47–49)

It impressed me that both houses heard the word, but only the one built on the rock actually did it. *"But be doers of the word, and not hearers only, deceiving yourselves"* (Jas. 1:22). There are many ministries today, especially on the mission field, where Jesus is working through His servants, doing miracles, healings, and deliverance. Sometimes there are medical reports to confirm the genuineness of them. Jesus can also lead in other giftings and ministry, like hospitality, giving, administration, counseling, etc.

Jesus Gives Prophetic Warnings So the Wise Can Repent

I remember hearing a prophetic word spoken before us all at a charismatic conference: *"My little ones, My little one, I love you more than you know."* It really touched me as if it were a personal message to encourage my heart.

Not all prophecy is warm and fuzzy. Jesus prophesied of upcoming judgment to the women on the way to Calvary. Rather than give them false peace, He had warned the women as He carried His cross:

> *Daughters of Jerusalem, do not weep for Me, but weep for yourselves and for your children. For indeed the days are coming in which they will say, "Blessed are the barren, wombs that never bore, and breasts which never nursed!" Then they will begin to say to the mountains, "Fall on us!" and to the hills, "Cover us!" For if they do these things in the green wood, what will be done in the dry?* (Luke 23:28–31)

As Jesus predicted in this hard word, Jews who did not repent faced the wrath of God when the Romans invaded Jerusalem and destroyed the temple around 70 AD.

Thank God, Jesus is *"Faithful and True"* (Rev. 19:11) and *"able to save to the uttermost those who come to God through Him"* (Heb. 7:25). Because He stands in His counsel, He checks with the Father and knows His mind before issuing a word to us. Jesus still does His work of teaching us, leading those who are willing to follow Him. Part of this is by the Scriptures and part by His prophetic function of speaking to us through His Holy Spirit. Whatever He says to us today though will line up with existing Scripture. He gives us rest and divine assurance when we do His will and cast all our cares upon Him; and security in knowing He is our defense. *"And the rain descended, and the floods came, and the winds blew, and beat upon that house* [of those hearing and doing His word]; *and it fell not; for it was founded upon a rock"* (Matt. 7:25).

Being a prophetic evangelist, Jesus helps the church to prosper and gives warnings. This is evident in the letters Jesus sent to the seven churches in Revelation 2 and 3 and in prophetic words He has given today. Although Jesus came so that those who believe in Him and do His will do not have to get what they deserve, they still can reap judgment if they will not trust and obey Him. **We do well when we have a holy fear of the Lord, recognizing that Jesus taught what would lead to blessing in the lives of believers, but He also gave warnings of what could lead to curses with,** *"Woe to you..."* (see Luke 6:24–26; Matt. 23:13–23). We don't want people to miss the train to glory. **Being a loving Father, God can punish sin even in His disobedient children, but can forgive the sincere who come to Him.**

Although he was one of God's first chosen people, Saul had persecuted Christians until Jesus revealed Himself to him and he heeded His warning. He was knocked off his horse and afflicted with blindness for three days. But Jesus spoke to him, prophesied to him, and when he was mercifully healed, repented, and renamed, Paul began to preach wholeheartedly that Christ is the Son of God, even though it meant that Paul began to experience persecution and death attempts. Yet clothed in His righteousness he also experienced the goodness of God. He knew it was better to suffer for doing right than wrong.

Acts Christians were willing to even shed their blood in the battle against sin. Yet they also saw the protection and mercy of God and deliverance from evil. Paul preached to Jews and Gentiles and was saved from death time and again until God's purpose was fulfilled in his life and multitudes became disciples before he died as a martyr. *"Blessed be the God and Father of our Lord Jesus, the Messiah! He is our merciful Father and the God of all comfort"* (2 Cor. 1:3 NRS). *"Then the churches throughout all Judea, Galilee, and Samaria had peace and were edified. And walking in the fear of the Lord and in the comfort of the Holy Spirit, they were multiplied"* (Acts 9:31). **The fear of the Lord and the comfort of the Holy Spirit go hand in hand when we heed God's warnings, and can lead to church multiplication today too.**

"He who has an ear, let him hear what the Spirit says to the churches" (Rev. 3:22). We should hear what Jesus speaks to the various churches and learn from it. And when prophecy comes from the mouth of the Lord for you, it should involve not just hearing what God says, but actively **listening** to it. That is what young Samuel chose to do when

418 • Jesus the Bridge

he replied to God's call saying, *"Speak Lord! Your servant is listening"* (1 Sam. 3:10).

> **"Then the wicked one comes and snatches away what was sown in his heart."**
> (Matt. 13:19)
> [The devil steals the word to try to keep him from believing and being saved.]

This is he who received seed by the wayside.

Journaling helps us to hold on to His Word so the devil does not steal it from our hearts. Jesus sent word, *"Behold, I am coming quickly! Hold fast what you have, that no one may take your crown"* (Rev. 3:11).

Sometimes well-meaning friends can try to talk you out of what God has shown you, just as Peter did with Jesus. It is like they have on a devil costume. But Jesus rebuked Satan who was trying to act through Peter.

Jesus wants to break the bread of the Word with us, helping us overcome. As He told the Laodicean church, *"Behold, I stand at the door and knock. If anyone hears My voice and opens the door, I will come in*

Jesus the Prophet and Prophetic Evangelist • 419

to him and dine with him, and he with Me. To him who overcomes I will grant to sit with Me on My throne as I also overcame and sat down with My Father on His throne" (Rev. 3:20–21).

Depending upon what God wants to do, prophecy can **warn, encourage, comfort, and build up** the body of Christ. *"But he who prophesies speaks edification and exhortation and comfort to men"* (1 Cor. 14:3). It can also **uproot** what the enemy has planted through false words so that what **Jesus plants** can grow in freedom. That is what happened in my life when the Lord sent a man to minister to me with the words, *"They are dead. Do not contact them."* That very night, November 25, 1994, I began to have more understanding, repented of, and stopped praying the rosary. I determined to stop praying to Mary and the saints even for intercession in Jesus's name.

That idolatrous practice was uprooted from me, but had been so established that it took three and a half years. The Lord told me directly that the apparitions of a "Lady" promoting the rosary were *"Illusion! Illusion! Illusion!"* and in regards to the consecration to the Immaculate Heart of Mary, the Lord told me, *"Repudiate the consecration,"* and, *"Come out of her."* Then at the end of three and a half years of seeking Scriptural confirmation, He had also begun to plant in my life. **One of the most important seeds He gave me was the *rhema* word for not praying the "Hail Mary"**: *"I am the way, the truth, and the life. No one comes to the Father except through Me"* (John 14:6). **Thank God, I journaled it**, because I forgot the word at first and asked the Lord a second time. Then, seeing it in my journal twice, I could hold on to it. Glory be to God.

Prophecy can **give deeper understandings of things and tell what is coming to pass to give us warning or hope:**

> *O Jerusalem, Jerusalem, the one who kills the prophets and stones those who are sent to her! How often I wanted to gather your children together, as a hen gathers her chicks under her wings, but you were not willing! See! Your house is left to you desolate; for I say to*

you, you shall see Me no more till you say, "Blessed is He who comes in the name of the LORD!" (Matt. 23:37–39)

After Jesus prophesied the destruction of Jerusalem because of her refusal to come to Him, the apostles pointed out the beautiful, monumental temple Herod had built in place of Solomon's fallen temple, and Jesus prophesied its destruction too. *"Jesus said to them, 'Do you not see all these things? Assuredly, I say to you, not one stone shall be left here upon another, that shall not be thrown down'"* (Matt. 24:2).

When God judges a city, church, or a people because of its sinfulness, and brings it down, man cannot rebuild it to last unless God is in charge of the restoration. A word from Jesus the Prophet can bring re-creation and restoration.

The Lord prophesied the same word about *"not one stone shall be left here upon another, that shall not be thrown down,"* to the Catholic charismatic movement in Kingston, Ontario, in the late eighties or early nineties, when the leadership would not receive the words the Lord sent me to bring them. Then around 1995, a Protestant pastor in Kingston had a vision of me as a large stone sitting in the middle of a field of grass. I said nothing but knew I had been *"thrown down."* When I would try to go back to a Catholic Diocesan workshop or charismatic meeting, I would not fit in anymore because I only lifted the name of Jesus and no longer took part in any RC idolatry. They did not believe the Lord had sent me—yet. But God had prepared me for this.

In late 1994, the Lord had said to me, *"Humble yourself in the sight of the Lord, and He will lift you up,"* so I remember prostrating myself in worship in my hotel room at a Vineyard conference and beginning to pray like David that He would *"search me* [and show me] *if there is any wicked way in me, and lead me in the way everlasting"* (Ps. 139:23–24). Isaiah and John the Baptist prophesied the bringing down of proud things and raising up of the humble. **We can either humble ourselves or be humbled.** *"Every valley shall be exalted and every mountain and* *hill brought low; the crooked places shall be made straight and the rough places smooth"* (Isa. 40:4).

Jesus also prophesied His lifting up to the apostles, saying, *"The Son of Man must suffer many things, and be rejected by the elders and chief priests and scribes, and be killed, and be raised the third day"* (Luke 9:22), so they would remember that He had tried to prepare them for His death and rising. *"Now as He sat on the Mount of Olives, the disciples came to Him privately, saying, 'Tell us, when will these things be? And what will be the sign of Your coming, and of the end of the age?'"* (Matt. 24:3). So when they asked, Jesus also prophesied about His return and the end of the age and later revealed prophetic things to John which he recorded in the Book of Revelation so we would be prepared.

> *Surely the Lord GOD does nothing,*
> *Unless He reveals His secret to His servants the prophets.*
> *A lion has roared! Who will not fear?*
> *The Lord GOD has spoken!*
> *Who can but prophesy?* (Amos 3:7–8)

When *"the testimony of Jesus"* comes to someone as a prophetic word placed in his mouth today, *"For the testimony of Jesus is the spirit of prophecy"* (Rev. 19:10), it should not be quenched. It is GOD Himself, Jesus Himself, ministering today, speaking to one of His menservants or maidservants so he or she can utter the prophetic word, what he hears God say, passing it on to whomever God sends him. So Paul warned, *"Do not quench the Spirit. Do not despise prophecies. Test all things; hold fast what is good. Abstain from every form of evil"* (1 Thess. 5:19–22).

Just because someone says something is prophecy does not guarantee that it is. It can be tested against Scripture and should line up with it, and produce good fruit. When people receive a prophetic warning, they can always choose to repent and avoid the consequences of their actions because of God's saving grace—even today. He changed His mind and was merciful to Nineveh when they repented.

Prophecy also **equips** *"the saints for the work of ministry, for the edifying of the body of Christ"* (Eph. 4:12). But first **God builds up the prophet** by prophecy, speaking to him and showing him things to prepare him so he will be able to confidently release the words God gives him to speak.

> *I will utter My judgments*
> *Against them concerning all their wickedness,*
> *Because they have forsaken Me,*
> *Burned incense to other gods,*
> *And worshiped the works of their own hands.*
> *Therefore prepare yourself and arise,*
> *And speak to them all that I command you.*
> *Do not be dismayed before their faces,*
> *Lest I dismay you before them.*
> *For behold, I have made you this day*
> *A fortified city and an iron pillar,*
> *And bronze walls against the whole land—*
> *Against the kings of Judah,*
> *Against its princes,*
> *Against its priests,*
> *And against the people of the land.*
> *They will fight against you,*
> *But they shall not prevail against you.*
> *"For I am with you," says the* LORD, *"to deliver you."* (Jer. 1:16–19)

Jeremiah's prophecy from God was to restore the land for those who would believe, but first it foretold judgment for the household of God.

Sometimes prophecy foretells what is going to happen. Biblical prophecy is still being fulfilled today. Jesus **prophesied, foretelling judgments** in the Book of Revelation—Babylon's fall, seals, trumpets, and bowls of the wrath of God—**so that His people would flee evil and pursue His righteousness and peace, and understand** when they saw them come to pass, and He still does that today, speaking through His prophets. He also showed John **hopeful prophetic visions of the awesome joy in heaven** of those who repented and joined the heavenly hosts worshiping around the throne.

Although certainly the Lord will be giving the commendation, *"Well done, good and faithful servant"* (Matt. 25:23), to many, John saw no one shouting praise to any of the saints. Instead, he saw them shouting praise to God and going down on their faces in worship before God alone, even casting down crowns before Him and giving Him the glory due His name.

Sometimes **Jesus gives people personal prophecy** which is just for themselves, either speaking to them directly or through another person. I have had times when the Lord has given me a personal word, such as, *"Fear not,"* or *"You have need of endurance,"* which helped me in specific circumstances. And I have had times when a visiting prophet has spoken a word to me which confirmed something God was already teaching me or brought some fresh light on a situation, praise God. But sometimes prophecy is for a congregation, a city, or a nation too. **It connects us with God.**

Chapter 18
Jesus the King

Still King of Righteousness and Peace

Through David, the Father spoke of His Son, *"Yet I have set My King on My holy hill of Zion"* (Ps. 2:6). **Jesus is the greatest King of all,** *"KING OF KINGS AND LORD OF LORDS"* (Rev. 19:16). **By the greatness of His power His enemies submit themselves to Him and His name** like the demon-possessed man from the tombs did. Even demons bow to His name: *"When he saw Jesus from afar, he ran and worshiped Him"* (Mark 5:6).

As Son of God who is God, He is the Father's chosen Messiah or Christ, so He is anointed—Prophet, Priest, and King.

> *To the Son* [God] *says,*
> *"Your throne, O God, is forever and ever;*
> *A scepter of righteousness is the scepter of Your kingdom.*
> *You have loved righteousness and hated lawlessness;*
> *Therefore God, Your God, has anointed You*
> *With the oil of gladness more than Your companions."* (Heb. 1:8–9)

Kings chosen by God were anointed with a lot of oil—a flask or ram's horn full. Samuel anointed Saul and David that way. At His baptism, with the voice of His Father revealing that He truly was the Son of God, and with the people seeing the heavens opened and the Holy Spirit visibly coming upon Him, Jesus was publicly anointed by

God Himself with a large amount of spiritual oil, *"anointed ... with the oil of gladness more than Your companions."*

Later on the cross, Jesus, the spotless Lamb of God, *"bore the sin of many, and made intercession for the transgressors"* (Isa. 53:12). Pontius Pilate recognized His kingship by putting over His cross a sign which read, *"JESUS OF NAZARETH, THE KING OF THE JEWS"* (John 19:19–22), abbreviated as "I.N.R.I." in Latin. Jesus was unjustly crucified for being who He was, and died satisfying the legal penalty for everyone else's sin and rose triumphantly from the grave spotless again, a conquering hero defeating even death so believers could be made righteous, triumph over evil in His name and power, and live forever.

Just as Joseph was lifted up out of the pit and out of prison where he had unjustly been sent, lifted up to be seated next to royalty, Jesus was lifted up on the cross and lifted up out of Death and Hades to the Father's side. He was also lifted up again from the earth with a cloud at His ascension to be seated next to God Most High, the supreme royalty. And He still does what pleases the Father, fulfilling Scriptures about Him concerning the last days. Daniel saw in a vision:***And behold, One like the Son of Man, coming with the clouds of heaven!***

> *He came to the Ancient of Days, and they brought Him near before Him.*
> *Then to Him was given dominion and glory and a kingdom,*
> *That all peoples, nations, and languages should serve Him.*
> *His dominion is an everlasting dominion, which shall not pass away,*
> *And His kingdom the one which shall not be destroyed.* (Dan. 7:13–14)

"All peoples, nations, and languages should serve Him." All should, although some do not yet. How wonderful for those who realize now how wonderful Jesus is!

Jesus Christ is King of righteousness and peace and His kingdom shall have no end, like *"Melchizedek, king of Salem, priest of the*

Most High God ... to whom also Abraham gave a tenth part of all, first being translated 'king of righteousness,' and then also king of Salem, meaning 'king of peace'" (Heb. 7:1–2). **True peace comes after right relationship with God is restored.**

Jesus Is the King Who Is Meek and Humble of Heart, but with Holy Boldness

If a king came on a donkey, he came in peace; but if he came on a white horse, he came in war. The Father sends forth Jesus, the living *"Word of God,"* in whatever way He needs Him to obediently come—as the Lamb of God or as the Lion of Judah.

The first time, He fulfilled Zechariah's prophecy of Israel's King coming humbly, *"lowly and riding on a donkey,"* who *"shall speak peace to the nations; His dominion shall be from sea to sea, and from the River to the ends of the earth"* (Zech. 9:9–10). The Lamb was slain that believers may obtain His righteousness by faith and His peace that passes understanding, not getting what they deserve since He bore it.

"The Lord reigns" (Ps. 97:1). King Jesus humbles Himself to submit His will to the Father's and we should too. But for those who do not want Him to rule over them and whose sins are not forgiven, He comes again, the conquering King on *"a white horse"* with fire in His eyes to fulfill all righteousness as *"KING OF KINGS AND LORD OF LORDS."* (Rev. 19:16). *"Now out of His mouth goes a sharp sword, that with it He should strike the nations. And He Himself will rule them with a rod of iron. He Himself treads down the winepress of the fierceness and wrath of Almighty God"* (Rev. 19:15). He has authority over all leaders.

When *"the Word of God"* returns like the *"certain nobleman [who] went into a far country to receive for himself a kingdom and to return"* (Luke 19:12), He will receive an accounting of stewardship from His servants and reward them accordingly. Jesus is taking far countries today, and has given His servants *"minas,"* or resources, to steward and invest well, desiring a good return, and has given them authority to *"do business* [occupy] *until* [He] *come*[s]*"* (Luke 19:13). Like those who got a tenfold or fivefold return, He will reward His profitable servants even here on earth, giving them increased authority. But those who wasted what He gave them, He will even strip them of those resources and give them to the ones who invest most wisely. Sadly, I have seen people like this. *"For I say to you, that to everyone who has will be given; and from him who does not have, even what he has will be taken away from him"* (Luke 19:26).

And to His enemies, like *"his citizens* [who] *hated him, and sent a delegation after him, saying, 'We will not have this man to reign over us'"* (Luke 19:14), Jesus will give judgment. *"But bring here those enemies of mine, who did not want me to reign over them, and slay them before me"* (Luke 19:27).

God knows what He is doing in each and every one who is slain in the spirit. But some are enemies inside because they do not really want Jesus to be Lord of their lives, or they might prefer some other god. He can cause some to physically die. (I remember one such worship leader who refused God's warning and died at the end of a prayer meeting. He was revived by paramedics and the Lord mercifully called me to intercede for him when I got home. I heard he died in hospital that same night, but I believe he was saved, glory be to God.)

Thanks be to God, Jesus is so righteous and yet rich in mercy, that for those who are only slain in the spirit, who take to heart the work He desires to do in them, there is another opportunity to surrender their lives to Him. Some profit by the experience and others act like it is only a joke, not taking it seriously, wanting to be knocked down again. *"He shall strike the earth with the rod of His mouth, and with the breath of His lips He shall slay the wicked"* (Isa. 11:4).

God spoke of His servants who acted like enemies through Hosea:

O Ephraim, what shall I do to you?

> *O Judah, what shall I do to you?*
> *For your faithfulness is like a morning cloud,*
> *And like the early dew it goes away.*
> *Therefore I have hewn them by the prophets,*
> *I have slain them by the words of My mouth;*
> *And your judgments are like light that goes forth.*
> *For I desire mercy and not sacrifice,*
> *And the knowledge of God more than burnt offerings"* (Hos 6:4–6)

Some who fall down under the power of God are enemies, but I am not saying that everyone is. John was only overcome by what he saw:

> *And when I saw Him, I fell at His feet as dead. But He laid His right hand on me, saying to me, "Do not be afraid; I am the First and the Last"* (Rev 1:17).

The King's Army Follows Him

People can be led astray by enemies from the world, the flesh, and the devil. *Satan* means "hostile opponent." He opposed Jesus when He came as the Son of Man and now he opposes Jesus as Christ the King and Lord of all, and opposes His followers too. He likes to work through people. But Jesus promised to build His church on the rock, *"and the gates of Hades shall not prevail against it"* (Matt. 16:18).

The King's faithful army might even look like they are losing some battles when they suffer persecution or martyrdom. **It might look like they are surrounded, but God has twice as many angels as the devil has, and God's armies have the final victory because Jesus is their Lord.** They win in the end, because King Jesus did and does. He either rescues them on earth, helping them become overcomers, or their victory comes in heaven. It is important to trust our Commander-in-Chief.

Satan as *"the dragon ... gave authority to the beast"* (Rev. 13:4) which carries Babylon, *"the beast ... that was, and is not, and yet is ... and is going to perdition* [destruction]*"* (Rev. 17:8, 11). **It is an illusion;** it *"is not, and yet is,"* but John saw that many people worshiped both the dragon and the antichrist beast who:...*was given authority to continue for forty-two months. Then he opened his mouth in blasphemy against God ... and those who dwell in heaven. It was granted to him to make war with the saints and to overcome them. And authority was given him over every tribe, tongue, and nation. All who dwell on the earth will worship him, whose names are not written in the Book of Life of the Lamb slain from the foundation of the world.* (Rev. 13:5–8)

God gave the devil permission to war against righteous Job, overcoming him for a time in many ways, but not to kill him; yet God gives permission for the Antichrist to war against righteous saints, and even to kill them. **However, God desires us to pass the test. Not all Christians will be martyred; some will die other deaths or be raptured. But those who follow Jesus, faithful to death however it comes, still have the victory, living forever with King Jesus who is** *"alive forevermore"* (Rev. 1:18).

It is better to suffer for doing right than for doing wrong. God's people ARE NOT TO TAKE THE MARK OF THE BEAST. As an angel cautions those who follow the Antichrist:

> *If anyone worships the beast and his image, and receives his mark on his forehead or on his hand, he himself shall also drink the wine of the wrath of God, which is poured out full strength into the cup of His indignation. He shall be tormented with fire and brimstone in the presence of the holy angels and in the presence of the Lamb. And the smoke of their torment ascends forever and ever; and they have no rest day or night, who worship the beast and his image, and whoever receives the mark of his name.* (Rev. 14:9–11)

Some might escape the wrath of the beast by submitting to idolatry, but the wrath of God is much worse.

This is a warning not to go along with evil rulers to try to save your own skin: *"For whoever desires to save his life will lose it, but whoever* *loses his life for My sake and the gospel's will save it"* (Mark 8:35). Thank God, not only is:*...the patience* [steadfastness, perseverance] *of the saints* [manifested]; *here are those who keep the commandments of God and the faith of Jesus. Then I heard a voice from heaven saying to me, "Write: 'Blessed are the dead who die in the Lord from now on.'" "Yes," says the Spirit, "that they may rest from their labors, and their works follow them."* (Rev. 14:12–13)

Obeying the Word of God leads to everlasting life and joy for martyrs *"who have the victory over the beast, over his image and over his mark and over the number of his name"* (Rev. 15:2). John saw them in heaven standing on *"a sea of glass mingled with fire ... having harps of God. They sing the song of Moses, the servant of God, and the song of the Lamb"* (Rev. 15:2–3).

Jesus Fights on Our Behalf, and He Glorifies God

Jesus even stands up for the faithful at the Father's side as He did for Stephen and gives us the victory in His name. **We have only to follow in faith:** *"Therefore whoever confesses Me before men, him I will also confess before My Father who is in heaven. But whoever denies Me before men, him I will also deny before My Father who is in heaven"* (Matt. 10:32–33). **Stay loyal to King Jesus. If we are unashamed of Him, He will be unashamed of us.**

> *Trust in the Lord with all your heart,*
> *And lean not on your own understanding;*
> *In all your ways acknowledge Him,*
> *And He shall direct your paths.* (Prov. 3:5–6)

Rather than fear or give our allegiance over to God's enemies to avoid persecution, we are to be unashamed of Jesus and what He stands for, with a holy fear of the Lord and with our name written in the Lamb's Book of Life. To be true Christians, to come behind Jesus as His followers, we do what we see Him doing and telling us to do. That is truly acknowledging His reign over us: *"If anyone desires to come after Me, let him deny himself, and take up his cross, and follow Me. For whoever desires to save his life will lose it, but whoever loses his life for My sake will find it"* (Matt. 16:24–25). **Christians may be meek, but they are not cowards.** They can have a holy boldness for what is right, *"the Spirit of … might"* (Isa. 11:2).

He leads His army today and provides armour and strategies. *"[Our battle is not] against flesh and blood"* (Eph. 6:12). Jesus gave us the Beatitudes and other teachings plus His Spirit to lead us into battle against our enemies and into His righteousness, peace, rest, and provision. **Jesus won the battle against sin at the cross and helps us individually to win so we can continue to experience the divine exchange.** He took on our sin so we could take on His righteousness. The victory is the Lord's, and He counsels us so we can be overcomers and do the things He did in His power and authority.

His name is powerful:

> *Then the seventy returned with joy, saying, "Lord, even the demons are subject to us in Your name." And He said to them, "I saw Satan fall like lightning from heaven. Behold, I give you the authority to trample on serpents and scorpions, and over all the power of the enemy, and nothing shall by any means hurt you. Nevertheless do not rejoice in this, that the spirits are subject to you, but rather rejoice because your names are written in heaven."* (Luke 10:17–20)

There are times when Jesus gives His faithful followers, His army, authority to triumph over Satan and his demons and times when He may remove some of His protective cover and allow followers to be put to the test and for the enemy to appear to triumph for a time. But it is important to know that **those with King Jesus win in the end and His strategy is to** keep us faithful. *"The testing of your faith produces patience* [steadfastness, perseverance]*"* (Jas. 1:3).

Job 2:3 says, *"Then the L*ORD *said to Satan, 'Have you considered My servant Job, that there is none like him on the earth, a blameless and upright man, one who fears God and shuns evil? And still he holds fast to his integrity, although you incited Me against him, to destroy him without cause.'"*

Even though Jesus allowed some of His apostles and disciples to drink the same cup He drank and be martyred for their faith, they triumphed in the end, praising God, as He knew they would. So will we if we learn from Jesus who is confident in who He is in God, and yet meek and humble, or *"gentle and lowly in heart"* (Matt. 11:29). *"And they overcame him* [Satan, the accuser of the brethren] *by the blood of the Lamb and by the word of their testimony, and they did not love their lives to the death"* (Rev. 12:11). A day will come when we will see this fulfilled: *"Death is swallowed up in victory"* (1 Cor. 15:54), and, *"The devil, who deceived them, was cast into the lake of fire and brimstone where the beast and the false prophet are. And they will be tormented day and night forever and ever"* (Rev. 20:10). The devil is defeated and will be defeated by God.

King Jesus, our Saviour said, *"And this is the will of Him who sent Me, that everyone who sees the Son and believes in Him may have everlasting life; and I will raise him up at the last day"* (John 6:40). He is not saying everyone created will be saved, but those who believe in Him. So Jude admonished believers to maintain their lives with God: *"And on some have compassion, making a distinction; but others save with fear, pulling them out of the fire, hating even the garment defiled by the flesh"* (Jude 1:22–23). Some can be rescued from hell on earth and from suffering in Hades and the *"second death"* of *"the lake of fire"* (Rev. 20:14), that they may enjoy heaven forever with Christ.

David gave glory to God, even facing Goliath as a youthful believer and worshiper of the Most High God. David's training began by learning that the Lord is his Shepherd who helped him conquer the lion and bear, enemies of the sheepfold. **David knew from experience from whence His strength and abilities came and who would fight for him, so he boasted of his God, not himself.** He told Goliath:

> *You come to me with a sword, with a spear, and with a javelin. But I come to you in the name of the L*ord *of hosts, the God of the armies of Israel, whom you have defied. This day the L*ord *will deliver you into my hand, and I will strike you and take your head from you … that all the earth may know that there is a God in Israel. Then all this assembly shall know that the L*ord *does not save with sword and spear; for the battle is the L*ord's *and He will give you into our hands.* (1 Sam. 17:45–47)

In training us to lay down our lives for our friends, Jesus might train us with something little. I had a swollen foot and leg as a result of a spider bite as a teen. I remember how the Lord trained me later as a mother to call on His name if I had to face my fears with large spiders or wasps so that my children and grandchildren would be protected. I would tell spiders **they were out of my house or under my feet, in Jesus's name**. Thank God, they would sometimes present themselves when the time was right to be snatched up with a tissue and squashed under my feet. Glory be to God! Likewise with wasps that came into the yard looking for the flowers and fruit growing there. **I also told them that they were to do us no harm.** After I began to take authority over them in Jesus's name, no more was anyone stung for several years. Thanks be to God! There is power in the name of Jesus!

Jesus Reveals God's Beauty and Lets Us Ask Him Questions

King Jesus, our eternal High Priest and Bridegroom, still lives in the real sanctuary in heaven and in the temple of His Holy Spirit in our hearts.

> *One thing I have desired of the L*ord,
> *That will I seek:*
> *That I may dwell in the house of the L*ord *All the days of my life,*
> *To behold the beauty of the L*ord,
> *And to inquire in His temple.* (Ps. 27:4)

Praise God, thousands of young people have learned to put first things first, to seek that *"one thing"* like David, and for years thousands even spent their New Year's Eves at an IHOP conference in Kansas City doing that.

While flying to Lethbridge in 2002, I asked the Lord if I could see some of His beauty and kept desiring to see **His "purple mountain majesty."** Although I could only see the mountains outlined on the horizon when I landed, the Lord surprised me. A stranger I met, Jean Bohne, graciously offered to drive me into the Rocky Mountains. She even lent me her camera and I took this picture in the Rockies.

The works of His creation are like glimpses of His beauty and majesty, but the Lord brought more out of the photo than I expected. Looking at it, I thought of His Majesty, Jesus, who is the Most Beautiful One, our Rock of Salvation, purple reminding me both of His kingly majesty and of His unjust suffering for our sake. Kings used to lead their troops into battle, willing to lay down their lives for their people. *"Jesus of Nazareth, King of the Jews,"* certainly did that. He leads us in battle today and bore His suffering like a king, the joy of the Lord being His strength as He thought on those who would be saved because of His sacrifice and victorious resurrection. That is beautiful!

Like a beautiful rose, He was crushed and trampled for us, releasing the fragrance of heaven. He still lives to give believers His saving grace and mercy and glimpses of His beauty, just as Solomon's bride saw glimpses of her beloved's beauty. *"Strength and beauty are in His sanctuary"* (Ps. 96:6).

That is where true beauty is found. The works of His creation, including the aurora borealis, even proclaim it. **How Beautiful Jesus is that He would show such love for His bride that He would lay down His life for her even before she had changed into her wedding clothes!** So now He has become our First Love and wants us to lovingly respond to His love by obeying His Word and commands. Just knowing how much our Beloved loves us individually and corporately can cause us to glow. By spending time with Him in the secret place and doing His will in love, we can begin to look like our Beloved, taking on aspects of His beauty. After all, Jesus did that with His Father and is *"the brightness of His glory and the express image of His person"* (Heb. 1:3).

That does not mean we will not have difficulties to go through, but like rebar, Christ living in us will strengthen us with joy and the Spirit of might. He warned His disciples that problems and persecution would come upon them for His name's sake and they would be scattered when His time came, but, *"These things I have spoken to you, that in Me you may have peace. In the world you will have tribulation; but be of good cheer, I have overcome the world"* (John 16:33). Some Christians are persecuted even today, but those who keep their eyes on Jesus have His peace. *Shalom* peace is "nothing missing, nothing broken." That is the wholeness of salvation that I have found.

Praise God, just as Jesus encouraged His disciples to ask, seek, and knock, we can ask today, and learn from Him many things we did not know. As I sought Him, desiring to see His beauty, I realized that **not only is Jesus beautiful but He has beautiful clothes for us.**

As has been said, in Old Testament times only a very holy high priest in the order of Aaron could even enter the Holy of holies and stand before the presence of God to intercede. The bronze sea contained water so he could wash his hands and feet first, and put on beautiful, holy garments, designer garments designed by Almighty God Himself: *"And you shall make holy garments for Aaron* [and his sons], *for glory and for beauty"* (Ex. 28:2).

It was a foreshadow of the real thing to come with our resurrected High Priest Jesus washed clean of the stain of our sin by His own blood, ready to baptize us, and wearing His designer garments of salvation and righteousness, beautiful and glorious clothes. When we seek a right relationship with God and let Him wash us, *"like the lilies of the field,"* He will clothe us too, more radiantly than *"even Solomon in all his glory"* (Matt. 6:29).

> *I will greatly rejoice in the LORD,*
> *My soul shall be joyful in my God;*
> *For He has clothed me with the garments of salvation,*
> *He has covered me with the robe of righteousness,*
> *As a bridegroom decks himself with ornaments,*
> *And as a bride adorns herself with her jewels.* (Isa. 61:10)

Marriage is a picture of the relationship Jesus wants to have with His church. Wanting to look beautiful for my husband, Attilio, I used to search for beauty by enhancing my outward appearance with boutique clothes and by wearing jewellery every day, plus makeup for special occasions. Then a godly woman, Dora Cornu, brought me a word from God about how to win my husband to the Lord. (He believed in God, but we had no fellowship of the Spirit yet.) This included, *"Do not let your adornment be merely outward.... Rather, let it be the hidden person of the heart, with the incorruptible beauty of a gentle and quiet spirit, which is very precious in the sight of God. For in this manner, in former times, the holy women who trusted in God also adorned themselves, being submissive to their own husbands, as Sarah obeyed Abraham, calling him lord, whose daughters you are if you do good and do not let anything terrify you"* (1 Pet. 3:3–6).

Interestingly, around this time the Lord began to purge me from my dependence on worldly beauty methods and began to strip away the wearing of jewellery and even occasional makeup from my life. (I do not mind if others wear some jewellery or makeup, but I know it is not for me anymore.) The daily earrings and lipstick were the last to go, although I would occasionally wear a cross the family gave me—but not every day because I used to wear one superstitiously, thinking it would save me. Now I know it is what Jesus did on the cross that saves me.

The Lord even led me to wear "sackcloth," which for me was often things from a sack which others gave me, new or old, and used clothing from a thrift shop. Eventually, when I learned that "sackcloth" was often black, maybe with some white, it began to be mostly dark clothes, as a reminder that I am mourning for so many of my people, Jesus's people. Yet there were times when I was led to also wear some *"beautiful garments"* (Isa. 52:1) which He supplied, because I mourn, not without hope.

The Lord taught me that true beauty came not from the clothes or jewellery I used to wear, but from within when Christ, the Beautiful One, was within me. It comes from spending time with Jesus and seeking His character, doing His will, keeping a short account with God. Righteousness produces peace. His Word teaches us today.

Jesus's Word is powerful. Besides to *"do good"* like Sarah, I also would often remember, *"Do not let anything terrify you."* I learned to conquer many fears by knowing that King Jesus was with me, **calling on His name for help**. For instance, when I would clean the family cottage in May, I used to find that wasps had gotten in and were alive on the bedroom floors upstairs. Thank God, it was still cold so they were not very active. So I would call on the name of Jesus for protection and step on them so our children would be protected, and He gave me victory. Later, my husband fixed the roofline so wasps could not get in anymore, but mice still did. Many a spring the Lord helped me face the mess they had made and clean it up too, unafraid. Praise God!

A ship needs a captain and so does a home. I was my earthly husband's equal, free to choose to submit to him, and he allowed me to take responsibility in many decisions. I began to learn to trust his judgment, especially in matters of household maintenance, but occasionally to submit my ideas on matters beforehand rather than afterwards. Sometimes he agreed that my suggestion was worth trying. However, he was a carpenter and sometimes I could not see how something would turn out and he could. Other times I could see little details that would later be significant, helping him. Although we sometimes had disagreements to work through, I truly wanted to be a blessed, meek *"helpmate,"* partnering with him in love. The Lord also said once, *"You need a fresh submission, the one to another."*

As I pursued the Lord's righteousness and a peaceful, forgiving heart *"with the incorruptible beauty of a gentle and quiet spirit"* (1 Pet. 3:4), people began to comment on the peace flowing out of me even in times of trial. Praise the Lord! Jesus was giving me true beauty, and I had much for which I was thankful. After my husband died, the Lord told me that *"he was a gift of love."* And he truly was.

King Jesus is returning for His corporate bride. She will be adorned in beautiful clothes, knowing that His righteousness is beautiful. She may not understand all our Beloved's decisions, but can trust our Lord, our Kinsman Redeemer. *"'His wife has made herself ready.' And to her it was granted to be arrayed in fine linen, clean and bright, for the fine linen is the righteous acts of the saints"* (Rev. 19:7–8). Like Solomon in Song of Songs, Jesus praises her beauty and may she praise His.

He can give us revelation knowledge: *"Call to Me, and I will answer you, and show you great and mighty things, which you do not know"* (Jer. 33:3).

I asked the Lord for a word for 2013 as I often do at the start of the year and He said, *"Trust, trust, trust in Me."* Just as it is good to spend time with an earthly spouse, it is good to make time to spend with the Lord, who is also our Beloved, praising His name, seeking His face, touching His grace, dwelling in the secret place with Him (see Psalm 91). He is Truth and does not tell lies like a mere mortal. He and His Word are entirely trustworthy—no matter what comes. We grow in trust.

Jesus showed in the Beatitudes that when we seek Him, His kingdom, and His righteousness before we seek to have our own material needs met, that we will truly be blessed and live in the peace and provision of God. This is the peace that passes understanding: *"Peace I leave with you. My peace I give to you; not as the world gives do I give to you. Let not your heart be troubled, neither let it be afraid"* (John 14:27). That does not mean there will never be obstacles, but confident faith in Him and His name overcomes them.

He showers blessings of mercy and grace on His people, whether it is deserved or not, beginning with the Jews. Righteous deeds done through members of His body can draw nations to Christ. **He has been extending the scepter.**

> *For You will arise and have mercy on Zion;*
> *For the time to favour her,*
> *Yes, the set time, has come.*
> *For Your servants take pleasure in her stones,*
> *And show favor to her dust.*
> *So the nations shall fear the name of the* Lord,
> *And all the kings of the earth Your glory.*
> *For the* Lord *shall build up Zion;*
> *He shall appear in His glory.*
> *[He will reveal His greatness.]*
> *He shall regard the prayer of the destitute,*
> *And shall not despise their prayer.* (Ps. 102:13–17)

The King Owns It All and Is Victorious

Psalms 24:1 says, *"The earth is the Lord's and all its fullness, the world and those who dwell therein."* Our Most Highly exalted God owns and possesses both heaven and earth, even though some of His creation has rebelled. We do not see it in the natural yet, but it all belongs to Him and He has a right over what is His. Jesus is our Shepherd-King.

> *Today if you will hear His voice;*
> *"Do not harden your hearts as in the rebellion,*
> *As in the day of trial in the wilderness,*
> *When your fathers tested Me;*
> *They tried Me, though they saw My work."* (Ps. 95:7–8)

God says that His is not only *"the cattle on a thousand hills"* (Ps. 50:10), but, *"'The silver is Mine, and the gold is Mine,' says the Lord of hosts"* (Hag. 2:8). The enemy has tried to take it away from Him, but for those who desire the Most High God to rule them, to be their Lord, the enemy's grasp is only temporary. God's grasp is eternal for those who become His children, and He provides for them, especially when they lovingly consider the needs of others. Then, they can say, *"And my God shall supply all your need according to His riches in glory by Christ Jesus. Now to our God and Father be glory forever and ever. Amen"* (Phil. 4:19–20). **In love, He even blesses His enemies, but He has special covenant blessings, some conditional, for His people.**

Jesus described kingdom living as recognizing that what we have comes from God, spiritual and material, like talents from a landowner which we can trade and invest and for which we must give an accounting one day. *"For the kingdom of heaven is like a man traveling to a far country, who called his own servants and delivered his goods to them"* (Matt. 25:14). Our hope is to hear Him say one day, *"Well done, good and faithful servant; you were faithful over a few things, I will make you ruler over many things. Enter into the joy of your lord"* (Matt. 25:21).

Our real enemy, Satan, may appear to win some battles against Christians but **it is important to remember that at the end of the Book, King Jesus wins the final battle. God has decreed it. God wins in the end.**

The psalmist Asaph wondered why it was that evil men sometimes prospered and seemed to get away with murder; he just could not figure it out—*"Until* [he] *went into the sanctuary of God; then* [he] *understood their end"* (Ps. 73:17). A time comes when they must answer to God and reap what they have sown if they do not repent. People will be judged by what they have done. It is all recorded in heaven. That will be evident when heavenly books are opened.

John saw Jesus reigning as the victorious King of the Nations when he saw the seventh angel prophetically sounding the trumpet:

> *And there were voices in heaven, saying, "The kingdoms of this world have become the kingdoms of our Lord and of His Christ, and He shall reign forever and ever!" And the twenty-four elders who sat before God on their thrones fell on their faces and worshiped God, saying:*
>
> *"We give You thanks, O Lord God Almighty,*
> *The One who is and who was and who is to come,*
> *Because You have taken Your great power and reigned.*
> *The nations were angry, and Your wrath has come,*
> *And the time of the dead, that they should be judged,*
> *And that You should reward Your servants the prophets and the saints,*
> *And those who fear Your name, small and great,*
> *And should destroy those who destroy the earth."*
> *Then the temple of God was opened in heaven, and the ark of His covenant was seen in His temple. And there were lightnings, noises, thunderings, an earthquake, and great hail.* (Rev. 11:15–19)

Also, Isaiah prophesied of a pay-back time in Isaiah 40:10: *"Behold the Lord God shall come with a strong hand, and His arm shall rule for Him; behold His reward is with Him and His work* [recompense] *before Him."*

John also described his vision of heaven opening and **King Jesus, crowned with many crowns, suddenly coming on a white horse.**

> [He] *was called Faithful and True, and in righteousness He judges and makes war. His eyes were like a flame of fire, and on His head were many crowns. He had a name written that no one knew except Himself. He was clothed with a robe dipped in blood, and His name is called The Word of God. And the armies in heaven, clothed in fine linen, white and clean, followed Him on white horses. Now out of His mouth goes a sharp sword, that with it He should strike the nations. And He Himself will rule them with a rod of iron. He Himself treads the winepress of the fierceness and wrath of Almighty God. And He has on His robe and on His thigh a name written:*
>
> *KING OF KINGS*
>
> *AND LORD OF LORDS.*
>
> *Then I saw an angel standing in the sun; and he cried with a loud voice, saying to all the birds that fly in the midst of heaven, "Come and gather together for the supper of the great God. That you may eat the flesh of kings, the flesh of captains, the flesh of mighty men, the flesh of horses and of those who sit on them, and the flesh of all people, free and slave, both small and great." And I saw the beast, the kings of the earth, and their armies, gathered together to make war against Him who sat on the horse and against His army. Then the beast was captured, and with him the false prophet who worked signs in his presence, by which he deceived those who received the mark of the beast and those who worshiped his image. These two were cast alive into the lake of fire burning with brimstone. And the rest were killed with the sword which proceeded from the mouth of*

Him who sat on the horse. And all the birds were filled with their flesh. (Rev. 19:11–21)

Evil is ultimately defeated.

The above passage reminds me of how **when it looked like all hope was lost** in the cowboy movies, that **there would still be a remnant of hope, and suddenly the cavalry would come riding into the rescue, blowing the bugle. Jesus saves! And His cavalry follows Him because of Calvary.** He is our shofar, our *"horn of salvation"* (Ps. 18:2; Luke 1:69). Hallelujah! Our God reigns forever!

King Jesus Will Come Again for Those Who Eagerly Await Him

An unknown person made the following banner:

Paul wrote of the rapture:

> *But I do not want you to be ignorant, brethren, concerning those who have fallen asleep, lest you sorrow as others who have no hope. For if we believe that Jesus died and rose again, even so God will bring with Him those who sleep in Jesus....* [When the archangel sounds the trumpet] *the dead in Christ will rise first. Then we who are alive and remain will be caught up together with them in the clouds to meet the Lord in the air. And thus we shall always be with the Lord.*
> (1 Thess. 4:13–17)

Jesus is also the great and Mighty Warrior King of kings who will come again in the final great day of the Lord. There have been small "d" days of the Lord, but there is a great Day coming:

> *Since it is a righteous thing with God to repay with tribulation those who trouble you, and to give* [believers who are persecuted] *rest with us when the Lord Jesus is revealed from heaven with His mighty angels, in flaming fire taking vengeance on those who do not know God, and on those who do not obey the gospel of our Lord Jesus Christ. These shall be punished with everlasting destruction from the presence of the Lord and from the glory of His power, when He comes in that Day, to be glorified in His saints and to be admired among all those who believe, because our testimony among you was believed.* (2 Thess. 1:6–10)

Paul went on to warn first century believers to stand firm in the faith and that **the rapture would not come until the Antichrist was revealed:**

> *Then the* [Antichrist] *king shall do according to his own will: he shall exalt and magnify himself above every god, shall speak blasphemies against the God of gods, and shall prosper until the wrath has been accomplished; for what has been determined shall be done. He shall regard neither the God of his fathers nor the desire of women, nor regard any god; for he shall exalt himself above them all.* (Dan. 11:36–37)

It appears that **Jesus will come once in the rapture to take to heaven those who are eagerly waiting for Him. Then He will come again with His heavenly cavalry,** *"the armies in heaven, clothed in fine linen, white and clean,* [who] *followed Him on white horses"* (Rev. 19:14), **as the conquering King to defeat evil.**

> *Concerning the coming of our Lord Jesus Christ and our gathering together to Him.... Let no one deceive you by any means; for that Day will not come unless the falling away comes first, and the*

> man of sin is revealed, the son of perdition, who opposes and exalts himself above all that is called God or that is worshiped, so that he sits as God in the temple of God, showing himself that he is God.... For the mystery of lawlessness is already at work; only He who now restrains will do so until He is taken out of the way. And then the lawless one [Antichrist] will be revealed, whom the Lord will consume with the breath of His mouth and destroy with the brightness of His coming.
>
> The coming of the lawless one is according to the working of Satan, with all power, signs, and lying wonders, and with all unrighteous deception among those who perish, because they did not receive the love of the truth, that they might be saved. And for this reason God will send them strong delusion, that they should believe the lie, that they all may be condemned who did not believe the truth but had pleasure in unrighteousness. But we are bound to give thanks to God always for you, brethren beloved by the Lord, because God from the beginning chose you for salvation through sanctification by the Spirit and belief in the truth, to which He called you by our gospel, for the obtaining of the glory of our Lord Jesus Christ. (2 Thess. 2:1–4, 7–14)

If believers realize they have been deceived, they can flee evil, wash their clothes, and follow the Lamb who told His disciples, *"Take heed that you not be deceived"* (Luke 21:8). They will be among the multitude of "praisers" around the throne of God:

> ...*of all nations, tribes, peoples and tongues, standing before the throne and before the Lamb, clothed with white robes, with palm branches in their hands, and crying out with a loud voice, saying, "Salvation belongs to our God, who sits on the throne, and to the Lamb!..." These are the ones who come out of the great tribulation, and washed their robes and made them white in the blood of the Lamb. Therefore they are before the throne of God, and serve Him day and night in His temple. And He who sits on the throne will*

> dwell among them. They shall neither hunger anymore nor thirst anymore; the sun shall not strike them, nor any heat; for the Lamb who is in the midst of the throne will shepherd them and lead them to living fountains of waters. And God will wipe away every tear from their eyes. (Rev. 7:9–10, 14–17)

I used to be very timid and shy. But since I found I had been deceived by the false apparitions of the "Lady" and the Lord told me to *"wash yourself in the public pool,"* now there are times when I have a newfound freedom to shout out my praise to the Lord in gratitude for all He is and all He has done for me. We can wave the palms of our hands now like palm branches as we worship. (Maybe that is why I like to wave banners in praise of Him.)

Our King Is the Just Judge

Acts 10:42 says, *"He commanded us to preach to the people, and to testify that it is He who was ordained by God to be Judge of the living and the dead."* There is a final judgment, but Jesus can also come with a preliminary judgment while we are still on earth. I know because it is written and I experienced it.

> *For the time has come for judgment to begin at the house of God; and if it begins with us first, what will be the end of those who do not obey the gospel of God? Now*
>
> *"If the righteous one is scarcely saved,*
> *Where will the ungodly and the sinner appear?"*
> *Therefore let those who suffer according to the will of God commit their souls to Him in doing good, as to a faithful Creator.* (1 Pet. 4:17–19)

After Jesus gave them a process of confronting sin in the hope of a reconciliation, Peter asked Him, *"'Lord, how often shall my brother sin against me, and I forgive him? Up to seven times?' Jesus said to him, 'I do not say to you, up to seven times, but up to seventy times seven. Therefore the kingdom of heaven is like a certain king who wanted to settle accounts with his servants'"* (Matt. 18:21–23). With His kingdom here on earth as it is in heaven, King Jesus can settle accounts sooner rather than later, like in the parable of the unforgiving servant.

Jesus is a Just Judge who knows whether to forgive or not forgive—to grant a pardon even mercifully when it is not deserved or to pass a sentence, and when to commend people. In the case when a brother, a part of the body of Christ, is found to be causing other members to sin, especially when he will not receive correction, it could be time to withhold forgiveness. *"If your hand of foot causes you to sin, cut it off and cast it from you. It is better for you to enter into life lame or maimed, rather than having two hands or two feet, to be cast into the everlasting fire"'* (Matt. 18:8).

Jesus has already given His New Covenant promise to the house of Israel and those associated with it who enter into covenant with Him that He would place His laws in their hearts and minds, and would be their God and they be His people. A time would come for His people when they *"all shall know Me, from the least of them to the greatest of them. For I will be merciful to their unrighteousness* [forgive their iniquity] *... and their sins and their lawless deeds I will remember no more"* (Heb. 8:11–12; 10:17). His forgiveness should be followed by our repentance. **The spotless Lamb of God was slain shedding His own blood so that the sin of the world could be taken away. Let us value that sacrifice by which we can receive mercy and grace.** It is up to us to remember the Golden Rule and live by it.

Jesus helps Christians to be very forgiving and unoffendable. Jesus told His disciples to pray, *"Forgive us our debts, as we forgive our debtors.... For if you forgive men their trespasses, your heavenly Father will forgive you. But if you do not forgive men their trespasses, neither will your Father forgive your trespasses"* (Matt. 6:12, 14–15).

Not everyone who sins is automatically forgiven by God or going to heaven. But in His name, baptized followers, members of His *"royal priesthood"* (1 Pet. 2:9), can pronounce forgiveness over a repentant believer. Visiting them after His resurrection, Jesus breathed the Holy Spirit onto His assembled, trained disciples, giving them the power to discern spirits in the peace of Christ. *"Receive the Holy Spirit. If you forgive the sins of any, they are forgiven them; if you retain the sins of any, they are retained"* (John 20:22–23).

That Word referred to forgiving themselves too, since they had all had trouble understanding His crucifixion and believing Jesus had risen. They began that day by receiving not only the power to forgive sins but both forgiveness for their own sins and the peace of God that Jesus gave them.

Although we should always be ready to forgive those who trespass against us, and to be reconcilers, there are times when a sin may not be forgiven. Jesus showed this in dealing with a sinning brother in Christ who acts like he is not part of the family.

> *Moreover if your brother sins against you, go and tell him his fault between you and him alone. If he hears you, you have gained your brother. But if he will not hear, take with you one or two more, that "by the mouth of two or three witnesses every word may be established." And if he refuses to hear them, tell it to the church. But if he refuses even to hear the church, let him be to you like a heathen and a tax collector. Assuredly, I say to you, whatever you bind on earth will be bound in heaven, and whatever you loose on earth will be loosed in heaven. Again I say to you that if two of you agree on earth concerning anything that they ask, it will be done for them by My Father in heaven. For where two or three are gathered in My name, I am there in the midst of them.* (Matthew 18:15–20)

When someone sins against us, we are not responsible for their sin but for our own reaction. Binding and loosing here seem to be connected to retaining and forgiving. Then Jesus told Peter to keep forgiving a brother who asks him, who receives what he says, even *"seventy times seven"* (Matt. 18:22). By forgiving the brother, we are set free ourselves.

Another time, Jesus warned His disciples against giving offense or they could be judged. **He told them to rebuke one who offends them, ready to forgive if he repents:** *"It is impossible that no offenses should come, but woe to him through whom they do come!... Take heed to yourselves. If your brother sins against you, rebuke him; and if he repents, forgive him. And if he sins against you seven times in a day, and seven times in a day returns to you, saying, 'I repent,' you shall forgive him"* (Luke 17:1–4).

Often, we need to prayerfully look at more than one Scripture if we really want to understand what Jesus is saying to us. For instance, He says to rebuke a Christian who sins against you, one who should know better, in the hope of restoring him: *"Moreover if your brother sins against you, go and tell him his fault between you and him alone"* (Matt. 18:15). And yet it is also true that Holy Spirit, *"will convict* [convince] *the world of sin"* (John 16:8). **So there are times when the Holy Spirit Himself will convince someone that something is sin, and other times when we ourselves need to give appropriate feedback, in love, to a brother. And if he takes it well, and repents, and we forgive, our King will be pleased that we are reconciled—and the brother will have avoided having God judge him. There are other times when we are called to forgive, even when he has not repented yet, and leave him to deal with God.**

In the parable of the unforgiving servant, when he refuses to forgive a brother believer who asks him, the other servants, like intercessors, plead the case of the second servant seeking righteousness with the king—who does the judging. Originally the first servant had received mercy and debt cancellation of an enormous debt when he had begged for mercy and the king gave him forgiveness and freedom. However, then he cruelly refused to forgive his fellow servant a much smaller debt even though the man likewise pleaded with him for mercy and patience until he could repay him.

When the king was told about it, he had to deal with the first servant differently and punish him, retaining his sins this time until the debt was paid. Possibly in this second court appearance he had cried out, *"Lord! Lord!"* But this time since he would not forgive the man who trespassed against him, the servant not only forfeited the mercy he could have received but he was handed over *"to the torturers until he should pay all that was due to him"* (Matt. 18:34). Jesus wants us to love others as He has loved us. He grants us more mercy when we are merciful to others.

Satan is the father of lies. Today, judges have authority to sentence guilty people to jail and/or a fine until they pay their debt to society. (Unfortunately, some judges have abused the authority by sentencing some people, including pastors, who are wrongly accused.)

In the Scriptures, we also see Holy Spirit-led church leaders exercising the authority of the believer. Peter judged Ananias and Sapphira, retaining their sin when they conspired to lie to the Holy Spirit. Both died. The apostle Paul also retained the sin of the unrepentant man who was having sex with his mother. Paul told the church, *"In the name of our Lord Jesus Christ, deliver such a one to Satan for the destruction of the flesh, that his spirit may be saved in the day of the Lord Jesus"* (1 Cor. 5:5–6). The gift of *"fear of the Lord"* came upon the people as a result.

Sexual immorality defiles a church. Sadly, some today believe that what is wrong is right. But if one caught in this sin repents, there is forgiveness as with the woman caught in adultery. She was convicted of sin, and the lawful penalty was stoning to the death; but believing, she was willing to repent. Jesus did not condemn her. Instead, forgiving, He told her, *"Go and sin no more"* (John 8:11), knowing the just penalty of the law would be paid for believers by His cleansing blood.

When God showed His glory to Moses, He showed both His bountiful mercy and His refusal to clear the guilty. No wonder Jesus called people to repentance and belief! His glorious goodness

passed before Moses: *The* L*ORD* *God, merciful and gracious, longsuffering, and abounding in goodness and truth, keeping mercy for thousands, forgiving iniquity and transgressions and sin, by no means clearing the guilty, visiting the iniquity of the fathers upon the children to the third and the fourth generation.* (Ex. 34:6–7)

Sin deserves punishment, so in time He mercifully sent His Son to be the Saviour, satisfying the Law for those who believe in Him, atoning for sin with His blood. However, **both forgiven and unforgiven sin affects our family**. When I realized this many years ago, **although I had trouble repenting just for me, I did it for my family's sake.**

Our Father wants to bring His kingdom living here on earth. It is good for His servants to keep a short account with Him, repenting quickly and walking in righteousness. None of us can pay all we owe, so we should appreciate the Father's sacrifice of His Son. God is like a king who wants to:

> *…settle accounts with his servants.* [When the servant] *was not able to pay, his master commanded that he be sold, with his wife and children and all that he had, and that payment be made. The servant therefore fell down before him, saying, "Master, have patience with me, and I will pay you all." Then the master of that servant was moved with compassion, released him, and forgave him the debt.* (Matt. 18:23–27)

His family was affected too when his huge debt was unpaid, with his impoverished wife and children to be sold into slavery and all that they owned to be taken away to repay the debt. But his repentance allowed blessings of mercy to flow to them too. Fathers need to care about their children.

Sin makes people slaves, taking away their freedom. But repentance allows them to receive the forgiveness and debt cancellation that Jesus purchased for them as a free gift and start fresh to do what Jesus says. *"If the Son makes you free, you shall be free indeed"* (John 8:36).

When Jesus is willing to forgive us, we should be willing to forgive ourselves too.

But if we refuse to deal with sin habits in our own lives, those iniquities or weaknesses towards those sins can be passed down, showing up in a greater measure in our children to four generations. It is like growing weeds. That is why we exhort the parents to repent, not just for their own sakes but for their children's sake, so they will not reap the consequences of the sin; so the Lord will not *"come and strike the earth with a curse."* Was not Covid19 a curse over all the earth?

It is written:

Behold, I will send you Elijah the prophet
Before the coming of the great and dreadful day of the LORD.
And he will turn
The hearts of the fathers to the children,
And the hearts of the children to their fathers,
Lest I come and strike the earth with a curse. (Mal. 4:5–6)

The Just Judge can set families free today. Fathers and children need to look to one another. Children, grandchildren, and great-grandchildren of believers no longer have to suffer for the sins of their fathers because of what Jesus did at the cross. Blessings can go down to thousands of generations by faith. *"'Now the just shall live by faith; but if anyone draws back, My soul has no pleasure in him.' But we are not of those who draw back to perdition* [destruction]*, but of those who believe to the saving of the soul"* (Heb. 10:38–39).

Forgiveness is a free gift. We don't have to do anything to earn it, but if we need to make amends to someone, we still should. Forgiveness does not mean that justice should not be served. For instance, if someone has been defrauded, restitution should be made if possible, and for some crimes a prison sentence is necessary or possible. But good behaviour in prison can merit early release, and judges can even grant mercy to someone on death row if they believe it is warranted. Like Jesus, people may even choose to give a truly repentant person a gift of debt cancellation, as Corrie Ten Boom did. **We can pray as Jesus did,** *"Father forgive them, for they know not what they do"* **(Luke 23:34 KJV), leaving forgiveness or vengeance in the Father's hands.**

Jesus said the kingdom of God is like how the king handled his servant. There are times when He sets people free and other times when He leaves them bound for a time until the debt is paid. Hopefully people will realize as I did many years ago that it was impossible for me to be good enough to save myself, to fully pay my debt to Him on my own; so I set out to forgive others and accept His undeserved gift of amazing grace so my account would be paid in full. Jesus gave His Spirit to apostles and disciples, and gives Him to believers today, to help discern and to give good wisdom and counsel, with a holy fear of the Lord. That is the beginning of wisdom and understanding.

Being not only the Judge but our lawyer for the defense, our Advocate, Jesus knows the truth about us and can defend us. He can tell us when to plead innocent and when to plead guilty. He told people to make peace with their accuser if he really had something against them, even before offering their gift to God. It is like settling out of court:

> *First be reconciled with your brother, and then come, and offer your gift. Agree with your adversary quickly, while you are on the way with him, lest your adversary deliver you to the judge, the judge hand you over to the officer, and you be thrown into prison. Assuredly, I say to you, you will by no means get out of there till you have paid the last penny.* (Matt. 5:24–26)

Unforgiveness can be an obstacle to having our own sins forgiven, so we must be wise and compassionate: *"Therefore I say to you, whatever things you ask when you pray, believe that you receive them, and you will have them. And whenever you stand praying, if you have anything against anyone, forgive him, that your Father in heaven may also forgive you your trespasses"* (Mark 11:24–25).

People should respond to God's mercy by forgiving their debtors the same way they would like to be treated, loving one another as Jesus has loved them and not taking offense easily. Forgiving sets us free and leaves the other party to deal with God. If vengeance is necessary, God will see to it. Jesus already paid the price for those who will believe. Let us not only hear the Word, but be doers of it.

Although Jesus did give power to His disciples to forgive sin, it is in His name as parts of His body, and no one, **not even a Catholic priest, is "another Christ" on earth, as if he were taking Jesus's place in forgiving.** As Jesus warned, *"Then if anyone says to you, 'Look, here is the Christ!' or 'There!' do not believe it"* (Matt. 24:23–24).

I was so happy to learn in our Kinsman Redeemer's fields that we do not even need to wait for an earthly priest to mediate for us. **We can go right to God our Father to confess our sins through Jesus, our real Mediator and High Priest**: *"Let us therefore come boldly to the throne of grace, that we may obtain mercy and find grace to help in time of need"* (Heb. 4:16). Like a child we can come before the Father. There are times though when it is good to *"confess your trespasses to one another, and pray for one another, that you may be healed. The effective, fervent prayer of a righteous man avails much"* (Jas. 5:16).

It is especially good to confess to the person you have sinned against, mindful also that all sin is against God. But we can confess to a believer, a disciple of Jesus who has put on the righteousness of Christ and a righteous lifestyle, and so is *"a righteous man."* Sometimes, after some sins have been publicly confessed, it is easier to overcome *"the accuser of the brethren"* and receive the forgiveness of God for oneself. **Jesus washes away the stain and shame. It was done two thousand years ago, and it is received today.** The Bible says, *"As far as the east is from the west, so far has He removed our transgressions from us"* (Ps. 103:12).

Once we have received the Father's forgiveness for particular sins, they are gone and so is condemnation, His mercy is so great. Let us walk in repentance and **let Jesus guide us**. *"For I, the L*ORD *your God, will hold your right hand, saying to you, 'Fear not, I will help you'"* (Isa. 41:13). What a comfort that is!

Praise God, the RC Church taught us to love God and to hate sin and to seek to be in right relationship with God. However, when I was a child, when I confessed my sins to a priest I was told to do penance like a sin offering in reparation for sins. It might have been to say certain prayers a certain number of times or to do some good deed. But **Scripture does not say that a penance is necessary.** The Lamb of God was our sin offering, so we do not have to make one. Jesus made atonement with His blood. No penance is necessary. **Much more important than that, Jesus calls us to repentance, to do it the right way the next time with a change of heart.** We used to call it *Metanoia*: having a firm purpose of amendment. Jesus said, *"Repent for the kingdom of heaven is at hand"* (Matt. 4:17).

He is always ready to intercede for us and paid the price for our forgiveness, but He wants us to follow Him with a change of heart, to seek to make our will coincide with His in kingdom living.

King Jesus Can Reward and Execute Judgments

Paul said to Timothy, *"I charge you therefore before God and the Lord Jesus Christ, who will judge the living* [quick] *and the dead at His appearing and His kingdom.... Finally, there is laid up for me the crown of righteousness, which the Lord, the righteous Judge, will give to me on that day, and not to me only but also to all who have loved His appearing"* (2 Tim. 4:1, 8).

Kings and judges can reward good actions and punish evil, and Jesus can too. It is by faith that we are saved, but it is by our works that we are rewarded—or punished. Those who love His appearing can receive a *"crown of righteousness."* Jesus was crucified so believers could receive blessings instead of curses, escaping receiving what we deserve. But if we then do not repent but deliberately sin, we risk being chastised according to what we deserve. It is written:

> *He who is unjust, let him be unjust still; he who is filthy, let him be filthy still; he who is righteous, let him be righteous still; he who is holy, let him be holy still. "And behold, I am coming quickly, and My reward is with Me, to give to everyone according to his work. I am the Alpha and the Omega, the Beginning and the end, the First and the Last."*
>
> *Blessed are those who do His commandments* [wash their robes], *that they may have the right to the tree of life, and may enter through the gates into the city. But outside are dogs and sorcerers and sexually immoral and murderers and idolaters, and whoever loves and practices a lie.*
>
> *"I, Jesus, have sent My angel to testify to you these things in the churches. I am the Root and the Offspring of David, the Bright and Morning Star."* (Rev 22:11–16)

Hebrews 10:30–31 says, *"For we know Him who said, 'Vengeance is Mine, I will repay,' says the Lord. And again, 'The Lord will judge His people.' It is a fearful thing to fall into the hands of the living God."* We need the love of God, but the holy fear of the Lord is important too.

Jesus can come suddenly to judge His servants and His enemies while they are still living. God would like to settle accounts with them sooner rather than later, even if it means they have to reap the just punishment that they deserve for a while. But the refining fire of God can make them fit to live or die. If they sincerely choose to repent, chastisement can end and they can be mercifully released from prison to enjoy the gracious benefits of kingdom living again, loving one another as He has loved us.

Our job is to walk humbly with Jesus, forgive as we would like to be forgiven, and leave the rest to God. He sees everything, judging even heart motives. God revealed His judgments to the Old Testament high priest who was only a foreshadow of Jesus. How much more will He now reveal His judgments to His Son so Jesus can intercede, pronounce, and execute His Father's will. He can reward or chastise His own children, but He can also judge His enemies.

King Jesus rewards behaviour, bad and good. He comes with rewards, to destroy those who destroy the earth and to honor His servants and those who fear His name. Salvation is a free gift, but some things we do deserve good rewards.

John saw that an angel *"laid hold of the dragon, that serpent of old, who is the Devil and Satan, and bound him for a thousand years, and he cast him into the bottomless pit, and set a seal on him, so that he should deceive the nations no more till the thousand years were finished. But after these things he must be released for a little while"* (Rev. 20:2–3). But the martyred saints will have a thousand years of rest and peace reigning with King Jesus with no devil to deceive them.

Afterwards, *"Satan will be released from his prison"* (Rev. 20:7) and deceive nations gathering them to battle from the four corners of the earth, and **the final satanic rebellion will be crushed:** *"They … surrounded the camp of the saints and the beloved city. And fire came down from God out of heaven and devoured them. The devil, who deceived them, was cast into the lake of fire and brimstone where the beast and the false prophet are. And they will be tormented day and night forever and ever"* (Rev. 20:9–10).

Unrepented evil is punished. At the **Great White Throne Judgment,** John saw that others were thrown in too: *"The dead were judged according to their works, by the things which were written in the books.… And anyone not found written in the Book of Life was cast into the lake of fire"* (Rev. 20:12, 15).

However, **the redeemed will live forever in the marvelous presence of God, in a place prepared for them by Christ in New Jerusalem.** How glorious that will be!

Our King Can Intercede and Is Mighty in Battle

No one calls for justice,
Nor does any plead for truth....
It displeased Him
That there was no justice.
He saw that there was no man,
And wondered that there was no intercessor;
Therefore His own arm brought salvation for Him;
And His own righteousness, it sustained Him.
For He put on righteousness as a breastplate,
And a helmet of salvation on His head;
He put on the garments of vengeance for clothing,
And was clad with zeal as a cloak. (Isa. 59:4, 15–17)

In the time of Isaiah, the Lord saw that the people were separated from God because of their sin, and **no one was standing in the gap so that judgments might be held back and righteousness restored. So God, Himself, made the plea for the restoration of righteousness**, and went forth as the Mighty Warrior King to accomplish it and bring salvation to His people.

Today again Jesus stands in the gap for us as eternal High Priest and fights for us as the Mighty Warrior King. Intercession can be spiritual warfare in prayer and deed. **He can come again spiritually** as *"the Word of God"* and conquering *"King of kings and Lord of lords"* with *"the sword of the Spirit"* (Eph. 6:17) and His rod of authority to save us from our enemies. John was shown in a vision that He is not alone. He saw a heavenly host riding with Him, who could include intercessors following His commands: *"The armies in heaven, clothed in fine linen, white and clean"* (Rev. 19:14). Those born again can *"sit together in the heavenly places in Christ Jesus"* (Eph. 2:6). Jesus is called *"Faithful and True, and in righteousness He judges and makes war"* (Rev. 19:11).

Although part of His job involves executing justice and truth, the righteousness of God can include mercy. *"For the law was given through Moses, but grace and truth came through Jesus Christ"* (John 1:17).

Jesus prayed for a true unity for His followers today. When there is no one to stand in the gap, Jesus can, and He can include members of His body who lift up prayer requests to the throne of grace in His name, interceding through them by His Spirit. Christians born again from above might become a part of *"His own arm"* and be trained in intercession as His helpmate, to shoot arrows of deliverance. The arm gets its directions from the head and Jesus is the head of the body of Christ.

The enemy has sometimes tried to puff up intercessors with flattery, to think they deserve all the credit for the power of prayer, but **what good is an arm unless it is attached to His body getting its lifeblood power from Jesus?** No one person or prayer team is the whole arm of Christ. They might be His arm on the micro level in a situation. But on the macro level—citywide, nationwide, worldwide—they are only a tiny portion. Without the power of the name of Jesus they could do nothing lasting, so He deserves the glory and honour.

Spiritual Warfare

God is good, all the time. We see from history that even His vengeance is love and He is rich in mercy and remembers His covenant. Let us appreciate what He does for us and in love, follow Him. Today, if He calls us, we can stand in the gap or ride with Him as part of His arm(y). We are in a spiritual battle and in Old Testament times, kings always led their troops into battle, stirring their zeal. King Jesus only does the will of the Father. Being the living Word of God, wearing many crowns, He can lead His intercessors into battle spiritually in His name. *"The Lord shall go forth like a mighty man; He shall stir up His zeal like a man of war. He shall cry out, yes, shout aloud; He shall prevail against His enemies"* (Isa. 42:13).

Our Shepherd-King wants us to study His Word, listen to His voice, and do His will. Jesus said, *"My sheep hear My voice, and I know them, and they follow Me. And I give them eternal life, and they shall never perish; neither shall anyone snatch them out of My hand"* (John 10:27–28). When we intercede in His name, we have to do it with faith that He is able to save all the sheep who are given to Him. He is Almighty God who can anoint us from above with all the power we need, His passionate love is so great for His bride.

The Royal Bridge Serves Humbly

The word of the Lord came to me to declare at a Kingston prayer breakfast for pastors and intercessors during the nineties revival when many of us were experiencing new power, stronger than we had ever experienced before:

> *"Once, twice, three times I have heard,*
> *'Power comes from the Lord.'"*

God's adopted children are to be part of a *"royal priesthood"* (1 Pet. 2:9) by our baptism becoming priest, prophet, and king with and in Jesus. Yet knowing that whatever we have comes from God, we are not to promote ourselves; rather let the Lord promote and honor us. *"The King's daughter is all glorious within the palace; her clothing is woven with gold. She shall be brought to the King in robes of many colours"* (Ps. 45:13–14).

We are to be little in our own eyes no matter what responsibility the King gives us and *"glorious within,"* beautiful on the inside. He will dress us beautifully. As Samuel told Saul, *"When you were little in your own eyes, were you not head of the tribes of Israel? And did not the LORD anoint you king over Israel?"* (1 Sam. 15:17). Because he did not humble himself later, God humbled King Saul.

We are to be who God has created us to be. In the micro view, we might be a hand or arm of Christ in our circle; but I realized one day that next to Jesus in the macro view, we are each only tiny cells in His worldwide body.

However, we are not to have a "grasshopper" mentality either like the Jews who felt like grasshoppers next to their enemies and were afraid to enter when God told them to. Since **we have a big God**, when He sends us with Christ in us we have the power to be overcomers and to be *"more than conquerors through Him who loved us"* (Rom. 8:37), and to do mighty deeds in His name. So our boast should be in our God, not in ourselves. Our confidence is in His Word.

> *Give to the LORD the glory due His name.* (Ps. 96:8)

> *For who makes you differ from another? And what do you have that you did not receive? Now if you did indeed receive it, why do you boast as if you had not received it?* (1 Cor. 4:7)

> *My soul shall make its boast in the LORD; The humble shall hear of it and be glad.* (Ps. 34:2)

Jesus is humility personified, still bowing His will to that of the Father. When we humble ourselves in the sight of the Lord, He lifts us up. Philippians 2:5–9 says:

> *Let this mind be in you which was also in Christ Jesus, who being in the form of God, did not consider it robbery to be equal with God, but made Himself of no reputation, taking the form of a bondservant, and coming in the likeness of men. And being found in appearance as a man, He humbled Himself and became obedient to the point of death, even the death of the cross. Therefore God also has highly exalted Him and given Him the name which is above every other name.*

When I realized in the late nineties how deeply RCs had been deceived by the "Lady," I also noticed how Daniel and Nehemiah had stood in the gap when the Father's House was in ruins because His people had gone astray. So, like them, I confessed the sins of my ancestors and myself, standing in the gap with Jesus asking God to forgive us by His blood, severing any ungodly ties in His name, but keeping godly ties. Then He confirmed this by leading me over the years to large assemblies of believers at the times of March for Jesus and The CRY where we prayed the prayers of Daniel and Nehemiah for our nation all together in identificational repentance, remembering also: *"If My people who are called by My name will humble themselves, and pray and seek My face, and turn from their wicked ways, then I will hear from heaven, and will forgive their sin and heal their land"* (2 Chron. 7:14).

If people humble themselves in the sight of the Lord, turning from wicked ways, they can receive forgiveness for their sins, their *"garments"* washed as white as snow, washed by the Word and blood of Christ, and they can start fresh to follow our Lord Jesus clothed in Christ and His righteousness. We should not put God into a box though. Just by humbling ourselves to come to Jesus, He could say, *"Your sins are forgiven"* (Luke 7:48).

Instead of curses, blessings can go down family lines. *"For as many of you as were baptized into Christ have put on Christ"* (Gal. 3:27). What a privilege to put to death our old sin practices, be crucified with Christ, raised to new life with Him, and be born again from above! Then, when we follow Jesus, listening to His Word, He helps us overcome sin tendencies on an ongoing basis, and if we fall into sin again we can repent with sorrow for having trespassed against God and receive His forgiveness. He will never let us down.

Like the bride in the Song of Songs, we are to celebrate that our Beloved brings us to His banqueting table and His banner over His body, His bride, is love, and He wants us to be ready with mature love to open the door to Him and to minister with Him spirit to Spirit.

Aaron had his sons, the priests, to minister with him in some duties. They had to humble themselves first and wash their hands and feet with water from the bronze laver, made from mirrors: *"Aaron and his sons shall wash their hands and their feet in water from it. When they go into the tabernacle of meeting, or when they come near the altar to minister, to burn an offering made by fire to the* LORD, *they shall wash with water, lest they die"* (Ex. 30:19–20). **Jesus and His Word are our mirror** and **He gives us living water.** Jesus had and has His chosen ones, those who have been born again of water and the Spirit and have become parts of His *"royal priesthood"* (1 Pet. 2:9). He trains them to minister unto God and men and He even washed their feet at the Last Supper. When Peter protested, Jesus told him, *"'If I do not wash you, you have no part with Me.' Simon Peter said to Him, 'Lord, not my feet only, but also my hands and my head!' Jesus said to him, 'He who is bathed needs only to wash his feet, but is completely clean; and you are clean, but not all of you'"* (John 13:8–10).

Interestingly, it was His trained leaders, His chosen ones, whose feet He washed. He can baptize us and wash our heart and minds further with His Word, Spirit, and blood. *"You are already clean because of the word which I have spoken to you"* (John 15:3). As Mary said at Cana, *"Whatever He says to you, do it"* (John 2:5). After the servants filled the vessels, He turned the water for cleansing into wine.

Just as the apostles wore sandals and sometimes picked up the dust of the road, and were to shake off the dust of places which would not receive them, our feet are supposed to be shod *"with the preparation of the gospel of peace"* (Eph. 6:15). When we travel, mixing with others, sometimes we pick up dust of their wrong doctrines or practices. So Jesus warned of coming deception and instructed His trained servant-leaders not only to submit to having Him wash their feet, but to let other leaders wash them and to wash those of others themselves:

> *If I then, your Lord and Teacher, have washed your feet, you also ought to wash one another's feet. For I have given you an example, that you should do as I have done to you. Most assuredly, I say to you, a servant is not greater than his master; nor is he who is sent greater than he who sent him. If you know these things, blessed are you if you do them.* (John 13:14–17)

There are times when we might be called to wash feet by doing an act of charity and other times by speaking a word in love, or even by physically cleansing someone's feet. *"Perfect love casts out fear"* (1 John 4:18). A widow who was worthy of honour was one who *"has washed the saints' feet ... [and] she has diligently followed every good work"* (1 Tim. 5:10).

We should always remember that Jesus is the greatest of all and He humbly serves as God's holy adult Child. When they argued over who was greatest amongst them, Jesus told the twelve, *"If anyone desires to be first, he shall be last of all and servant of all"* (Mark 9:35). He gave them the example of a little child whom He set in their midst and took in His arms, and said, *"Whoever receives one of these little children in My name receives Me; and whoever receives Me, receives not Me but Him who sent Me"* (Mark 9:37). They were to serve and be on guard to receive the little ones whom Jesus would send among them. Receiving the sent one, you receive the Sender.

Jesus commended humility in His trained leaders: *"The kings of the Gentiles exercise lordship over them, and those who exercise authority over them are called 'benefactors.' But not so among you; on the contrary, he who is greatest among you, let him be as the younger, and he who governs as he who serves. For who is greater, he who sits at table, or he who serves? Is it not he who sits at the table? Yet I am among you as the One who serves"* (Luke 22:25–27).

A weapon of pride brought down King Hezekiah after he had done many good deeds to tear down idolatry and restore loyal worship. But he *"humbled himself for the pride of his heart, both he and the inhabitants of Jerusalem, so that the wrath of the Lord did not come upon them in [his days]"* (2 Chron. 32:26).

Jesus Teaches Us to Pray

We do not need to pray in legalistic, formal prayers, although sometimes they can be good to train us up. As a child I learned to pray the

Our Father, memorizing every word and comma. But then I learned that with it Jesus was actually showing His disciples **the manner, how to pray**. It was meant to be a template, not an absentminded ritual. Our prayers should glorify God and seek that His will be *"done on earth as it is in heaven."* We can pull down the will of God.

> *In this manner, therefore, pray:*
> *Our Father in heaven,*
> *Hallowed be Your name.*
> *Your kingdom come.*
> *Your will be done*
> *On earth as it is in heaven.*
> *Give us this day our daily bread.*
> *And forgive us our debts,*
> *As we forgive our debtors.*
> *And do not lead us into temptation,*
> *But deliver us from the evil one.*
> *For Yours is the kingdom and the power and the glory forever.*
> *Amen.* (Matt. 6:9–13)

Chapter 19
The Ministry of Reconciliation

Jesus shares with believers His ministry of reconciling people to the Father. As preparation, it is good to be reconciled ourselves. We can pray like David, asking God to reveal to us any way we might have displeased Him so we can repent.

> *Cleanse me from secret faults.*
> *Keep back Your servant from presumptuous sins;*
> *Let them not have dominion over me,*
> *Then I shall be blameless,*
> *and I shall be innocent of great transgression.* (Ps. 19:12–13)

Mark 11:25–26 says, *"And whenever you stand praying, if you have anything against anyone, forgive him, that your Father in heaven may also forgive you your trespasses. But if you do not forgive, neither will your Father in heaven forgive your trespasses."* Jesus cleanses and reconciles us, making us new creations ready to serve Him.

Intercessors should keep a clear conscience before God, repenting when necessary. Therefore, when coming into the Lord's presence with praise and thanksgiving, it is good to ask Him to forgive our trespasses, and for us to forgive those who trespass against us. People can be reconciled because God will grant them forgiveness for their sins or trespasses against Him, in the same way that they forgive those who trespass against them. Unforgiveness could block their prayers.

It is good to pray from an attitude of gratitude. *"In everything give thanks; for this is the will of God in Christ Jesus for you"* (1 Thess. 5:18). We can pray Scriptures or from the heart, be led by the Spirit, or ask the Father for a need in the name of His Son, the Mediator. The psalms and epistles include many prayers which we can personalize and pray.

> *Therefore strengthen the hands which hang down, and the feeble knees* [drooping hands and weak knees], *and make straight paths for your feet, so that what is lame may not be dislocated, but rather be healed. Pursue peace with all people and holiness, without which no one will see the Lord: looking carefully lest anyone fall short of the grace of God; lest any root of bitterness springing up cause trouble, and by this many become defiled; lest there be any fornicator or profane person like Esau, who for one morsel of food sold his birthright.* (Heb. 12:12–16)

We are called to be pray-ers in unity, bending our knees only to the Lord, not to idols, repenting quickly if Holy Spirit convinces us of sin in our life, and forgiving others the way we would like God to forgive us. We need His revelation, love, and grace.

We are *"to walk worthy of the calling with which you were called, with all lowliness and gentleness, with longsuffering, bearing with one another in love, endeavoring to keep the unity of the Spirit in the bond of peace.... One God and Father of all, who is above all, and through all, and in you all. But to each one of us grace was given according to the measure of Christ's gift"* (Eph. 4:1–3, 6–7). We may not all agree on every detail, but in humility we should seek the Lord's leading when we pray, pouring out our hearts to God, and endeavour *"to keep the unity of the Spirit in the bond of peace."*

God Was in Christ Reconciling the World to Himself

> *Therefore, if anyone is in Christ, he is a new creation; old things have passed away; behold, all things have become new. Now all things are of God, who has reconciled us to Himself through Jesus Christ, and has given us the ministry of reconciliation, that is, that God was in Christ reconciling the world to Himself, not imputing their trespasses to them, and has committed to us the word of reconciliation. Now then, we are ambassadors for Christ, as though God were pleading* [making his appeal] *through us: we implore you on Christ's behalf, be reconciled to God. For He made Him who knew no sin to be sin for us, that we might become the righteousness of God in Him.* (2 Cor. 5:17–21)

Jesus imputes righteousness to believers. Though innocent, at the cross He became like the two goats at the Day of Atonement. One became the scapegoat upon whom the high priest imparted the sins of the people and sent it outside the city to die. The other one was put to death as a sin offering and it's blood was brought into the Holy of holies in atonement for the sins of *"the people"* (Lev. 16:15). Jesus, though innocent, had our sin imparted to Him, drawing it unto Himself like iron filings to a magnet, and was put to death, His blood making atonement so that we could start out with a clean slate, a pure heart, His righteousness upon us.

Impute means "to set to the account of a person, or charge."[20] **The repentant, though guilty, are given the privilege of having their sins and trespasses not set to their account, but having the righteousness of God set to their account instead.** Therefore, they are able to lead others to become reconciled with God as well, with the help of the Lord.

---

20   James Fernald, LHD, *Concise Standard Dictionary* (New York & London: Funk and Wagnalls Co. 1942), 267

He became a sin offering for us, taking our sin and punishment upon Himself, and we become a righteousness offering with Him if we are *"in Christ,"* taking His righteousness and grace upon ourselves so we can serve God and help others to do likewise. We can resolve, with Jesus: *"I have come to do Your will, O God"* (Heb. 10:9). **Charles Wesley's Explanatory Notes** says for 2 Corinthians 5:21 that we **"might through Him be invested with that righteousness, first imputed to us, then implanted in us, which is in every sense the righteousness of God."** [21]

Jesus also implants righteousness in believers over time. Some people like to say, "I am the righteousness of God." But technically, I believe **only Jesus can truly make that claim** as it stands because **only God is *"I Am Who I Am"* (Ex. 3:14) all the time.** Let us remember that **it is not that God gets His righteousness from us, but that we get ours from Him** if we are *"found in Him, not having my own righteousness, which is from the law, but that which is through faith in Christ, the righteousness which is from God by faith"* (Phil. 3:9).

> *I will greatly rejoice in the* Lord,
> *My soul shall be joyful in my God;*
> *For He has clothed me with the garments of salvation,*
> *He has covered me with the robe of righteousness,*
> *As a bridegroom decks himself with ornaments,*
> *And as a bride adorns herself with her jewels.*
> *For as the earth brings forth its bud,*
> *As the garden causes the things that are sown in it to spring forth,*
> *So the Lord* God *will cause righteousness and praise to spring forth before all the nations.* (Isa. 61:10–11)

Obedience to God's Law made one righteous, but His people found that occasionally they disobeyed the Law. If we sin, which is disobeying God's Word, thank God by faith we can be made righteous

---

21   Rick Meyers, e-Sword, *John Wesley's Explanatory Notes*, commenting on 2 Corinthians 5:21. https://www.e-sword.net/.

again when we confess to God because, *"He made Him who knew no sin to be sin for us, that we might become the righteousness of God in Him"* (2 Cor. 5:21). *"Might become"* or *"be made"* (KJV) righteous are active verbs. It is done already at the cross, and it is being done in the lives of those in Christ. **Jesus is Yahweh Tsidkenu: *"The Lord [is] our righteousness."***

> *"Behold, the days are coming," says the Lord,*
> *"That I will raise to David a Branch of righteousness;*
> *A King shall reign and prosper,*
> *And execute judgment and righteousness in the earth.*
> *In His days Judah will be saved,*
> *And Israel will dwell safely,*
> *Now this is His name by which He will be called:*
> THE LORD OUR RIGHTEOUSNESS." (Jer. 23:5–6)

His righteousness comes on us by faith when we are justified by faith, not because of any good works; but that does not mean that we should not do the good works that God has for us to do. Jesus will separate His sheep from the goats on the basis of deeds done in loving compassion. We are clothed in His righteousness by faith as a free gift, but we become His righteousness, grow into it, as we follow Jesus, doing what He does, being sanctified and transformed from glory to glory. *"But we all ... beholding as in a mirror the glory of the Lord, are being transformed* [changed] *into the same image from glory to glory, just as by the Spirit of the Lord"* (2 Cor. 3:18).

> *And this I pray, that your love may abound still more and more in knowledge and all discernment, that you may approve the things that are excellent, that you may be sincere and without offense till the day of Christ, being filled with the fruits of righteousness which are by Jesus Christ, to the glory and praise of God.* (Phil. 1:9–11)

Believers *"become the righteousness of God in Him"* (2 Cor. 5:21). When we are *"baptized into Christ,"* we *"put on Christ"* (Gal. 3:27). We put off the old man and his ways, are renewed in the spirit of our minds, and *"put on the new man which was created according to God, in true righteousness and holiness"* (Eph. 4:24). **Those words, "become" and "in Him," are important.** We can grow in His character, and in overcoming sin patterns, being made righteous by faith **because we are parts of His body**, and we can wear His righteousness as a *"breastplate"* (Eph. 6:14). *"For in* [the gospel of Christ] *the righteousness of God is revealed from faith to faith; as it is written, 'The just shall live by faith'"* (Rom. 1:17).

But *"faith without works is dead"* (Jas. 2:19). James said that Abraham was *"justified by works when he offered Isaac his son on the altar. Do you see that faith was working together with his works, and by works faith was made perfect?"* (Jas. 2:21–22). Although a believer should choose obedience and to remain righteous, God knows that there are times when we will miss the mark. Jesus told us to **seek** His righteousness; so we are to be made right with God, to be in right relationship with Him, and to practice righteousness going from *"faith to faith"* as more of His righteous ways are revealed to us. *"But seek first the kingdom of God and His righteousness, and all these things shall be added to you"* (Matt. 6:33). One day we will receive a white robe that will never have a stain on it again. In the meantime, thank God the blood of the Lamb and doing His will keeps us clean, following Christ.

Therefore, doing certain live works is important too, the *"good works, which God prepared beforehand that we should walk in them"* (Eph. 2:10). The bride of Christ will have a wedding gown of *"fine linen, clean and bright, for the fine linen is the righteous acts of the saints"* (Rev. 19:8). **The bride will also take on her husband's name: *"And this is the name by which she will be called: 'THE LORD OUR RIGHTEOUSNESS'"*** (Jer. 33:16). She will not be called, "I am His righteousness."

As we are transformed, we *"become"* more like His righteousness inside, doing righteous deeds under His direction. Pieces of righteous material are being sewn together now for the bride. Obedience to God's loving will is still important for those who want to be intercessors with and in Christ, under His Lordship. *"Whoever does not practice righteousness is not of God, nor is he who does not love his brother"* (1 John 3:10). Noah believed God and obeyed Him. *"By faith Noah, being divinely warned of things not yet seen, moved with godly fear, prepared an ark for the saving of his household, by which he condemned the world and became heir of the righteousness which is according to faith"* (Heb. 11:7). May the Good Shepherd lead. *"He leads me in the paths of righteousness for His name's sake"* (Ps. 23:3).

As the *"chief cornerstone,"* **a connector**, Jesus is not only the true bridge between mankind and God, but between men. Just as the Father was in the Son reconciling the world to Himself, now Jesus and the Father and His Spirit are in true believers performing the reconciliation ministry which He entrusts to His disciples in His name. Because people's trespasses will no longer be imputed to them once forgiven, they can walk in the freedom of adopted sons of God. He will not call their forgiven sins to mind.

> *Judge not, that you be not judged. For with what judgment you judge, you will be judged; and with the measure you use, it will be measured back to you. And why do you look at the speck in your brother's eye, but do not consider the plank in your own eye? Or how can you say to your brother, "Let me remove the speck from your eye"; and look, a plank is in your own eye? Hypocrite! First remove the plank from your own eye, and then you will see clearly to remove the speck from your brother's eye.* (Matt. 7:1–5)

We can ask our Big Brother Jesus for help to remove any plank from our eye so we can help others in the way that God has helped us. We are not to judge others on our own, because appearances can be deceiving. We need to check our own hearts first. But if God shows us something, like dirt they have picked up on the road, we can pray that God will mercifully shower them with His love, washing away filthy stains. If God opens the door for us to speak to them in love, then we can wash their feet in His name. *"Brethren, if a man is overtaken in any trespass, you who are spiritual restore such a one in a spirit of gentleness, considering yourself lest you also be tempted. Bear one another's burden and so fulfil the law of Christ"* (Gal. 6:1–2).

There are times though when the Lord wants us to say nothing; that happened to me once with a traveling evangelist. When a sin was evident, the Lord called me to intercede privately and to say nothing to anyone including the person. Praise God, I noticed a difference the next time the evangelist spoke. God had answered my prayer.

Also, if the door is closed, we must wait on Him. Some people are just not ready yet to hear His Word or sound teaching, even if it could bring reconciliation with God and possibly with others. *"Do not give what is holy to the dogs; nor cast your pearls before swine, lest they trample them under their feet, and turn and tear you in pieces"* (Matt. 7:6).

Jesus Helps His People Carry Their Cross

> *Jesus said to His disciples, "If anyone desires to come after Me, let him deny himself, and take up his cross, and follow Me. For whoever desires to save his life will lose it, but whoever loses his life for My sake will find it. For what profit is it to a man if he gains the whole world, and loses his own soul? Or what will a man give in exchange for his soul? For the Son of Man will come in the glory of His Father with His angels, and then He will reward each according to his works."* (Matt. 16:24–27)

The King came on Palm Sunday and He is coming again and is with believers always.

I asked the Lord around 1981 what it meant to carry my cross and He told me, *"Fulfill the duties of your state in life."* He gave me a little glimpse of what that meant over the next years, and it was truly overwhelming to me. But God is so gracious! It is Jesus who is the Saviour of the world. He reminded me that when His cross became too heavy for Him, that His Father provided Simon the Cyrene to help Jesus shoulder it, and if my cross got to be too much for me, He would provide help, and He has, thanks be to God.

Whether we are a housewife for Jesus, a construction worker as my husband was, a politician, or a missionary, a disciple should choose to pick up his or her cross with the strength of the joy of the Lord, trusting Jesus to lead. *"Behold, I have come to do Your will, O God"* (Heb. 10:9). And **yoked to Jesus, He will carry the heaviest part.** If it is too heavy, then perhaps it is not for us and we should just leave it with Him. He truly lightens any burden He has designed for us when we bring it to Him because He will carry it with us. He will lead and give us rest when we trust Him to do so. After all, He succeeded because He came to the Father.

Even while trying to bring others to Christ, we are not to compromise with the world (*"Babylon"*) and seducing spirits. *"For what profit is it to a man if he gains the whole world, and loses his own soul?"* (Luke 9:25). But willing to risk our lives that lives may be saved, we are to follow Jesus and do what He says to do in humility, purity, and truth, giving Him the praise He is due.

> *I beseech you therefore, brethren, by the mercies of God, that you present your bodies a living sacrifice, holy, acceptable to God, which is your reasonable service. And do not be conformed to this world, but be transformed by the renewing of your mind, that you may prove what is that good and acceptable and perfect will of God.* (Rom. 12:1–2)

Interceding

He taught His disciples **how to join with Him in intercession and to pray in His name effectively. They were to abide in His love and He in them by keeping His commandments.**

> *If you keep My commandments, you will abide in My love, just as I have kept My Father's commandments and abide in His love. These*

things I have spoken to you that My joy may remain in you, and that your joy may be full. This is My commandment, that you love one another as I have loved you. Greater love has no one than this, than to lay down one's life for his friends. You are My friends if you do whatever I command you. [He chose and appointed them and disciples today to] *go and bear fruit, and that your fruit should remain, that whatever you ask the Father in My name He may give you. These things I command you, that you love one another.* (John 15:10–14, 17)

The high priestly job of interceding, reconciling His people to the Father, belongs to Jesus; yet He allows His disciples to work with Him as God makes His appeal through us.

When I made a banner illustrating a *rhema* word of God with a picture of Jesus carrying His cross with Simon's assistance, the Holy Spirit gave me a song: *"Hold your head up high."* It helped me to see that we should hold our head up high carrying our cross as Jesus would have, with a holy confidence, not arrogance. So that is how I pictured Him.

"You can choose to rejoice," was a prophetic word at a charismatic conference. It has encouraged me in some of the hardest moments of my life making it easier to pray. I found that when I chose to rejoice, I could always find something about which to praise God. I would put my problem in Jesus's hands and remember the song, *"Put on a garment of praise for a spirit of heaviness, lift up your heart and sing,"* and the Lord would lift my drooping spirit as I sang His praise. God is so good and so wise.

"Blessed are you when they revile and persecute you, and say all kinds of evil against you falsely for My sake. Rejoice and be exceedingly glad, for great is your reward in heaven, for so they persecuted the prophets who were before you" (Matt. 5:11–12). **Knowing this word has saved my soul, the seat of my emotions, mind, and will, and kept me from going into a deep depression.** You can be sad and happy at the same

time if you believe this word and rejoice in the Lord. The mourning soon turns into dancing. Praise the Lord! So then you can intercede for someone else experiencing persecution, asking God to strengthen them with His joy that they may stand firm in their faith and respond appropriately.

I remember being verbally persecuted by my husband one day. I was very disappointed but forgave him because he did not know what he was doing. Then I went over to a friend's house for prayer. As I stood there weeping while we four women prayed, the Lord said to me, *"Rejoice and leap on high on that day."* So, trusting His word, I began to jump, leaping up, and it seemed so comical that we all started to laugh and sadness vanished. Praise the Lord! **God knows best! Follow His Word.**

Join Jesus in Warfare Praying

Praise that is radically rooted in Christ is warfare.

> *Rejoice in the Lord always. Again I will say, rejoice! Let your gentleness be known to all men. The Lord is at hand. Be anxious for nothing, but in everything by prayer and supplication, with thanksgiving, let your requests be known to God; and the peace of God, which surpasses all understanding, will guard your hearts and minds through Christ Jesus. Finally brethren, whatever things are true, whatever things are noble, whatever things are just, whatever things are pure, whatever things are lovely, whatever things are of good report, if there is any virtue and if there is anything praiseworthy—meditate on these things.* (Phil. 4:4–8)

The Lord told me in the nineties at a March for Jesus prayer rally, *"That is spiritual warfare."* **Cast your cares on the Lord and magnify the good things God is doing.** The peace and faithfulness of God is your defense as you place your trust in Him and His Word. It is a shield about you so everyone's problems do not get you down. You lift them up to Jesus and stand ready to labour in prayer and deed with

Him, letting His Spirit lead you. **Trusting Him to help** is like putting the requests into a file folder in the filing cabinet and shutting the door after dealing with them, resting in Christ as you wait on Him, ready for Him to act and to do His bidding. This rest conquers anxiety. I am a witness of that because I used to be a great worrier, but now have the peace of Christ. Praise God! As He told me years ago, *"In returning and rest you shall be saved, in quietness and confidence shall be your strength"* (Isa. 30:15).

A decade later, as we were singing songs of praise to Him at a prayer meeting at Kingston Gospel Temple, the word of the Lord came to me, *"Praise is a powerful weapon."* Listening to the Lord, we were prophetically pray-singing out any songs the Holy Spirit gave us, and others were just singing from the heart. **Praising His name in faith for what He will do in answer to your prayers is warfare, especially if you have received a *rhema* word from Him.** When you align your actions with God's prophetic word, you are in alignment with His will. I love the next passage because that is what King Jehoshaphat did. Going into battle, he sent Judah (the "praisers"), out first because **he believed God and knew they would not have to fight. The battle was the Lord's and victory was assured.**

Powerful enemies had begun to come against him with a multitude of troops; so with a holy fear of the Lord, Jehoshaphat humbled himself to call on the Name, calling all Judah to fast and gather to *"ask help from the L*ORD*"* (2 Chron. 20:4). He asked God to judge these three, the people of Ammon and Moab (from Lot's daughters' incest) and Mount Seir (descendants of Esau). (See 2 Chronicles 20:1–12.) (It is like an approaching onslaught of lust against a faithful leader.) He prayed:

> *"O our God, will You not judge them? For we have no power against this great multitude that is coming against us; nor do we know what to do, but our eyes are upon You."* Now all Judah, with their little ones, their wives, and their children, stood before the L*ORD*. [And Jahaziel prophesied,] *"Do not be afraid nor dismayed*

because of this great multitude, for the battle is not yours, but God's. Tomorrow go down against them. You will not need to fight in this battle. Position yourselves, stand still and see the salvation of the LORD, *who is with you, O Judah and Jerusalem!' Do not fear nor be dismayed; tomorrow go out against them, for the* LORD *is with you."* [God caused His people to go down there by assuring them of His presence with them in the battle and gave them strategy. God would fight for them.] *And Jehoshaphat bowed his head with his face to the ground, and all Judah and the inhabitants of Jerusalem bowed before the* LORD, *worshiping the* LORD. [Worship gets God's attention, especially when it is done with a heart of loving appreciation.] *Then the Levites ... the Korahites, stood up to praise the* LORD *God of Israel with voices loud and high....* [The king encouraged them early the next morning to trust God.] *And when he had consulted with the people, he appointed those who should sing to the* LORD, *and who should praise the beauty of holiness, as they went out before the army and were saying:*

"Praise the LORD,
For His mercy endures forever."

Now when they began to sing and to praise, the LORD *set ambushes against the people of Ammon, Moab, and Mount Seir, who had come against Judah; and they were defeated.... They helped to destroy one another ...* [and the army of Judah found] *their dead bodies, fallen on the earth. No one had escaped.... They found among them an abundance of valuables ... and they were three days gathering the spoil because there was so much.* [So the Valley of Jehoshaphat was named] *the Valley of Berachah* [Blessing], *for there they blessed the* LORD. (2 Chron. 20:12–26)

Jehoshaphat had given them some key advice, giving 20/20 vision: "Believe in the LORD *your God, and you shall be established; believe His prophets, and you shall prosper"* (2 Chron. 20:20). They walked in faith and God gave them the victory as He said He would. **It is like praying**

without doubting. And they made sure to **express their gratitude**, both praising Him for His mercy beforehand and blessing Him when all was done. That is good for us to do when we want to see someone reconciled with Christ. Doubtless, *"He who continually goes forth weeping, bearing seed for sowing, shall doubtless come again with rejoicing, bringing his sheaves with him"* (Ps. 126:6).

> **But thanks be to God, who gives us the victory through our Lord Jesus Christ.**
>
> **Therefore, my beloved brethren, be steadfast, immovable, always abounding in the work of the Lord, knowing that your labor is not in vain in the Lord.** (1 Cor. 15:57–58)

Having received mercy, we can dispense it in love. Through Christ, with Christ and in Christ the Mediator, we take our place before God, able to sympathize with others in their weakness, to love our neighbour as ourselves. *"Christ in you, the hope of glory"* (Col. 1:27).

Let us join Jesus in warfare prayer, believing His Word. Sometimes it is through praise songs. Paul made it plain to Timothy that Christians are to pray various types of prayers to God, and to stand in the gap between God and people interceding as parts of the body of Christ, keeping in mind that Jesus is the one true Mediator between us. Prayers were to be made for all people, including spiritual and governmental leaders, *"for kings and all who are in authority"* (1 Tim: 2:2). In their blessing is our blessing that *"we may lead a quiet and peaceable life in all godliness and reverence"* (1 Tim. 2:2). We are to pray in Christ, in His name, according to His will, with an attitude of gratitude giving thanks to God, and Jesus does the work of interceding through us. Whether a leader is good or bad, he would have no authority if God had not given it to him. The children of Israel were even commanded by God to pray for their enemy, the king of Babylon, when they were captives there. We are to bless and love our enemies. *"The king's heart is in the hand of the* Lord, *like the rivers of water; He turns it wherever He wishes"* (Prov. 21:1).

Jesus said, *"Blessed are the peacemakers, for they shall be called sons of God"* (Matt. 5:9). The apostle Paul said, *"I desire therefore that the men pray everywhere, lifting up holy hands, without wrath or doubting, in like manner also, that the women adorn themselves in modest apparel ... with good works"* (1 Tim. 2:8–9). And it is pleasing to God that we desire to work with His Son, the Mediator, because He *"desires all men to be saved and to come to the knowledge of the truth"* (1 Tim. 2:4).

Praying in confident humility, whatever our prayer posture, is great. However, the spirit of what Moses did is important, because as long as he remained praying with uplifted hands, his two friends supporting him, Joshua had victory over the Amalekites. Sometimes we need the **power of agreement** when battles are tough, and to stay put on Jesus the Rock.

Moses began standing, but his *"hands became heavy; so they took a stone and put it under him, and he sat on it. And Aaron and Hur supported his hands, one on one side, and the other on the other side; and his hands were steady until the going down of the sun. So Joshua defeated Amalek and his people with the edge of the sword"* (Ex. 17:12–13).

Arms can get "heavy" when a weapon of discouragement or disappointment is forged against us. **But if we recognize the tactic, we can trust God and pray in the opposite spirit.** Abraham waited twenty-five years, but Isaac was born. *"Hope deferred makes the heart sick, but when the desire comes, it is a tree of life"* (Prov. 13:12). So we must remember that if we are following the Lord as His servants, *"No weapon formed against you shall prosper, and every tongue which rises against you in judgment you shall condemn"* (Isa. 54:17).

Reminding someone of a pertinent word of the Lord, our Rock, especially a *rhema* word, is like putting a stone under Moses; and agreeing with the person in prayer is like holding up his hands. It encourages him to remain confident in hope. And when God gives us a prophetic word to fight with, it is like Joshua defeating the enemy with the edge of the sword. When we battle in prayer and deed, we need to put on the full armour of Christ, and to be abiding in the vine. *"If you abide in me, and my words abide in you, ask whatever you will and it shall be done for you. By this my Father is glorified, that you bear much fruit, and so prove to be my disciples"* (John 15:7–8 RSV).

John 14:12–14 says, *"Most assuredly I say to you, he who believes in Me, the works that I do he will do also; and greater works than these he will do, because I go to My Father. And whatever you ask in My name, that I will do, that the Father may be glorified in the Son. If you ask anything in My name I will do it."*

Jesus will eternally keep His position of Mediator, High Priest, Intercessor, Reconciler, bridging the gap. He gave authority to His disciples who do His will, saints alive on earth, to stand with, within, under, and on Him, our Rock, **in His name**, like mighty warriors, because He is the Mighty Warrior King who dwells within us and reigns over us. **We can be like mighty trestlework because He is like a mighty trestle bridge and the strengthening rebar within it.** *"Do you not believe that I am in the Father and the Father in Me? The words that I speak to you I do not speak on My own authority; but the Father who dwells in Me does the works"* (John 14:10). (See also John 14:20, 23.) With Him in us and us in Him, the weak can say, in truth, *"I am strong"* (Joel 3:10), because He enables us to overcome our weakness. **His brethren will do greater works in His name because Jesus, through His Spirit, is doing them through them in many places at the same time.** He has multitudes to redeem with His prophetic evangelism through His servants.

The worshipful prayers of the faithful saints on earth ascend to God as a sweet-smelling offering, which is gathered in heavenly bowls. The twenty-four elders worshiping prostrate around the throne in heaven, *"each having a harp, and golden bowls full of incense, which are the prayers of the saints,"* look forward to the coming of New Jerusalem and praise the Lamb for being worthy, saying He *"redeemed us to God by* [His] *blood out of every tribe and tongue and people and nation, and have made us kings and priests to our God; and we shall reign on the earth"* (Rev. 5:8–10). Jesus will come again with all His holy ones. His royal priesthood shall reign with Him and we can train for that now, receiving and using the gifts God chooses for us.

> *And who is he who will harm you if you become followers of what is good? But even if you should suffer for righteousness' sake, you are blessed. "And do not be afraid of their threats, nor be troubled."* [Jesus knows the truth about you and can encourage and defend you and even give you the words to say, so rejoice.] *But sanctify the Lord God in your hearts, and always be ready to give a defense to everyone who asks you a reason for the hope that is in you, with meekness and fear; having a good conscience, that when they defame you as evildoers, those who revile your good conduct in Christ may be ashamed. For it is better, if it is the will of God, to suffer for doing good than for doing evil.* (1 Pet. 3:13–17)

His Word is still speaking to us.

Part of Jesus's Work Is in the Restoring of Ruined Cities

Sin can affect a person plus his family and even the land, especially when the sin is widespread. **Many cities have been destroyed by fire and by storms of biblical proportions in recent years. Yet so many times you also hear of the faithful being spared or receiving mercy.** Cities are not ruined because of God who judges them, sometimes leveling them—that is, **it is not God's fault**; but rather they can be ruined because of unrepented sinfulness bringing down curses on the land. That happened to all of Jericho, except for Rahab's family, and when all of Israel suffered because of the deliberate sin of Achan at Jericho.

Jesus:*...began to rebuke the cities in which most of His mighty works had been done, because they did not repent: "Woe to you, Chorazin! Woe to you, Bethsaida! For if the mighty works which were done in you had been done in Tyre and Sidon, they would have* *repented long ago in sackcloth and ashes. But I say to you, it will be more tolerable for Tyre and Sidon in the day of judgment than for you. And you, Capernaum, who are exalted to heaven, will be brought down to Hades; for if the mighty works which were done in you had been done in Sodom, it would have remained until this day. But I say to you that it shall be more tolerable for the land of Sodom in the day of judgment than for you."* (Matt. 11:20–24)

People ran after the prophet Ezekiel to hear what God was saying, but did not act on it. God said, *"So they come to you as people do, they sit before you as My people, and they hear your words, but they do not do them; for with their mouth they show much love, but their hearts pursue their own gain"* (Ezek. 33:31). **To avoid ruining our cities**, people are to *"be doers of the word, and not hearers only, deceiving yourselves"* (Jas. 1:22).

The Lord said to me once, *"Nancy Salvador, desolations are decreed!"* Sin has ruined many cities and many have been ripe for judgment. Thank God for the times when in wrath He has remembered mercy. But our God is both just and in the restoration business.

We are called to have such love that we are willing to *"lay down one's life for his friends"* (John 15:13), upholding faith in Jesus. **Some might run in to an area to help after a disaster or risk their lives that lives may be saved and cared for** (like frontline health staff in the COVID-19 pandemic). And others might send resources so others can go. I remember a Christian couple who often went into disaster areas as part of a team **to physically rebuild it, and some go to spiritually rebuild**. Sometimes Christians endure persecution, willing to even have their lives unjustly restricted or taken from them if need be, that sin may be resisted and overcome, and sheep cared for in ruined cities. Suffering in some form is part of a disciple's job description.

Some, even today, have so completely surrendered their lives to Jesus in the battle against sin that they have suffered unjustly and even have shed their blood with the holy boldness God gives rather than deny Him. They know that they will have eternal life with Christ and

God will deal with their oppressors. *"For consider Him who endured such hostility from sinners against Himself, lest you become weary and discouraged in your souls. You have not yet resisted to bloodshed, striving against sin"* (Heb. 12:3–4).

A true martyr is a faithful witness for Jesus and loves Him and His sheep passionately. Nothing can separate him from God's love, for *"we are more than conquerors through Him who loves us"* (Rom. 8:37). **A true martyr is persecuted and killed for his faith, but a true martyr does not commit suicide or purposely kill innocent people**, because that would be sin. Instead, he shoulders the cross given him by God with the joy of the Lord and blesses *"those who curse* [Him], *and* [prays] *for those who spitefully use* Him]*"* (Luke 6:28).

Peter had been a ruined individual, a *"waste place,"* after denying Christ. Knowing Peter's sorrow, Jesus forgave and restored him with His love and willingness to work with Peter again. Jesus told him that if he loved Him, to feed and tend His sheep and lambs. *"Break forth into joy, sing together, you waste places of Jerusalem! For the* LORD *has comforted His people, He has redeemed Jerusalem"* (Isa. 52:9).

Jesus also told Peter, *"'Most assuredly, I say to you, when you were younger, you girded yourself and walked where you wished; but when you are old, you will stretch out your hands, and another will gird you and carry you where you do not wish.' This He spoke, signifying by what death he would glorify God. And when He had spoken this, He said to him, 'Follow Me'"* (John 21:18–19). Peter preached boldly after Pentecost and later was crucified for his faith, choosing that it be upside down, and the other apostles too were martyred, except John, although he too was persecuted.

We are saved by faith to walk in the works God has prepared for us: *"And the King will answer and say to them, 'Assuredly I say to you, inasmuch as you did it to one of the least of these My brethren, you did it to Me'"* (Matt. 25:40). **The least of Jesus's brethren, even *"old waste places,"* have the potential of being the great ones of His brethren.** We can cooperate with Jesus in their restoration by showing them love, pouring ourselves out for them in their time of need—be it spiritual or physical, food, clothing, justice—investing into their future, by fasting as in Isaiah 58.

> *Those from among you*
> *Shall build the old waste places;*
> *You shall raise up the foundations of many generations;*
> *And you shall be called the Repairer of the Breach,*
> *The Restorer of Streets to Dwell In.* (Isa. 58:12)

There are actual cities in our time which have undergone transformation by repentance and the outpouring of the Holy Spirit.

After the Lord has given His people a new heart and His Holy Spirit and washed them clean as He promised in Ezekiel 36, restoring people and the land: *"Thus says the Lord GOD: 'I will also let the house of Israel inquire of Me to do this for them: I will increase their men like a flock. Like a flock offered as holy sacrifices, like the flock at Jerusalem on its feast days, so shall the ruined cities be filled with flocks of men. Then they shall know that I am the LORD'"* (Ezek. 36:37–38). **Restored cities will have believers full of the love of God, unafraid to lay down their lives for the gospel and their friends.**

When ruined cities are restored by Christ with the aid of Christians, consecrated in the truth of God's Word, it is a witness that Jesus is Lord. Part of the Elijah task is the restoration of all things, but not without the help and grace of the Lord. **In the beginning, God created mankind perfectly and Jesus came so that refining fellowship with Him could be restored, causing His bride to be perfected.** John saw that a day will come when there will be a thousand years of peace with no devil, and then even a better day when His people will be completely restored in New Jerusalem. *"Nevertheless we, according to His promise, look for new heavens and a new earth in which righteousness dwells. Therefore, beloved, looking forward to these things, be diligent to be* *found by Him in peace, without spot and blameless"* (2 Pet. 3:13–14; see Eph. 5:27).

Character of Intercessors

Ministering in faith and love is important. Jesus made it clear that He wanted His disciples to join Him in His priestly function of ministering unto the Father, exhorting His disciples, since He would no longer be bodily on earth. But we are to be faithful—asking in faith and believing, for *"he who believes on Him will by no means be put to shame"* (1 Pet. 2:6). James warned about being double-minded: *"But let him ask in faith, with no doubting, for he who doubts is like a wave of the sea driven and tossed by the wind. For let not that man suppose that he will receive anything from the Lord; he is a double-minded man, unstable in all his ways"* (Jas. 1:6–8).

"Now faith is the substance of things hoped for, the evidence of things not seen" (Heb. 11:1). Faith is like ordering a new stove, paying for it, and waiting to have it delivered. Even before you see it in your kitchen, you know that stove is yours. *"But without faith it is impossible to please Him, for he who comes to God must believe that He is, and that He is a rewarder of those who diligently seek Him"* (Heb. 11:6).

Jesus wants believers to be like a faithful tree planted by living water that has leaves for the healing of the nations and bears fruit in its season for when He is hungry. After Jesus cursed the unresponsive fig tree and it withered, He told His disciples, *"Have faith in God. For assuredly, I say to you, whoever says to this mountain, 'Be removed and be cast into the sea,' and does not doubt in his heart, but believes that those things he says will be done, he will have whatever he says. Therefore I say to you, whatever things you ask when you pray, believe that you receive them, and you will have them"* (Mark 11:24). Intercessors must believe that when they use the authority of the believer, in Jesus's name, and speak to problems which are like mountains or unresponsive fig trees, that a change will occur. What we pray for, we will receive if we only believe.

Eternally, Jesus lives to make intercession for us, to guide and save us from our sins by His Holy Spirit. **His character is spotless, and ours should be too.**

> *Therefore, as the elect of God, holy and beloved, put on tender mercies, kindness, humility, meekness, longsuffering; bearing with one another, and forgiving one another, if anyone has a complaint against another; even as Christ forgave you, so you also must do. But above all these things put on love, which is the bond of perfection. And let the peace of Christ rule in your hearts, to which also you were called in one body; and be thankful. Let the word of Christ dwell in you richly in all wisdom, teaching and admonishing one another in psalms and hymns and spiritual songs, singing with grace in your hearts to the Lord. And whatever you do in word or deed, do all in the name of the Lord Jesus, giving thanks to God the Father through Him.* (Col. 3:12–17)

The first time I went to Dominion Conference in Lethbridge, in 2002, I remember going up for prayer and a woman prophesying over me, *"You are different!"* Remembering all the times I had been rejected in my life, and feeling lonely as a widow, miles from family—all alone, but with Jesus—I began to cry. She explained that I was not different in a bad way, but in a good way; so then I could smile and thank God knowing I am a work in progress, *"His workmanship"* (Eph. 2:10).

Like Daniel, we are to be "different" in the sense of not being afraid to publicly choose to do what is right and pure and holy, with an attitude of humility, yet confident of who we are in Christ. Not being equal to Jesus, if we do wrong, we should repent quickly, knowing that God looks at the heart and not outward appearance, and loves when we lovingly do His will. Another way to put it is that if we want to stand with Him in the battle against evil, then our armour must not have holes in it.

Trestlework on the True Bridge

All can pray but some are chosen specifically to stand in the gap with Him interceding, like support beams under a bridge which has trestles grounded on rock. Paul knew that we could not bear the load on our own. Marks of the ministry of reconciliation are spoken of in 2 Corinthians 6:1–10, including:

> *We then, as workers together with Him also plead with you not to receive the grace of God in vain. For He says,*
> *"In an acceptable time I have heard you,*
> *And in the day of salvation I have helped you."*
> *Behold, now is the accepted time; behold, now is the day of salvation.*
> (2 Cor. 6:1–2)

Jesus wants us to continue walking with Him, to be holy as He is holy. And, *"Do not be unequally yoked together with unbelievers"* (2 Cor. 6:14).

Having turned away from the idolatry of trying to intercede with the Father through saints who had died, and having sought truth and wholeness, I found it in the salvation that Jesus purchased by His blood sacrifice. This allowed me to join with Jesus in intercession. His yoke is easy and His burden is light. I also found that the wholeness of salvation includes "health" and *"liberty, deliverance, prosperity: - safety, salvation, saving."* [22] Thank God, having experienced these in my life, it is easier to intercede for others.

Led by Jesus, we ask God for mercy and grace for the people and we plead with people to appreciate God's gift and make good use of the saving grace which the Lord supplies. With integrity we are to speak openly to people when Jesus opens the door. We are to seek His righteousness: truth and justice tempered by mercy, being firmly

---

22   James Strong, *Strong's Hebrew and Greek Dictionaries, in* Rick Meyer's e-Sword. G4991, H3468.

grounded in Christ, in the love and Word of God, just as trestlework is to be firmly cemented into place so it can withstand whatever comes.

Jesus functions as Chief Minister of Reconciliation *"and has given us the ministry of reconciliation"* (2 Cor. 5:18). Intercessors are to let Him work through them, using the authority of the believer. By faith in His blood and name, other believers are justified too, just as if they had never sinned, by the finished work at the cross. Peace with God is restored.

Now is the time when **one of Jesus's functions is to ask for the nations, and we can agree with Him in asking for them.** I remember a time when the Lord called me to pray for Africa, I think in late 2000, giving me a drum beat to play on my coffee table and the *rhema* word to sing, *"Holy Spirit, come."* So I prayed it over and over, faithfully in the middle of the night when He called me, and glory be to God, I began to see ministries expanding more and more in Africa as the Holy Spirit would come and work with them. Now I am sure I was not the only one He called to pray for Africa, but Jesus is the Chief Intercessor and deserves the glory, orchestrating His intercessors. He can speak similar words to people miles apart. **It is as if the trestlework can vibrate on the same frequency as the top of the bridge, knowing that Jesus is the true bridge between God and mankind.**

Bibliography

Fernald L,HD, James C. *Concise Standard Dictionary* (1942) New York & London: Funk and Wagnalls Co.

Kylstra, Chester and Betsy. *Restoring the Foundations: An Integrated Approach to Healing Ministry 2nd Edition.* (2,000) Hendersonville, NC: Restoring the Foundations Publications. Copying of material allowed for limited use within a teaching.

Meyers, Rick. *John Wesley's Explanatory Notes,* in e-Sword, a downloaded Bible platform from https://www.e-sword.net/.

Meyers, Rick. *Webster's Dictionary of American English* (1828) in e-Sword, https://www.e-sword.net/.

Strong, LL.D., S.T.D., James. "Nave's Topical Bible Reference System." In *The Strongest Strong's Exhaustive Concordance of the Bible* (2001) edited by JR Kohlenberger III and JA Swanson, 1545-1707. Grand Rapids, Michigan: Zondervan.

Strong, LL.D., S.T.D., James. In *Strong's Hebrew and Greek Dictionaries,* in Rick Meyer's e-Sword. https://www.e-sword.net/.

If This Book Blessed You, Will You Help Me Spread the Word?

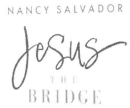

- Share my website, JesusTheBridge.info.

- Post a 5-Star review on Amazon, Goodreads and other online review venues.

- Post the book's title on your social media such as Facebook, X, Truth Social, Instagram, Google+, etc.

- Post a photo of yourself with your copy of the book.

- If you blog, reference the book, with a link to JesusTheBridge.info

- Recommend the book to friends – word of mouth is still the more effective form of advertising.

- Ask your bookstore if they carry the book. Word of mouth with booksellers causes them to stock the book. Any bookstore can easily order it.

- Do you know a journalist, podcaster or media influencer seeking guests on my topic? Send them my website, JesusTheBridge.info.

- Purchase additional copies for gifts to people you care about.

Order Your Copy of Volume Two

Jesus the Bridge: Finding the Kingdom with His Presence

The companion of this book, Volume Two helps you...

- **Live in God's Kingdom**
- **Discern and Resist Evil**
- **Enjoy His Presence**

The second installment of this powerful testimony is like the first: a friend and mentor. As you know now, Nancy writes like she talks with you. Find yourself in her pages, once again portraying God's presence with a trestle bridge. How can Jesus be your bridge?

Learn from her how you can walk with God in our society, discerning its idolatry and injustices to children. With parables and images, be forewarned about the Antichrist—and ready for the loyalty of love.

Everyone needs an honest role model for living in God's Kingdom—an example of how He speaks to us. Witness how the Holy Spirit manifests God's presence. Nancy is candid and direct, a practical model for your own spiritual vitality.

Purchase Volume Two where you bought this Volume One or online.